SIMON BALL is the Head of the Department of History at the University of Glasgow. His previous book, *The Guardsmen*, was published to critical acclaim in 2004.

By the same author

The Guardsmen
The Cold War: An International History
The Bomber in British Strategy

THE BITTER SEA

SIMON BALL

Harper
Press

To Helen

Harper*Press*
An imprint of HarperCollins*Publishers*
77–85 Fulham Palace Road
Hammersmith, London W6 8JB

Visit our authors' blog: www.fifthestate.co.uk
Love this book? www.bookarmy.com

This Harper*Press* paperback edition published 2010
1

First published in Great Britain by Harper*Press* in 2009

A catalogue record for this book
is available from the British Library

ISBN 978-0-00-720305-5

Typeset in Minion by Palimpsest Book Production Limited,
Grangemouth, Stirlingshire

Printed and bound in Great Britain by Clays Ltd, St Ives plc

CONTENTS

ILLUSTRATIONS

SECTION I

Ingress: Gibraltar as seen from a *Luftwaffe* aircraft, 21 August 1942. (Imperial War Museum, IWM C5676)

Egress. (Popperfoto/ Getty Images)

The Sword of Islam: Mussolini drives along the Balbia. (Mary Evans Picture Library)

The Sword of Islam: Mussolini bears the sword,. (Bettmann/CORBIS)

The Spider. (Bettmann/CORBIS)

The Brutal Friendship: Hitler. (Imperial War Museum, IWM HU2791)

The Dream and the Nightmare. (Solo Syndication/Associated Newspapers Ltd)

Gog. (Imperial War Museum, IWM A7522)

Mediterranean hero. (Imperial War Museum, IWM A7293)

Magog. (Imperial War Museum, IWM A4115)

The sinking of the Italian cruiser *Bartolemeo Colleoni*. (Imperial War Museum, IWM A219)

A distant view of the Italian fleet. (Imperial War Museum, IWM A2412)

Running the Narrows. (Imperial War Museum, IWM HU43447)

Lovely Derna. (Imperial War Museum, IWM F1871)

The Coast Road. (Imperial War Museum, IWM E19936)

The Balbia. (Imperial War Museum, IWM E20579)

Two Mediterraneanists. (Imperial War Museum, IWM HU86147)

New Enemies. (Imperial War Museum, IWM HU636611)

Two kinds of Frenchman? (Imperial War Museum, IWM E4131)

Eden in Cairo. (Imperial War Museum, IWM E2215)

Holding the East in Fee. (Imperial War Museum, IWM E8971)

The Face of Defeat. (Imperial War Museum, IWM GM1245)

SECTION II

SOURCES AND ACKNOWLEDGEMENTS

I have been thinking about the Mediterranean for a long time. I began my academic career researching Anglo-American strategic relations during the early Cold War. Later, I wrote about the careers of politicians who made their name in the Mediterranean. In particular, I became fascinated by the systems by which the British tried to combine direct and indirect, military and civil rule during the Second World War. These systems came to centre on the expedient of sending cabinet ministers to take up residence in the Mediterranean, first in Cairo but subsequently in Algiers and Naples. The papers of the ministers resident have been available in the British archives since the 1970s. Their activities were hard to understand fully, however, because they were so entangled with the 'hidden hand', the various covert departments of the British government. The papers of these organizations only began to be released in the late 1990s and these releases are still ongoing. The Mediterranean bred a rich collection of such organizations, to name but a few: CBME tackled signals intelligence; SIME, counter-espionage; A Force, deception; SOE, covert operations; PWE, propaganda; CSDIC, interrogation; ISLD, spying. Most of these bodies were offshoots of established organizations in the UK, but they operated with a degree of autonomy. They also expanded and moved over time. CSDIC, for instance, opened for business at Maadi, near Cairo in December 1940. A sister centre was established at Birkadem near Algiers in May 1943. Most of the staff moved to Porici near Naples in January 1944. A further move took CSDIC to Centrocelle on the Rome–Frascati road in June 1944.

The British (and American) documents, with their mass of decrypts and interrogation reports, provide such good insights into the 'other side of the hill' that they have been taken up with enthusiasm by non-Anglophone historians. The insights gleaned are joining generations of work in the archives of all the powers with an interest in the Mediterranean. Arguably, the British – latterly Anglo-American – version of the Mediterranean was the most important, but it was far from alone. The works of scholars of France, Germany, Italy and Turkey, amongst others, reveal alternative visions. In producing an 'inner' history of those who tried to rule the Mediterranean I have made particular use of the remarkable range of diaries that have been published over the past half century. This book begins with the diary of Galeazzo Ciano, Mussolini's son-in-law and Fascist Italy's Foreign Minister; it ends with the diary of James V. Forrestal, the US Secretary of the Navy and inaugural Secretary of Defense. Ciano's diary was first published in 1948; Forrestal's in 1952 (although much fuller and better editions have become available in recent years). The combination of old and new sources reveals a rather different version of Mediterranean history from that handed down to us, not least in the great 'Churchillian tradition', the master narrative created in the late 1940s and early 1950s. The great battles still reverberate; but the manner in which contemporaries thought about these events is at variance with later tradition. The Mediterranean world did a lot of forgetting during the Cold War.

I would like to thank everyone who has helped with encouragement and advice over the course of a complex project. The first draft of this book was written whilst on academic leave granted by the University of Glasgow. I am very grateful to the University and in particular to the Department of History for allowing me the time to write. At Glasgow it is my pleasure to work as part of a close-knit team. I would particularly like to thank Dr Phil O'Brien and Dr Will Mulligan of the Scottish Centre for War Studies for constantly discussing ideas and details. Professor Sönke Neitzel of the Johannes Gutenberg-Universität, Mainz and Dr Klaus Schmider of the RMA, Sandhurst patiently answered my questions about the Axis powers. Sönke did a great deal to keep my enthusiasm for studying the war high. I am extremely grateful to Professor Richard Aldous of University College Dublin, not only for bringing his own expertise in Anglo-American relations to bear but also for reading the draft manuscript. Richard took a great deal of valuable time away from his own writing and his headship of a large university department to help. The finished product is a lot better thanks to his contribution. I am most grateful to Jonny Pegg for becoming my agent after the tragic death of Giles Gordon. I was grateful when Jonny put me, once more, in the capable hands of Arabella Pike at Harper Press. Arabella's long-term support of my attempt to bridge the gap between academic and professional history has been an enormous boon and is heartily appreciated. Michael Upchurch and Georgia Mason picked up the task of preparing *The Bitter Sea* for publication with enthusiasm and skill. My greatest thanks go to Helen, my wife, who not only read drafts of the manuscript with meticulous care but lived *The Bitter Sea* experience. This book is dedicated to her with love.

MAPS

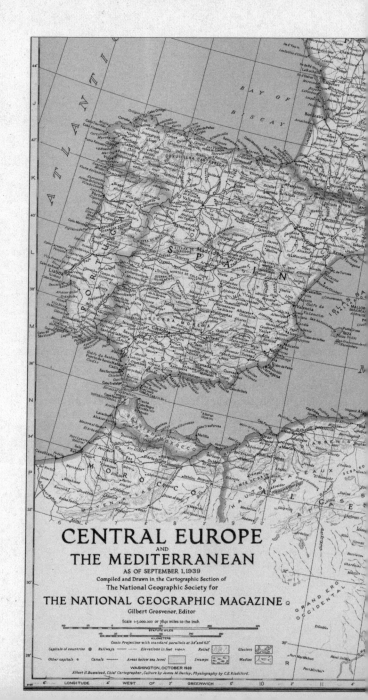

CENTRAL EUROPE
AND
THE MEDITERRANEAN
AS OF SEPTEMBER 1, 1939
Compiled and Drawn in the Cartographic Section of
The National Geographic Society for

THE NATIONAL GEOGRAPHIC MAGAZINE
Gilbert Grosvenor, Editor

Scale 1:5,000,000 or 78.91 miles to the inch

WASHINGTON, OCTOBER 1939
Albert H. Bumstead, Chief Cartographer, Culture by James M. Darley, Physiography by C.E. Riddiford.

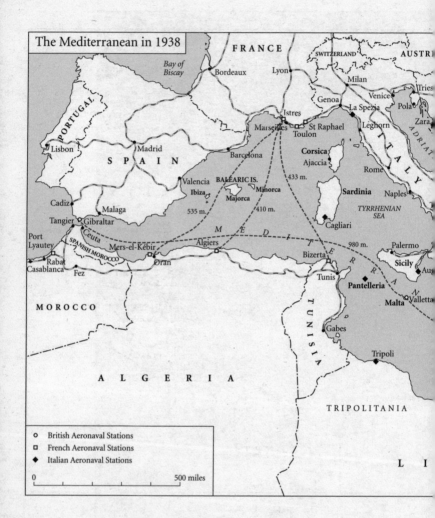

The Mediterranean in 1938

FRANCE
SWITZERLAND
AUSTR
Bay of
Biscay
Bordeaux
Lyon
Milan
Tries
Genoa
Venice
Pola
Istres
La Spezia
Zara
Marseilles
St Raphael
Leghorn
PORTUGAL
Toulon
Lisbon
Madrid
Corsica
Ajaccio
ADRIAT
SPAIN
Barcelona
Rome
Valencia
BALEARIC IS.
433 m.
ITALY
Ibiza
Minorca
Sardinia
Naples
Cadiz
Majorca
410 m.
TYRRHENIAN
Malaga
535 m.
SEA
Tangier
Gibraltar
Cagliari
Ceuta
M
E
D
I
T
Port
SPANISH MOROCCO
Mers-el-Kébir
Algiers
Palermo
Lyautey
980 m.
E
Rabat
Oran
Bizerta
R
Sicily
Au
Casablanca
Tunis
R
Fez
Pantelleria
A
Valletta
N
Malta
MOROCCO
Gabes
TUNISIA
ALGERIA
Tripoli
TRIPOLITANIA
L
I

○ British Aeronaval Stations
□ French Aeronaval Stations
◆ Italian Aeronaval Stations

0   500 miles

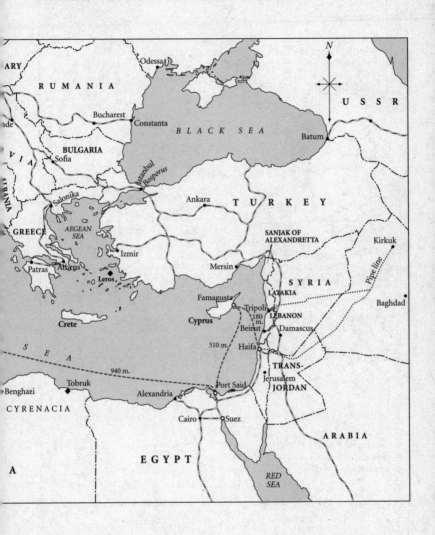

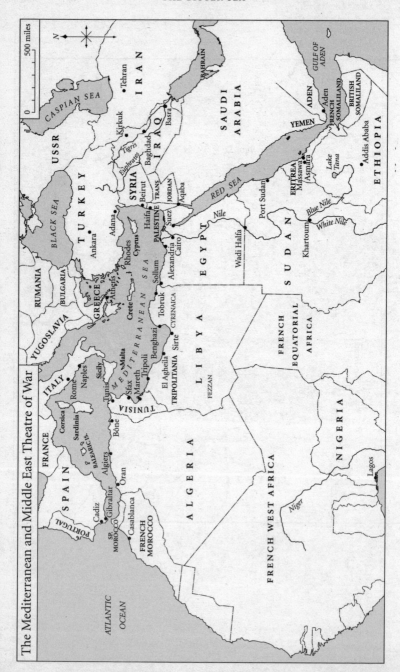

The Mediterranean and Middle East Theatre of War

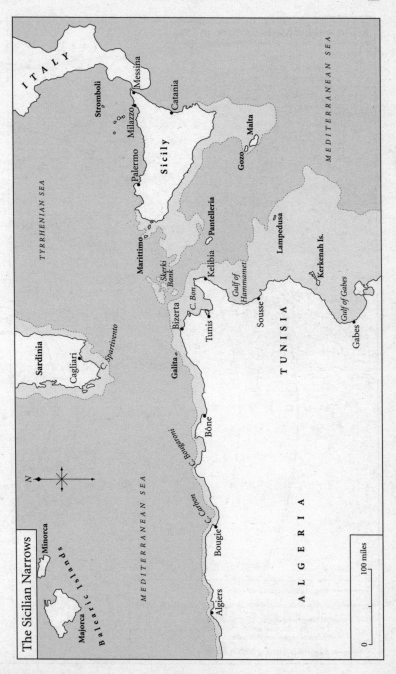

The Sicilian Narrows

MEDITERRANEAN SEA

TYRRHENIAN SEA

ITALY

Messina
Stromboli
Milazzo
Catania
Palermo
Sicily
Malta
Gozo
Marittimo
Pantelleria
Skerki Bank
Kelibia
Gulf of Hammamet
Lampedusa
Kerkenah Is.
C. Bon
Bizerta
Tunis
Sousse
Galita
Gulf of Gabes
Gabes
TUNISIA
Sardinia
Cagliari
C. Spartivento
C. Bougaroni
Bône
C. Carbon
Bougie
ALGERIA
Minorca
Majorca
Balearic Islands
Algiers
MEDITERRANEAN SEA

N

0   100 miles

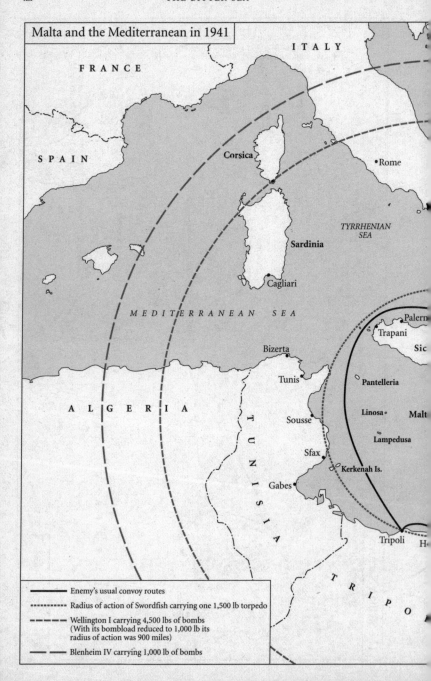

Malta and the Mediterranean in 1941

FRANCE

ITALY

SPAIN

Corsica

• Rome

TYRRHENIAN
SEA

Sardinia

Cagliari

MEDITERRANEAN   SEA

Palerm

Trapani

Sic

Bizerta

Pantelleria

Tunis

Linosa   • Malt

ALGERIA

Sousse   Lampedusa

Sfax

T   Kerkenah Is.

U

N   Gabes

I

S

I

A

Tripoli   H

TRIPO

——— Enemy's usual convoy routes

············· Radius of action of Swordfish carrying one 1,500 lb torpedo

— — — Wellington I carrying 4,500 lbs of bombs
(With its bombload reduced to 1,000 lb its
radius of action was 900 miles)

— — Blenheim IV carrying 1,000 lb of bombs

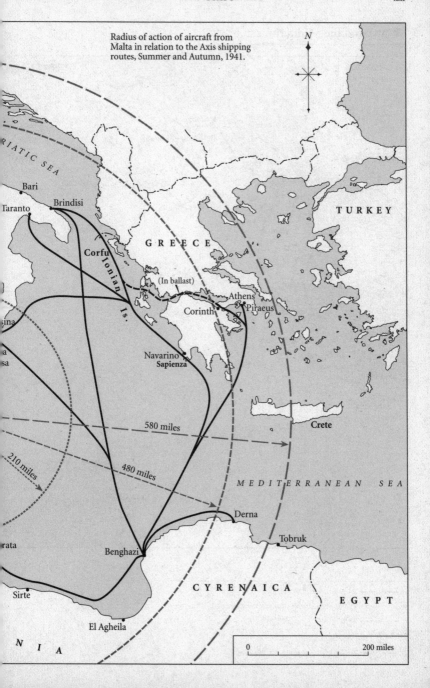

Radius of action of aircraft from
Malta in relation to the Axis shipping
routes, Summer and Autumn, 1941.

N

RIATIC SEA

Bari

Taranto   Brindisi

Corfu

Ionian Is.

G R E E C E

T U R K E Y

(In ballast)

Athens

Corinth   Piraeus

ina

sa

Navarino
Sapienza

580 miles

480 miles

Crete

M E D I T E R R A N E A N   S E A

210 miles

Derna

Tobruk

rata

Benghazi

C Y R E N A I C A

E G Y P T

Sirte

El Agheila

N   I   A

0   200 miles

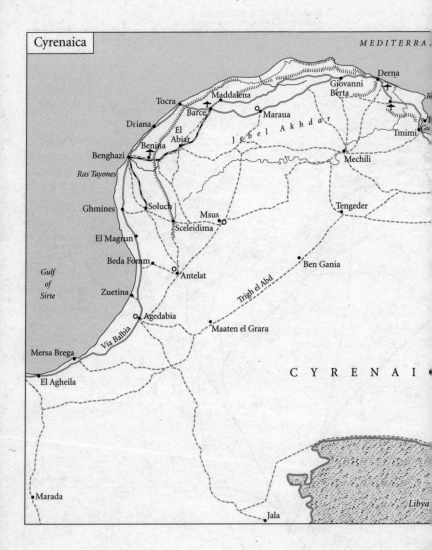

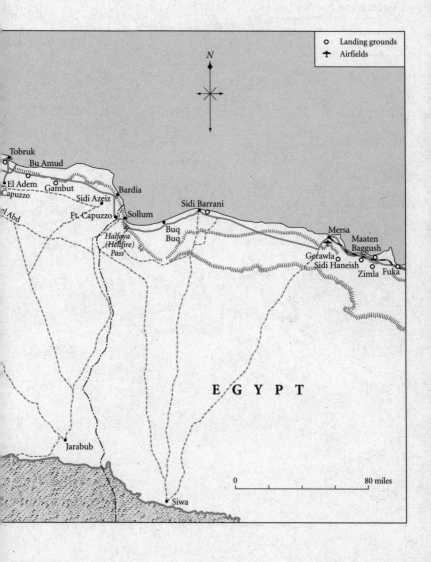

Landing grounds

Airfields

N

Tobruk
Bu Amud
El Adem
Gambut
Capuzzo
Sidi Azeiz
Bardia
l Abd
Ft. Capuzzo
Sollum
Sidi Barrani
*Halfaya
(Hellfire)
Pass*
Buq
Buq
Mersa
Maaten
Baggush
Gerawla
Sidi Haneish
Zimla
Fuka

E G Y P T

Jarabub

0   80 miles

Siwa

Greece and the Aegean

ITALY

ADRIATIC SEA

Foggia

Naples

Bari

Brindisi

Taranto

Gulf of Taranto

Durazzo

ALBAN

Valona

Lesko

Santa Quàranta

Argyró

Corfu

Sea of Otranto

CALABRIA

Str. of Messina

Sicily

I O N I A N

S E A

I
o
n
i
a
n

I
s.

Cephalonia

Argostoli

Za

Malta

M E D I T E R R A N E A N

0   200 miles

The Partition of Yugoslavia in 1941

AUSTRIA

HUN

PREKOMURJE

MEDJIMURJE

Drava R

Trbovlje

Zagreb

ITALY

Ljubljana

SLOVENIA

INDEPENDE

Rijeka

KORDUN

BANIJA

Sava R

STATE OF

Una R

Bihać

CROA

LIKA

Jajce

Zara

(IT.)

I

II

III

A D R I A T I C

S E A

Vis

(IT.)

Annexed to Hungary		German occupied
Annexed to Bulgaria		State borders
Annexed to Albania		Zone border
Italian occupied		German-Italian demarcation line
Annexed to Italy		

II and III Italian occupied zones of Croatian State Territory

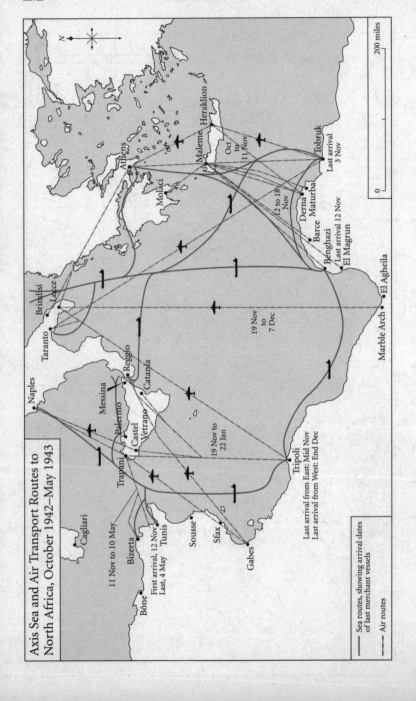

Axis Sea and Air Transport Routes to
North Africa, October 1942–May 1943

200 miles

0

N

Athens
Maleme
Heraklion
Molaoi
Oct to 11 Nov
12 to 18 Nov
Tobruk
Last arrival 3 Nov
Derna
Maturba
Barce
Benghazi
Last arrival 12 Nov
El Magrun
Brindisi
Lecce
Taranto
19 Nov to 7 Dec
Marble Arch
El Agheila
Naples
Reggio
Messina
Catania
Palermo
Castel Vetrano
Trapani
19 Nov to 22 Jan
Tripoli
Last arrival from East: Mid Nov
Last arrival from West: End Dec
Cagliari
Bizerta
Bône
11 Nov to 10 May
Tunis
First arrival, 12 Nov
Last, 4 May
Sousse
Sfax
Gabes

Sea routes, showing arrival dates
of last merchant vessels

Air routes

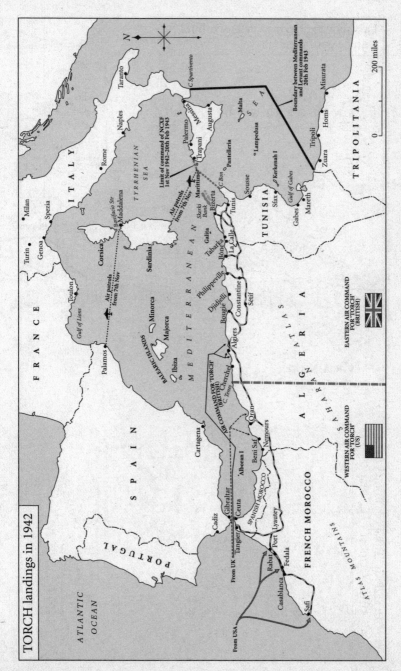

TORCH landings in 1942

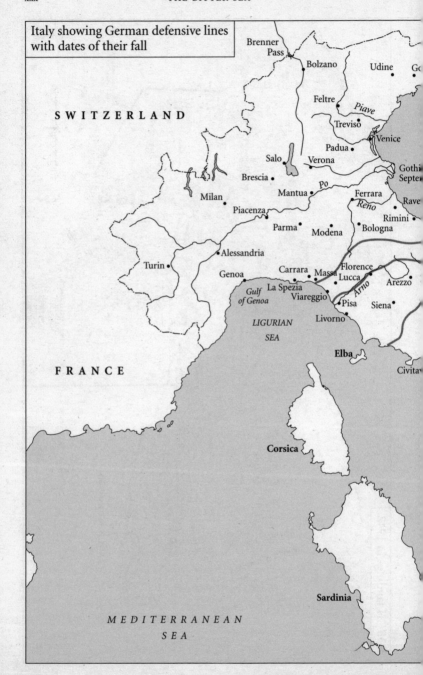

Italy showing German defensive lines with dates of their fall

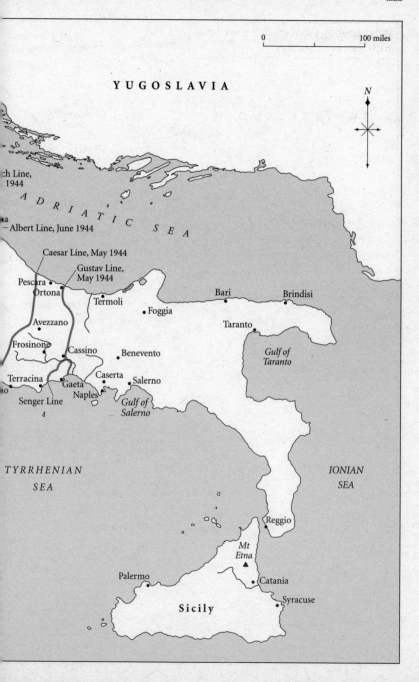

0   100 miles

N

YUGOSLAVIA

ch Line,
1944

A D R I A T I C   S E A

a
— Albert Line, June 1944

Caesar Line, May 1944
Gustav Line,
May 1944

Pescara
Ortona
Termoli
Bari   Brindisi
Foggia
Avezzano
Taranto
Frosinone
Cassino
Benevento   *Gulf of Taranto*
Terracina
Caserta
Gaeta   Salerno
Naples
Senger Line
Gulf of Salerno

*TYRRHENIAN
SEA*

*IONIAN
SEA*

Reggio

*Mt
Etna*

Palermo
Catania

Sicily   Syracuse

INTRODUCTION

In July 2008 the Libyan tyrant Muammar Gaddafi announced that he would boycott the inaugural meeting of the Union for the Mediterranean, or 'Club Med' as it was invariably known. The President of France, Nicolas Sarkozy, had summoned forty-two Mediterranean leaders to Paris to create the Union. Newly elected, he wanted an alternative to the faltering 'Barcelona process' that, since 1995, had been a vehicle for transferring aid from the European Union to the Arab world. Something grander and more heroic was required to capture the imagination of Europe and the Middle East, Sarkozy believed. Gaddafi was appalled. The initial invitation to Club Med, issued in December 2007, was grandly entitled, in the worst possible taste, the 'Appeal from Rome'. Libya had been created from the ashes of Mussolini's Roman Empire. Sarkozy had flanked himself with the leaders of Spain and Italy, an echo of the unrealized Mediterranean Axis of 1940. 'We shall have another Roman Empire and imperialist design,' Gaddafi snarled from his palace in Tripoli. 'There are imperialist maps and designs we have already rolled up. We should not have them again.'[1]

This is a book about an idea and its time. The idea was that there was a place called the Mediterranean and that the Mediterranean was worth fighting for. The time was the mid-1930s to the late 1940s.

The existence of the Mediterranean is embedded in the modern imagination.[2] Long before the aeroplane or the satellite created aerial pictures of the Mediterranean, the Victorian art critic John Ruskin urged his reader to rise with him higher than the birds. Together they would see 'the Mediterranean lying beneath us like an irregular lake, and all its ancient promontories sleeping in the sun'. Beneath them were 'Syria and Greece, Italy and Spain, laid like pieces of a golden pavement into the sea blue'.[3] This vision of the 'golden pavement' and 'sea blue' was endorsed by the most famous twentieth-century history of the Mediterranean. In *The Mediterranean and the Mediterranean World in the Age of Philip II*, published in 1949, the French historian Fernand Braudel insisted that the Mediterranean was a unit of 'creative space': its amazing freedom of sea-routes and 'complementary populations' shaped human actions. Braudel's putative subject was the sixteenth century, but few were in any doubt that he was addressing his own times.[4] As Braudel himself remarked, his view of the historical Mediterranean was formed by his years as a teacher in Algeria. He imagined a Mediterranean seen from the 'other bank', 'upside down'.[5]

Yet there were sceptics about 'the Mediterranean'. What, writers from Mediterranean countries asked, did all this talk about 'Mediterranean culture' amount to, beyond chatter worked up into an intellectual system? The Mediterranean was not a good 'unit of analysis'. The unity of its populations was illusory. National histories mattered more than an ill-defined Mediterranean identity.[6] The Mediterranean did not make much sense. A central tenet of 'Mediterraneanness' was that religious differ-ence, though not religions, was essentially unimportant. As Braudel put it, the Islamic Mediterranean lived and breathed with the same rhythms as the Christian. Yet at the very moment he wrote, the whole concept of the 'the Middle East', a different, identifiable, Muslim, world incorpo-rating eastern Mediterranean lands, had colonized the imagination of politicians and journalists. Efforts to halt or reverse the spread of the concept proved fruitless. Winston Churchill told cavillers: 'a million or so Englishmen had fought, and many died, in what they knew as the *Middle East*, and the *Middle East* it was to remain!' By the late 1940s the term Middle East was in universal circulation, and has retained its grip ever since.[7]

One group able to write about the Mediterranean and the Middle East, without worrying too much about questions of identity, has been mili-tary historians.[8] For them the Mediterranean was not a culture area but a theatre. Rather than doubt the self-evident existence of the Mediterranean 'theatre', they instead gnawed away at the question of whether the Mediterranean was important to the outcome of the Second World War. The argument stretched back to Anglo-American disputes about strategy in the middle years of the war.[9] These arguments did not long remain private. Elliot Roosevelt, the officer in charge of the air-force photographic reconnaissance in the Mediterranean, but more prominently the son of the President of the USA, published a bilious caricature of foolish British Mediterraneanists and wise American Europeanists as early as 1946.[10] More in the same vein was to follow. The Americans claimed that arms and men had been wasted on a sideshow. The British retorted that American foot-dragging had prevented the exploitation of victory. The burgeoning literature on 'total' war dismissed the Mediterranean war as 'second class' because of its political and limited nature. 'Mediterraneanists' were left to argue that their theatre was of primary importance for short, but pivotal, periods.[11]

This book does not assume that the unity of the Mediterranean rested on deep structures. Rather it suggests that any such unity was fleeting. The Mediterranean was the product of competing notions of thalassocracy – 'rulership of the sea'. These ideas were ebbing away by the late 1940s. Whilst belief in the Mediterranean existed, however, there were genuine attempts to wield pan-Mediterranean authority. This is a history of the Mediterranean told from the point of view of those who attempted to rule it. Their Mediterranean was a crucible of modernity. The key features of the Mediterranean crisis – shifting coalitions held together by contingent loyalty, information warfare, the projection of air and sea power, civil war and terrorism – remained crucial long after the Mediterranean itself had become a fantasy of western tourist brochures.

ONE

The Dead Dog

Eyeless in Gaza, Aldous Huxley's 1936 novel, opens with a metaphor for the Mediterranean: the lazy, ripe, sea-girt lands, beloved of travellers, and Mussolini's hell-hole. Two sunbathers' eyes are drawn to the west, to 'a blue Mediterranean bay fringed with pale bone-like rocks and cupped between high hills, green on their lower slopes with vines, grey with olive trees, then pine-dark, earth-red, rock-white or rosy-brown with parched heath'. To the east they observe 'the vineyards and the olive orchards mounted in terraces of red earth to a crest'. The 'sunlight fell steep out of flawless sky', and they dozed, until 'a faint rustling caressed the half-conscious fringes of their torpor . . . and became at last a clattering roar that brutally insisted on attention'. Annoyed, they closed their eyes once more, 'dazzled by the intense blue of the sky'. Suddenly, 'with a violent but dull and muddy impact the thing struck the flat roof a yard or two from where they were lying'. 'The drops of a sharply spurted liquid were warm for an instant on their skin, and then, as the breeze swelled up out of the west, startlingly cold.' 'In a red pool at their feet lay the almost shapeless carcass of a fox-terrier. The roar of the receding aeroplane had diminished to a raucous hum, and suddenly the ear found itself conscious once again of the shrill rasping of the cicadas.' *Eyeless in Gaza* prophesies a Mediterranean war in 1940.[1]

Huxley's aeroplane was indeed an apt metaphor for Italian Fascism. Sowing chaos from the air was central to Mussolini's regime.[2] *Il Duce*'s collected writings and speeches on the subject were published in March 1937.[3] Flying was dynastic aggrandizement for Mussolini. When he took flying lessons in the 1920s he took his sons, Vittorio and Bruno, to the aerodrome. In 1935 the Mussolini clan 'volunteered' to fly in the conquest of Abyssinia. Vittorio Mussolini was nineteen, Bruno only seventeen but worthy of bombing Abyssinians. Their cousin, Vito, son of Mussolini's late brother, went as well. They were chaperoned by Galeazzo Ciano, the husband of Vittorio and Bruno's sister, Edda. 'We have carried out a slaughter,' Ciano boasted. Vittorio's shadowed autobiography was rushed out in celebration. He admitted to being a little disappointed by his first bombing raid; the Abyssinians' feeble huts collapsed without any spectacular strewing of rubble. The Mussolini boys were not, however, good pilots: their true love was brothels rather than aerodromes. On their return from the front they lorded it around Rome, raping girls, crashing fast cars and treating the professional head of the *Regia Aeronautica*, Giuseppe Valle, like a flunkey.[4] Only Ciano stayed the course, returning to Abyssinia for the final victory in the spring of 1936. The fawning Italian press gave his exploits so much coverage that eventually he ordered them reined in lest he become a laughing stock at his golf club.[5] Nevertheless, Ciano, at the age of thirty-three, emerged from Abyssinia as the 'hero' of the dynasty. In the summer of 1936 Mussolini not only made him Italian foreign minister but put him in charge of the Fascist project for Mediterranean conquest.[6] Ciano was a monster: vain, corrupt and murderous. Nevertheless, most people liked his 'winning ways'.[7] He was good-looking and fun to talk to. Ciano had a low, and usually accurate, opinion of his fellow man, Fascist, Nazi or democrat. He had a gift for self-reflection, as well as self-deceit. Both characteristics were reflected in a diary he began to keep, with Mussolini's blessing, once he had firmly established himself at the foreign ministry.

Mussolini 'dropped the dog' on 3 October 1935 when Italy invaded Abyssinia. The Mediterranean may not have been a peaceful place in the decade before 1935: monarchy was overthrown in Spain, but preserved by a military dictatorship in Greece; the French ruthlessly suppressed colonial peoples in Morocco and Syria; terrorists murdered their ethnic enemies in Yugoslavia and Palestine. Its quarrels were, however, parochial. The Mediterranean itself played little part in these struggles beyond that of a means of departure and arrival. It was Mussolini's challenge to Britain that plunged the Mediterranean as a whole into its fourteen-year crisis.

The British described their Mediterranean as an 'artery'.[8] Armies and navies made the passage to the East through the artery, raw materials, tin, rubber, tea and, above all, oil, made their way west. On any given day in the mid-1930s the tonnage of British shipping in the Mediterranean was second only to that found in the North Atlantic. The Mediterranean was not, however, Britain's only arterial route. Many of the same destinations could be reached by sailing the Atlantic–Indian Ocean route around Africa via the Cape of Good Hope. The Mediterranean's chief attraction was speed. A ship steaming from the Port of London to Bombay would take a full fortnight longer, and travel nearly 4,500 miles more, to reach its destination if it did not pass through the Mediterranean.

The British artery had three main choke points: Gibraltar, Malta and Port Said. The first port of call for a ship entering the Mediterranean was Gibraltar. Seven million tons of commercial shipping called at Gibraltar every year. The Rock, a mere one-and-seven-eighths square miles in area, had been a British possession since the early eighteenth century. It housed a large naval base for the use of the Home Fleet. Nearly a thousand miles to the east, the small island of Malta lay at a point almost equidistant between Gibraltar and the entrance to the Suez Canal at Port Said in Egypt. It also sat astride the narrowest point in the Mediterranean, the Strait of Sicily. Valletta was one of the great harbours of the world, providing the main base of the Mediterranean Fleet, comprising, at the beginning of 1935, five battleships, eight cruisers and an aircraft-carrier. Apart from its strategic importance, the British dominance of Malta irritated Mussolini. In the early 1930s the British started a campaign to encourage the Maltese language to replace Italian in the schools and law courts.[9] Pro-Italian Maltese 'traitors' were imprisoned, and Italian diplomats were expelled from the island for indulging in subversion and espionage. Italian was expunged as a legitimate language.[10]

A few ships left the main artery at Malta and headed into the northeastern Mediterranean, to the British possession of Cyprus, 'off the main track of sea communications . . . unfortified and garrisoned only by native police, together with one company of British troops'. Unlike Gibraltar and Malta, Cyprus had a large land mass capable of supporting a substantial population – nearly 350,000 in 1935. Its coast was dotted with harbours but they were little more than 'open roadsteads' or 'small and silted up'. The only substantial port was Famagusta on the east of the island. In the mid-1930s the British did consider turning Famagusta into a major naval base.[11] In the end they decided that Cyprus was 'out of the question for the immediate needs of the moment'. A base at Famagusta would have taken over a decade to complete.[12]

Most ships did not divert to Cyprus. They travelled on for another thousand miles from Malta. At Port Said they entered the Suez Canal. A great feat of nineteenth-century engineering, the Canal ran for 101 miles through Egypt, providing a single-lane highway, with passing places to accommodate both north-and southbound traffic. A ship would take – on average – fifteen hours to pass through the Canal before debouching into the Red Sea at Port Suez.

Thus for the British the Mediterranean comprised a seamless whole. The sea was a journey from west to east, and the Mediterranean coast comprised the north and south banks of an eastward-flowing river.[13]

By the time 'major combat operations' in Abyssinia ended on 9 May 1936, the British had been thoroughly spooked.[14] They could no longer 'despise the Italians and believe they will never dare to put to and face us', wrote Winston Churchill. 'Mussolini's Italy may be quite different to that of the Great War.'[15] Major-General Robert Haining, the British army officer charged with assessing his Italian opposite numbers, described the campaign as a 'masterpiece'. 'There has been a great tendency in this country', he warned, echoing Churchill, 'to think that the Italian of today is still the Italian of Caporetto [whereas] the Italian, from what one has seen of him, is a very different individual to what he used to be.'[16]

The British response to the war was characterized by Sir Warren Fisher, the head of the civil service, as feeble. British officials had stood on the dockside at Port Said as Italian troop ships sailed through the Suez Canal carrying, by their estimation, nearly a quarter of a million men.[17] One in five ships that sailed through the Canal in 1936 were Italian.[18] Italy was able to send three hundred tons of poison gas through the Suez Canal on a refrigerated banana boat. Despite attempts to cover up the shipments, the British were well aware of the weapons of mass destruction passing under their noses. Abyssinia was a honeypot for ambitious writers hoping to make a name for themselves. The most famous, subsequently, of these writers, Evelyn Waugh, wrote to the wife of a British cabinet minister: 'i have got to hate the ethiopians more each day goodness they are lousy & i hope the organmen gas them to buggery'.[19] The 'organmen' did Waugh proud. Sir Aldo Castellani, a prominent Harley

Street surgeon and father-in-law of the British High Commissioner in Egypt, discredited British reports about gassing by claiming that the photographs of gas victims actually showed lepers. He admitted the truth, in private, to his English friends.[20] 'No country believes that we ever intended business,' lamented Sir Warren, 'and our parade of force in the Eastern Mediterranean, so far as impressing others, has merely made a laughing stock of ourselves. All that is now needed to complete the *opera bouffe* is a headline in the newspapers, "Italians Occupy Addis Ababa, British evacuate Eastern Med".'[21] Dino Grandi, the Italian ambassador in London, reported that although the British realized, 'the Italian empire in Ethiopia was also the Italian Mediterranean empire', they feared to act.[22]

The Fascists oriented their Mediterranean quite differently from that of the British: north–south rather than west–east. Apart from metropolitan Italy, the pre-Fascist Italy – stretching around the northern end of the Adriatic to Pola, a naval base, and the city of Zara in Dalmatia – had acquired colonies from the dying Ottoman Empire: the twin lands of Tripolitania and Cyrenaica in North Africa, and the islands of the Dodecanese in the Aegean, chief amongst them Rhodes, Cos and Leros.

Mussolini developed this existing empire. In 1936 he sent Cesare Maria De Vecchi, one of the 'heroes' of the Fascist seizure of power, to govern the Dodecanese. De Vecchi built himself a huge palace on Rhodes and managed to alienate the native population through a combination of excess and incompetence. He pursued, for instance, assimilation – banning all newspapers in Greek – and segregation – banning intermarriage – at the same time.[23] The Italians fortified the islands, building airfields and naval facilities. Leros had a deep-water harbour from which destroyers, torpedo boats and submarines could operate.[24] The island became known as 'the Malta of the Aegean'. The Turks called it the 'gun' pointing at Turkey. They suggested to anyone who listened that the base was the first link in the chain that would give Italy dominance in the eastern basin of the Mediterranean.[25]

Ciano's nascent *Ufficio Spagna* also fell greedily on the idea of a base in the western Mediterranean. The outbreak of the Spanish Civil War in July 1936 gave the Fascists the chance to seize such a base. For the Italians the war was as much about bases in the Balearics as it was about Madrid.[26]

Months before any Italian armies went to Franco's aid on the mainland, the Italians were already fighting a parallel war for the Balearic islands of Majorca, Minorca and Ibiza. A particularly brutal Black Shirt leader, Arconovaldo Bonaccorsi – known as the *Conte Rossi* because of his red hair and beard – was sent to Majorca, announcing that he was there to ensure 'the triumph of Latin and Christian civilization, menaced by the international rabble at Moscow's orders that want to bolshevize the peoples of the Mediterranean basin'. Rossi carried out a reign of terror, murdering about three thousand people during his occupation of the Balearics. 'Daily radical cleansing of places and infected people is carried out,' he boasted.[27] Soon Rossi was reinforced by a small air force. The aircraft operated to such good effect that the Republicans were forced to withdraw at the beginning of September 1936.

For years, those who observed Fascist ambitions had suspected that Mussolini coveted the Balearics: now the Fascists were firmly in charge.[28] Indeed Mussolini opened his November 1936 oration on the need for an expanded war in Spain with the cry, 'the Balearics are in our hands'.[29] It was only in the light of the triumph in the Balearics that Mussolini fully embraced Franco. The *Duce* ordered that Franco should receive both an Italian air force and army. One month later the Black Shirts surreptitiously set sail from the port of Gaeta, north of Naples. Within months nearly 50,000 Italian troops were fighting in Spain. Their first mission was to seize Spain's Mediterranean coastline.[30]

Bruno Mussolini was sent to Majorca to command a squadron of bombers. 'I envy them,' Ciano wrote of his old colleagues from Abyssinia, 'but I am, at least for the moment, nailed to this desk.' Still, he could give them a satisfying mission since 'we must seize the moment to terrorize the enemy'.[31] Valencia, and even Barcelona, the heart of the most hardcore Catalan resistance to Franco, were within easy bombing range of Majorca. The aircraft had less than an hour's flying time to their targets and could approach, unobserved, over the water.[32] The Italian pilots boasted incessantly – and inaccurately – about the amount of damage they were doing. Mussolini was so delighted with the results that he doubled the bomber force on Majorca at the beginning of 1938.[33] In March the aircraft were 'unleashed' on the civilian suburbs of Barcelona, causing many casualties. *Regia Aeronautica* chief Giuseppe Valle, the butt of the younger Mussolini's taunt that he no longer had what it took to be a man in the cockpit, even flew a lone aircraft at night from Rome to bomb Barcelona.[34] Whenever the world talked about bombing they did not get much beyond the Nazi Condor Legion's devastating attack on the Basque town of Guernica in April 1937 – an attack in which Italian bombers, unnoticed, took a minor part.[35] Surely, the Italian ambassador in Berlin claimed with some satisfaction, 'the whole world knew that those involved in the bombing attacks on harbour cities, especially Barcelona, had been Italian fliers'.[36]

Fascist propagandists lamented the fact that the Italian Empire, emasculated by 'morbid parliamentarism', had not hitherto been regarded as 'an immediate menace to the great imperial artery from Gibraltar to Port Said'.[37] For the Italians too, the Mediterranean comprised a whole. To them, however, the proper orientation of the sea was not west to east but north to south. Their ambition to reorientate the Mediterranean had been constantly thwarted by Britain's west–east stranglehold. As early as May 1919 Mussolini had travelled to Fiume, the heart of *Italia irredenta*, to tell his supporters that 'the first thing to be done is to banish foreigners from the Mediterranean, beginning with the English'.[38] Now that Fascism had 'incalculably strengthened Italy's spiritual, political and military efficiency', Britain would discover that Italian possession of the north–south 'trans-Mediterranean lines Sicily–Tripoli and Dodecanese–Tobruk' rendered its own Mediterranean artery forfeit. Britain was *hegemon* of the Mediterranean, but that hegemony would be challenged. For anyone with a smattering of classical learning – and no account of the Mediterranean in the 1930s could resist extensive reference to ancient history – the implication was clear. Athens's hegemony in the Aegean had – according to Thucydides – inevitably led to war with Sparta. The war had dragged on for decades, leaving Athens enfeebled. Italy was Sparta to Britain's Athens.[39]

Britain was the *hegemon* of the Mediterranean; Fascist Italy was its would-be successor. At either end of the Mediterranean, however, lay two major powers each with claims to eminence in their own half of the sea, with some, albeit limited, ability to project power into the other half. Such an evaluation may seem unfair to the French who possessed a formidable Mediterranean Fleet docked on both shores of the Mediterranean. The French Fleet had naval bases at Marseilles and Toulon in France, Bizerta in Tunisia, and Oran in Algeria. In addition the French had a complex series of alliances with the smaller powers, not least, since 1927, Yugoslavia. It held the 'mandates' for Syria and Lebanon in the eastern Mediterranean. The further east one went, however, the less apparent was French power.[40] Regretfully, the French themselves realized that their naval power made sense in the western Mediterranean only in conjunction with that of Britain, and operated in the east entirely on the sufferance of the English. Although the *Marine* did not like to admit it they were, for all their gleaming new warships and well-appointed ports, merely an escort force for the French Army. Their mundane task was to transport thousands of 'black' African troops across the Mediterranean to serve in Europe. If the French ever had to fight the Germans they intended to rerun the war of 1914–1918, this time bleeding Africa, rather than France, 'white'. By the end of the first year of a European war, half a million Africans would be fighting for France, with millions more to come if necessary.[41] 'If we use the base in Majorca', Mussolini assured Hitler's foreign minister, Joachim Ribbentrop, 'not one negro will be able to cross from Africa to France by the Mediterranean route.'[42] The head of the French navy, Admiral François Darlan, believed that Majorca was more important than Spain.[43]

The embarrassment, for some a humiliation, of the navy's subordinate position made for a streak of vicious Anglophobia that ran through the *Marine* and other elements in French life. Many Britons, on the other hand, admired France's Mediterranean empire. Winston Churchill, wintering in North Africa, remarked that 'you would be staggered by what the French have done out here in twenty years . . . an extraordinary effort'. 'The French are not at all infected with the apologetic diffidence that characterizes British administration,' he assured the readers of the *Daily Mail* in February 1936, 'they offer [indigenous] inhabitants logical, understanding modern solutions.'[44]

The Mediterranean's other major power, Turkey, revived by the successful Kemalist revolution, had had its right to the Sea of Marmara – and to the city of Constantinople on its west shore – acknowledged by the other powers after it had gone to the brink of war with Britain in 1922. Turkey sat astride the third egress from the Mediterranean. The Straits, the Dardanelles running from the Mediterranean into the Sea of Marmara, and the Bosphorus running from the Sea of Marmara into the Black Sea, remained under international control. The Turks could not deploy a formidable navy, but their huge army lay at the heart of the Kemalist regime.[45]

Both the French and the Turks knew that for Italian ambitions to be realized, they themselves would need to be displaced. In 1926 the *Duce*'s brother, Arnaldo, was honest about family intentions. Italy would predate both the French and the Turks. Italian expansion had many avenues to pursue. 'There's the entire eastern basin of the Mediterranean, where the remnants of the old Turkish empire are to be found,' Arnaldo wrote glee-fully in the *Popolo d'Italia*. 'There's also Syria, which France won't even colonize because she has no excess population. Then there's Smyrna which should belong to us. And finally there's Adalia.'[46] The French continually toyed with the idea of an alliance with Italy against the Germans in Europe, to the disadvantage of the British in the Mediterranean, but they could never bring themselves to trust a country whose ambitions ran so obviously counter to their own. In the autumn of 1933, for instance, the Army's *Deuxième Bureau* reluctantly concluded that the destruction of France would be 'a fundamental objective of Italian policy as long as France remains a Mediterranean power'.[47]

The Turks, unlike the French, never tried to convince themselves that the Italians were friends.[48] Kemal Ataturk had a nice line in Mussolini appreciation: 'the swollen bullfrog of the Pontine Marshes'. The Turks also had a cynical view of the Italian threat: 'It is unlikely that there will be any serious trouble between Italy and Turkey,' Ataturk commented in 1935, 'madmen don't as a rule fall foul of drunkards.'[49] Indeed, the Turks adroitly turned the geopolitical obsessions of the other powers to their own advantage. With astonishingly little resistance they persuaded other countries to allow them to reoccupy the Straits. The signature of the Montreux Straits Convention in July 1936 was the signal for remarkable manifestations of joy throughout Turkey. Turkish troops were greeted on the Dardanelles with garlands and streamers, the Turkish Fleet was met by cheering crowds. In September 1936 King Edward VIII, travelling 'incognito' as the Duke of Lancaster, arrived off Turkey in his steam yacht; he and Ataturk paid each other carefully choreographed mutual visits. The Turkish Fleet steamed into the Mediterranean for the first time since the Great War. They were warmly received at Malta. British diplomats were delighted by their coup; the British military was not. British interest in the new situation and the assistance Britain would receive from it, they complained, could be summed up in one phrase: 'very small'. 'This country', the military observed wearily, 'would give more than it receives.'[50]

Many post-war Italian historians have doubted the seriousness of Mussolini's Mediterranean ambitions. Citing his undoubted tergiversations, they have questioned whether a master plan for Italian hegemony in the Mediterranean ever really existed. Their Mussolini is a restless opportunist, constantly searching for a status that Italy's military and economic power did not deserve. This Mussolini was potentially as interested in the Danube and the Brenner Pass as in a new Roman Empire. He was a 'Stresa' Mussolini, as likely to make a deal with Britain against Germany in Europe as he was to make a pact with Germany against Britain in the Mediterranean. Refuting these unconvincing apologetics has made work for generations of counter-revisionists.[51]

Mussolini's apologists were able to make a case because of the self-contradictions at the heart of Fascist plans for the Mediterranean. Mussolini contradicted himself about the purpose of a Mediterranean empire. Often he celebrated Italy's Mediterranean destiny. He spoke of the Mediterranean as Italy's natural space. Italy, Mussolini declared, was 'an island which juts into the Mediterranean'. What was the Mediterranean to Italy, he asked: 'it is life'. For the British, on the other hand, the Mediterranean was no more than 'a short cut whereby the British empire reaches more rapidly its outlying territories'.[52] He would, he boasted, recreate *Mare Nostrum* – 'our sea' – as part of the great Fascist crusade to rebuild the Roman Empire. That empire had bound together the north and south of the Mediterranean; Italy and North Africa had been an organic whole.[53] Now Fascism would rebuild 'the fourth shore', the empire in North Africa. It would be peopled by Italian colonists.[54] One could only admire, wrote a British expert, 'the courage of the Italian nation in boldly applying new methods to this old problem of colonization, and in setting examples which, if they succeed, will furnish models for others to follow'.[55] Freed of land hunger the Italian population would increase exponentially. In decades to come the Mediterranean, purged of the British, would house an Italian population rivalling that of the British Empire, the United States or the Soviet Union.

At other moments Mussolini disdained the Mediterranean. Far from being a natural space, it was a prison. The Fascists could not confine themselves to repopulating the Fourth Shore. They needed to escape the Mediterranean altogether. In 1934 he told the Second Quinquennial Assembly of the Fascist Party that Italy would 'find the keys of the Mediterranean in the Red Sea'. 'The historical objectives of Italy have two names,' he declared, 'Asia and Africa.'[56] In 1938 Mussolini had 'The March to the Oceans' included in the official record of the Fascist Grand Council. It claimed that Italy was imprisoned in the Mediterranean:

> The bars of this prison are Corsica, Tunisia, Malta, and Cyprus. The guards of this prison are Gibraltar and Suez. Corsica is a pistol pointed at the heart of Italy; Tunisia at Sicily. Malta and Cyprus constitute a threat to all our positions in the eastern and western Mediterranean. Greece, Turkey, and Egypt have been ready to form a chain with Great Britain and to complete the politico-military encirclement of Italy. Thus Greece, Turkey, and Egypt must be considered vital enemies of Italy and of its expansion . . . Once the bars are broken, Italian policy can only have one motto – to March to the Oceans.[57]

What did Mussolini want? A Mediterranean Empire? Or was the Mediterranean merely a prison from which he must break free to achieve *Weltmacht*? Whatever the answer, the first step was the same: Italy had to defeat the British.

The contradiction in Fascist goals was actually less important than the contradiction in Fascist methods. Whereas the difference between *Mare Nostrum* and the Prison was only intermittently debated, arguments within the Fascist elite about methods of expansion were constant. There were two main schools of thought. On one side were those who advocated *mezzi insidiosi*, 'insidious methods', the use of stealth and dissimulation to achieve long-term goals. The driving force behind Mediterranean expansion should be political warfare. Through subversion, propaganda and espionage the Fascists could undermine their rivals. Self-doubt and internal divisions would cause them to collapse. If military force was to be used, it should be limited and aimed at weak opponents. The most useful type of military power was provided by special forces. They would engage in asymmetric warfare, using a few men armed with innovative weapons to cause disproportionate amounts of damage to the enemy. The Italians were pioneers in special forces. The navy's 'Special Weapons Section' was tasked with using explosive-filled motorboats and 'human torpedoes' to bring the British Mediterranean Fleet to its knees.[58] Large conventional armed forces were also important but they were a 'luxury fleet', cowing and deterring potential enemies whilst the *mezzi insidiosi* took their toll. 'Our fleet has no battleships; it has fast cruisers with little or no defences; it has good destroyers, good submarines. It is thus able to engage in little more than . . . guerrilla warfare at sea,' the head of Italy's armed forces, Pietro Badoglio, warned Mussolini in 1935.[59]

This cannot be true Fascism, others objected. The practice of diplomacy, albeit laced with terrorism, hardly suited the needs of a regime whose claims to violent, masculine *squadrismo* were beginning to look distinctly middle-aged. The Second Quinquennium reminded everyone that Fascism had done nothing violent or heroic for at least ten years.[60] Fascism would thrive on heroic conflict. The road to world power was paved by catalytic wars rather than sneaky subversion.[61] The Italian armed forces should be expanded and re-equipped, most especially with the weapons of total war, the bomber and the battleship. These forces were far from a luxury. They were there to be used. If the democracies showed signs of coalescing to face the threat, then Italy too would need to seek congenial allies, most notably Nazi Germany.

Throughout the 1930s the dispute over methods was a closely fought battle. In 1936 Admiral Domenico Cavagnari, the professional head of the Italian navy, declared that *mezzi insidiosi* showed a lack of ambition. Responding to Badoglio's scepticism, in August 1936 he ordered his officers to concentrate on building a battlefleet capable of attacking the British in conjunction with the Nazi *Kriegsmarine*.[62] The predicted date for a war was 1942. The *Duce* formally proclaimed the Italian-German Axis on 1 November 1936 to 'an immense and enthusiastic crowd' in a speech in the *Piazza Duomo* of Milan. His words were later broadcast in the major Mediterranean languages – English, French, Greek, Spanish and Arabic. He told Hitler's personal representative that 'our relations with London are very bad and cannot improve'. In return Hitler's message was: 'that we should know that he regards the Mediterranean as a purely Italian sea'.[63] Mussolini's 'tragedy' was that his regime was supremely well equipped for *mezzi insidiosi* whereas its lack of material resources hobbled its preparation for total war.

Mezzi insidiosi continued in full force despite the Axis. In August 1935, the Royal Navy had decided that its great base at Malta was too dangerous as a wartime berth for the Mediterranean Fleet. Whenever there was a crisis the Fleet would have to steam to Alexandria, its main harbour in Egypt. Unlike Malta, however, Alexandria was far from being an ideal anchorage. Although offering the charms of a cosmopolitan and well-stocked city to sailors, it had real military disadvantages. Alexandria did not have a dockyard that could repair any damaged ships. Any warship damaged by accident or enemy action would have to leave the Mediterranean altogether. And Alexandria's harbour mouth was notoriously narrow. If a ship was sunk within it, the entire British fleet would be trapped. Indeed, days after war in Abyssinia was declared, the Italian liner *Ausonia* – 'the most luxurious steamer on the Europe–Egypt service' – mysteriously caught fire in the entrance to Alexandria Bay.[64] British destroyers raced to the scene and, at considerable risk to themselves, nosed up to the Italian ship and pushed it out of the way. 'British naval men', remarked a journalist who reported the story, 'have their own private opinion of the burning of this ship in this particular place.'[65]

A final flaw of Alexandria was created by its position on the Nile Delta. The outpouring of the Nile created complex eddies, currents and water densities. By developing a method – called sonar – of 'pinging' artificial bodies underwater with sound waves, and picking up the echo, the British possessed what they hoped was the decisive weapon against submarines. The hydrology of Alexandria, however, crippled this brilliant new British invention.[66] Alexandria was the perfect laboratory for *mezzi insidiosi*. Italian submarines operated at the harbour mouth, shadowing British battleships whenever they left port.[67]

In the event, however, Italian submariners demonstrated the value of *mezzi insidiosi* elsewhere in the Mediterranean. In August 1937 Mussolini and Ciano ordered them to launch a 'pirate war' in the Mediterranean against Spanish and Soviet shipping.[68] In Rome, they would maintain 'plausible deniability'. Merchantmen would be sent to the bottom by desperadoes of unknown origin. Fifty-nine submarines fanned out through the Mediterranean. Some daring submariners made it as far as the Black Sea Straits where they attacked Soviet ships, proving that the Turks could not defend the Straits they had, with such fanfare, remilitarized. Cruisers and destroyers entered the Straits of Sicily, the choke point between eastern and western Mediterranean, attacking any Spanish ship that passed. Torpedo boats ranged along the North African coast doing the same.[69] The operation also was not without its risks. At the end of August the submarine *Iride* attacked the Royal Navy ship HMS *Havock* in error. Up until that point British destroyer crews had largely enjoyed their posting in the western Mediterranean. Memorably, Miss Czechoslovakia had embarked on a warship during a stop-over at Palma by the First Destroyer Flotilla. The beauty queen had 'enjoyed her passage enormously and even joined us in the water when we stopped and piped hands to bathe'.[70] The contrast with a sudden attack was a shock. The enraged destroyer captain hunted the submarine for hours, although in the end neither vessel was sunk. Even Ciano admitted, 'we are in deep trouble'.[71]

The foreign ministers of the 'Mediterranean powers' assembled in the Swiss town of Nyon to discuss what should be done about the 'piracy'.[72] Nyon was an appeasers' paradise. The fiction that attacks on merchant shipping in the Mediterranean was the fault of 'pirates unknown' was fully indulged. Italy was even invited to the meeting, although it declined to attend. Not one word of criticism of Mussolini was allowed to emerge. The Mediterranean powers agreed to set up anti-submarine patrols. Italy was invited to take part in these patrols, in effect allowing her destroyers to search for her own submarines. The Royal Navy accorded the *Regia Marina* equality of status in the Mediterranean.[73] Nyon was hailed as a triumph of 'collective security'. England: 'a nation which thinks with its arse', was Mussolini's rather more robust verdict. 'It is a great victory,' chuckled Ciano, who only a fortnight before had been scared by the thought of British action, 'from accused torpedoers to Mediterranean policemen, with the exclusion of the Russians, whose ships have been sunk.'[74] Nyon preserved the naval status quo in the Mediterranean until the end of the Spanish Civil War: the Francoists received whatever they wanted, the Republicans got very little.[75]

Mezzi insidiosi rested on a clear understanding of the psychological weakness of enemies. Mussolini could look deep inside the British military, political and diplomatic establishment. The Italians had an outstanding intelligence network that fed Mussolini timely and accurate accounts of British deliberations about the Mediterranean. Mussolini often dressed up the sources of his information in picaresque stories; he ascribed his – accurate – information about ammunition shortages of the Royal Navy in the Mediterranean to a letter from 'a lady' in London.[76] In fact the intelligence-gathering was not fortuitous but the result of a professional and systematic effort. In 1924 Italian military intelligence – SIM – had introduced its first mole into the British Embassy in Rome. The treacherous

Embassy servant was, in due course, succeeded by his brother, who kept Mussolini supplied with British diplomatic correspondence until Italy entered the Second World War in June 1940.[77] At the post-war trial of the head of SIM, General Mario Roatta, it was claimed that his agency removed 16,000 documents a year from embassies in Rome. They also ran operations in other capitals. Italian employees of the Marconi company in Egypt, for instance, copied sensitive telegrams and fed them to Italian intelligence.[78] When Galeazzo Ciano met Hitler on 24 October 1936 he was able to hand him a dossier of thirty-two British Foreign Office documents. 'Today,' Ciano recorded the Führer as saying, 'England is governed merely by incompetents.'[79]

Hitler had a point: the damage caused by Italian espionage went far beyond diplomatic documents, however revealing of national policy. The haul from the British Embassy in Rome included diplomatic and consular codes, the naval attaché cipher, the India cipher and the interdepartmental cipher. Even without these windfalls the Italian cryptanalysts found communications between London and Athens, Belgrade, Rome and Addis Ababa easy to break. SIM could read British, French and Ethiopian diplomatic traffic. Naval codebreakers had similar successes. From the summer of 1935 they were reading signals from the Admiralty to Royal Navy units in the Mediterranean and the Red Sea.[80] The decrypts often reached Mussolini's desk within twenty-four hours of interception. Ignorant of how compromised they were, even the British recognized that Mussolini knew a great deal about their military plans and dispositions, 'for', Sir Robert Vansittart, the professional head of the Foreign Office, conceded, 'they have a decent Intelligence service.'[81]

TWO

Death on the Nile

In October 1937 another famous novelist paid tribute to the impact of *mezzi insidiosi* on the English imagination. 'The best of the new autumn crop' of thrillers was Agatha Christie's *Death on the Nile*. It told a story of theft and murder in Egypt, unravelled by Christie's Cartesian *alter ego*, the mincing Belgian, Hercule Poirot. *Death on the Nile* proved an entertainment of such enduring charm that few noticed how timely was the central plot. A group of western tourists escape the cold of the western Mediterranean for Egypt, 'real warmth, darling. Lazy golden sounds. The Nile.' On board the steamer *Karnak*, Poirot encounters two characters whose politics intrude into the murderous private affairs of their fellow passengers. His old friend Colonel Race, 'a man of unadvertised comings and goings . . . usually to be found in one of the outposts of empire where trouble was brewing', was on the trail of those who sought to undermine British power. There had been 'a good deal of trouble out here'. But it was not, the Colonel revealed, 'the people who ostensibly led the rioters we're after'. Race's prey were the men who 'very cleverly put the match to the gunpowder'. He was seeking one of the 'cleverest paid agitators that ever existed . . . a man with five or six cold-blooded murders to his credit . . . bit of a mongrel'. That clever, murdering, mongrel turned out to be an Italian fellow passenger. There was something not right about Signor Guido Richetti, *Archeologo*. He used 'hair lotions of a highly scented kind' and carried a lady's gun, the 'Mauser automatic twenty-five'.[1] Most damning was the discovery of Richetti's telegraphed instructions from the Italian secret service in Rome. Once their code had been broken, it revealed that an innocent discussion of vegetables was something much more sinister, a plan for violent revolution, for 'potatoes mean machine guns and artichokes are high explosives'.

Christie's thriller was unusually well informed. At the time of publication official opinion had judged that the threat of subversion in Egypt was great enough to require the institution in Cairo of the 'the only purely MI5 organisation in the area'. The real-life counterpart to Colonel Race, Major Raymond Maunsell, was soon 'deeply implicated in Egyptian politics'.[2] Few informed observers doubted that, by 1937, Britain was faced by a serious crisis in the Muslim Mediterranean.[3] After decades of toying with the Eastern Question the British had definitively displaced the Ottomans as the master race at the end of the First World War. Since then she had requited none of the hopes, bizarre and impractical as her officials saw them, invested in her rule. It was Britain which was seen as a tyrannical and destructive force. Many found her representatives arrogant and hateful. They longed to be done with the British. In 1937 it was hard to judge, however, the depth and importance of such malcontent. Some said that the problem went no further than members of the traditional elite, both secular and religious, disgruntled that the British insisted on a modicum of good governance. Others looked deeper and said that the maintenance of such traditions, especially the indulgence of corruption, was in the British interest. The pashas and notables might make spiteful complaint, plot and curse in private, but in the end they were no real threat. If politics ever took to the street, the masses would not thank Britons for their reforming efforts; rather they would string the unbelievers from the recently provided lampposts.[4]

The same informed observers were in little doubt that Britain's enemies were fishing in these foetid waters. Propaganda, money and weapons flowed into the eastern Mediterranean. Signor Richettis aplenty plied their subversive and violent trade. In 1935 Captain Ugo Dadone, dashing traveller, explorer, journalist and zealous Fascist, set up a propaganda office in Cairo.[5] The Italians financed the radical Young Egypt movement. Young Egypt organized its paramilitary Green Shirts to ape the Black Shirts. The Ministry of Propaganda, then headed by Galeazzo Ciano, set up a radio station, Radio Bari, to appeal directly to Arab malcontents. In the summer of 1935 it began daily broadcasts that proved wildly successful because 'adapted to the average puerile Arab mind'. Bari declared that: 'the Arab populations of the Levant must be freed from the yoke of their present masters'. It traded on the message that 'Arab patriots . . . all those not contaminated by British gold – know well the consequences of Britain's rule, they know how much grief and blood-shed Britain has caused . . . that it is in the interest of Fascist Italy that the Arab nations of the Levant attain their freedom and independence'.[6] The British soon noticed that Bari was 'becoming increasingly popular in Arab cafes'. Arabs 'sipped their coffee and swallowed Italian propa-ganda with every mouthful'. In 1937 it was calculated that over half of all the radios in Palestine were tuned into Bari.[7]

Mussolini made a spectacular appeal for a Fascist-Muslim alliance in March 1937. Marshal Italo Balbo, the Governor of Libya, had complained that the dreams of a Fourth Shore were far from realization. Not only was it actually hard to get to Libya from Italy, but it was virtually impos-sible to travel along the Mediterranean coast. The two halves of Libya, Tripolitania and Cyrenaica, were bisected by the inhospitable Sirtean desert. If one wished to travel from the capital in Tripoli to Benghazi, Cyrenaica's main port, all that was on offer was a weekly boat. He devised a grand plan, a road that would run the length of Libya's Mediterranean coast, all the way from the Tunisian to the Egyptian border. The gleaming thousand-mile-long highway was completed at the beginning of 1937. An arch of triumph was erected in the middle of the desert. The road was so much Balbo's project that it was nicknamed the *Balbia*. Though irritated by the name, Mussolini grasped the symbolic importance of Balbo's achievement. Determined to claim the glory for this great monu-ment of civilization, he agreed to preside over the festivities.[8]

A celebration of the civilizing mission, and the unveiling of plans for a mass influx of colonists from Italy, might have seemed an unlikely occa-sion for a celebration of Islamo-Fascist friendship. But in Balbo's fertile mind he was to be the architect of pan-Mediterranean syncretism. Buildings, he decreed, were no longer to espouse European modernism but a 'Mediterranean' style. The minaret of the mosque and the tower of the Italian town were part of the same culture.[9] The Islamic part of that heritage must be respected. The Governor funded religious schools and banned the sale of alcohol in Ramadan. What better place than Tripoli, 'the new pearl of the Mediterranean', Balbo convinced Mussolini, as a centre for *mezzi insidiosi*.[10]

The fondouks of the old town of Tripoli were torn down to make way for the new Mediterranean metropolis. The city was subject to a phantasmagoria of lighting effects. Balbo's palace, the Cathedral and long stretch of the embankment were floodlit. An immense *Dux* was laid out in powerful electric lights attached to the newly constructed grain silo. The motto 'Believe, Obey, Fight' was picked out in twelve-feet-high lighting on the customs warehouse. A steel tower was erected in the castle square with a huge searchlight mounted on top. The light beam was visible for thirty miles all around. When everything was ready, Balbo left Tripoli for Cyrenaica. At Benghazi, he proclaimed that Mussolini was the 'Protector of Islam'. Two days later the *Duce* himself stepped ashore at Tobruk. Accompanying him to Libya was a cruise ship filled with 120 journalists. Each journalist was provided with a car and servants so that they might follow Mussolini along the *Balbia* from east to west. The journey, by car and aeroplane, took four days.

On the evening of 16 March 1937 Mussolini made a triumphal entrance into Tripoli. He was accompanied by a bodyguard of Arab cavalrymen. The route was lined by tens of thousands of Arabs brought in from the countryside. It was said that political officers had rounded up nearly the entire pastoral population. For weeks afterwards, 'little columns of dust [would] betray the presence of nomads making the weary journey back'. Each group was equipped with banners to represent their particular Islamic religious society. The procession ended in the castle square. There, Mussolini was greeted by the dug-out son of the last Ottoman ruler of Tripoli and the Kadi, the head of the sharia courts. The Kadi in particular had a major role in driving home the point of the visit. The next afternoon he once more greeted Mussolini, at the mosque. 'I take the opportunity presented by your presence among us', the venerable judge intoned via a 'slick Arabic interpreter', 'to express our profound gratefulness for the favour which Fascism has showered upon these our countries which enjoy the benefits of progress, well-being, justice and perfect respect for our Sharia courts.' 'We declare', he continued, 'that we are truly happy to lie under the shadow of the glorious Italian flag, under the Fascist regime. And how can we forget all that you have said and done in favour of Islam in such important circumstances of international politics, thus acquiring such lively sympathy among the 400 million of Moslem believers.'

Balbo and Mussolini were far from finished, however. On the next afternoon, yet another group of Muslims pledged their loyalty. Arab soldiers of the Italian colonial army were drawn up in mounted array. One of their number rode forward towards Mussolini. 'In the name of the soldiers and Moslems of Libya,' he bellowed, 'I have the honour to offer to you, Victorious *Duce*, this well-tempered Islamic sword. The souls of the Moslems of all the shores of the Mediterranean . . . thrill with emotion at this moment, in sympathy with our own.' Mussolini pulled the sword from its scabbard and ululated a war cry. Then the mounted men made a second triumphal entrance into Tripoli, where Mussolini addressed the Muslim crowd from the saddle, his words followed by running translation in Arabic, each sentence being greeted in turn by cries of 'Dushy, Dushy'.[11]

In the wake of Fascism's victory over the Christians of Abyssinia, important Muslim leaders were ready to heed Mussolini's appeal for an anti-British alliance. First amongst them was Amin al-Husseini, Grand Mufti of Jerusalem, leader of radical Islam in Palestine. The Mufti was an elusive character. People tended to see in him what they wanted. He was regarded by some as a charming moderate. Those who crossed him found that he was cruel, merciless and unbalanced: they would fear his assassins for the rest of their often shortened lives. The British High Commissioner in Palestine, Sir Arthur Wauchope, said of the Mufti that as time passed wicked Dr Jekyll became dominant over the more moderate Mr Hyde. It was a revealing slip: in Stevenson's original story Mr Hyde is evil personified. Hitler refused to believe that the Mufti was a Semite at all. In the skewed vision of the Nazis he became a blond, blue-eyed Aryan, albeit one spoilt by miscegenation. The Grand Mufti was known to his Palestinian enemies as 'the spider' or 'Rasputin'.[12]

The Mufti had once been Britain's favourite Muslim. The mandatory government had sponsored his rise during the 1920s as a traditional aristocrat willing to collaborate with them in crushing secular militants. In 1934 the Mufti's power base, the Supreme Muslim Council of Palestine, was given an astonishingly generous financial settlement. The British congratulated themselves that the Mufti's religious charisma gave him dominion over the peasantry, inoculating them against the dangers of extremism. The Mufti put it differently. He had always hated the English. His goal was their total overthrow, but it was foolish to launch a revolt unprepared. The best approach was to undermine British power covertly, whilst preparing the jihad. With British money the Mufti created cohorts of officials loyal to him. One of his relatives toured the villages around Jerusalem, as a member of the land settlement department, creating a jihadist organization, known as the Sacred Holy War. Sacred Holy War created training camps where members of the Palestine police and the Syrian army trained insurgents.[13] As the Mufti told a Nazi diplomat, the Muslims of Palestine hoped fervently for 'the spread of fascist and anti-democratic leadership to other countries'.[14]

Britain's second foe was Ali Maher Pasha, minister of the royal household, *éminence grise* to the monarchs of Egypt.[15] Radio Bari blared that the English hypocrites took risks for infidel savages, the Abyssinians, but reduced civilized Muslims to slavery. Ali Maher's mobs cheered Mussolini as a Copt killer – the Patriarch of the Abyssinian church being traditionally chosen from amongst the Coptic monks of Egypt. Unlike the Grand Mufti, Ali Maher's espousal of violent Mohammedanism was not particularly sincere. His loathing of democracy, however, was just as real. In his view the 'illiterate electorate' should be no more than the attendees of disciplined rallies as in Fascist Italy. His main purpose was to recruit zealous thugs. Like the Italians he looked to the Green Shirts of Young Egypt as potential shock troops. His alliance with the sheikhs provided him with squads of embittered young men who found that their religious education was mocked by secular technocrats. Ali Maher could put violent gangs on the streets. He knew, however, that he had to bide his time.

The true mass movement in Egypt was the Wafd, 'the Delegation', the secular anti-royalist nationalist party created at the end of the First World War. The Wafd, too, was determined to make use of the Abyssinian War to its best advantage. Enemies of the Wafd charged that it was a Coptic conspiracy, its second-in-command and most outspoken radical, Makram Ubeid, was a Christian, reviled as 'Master William' by his Muslim opponents. Ubeid too, however, admired the Black Shirts. He raised his own paramilitary militia, the Blue Shirts. Egypt proved one of the most prolific creators of movements which looked to Fascist Black Shirt street violence as a model for emulation. Ciano's agents had great success in recruiting genuine Black Shirts from amongst the Italian population in Egypt. When Ciano visited in 1936, twenty thousand Black Shirts greeted him.[16] The appeal of Fascist methods was potent. The Wafd leadership remained, however, Italophobes. They saw little advantage in swapping British imperialism for the Italian variety.[17] After much thought, the leader of the Wafd, Nahas Pasha, denounced the Italian bogey. The Blue Shirts were turned upon the Green Shirts. Nahas and the British High Commissioner in Egypt, Sir Miles Lampson, agreed that the best answer to 'Italian intrigue' was an Anglo-Egyptian treaty.[18] The treaty would serve both their interests. The British could tell the world that they had secured untrammelled rights to bases around the Suez Canal. Nahas could tell the Egyptians that he had secured independence.[19]

The tawdry insincerity of the Anglo-Egyptian negotiations provided fertile ground for Ali Maher and his Fascist allies to exploit. In Farouk, the boy-king of Egypt, Ali Maher saw the perfect blank canvas from which he could create an Islamo-Fascist monarchy. The Wafd's elderly candidate for head of the royal household was discredited by his dalliance with a seventeen-year-old Austrian girl. With his competitor disposed of, Ali Maher became once again officially the King's chief adviser. Farouk invited a circle of Italian Fascist advisers to the Palace. Chief amongst them was the 'royal architect'. He did little design work. Instead he was a conduit for intelligence and influence to flow between Rome and Cairo. His influence was cemented by his equally important role of royal pander, supplying the young European girls so prized at Court.[20]

Fascists in the Palace were not Nahas's only problem. The Wafd had won power by aping Fascist models of street violence. Yet it was unclear whether they controlled the power on the streets that they had unleashed. The gangs created in the image of the Black Shirts did not necessarily agree with their leader's contention that the British, although repugnant, were better than the Italians. Although Nahas proclaimed himself 'supreme leader' of the Blue Shirts, they increasingly appeared as much a threat as a boon. The government of Egypt had declared against the Italians but contained elements of Fascist decay within it. The Blue Shirts turned on their own corrupt pashadom. The Party had to use all the powers of the State to destroy its own mass movement, to the benefit of Ali Maher and the Palace.

Egyptian Islamo-Fascism emboldened others.[21] The Mufti of Jerusalem himself had never had much in common with his fellow Islamic militants in Egypt. Egyptian clerics dreaming of a Caliphate in Cairo distrusted their more charismatic Palestinian brother, who made no secret of his own ambition to lead Sunni Islam. The Egyptian Islamo-Fascist successes, however, egged on the Syrians. The Syrian National Bloc created its own paramilitaries on the Fascist model, the Steel Shirts.[22] The Syrian Emir Shakib Arslan, the best-known spokesman of militant Arab nationalism, whose anti-French, anti-British propaganda was financed in equal measure by Mussolini and Hitler, goaded the Mufti in the Palestinian press.[23] The circumstances overrode the Mufti's preference for *mezzi insidiosi*.[24] The terrorist cells were activated. In April 1936 the Mufti himself arrived on the Mediterranean coast. Arabs started murdering Jews. The Mufti emerged as the head of the Arab Higher Committee. A general strike was declared.[25] The priority of the strike was to close down Palestine's modern commerce. The first target was the Mediterranean ports, and the railways which took imports inland. The struggle centred on Haifa, Palestine's great hope for modernity. It contained a new port built by the British and the railway workshops, the largest industrial site in Palestine.[26] Old Haifa was the base of the most notorious Islamic terrorists, the Black Hand. Modern Haifa was a heterogeneous place with many new immigrants. There, where the strike could have had most effect, its hold was patchy. On the other hand, the old Arab port of Jaffa was completely closed down. In order to solidify the strike in Haifa, and maintain it in Jaffa, the leaders of the revolt required a great deal of money. They needed to offer wavering Arab workers alternative incomes. Appeals to fellow Muslims raised very little.[27]

The Italians, on the other hand, were more than willing to provide the Mufti with 'millions'. Both the Italians and the insurgents got what they wanted. British troops were transferred from the Egyptian-Libyan border to Palestine, where they struggled to deal with terrorism. At last it seemed that money and violence would close down Haifa. *In extremis*, the British Army acted decisively. It sent troops into Haifa to protect those who kept working. But British success in Haifa provoked even more violence. Insurgents took to the countryside. If they could not close the ports they would sabotage the economy inland. In the towns the paramilitaries forced shops to close, preventing what arrived at the ports from being sold. Foreign fighters arrived from around the Arab world. Those with military training were able to deploy heavier weapons such as machine guns, making the bands even more deadly.

The British response was hobbled by disagreement over the nature of the revolt. Sir John Dill, the officer dispatched from Britain to deal with the insurgents, argued that the surest and most effective way of crippling the uprising was to decapitate it. He wanted to eliminate the Mufti. The High Commissioner in Palestine, Sir Arthur Wauchope, however, remained the Mufti's dupe. Wauchope's own desire that Palestine should become a peaceful, multi-racial, multi-religious society, led him astray.[28] The effect, one of his senior police officials remarked, was 'a

policy of glossing things over'.[29] In the autumn of 1936 London finally
agreed to overrule Wauchope. He was ordered to extirpate the leaders of
the revolt. Despite these orders Wauchope remained determined to subvert
the 'hard policy'. His first response was to wash his hands of his responsibilities, for he must remain 'the Kindly Father' of the Arabs. As the day
of martial law drew near, he warned the Arab Higher Committee that
he would soon be unable to protect them. The Mufti heeded Wauchope's
warning. Just before the Army moved in to arrest the leaders of the revolt,
the Arab Higher Committee decreed that they had won and the strike
would end. With his power intact the High Commissioner was able to
override any plans to hunt down the insurgents. Foreign fighters merely
crossed the border into Syria whilst home-grown terrorists returned
unmolested to their day jobs. As Dill bitterly observed, a great proportion
of the fighting power of the British army had been deployed to achieve
a paper victory.[30]

By the time Mussolini unsheathed the sword of Islam in Tripoli, the
Mufti was planning an even greater uprising in Palestine. His Italian lire
funded a meeting of militants at Bludan, well recorded since the 'Colonel
Race' of Syria, Colonel MacKereth, managed to sneak in an agent disguised
as an ice-seller.[31] Compromised, the Mufti fled. In the first of the escapes
that added glamour to his sinister fame, he climbed down the walls of
his Jerusalem mosque, sped to the Mediterranean coast by car and boarded
a boat for Lebanon. Once safely in Beirut he declared Jihad against the
British. It was launched on 26 September 1937.[32] In November 1937,
when the British decided to send more troops to the eastern
Mediterranean, the reinforcements went to Palestine. Far from deterring
Mussolini, the so-called 'Middle East strategic reserve' was tied down by
his Islamic allies in emergency counter-insurgency. Twenty thousand
troops, including eighteen infantry battalions, were deployed in the
country.[33] Mussolini's jihad even won the admiration of Hitler, who had
previously dismissed the Arabs as lacquered apes.[34]

Ciano, famously, dismissed the efficacy of political *mezzi insidiosi*. 'For
years,' he moaned to the German ambassador in Rome, 'he had maintained constant relations with the Grand Mufti, of which his secret fund
could tell a tale.' Sadly, Ciano lamented, 'the return of his gift of millions
had not been exactly great'. Militarily, all he had got for his money was

a few bands of Muslim insurgents willing to sabotage the oil pipeline that ran from northern Iraq to the Mediterranean coast at Haifa. But Ciano was speaking after Italy had declared war on Britain. Subversion was then of little importance to immediate military campaigns.[35] As Otto von Hentig, the premier German expert on oriental subversion, pointed out, the erosion of British power in the Mediterranean would take years rather than months. In Egypt, Ali Maher was Prime Minister, although he was too wily to twit British power openly. With the greatest difficulty the British had been able to smother the second *intifada*.[36] It was only in July 1939 that Britain, at last, managed to transfer troops from Palestine to the Egyptian-Libyan frontier. A remarkable amount had been achieved in only four years. Mussolini had acted as a beacon of hope for all those who hated the British. The tangible links between Islamic militancy and Fascism were actually less important than a vision of the future. The Italians had shown that British rule was not inescapable. 'The old impression of invulnerability has gone,' concluded one intelligence report, 'and while there are many who believe that England can still hold her own in the Mediterranean, there are just as many who question her ability to do so.'[37] It was possible to plan, and fight for, the illiberal, undemocratic bright horizon.[38]

THREE

Of Mice and Men

In the spring of 1939 the great Mediterranean navies had a burst of enthusiasm for killing each other. The Royal Navy found release from its own problems in fantasizing about giving the despised 'Itiy' a good drubbing.[1] The *Regia Marina* reached the height of its fervour for Fascist manliness. The most enthusiastic champion of a Mediterranean war was, however, the French *Marine* and in particular its charismatic leader Jean-François Darlan. Darlan had furiously politicked his way to the top. He cultivated an image as a 'liberal' ready to bring the navy out of the nineteenth century and into the twentieth. His fellow admirals did not altogether trust him. Most of them respected or feared his skills. They knew he had the ear of their political masters. They realized that Darlan had sedulously placed his own allies in positions of influence during his rise to the top.

The royal republicans of the *Marine* understood that France's best guarantee against Italian belligerence was the dominant power of Britain in the Mediterranean. This knowledge did not make them happy. France should have had a great role in the Mediterranean. She had a powerful fleet. That fleet had modern bases to both the north and the south: Toulon in metropolitan France, Oran in Algeria, Bizerta in Tunisia. Bizerta was the 'key naval base of the Middle Mediterranean', commanding the narrow seas between Sicily and Tunisia. Bizerta struck one British observer in the spring of 1939 as 'the most magnificent harbour on the whole African coast'. The bay was large and deep enough to accommodate the entire French fleet. Unlike the main British naval base in the central Mediterranean, Malta, its Tunisian hinterland could provision and support that fleet even in time of war.[2]

Unfortunately, however many great warships and magnificent facilities they possessed, at root the task of the French navy was to transport the French army from North Africa to southern France. This was hardly the glorious sea-spanning mission of a true battlefleet. But there was a golden scenario. If the Royal Navy was to fight Italy, it would seek an ally. French strength in the western Mediterranean would be indispensable; but so too would be France's assets in the eastern Mediterranean. The British would invite the French to sail, not just north and south on their unglamorous supply route, but east to glory. The odds in a naval war between France and Italy were too close to take the risk; the odds in a Mediterranean conflict between a Franco-British alliance and Italy were quite excellent. At the end of the struggle the French navy would be victorious, it would have achieved *gloire*. Most importantly of all, the *Marine* would have inserted itself into the eastern Mediterranean whence it was doubtful whether its erstwhile allies could dislodge it. The thought of the British fighting France's war to their own disadvantage was an appealing opportunity.

Darlan's plan was a difficult concept to sell to his own countrymen, let alone the British. Most French army and air-force officers were fixated on the defence of France's land frontiers, not ambitious naval operations far from home. Until the spring of 1939 the official position of the defence establishment was in favour of an alliance with Mussolini rather than for a war against him.[3] As the most enthusiastic military supporter of a campaign in the eastern Mediterranean, Maxime Weygand, put it: 'if one's range of vision were limited to distant horizons, one ran the risk of being like La Fontaine's astrologer who, walking with his eyes fixed on the stars, fell into a well'.[4] Why couldn't they see, Darlan demanded, that a war was coming in which France and Britain would be pitched against Germany, Italy, Japan and, he feared, Spain? That war would not be won by cowering behind the Maginot Line. War was about grand strategy, it was won by attack rather than defence and, Darlan maintained, the Mediterranean was the key to both. A great coalition war would not be a short affair. It would be a long struggle decided by which side was the most successful in mobilizing its resources. He argued that 'a significant part of British and French supplies and, in particular, almost all the oil extracted from the French, British and Russian oil fields in the East depends on the mastery of the Mediterranean'. More importantly still, the Mediterranean offered the avenue by which Germany and Italy could be outflanked. Now, 'above all,' Darlan observed, 'the Mediterranean constitutes the only communication line with our

Central European allies'. The pivot of such a line would be the city of Salonika in north-east Greece.[5]

Allied to his grand vision Darlan possessed a formidable talent for short-term political manipulation. Unable to convince the stolid military types, he appealed to worried politicians peering uncertainly into *l'âbime*. Rather nervously they agreed to consider his ideas. The political elite was far from endorsing Darlan's scheme but they did allow him to insert the *possibility* of a Mediterranean war into the machinery of planning.[6]

As ever it was Mussolini who transformed a dry debate about future possibilities into a pressing necessity for action.[7] At the end of November 1938, Mussolini ordered Ciano to terrify France. The Italian foreign minister presented himself in the Chamber of Deputies to espouse the 'natural aspirations' of the Italian nation. In response, the Deputies and those in the galleries erupted in chants of 'Tunisia, Corsica, Nice, Savoy'. These chants, if taken literally, reflected a series of territorial demands that would have made Italy the dominant power in the western Mediterranean, not to mention dismembering metropolitan and colonial France. To agree to these demands would have finished France as a serious power and provoked an internal revolution. Even the hardiest of French appeasers found it impossible to imagine how a compromise might be reached if Ciano's audience was a genuine sounding board for Italian ambitions – and Ciano affected to believe that he had 'expressed their aspirations, which are those of the nation'.[8]

One possible response was Nelsonian deafness. 'According to some accounts,' the British ambassador Lord Perth reported to London, the prolonged acclamations for Ciano, 'included cries of "Tunis, Tunis", though they were not distinguishable from the Diplomatic Gallery where I was seated.'[9] Even the Fascist stage-managers appeared a little confused as to what they should be demanding. The gallery claque were supposed to cry for Tunis and Corsica, but not only was Nice added for good measure but a few enthusiastic souls shouted a demand for Morocco as well.[10] Mussolini told the Fascist Grand Council, swearing them to secrecy, that his actual programme was to seize Albania and 'then, for our security needs in the Mediterranean which still constrains us, we need Tunis and Corsica'.[11] Even the *Duce* acknowledged that plans to dismember   ·

metropolitan France were unrealistic. Mussolini's real aim, he told Ciano, was to sow confusion in preparation for the invasion of Albania. The furore would 'distract local attention, allowing us a convenient preparation without stirring up any fear, and in the end induce the French to accept our going into Tirana'.[12]

Within a few days even Mussolini was moved to admit that they might have overdone it, since 'continuing at this rate cannon will have to be put to use and the time has not yet arrived'.[13] The damage, however, had already been done.[14] The French had no mean intelligence service working against the Italians: it was conservatively estimated that France had over one thousand agents in Italy by the late 1930s. The contents of Mussolini's 'March to the Oceans' found their way into French hands. Darlan's warnings about the inevitability of war against a German-Italian Axis were, even his detractors in the French army were moved to admit, appearing more and more prescient by the day. The French Prime Minister, Edouard Daladier, made a highly publicized trip to Tunis in January 1939 to emphasize French willingness to fight for its Mediterranean possessions. He approved extra spending to prepare Tunisia against Italian attack.[15]

Darlan was by no means finished with his manoeuvres. German and Italian bellicosity had finally convinced the appeasement-minded governments of Chamberlain and Daladier that their respective armed forces should be allowed to talk to one another. Darlan hoped to use these talks as a means of achieving his long-term goal of levering France into the eastern Mediterranean. In the short term he intended to use the British to clear away the objections of his colleagues. He found a willing ally in his British opposite number, the newly appointed First Sea Lord, Sir Roger Backhouse. Backhouse, too, was trying to overcome what he regarded as pusillanimous diplomatic appeasers in an attempt to get to grips with Mussolini. If anything he was even more aggressive than Darlan and advocated going straight for the Italian mainland. In the autumn of 1938 he had commissioned his chief planner, the grandiloquently named Sir Reginald Plunkett-Ernle-Erle-Drax, to start work on that basis. The French found Drax's plans rather strong meat.

Italian naval planners had also worked themselves into a lather, if not of aggression, at least of bellicosity. The planners pointed out that an unexpected surprise attack on the British, preceding the outbreak of a general war, might be the best way to achieve their goal. If no such 'knockout blow' was forthcoming then the Italians would wait until they had assembled a big enough army in Libya. The army would then advance eastwards towards Egypt and the Suez Canal to 'to defeat the main enemy at a vital point and open one of the doors that close Italy off from free access to the oceans'.[16] The navy did, however, add one important caveat to these ambitious plans. Although the 'system of defence' that would divide the Mediterranean was plausible, and could be erected in fairly short order, the deployment of the main battlefleet was more problematic. There were only two harbours capable of handling the most modern battleships, both of them historic hangovers more suited for the coastal operations of an earlier age. Genoa was too exposed to attack. Indeed both Darlan and Backhouse had identified it as one of their first targets for naval bombardment. Venice and the Adriatic seaboard were too far from the central Mediterranean. The answer to this problem was a new naval base at Taranto in the far south of the Italian mainland; but it was not due to come into full operation before 1942.

The perceived caution of the naval planners prompted derision from the other services. Mutual inter-service mud-slinging offered an opportunity for Marshal Badoglio, the Chief of Supreme General Staff, who, for all his prestige, was usually kept away from real decision-making, to intervene.[17] Badoglio thought that the war talk was dangerous nonsense. Mussolini's rhetoric, he assured the military chiefs, was just that. He himself had talked to Mussolini. He had assured Badoglio that Ciano's speech and his own statements to the Fascist Grand Council were merely a blind for the limited operation in Albania. Badoglio's timing was poor. On the day that the chiefs met, news arrived in Rome that Barcelona had fallen; victory in Spain, Mussolini said, bore only one name, his own. He had persevered when nay-sayers such as Badoglio had despaired. Mussolini always delighted in making the Marshal appear cowardly and foolish. The very next day the *Duce* contradicted his most distinguished soldier and declared that he was indeed intending to 'wage war and defeat France destroying everything and levelling many cities'.[18]

On 7 April 1939, Italian forces invaded Albania. The self-proclaimed king of the tiny Muslim nation on the Adriatic, Zog, had done his best to

accommodate Italian demands down the years, telling his countrymen that 'we must make speedy and strong paces towards occidental culture and civilisation'. He had even sent his sisters into the mountain strongholds of Islamic fanaticism dressed in tight-fitting skirts to propagate the new Italian way.[19] Despite Zog's willingness to please, Galeazzo Ciano had concluded that it would be much more satisfactory if he, rather than 'an Oriental', should receive the homage of Albania's feudal society. Formally, his intention was to annex the 'made up' nation to the Italian crown. In reality Albania would become the private playground of the Fascist elite. There they could build their hunting lodges, change the names of whole regions and enrich themselves by the exploitation of Albania's presumed oil reserves.[20] Albania, Ciano said, was a 'beautiful spectacle', the Mediterranean 'like a mirror' giving way to green countryside and then the snow-crowned mountains.[21]

Ciano's original plan was to have Zog assassinated, his only qualm a lingering fondness for Zog's wife, Queen Geraldine.[22] The assassination plot was discovered. In its place Ciano convinced Mussolini that a full-scale invasion could win the prize with minimum effort. Even the cautious Badoglio agreed that a war limited to Albania could be carried through without too much trouble. He merely insisted that an even larger body of troops should be used to be on the safe side.[23] The Albanian 'incident' itself was over within forty-eight hours. Zog fled to Greece without putting up any resistance. Observers described a triumph: the British military attaché in Rome reported that 'the invasion of Albania was an example of the great progress made by the Italian army in military organisation on a large scale'.[24]

Those closer to the action were less sure. One of Ciano's aides commented that 'if the Albanians had possessed a corps of well-trained firemen they would have thrown us into the Adriatic'.[25] Ciano himself, who made the short flight to Albania's Italian-built Mediterranean port Durazzo on the day of the invasion, was delighted. The situation in the country was 'excellent'. As Britain's senior diplomat in Tirana noted, 'whatever the deeper feeling of various sections of the Albanian people as a whole, the broad fact remains that on the political side the Italians carried through with much greater ease than might have been expected'.[26] What was even better, Ciano remarked, was that the 'international reaction was almost non-existent'.[27] But despite the cordiality of the Britons on the spot, he was wrong.[28] The invasion marked the start of feverish attempts by Britain to redefine the Mediterranean.[29] Before the spring of 1939 there was talk; between the summer of 1939 and the summer of 1940 there was, if not action, at least organization.

The very terminology used for Britain's new Mediterranean paid testimony to the now overriding concept of a 'closed sea' – impassable to merchantmen and difficult even for warships unless in great strength. If the Mediterranean was severed at the Sicilian Narrows, then British forces could still reach it from the east, albeit with difficulty. Thus, the argument went, the Mediterranean and the Middle East 'was clearly one strategic problem'. In the 1930s the RAF had started using the generic term 'Middle East' to refer to Egypt as well as Iraq, leading in turn to the application of the phrase to all British forces deployed around the eastern shores of the Mediterranean. Sadly no one could quite agree on the nature or geographical extent of that problem.[30] The Army's concept was to create a General Officer Commanding-in-Chief, Middle East. But until the crisis of the summer of 1939, the generals were unwilling to act on their own concept. The army commanders in Egypt and Palestine objected to having a commander imposed on them when their main challenge was internal revolt. They saw themselves as vice-regents of the eastern Mediterranean, in uneasy partnership with their diplomatic and gubernatorial opposite numbers. So the Army parked its commander-in-chief-elect at the other end of the Mediterranean in Gibraltar, ready to be rushed to Cairo in an emergency.[31] It was only in June 1939 that the GOC-in-C was activated. General Archie Wavell was finally dispatched to Egypt in August 1939. At that time he controlled two pieces of the Mediterranean littoral – Egypt and Palestine – and a major island, Cyprus. He was instructed to make arrangements to fight alongside three Mediterranean powers, France, Turkey and Greece; 'a bit hectic if we have a war', he commented with some understatement.[32]

The RAF already had a Mediterranean Command of sorts, since the Air Officer Commanding Malta also controlled air forces on Gibraltar. Some flyers wanted to move the Mediterranean west rather than east, arguing that Malta was indefensible and that Cairo was too far away from the real action. They were overruled, not least because the Army was moving east. The RAF, too, created an Air Officer Commanding-in-Chief, Middle East to sit alongside his Army counterpart.[33]

It was the Royal Navy who stood out for a true Mediterranean command. They had a Mediterranean Fleet and a Commander-in-Chief, Mediterranean. The sailors were purists. Their Mediterranean stretched from Gibraltar to Suez, with Malta as the half-way point. They would have no truck with ideas of a unified Middle East and Mediterranean. Anything south of the Suez Canal was in the Indian Ocean as far as they were concerned.[34] The navy also disliked the AOC-in-C Middle East. They wanted the AOC Mediterranean to be part of their organization; the RAF wanted him firmly under the command of their man in Cairo. The final compromise reached through the 'alembic' of the Chiefs of Staff placed the AOC Mediterranean under the 'command and general direction' of the AOC-in-C Middle East but with the authority to deal directly with the C-in-C Mediterranean.[35]

When the three commanders-in-chief met for the first time on 18 August 1939 on board the battleship HMS *Warspite* in Alexandria harbour they still couldn't agree exactly where the Mediterranean was, or where they were going to control it from. The Army and the RAF were busy setting up their headquarters in Cairo. The Royal Navy was still equivocating between Malta and Alexandria. The C-in-C Mediterranean, Andrew Cunningham, himself admitted that he was 'rather remote'.[36] Even when the time came to move 'lock, stock and barrel to Alexandria in a hurry', there would be real difficulties for the Mediterranean commanders in talking to each other.[37] Following naval tradition, Cunningham insisted on sleeping on his flagship. He was often at sea. Quite often when a Commanders-in-Chief meeting was called he would be unreachable, leaving behind a harassed and unauthoritative staff officer.

In the wake of the commanders-in-chief came a plethora of subsidiary organizations all seeking their place in the sun. For some years it had been acknowledged that commanders might need to know what was happening in the vast area they were supposed to control; equally they would probably need to know what the enemy intended to do to them. No one was collating such information, however. At the time of the Munich crisis in the autumn of 1938, naval intelligence detected troop ships sailing from Italy to Libya, but no one told the GOC Egypt who was supposed to defend Egypt against a surprise attack from Libya. Agents in Libya observed the troop ships arriving, but they communicated the information to the Foreign Office in London, who failed to decipher the telegram. When the telegram was finally read it was passed along Whitehall from the Foreign Office to the War Office. The War

Office then telegraphed Cairo. All the communications went via London, and no one in the Mediterranean seemed to talk to one another.[38]

There were three schools of thought on this issue. One maintained that all such high matters of state should be decided in London. The military could be given the information they needed and ordered to get on with whatever operations the government decided upon.[39] A second school retorted that this model of central control was unrealistic. Although London and Cairo could talk to each other fairly easily by telegraph, and personnel could be moved to and fro on aircraft, the Mediterranean was really a semi-autonomous world that needed its own sources of information.[40] A third school went even further and argued that military and civil rule in the Mediterranean should be integrated. Britain should create not merely short-term military expedients but political instruments devoted to the long-term maintenance of British power.[41]

These somewhat academic discussions were brought into focus by the embarrassing intelligence failure that was the Italian invasion of Albania. The Italian assault had come as such a complete surprise to the British that it found the capital ships of the Mediterranean Fleet paying courtesy calls in Italian ports, 'lolling about in Italian harbours', as Churchill put it, bitterly. Even if the British government had wanted to intervene, their own fleet was effectively hostage to good behaviour. The best the ships could do was to surreptitiously slip anchor and make their way back to Malta. By the time the Italian armada had sallied into the Adriatic from Brindisi, various British agencies had received upward of twenty warnings of Italian intentions. None had been taken seriously. It was all very well Chamberlain complaining that Mussolini had acted 'like a sneak and a cad', intelligence was supposed to spot the actions of those who were something less than gentlemen.[42]

Albania forced everyone to agree that it was no good limiting the 'men on the spot' to reporting back to London. There was finally agreement to create a self-contained regional intelligence organization.[43] Agreement in principle did not, of course, mean agreement in practice. The new body was to be called the Middle East Intelligence Centre – although it was usually referred to, not always kindly, as 'Mice'. The diplomats and spies refused to take part, in the hope that Mice would limit itself to military intelligence. The sailors and the airmen preferred to hand over as few resources to Mice as possible, the Royal Navy at one point saying rather insultingly that they couldn't spare a real naval officer and would send a Royal Marine instead. But the Centre did begin operating in October 1939. Despite attempts from London to insist that Middle East really did mean Middle East, Mice gaily included the northern littoral of the Mediterranean in its remit.[44] Although staffed almost wholly by soldiers, it was not deterred from offering political advice. The old-established bureaucracies in London suspected that once such agencies were created, they would slip away from central control; that suspicion was borne out in practice. Within months Wavell's GHQ had grown from a few officers lodging with the British army in Egypt to over a thousand men establishing themselves at Grey Pillars, a modern office building in the south of Cairo's Garden District. Slowly but surely, assets began to move eastwards. New pan-Mediterranean organizations began to burgeon around Grey Pillars.[45]

Those parts of the Mediterranean world not yet mortgaged to either side shifted uncomfortably. In the full spasm of their Mediterranean enthusiasm, the British courted the Turks. 'On no occasion does it appear to have been realised', they later chastised themselves, 'that we needed Turks more than they required us.'[46] A triple alliance was formed between Britain, France and Turkey.[47] In the person of Maxime Weygand, France had grand plans for this alliance. It was they who paid the direct price of the alliance, slicing off much of the Mediterranean coast of Syria – known as the Sanjak of Alexandretta – and gifting it to the Turks.[48] Appointed as commander of French forces in the eastern Mediterranean, Weygand imagined that he would lead a great expeditionary force into the Balkans from his base in Syria. The British demurred. They could find little appealing in the thought of Darlan harnessing British naval power and Weygand leading Britain's armies. The French had led the British a merry dance into the Balkans in the Great War, tying down a huge expeditionary force in Salonika for no military gain. The British felt that to play the same trick again lacked something in Gallic subtlety. The Kemalist regime begged to differ. They fêted Weygand and snubbed his British companions, asking why they had failed to draw up such valiant plans. The Turks and the French had a shared interest in British aid, shorn of British direction. Yet whatever their outward show, the Kemalists were playing the French as well. They swallowed the Sanjak but offered little in return. They made this calculation. If Britain and

France went to war with Italy in the Mediterranean, they were happy to join in. If Britain and France wanted to fight Germany in the Balkans then that was their problem. Turkey would pursue the strictest neutrality.[49] Right at the beginning of negotiations, Lord Halifax, the British foreign secretary, had noticed that the Turks always worded their commitments very, very carefully. They were willing to act only if a war *started* 'in the Mediterranean'. If Germany launched a war elsewhere, if Italy joined in, thereby spreading the fighting *to* the Mediterranean, Turkey would be under no obligation to fight. He then declared that he could not believe that the Turks were so deceitful.[50] Halifax should have heeded his inner voice. The Turks were that deceitful, and they had said exactly what they meant.[51]

Neutralism was equally popular at the other end of the Mediterranean. Recognizing the inevitable, Britain had acknowledged Franco as the legitimate ruler of Spain at the beginning of 1939. In the first flush of victory Franco had not been slow to declare that he was now one of the arbiters of the Mediterranean. Britain and France's attempts to 'reduce Spain to slavery in the Mediterranean' would lead to war.[52] He, Franco, now held the entrance to the sea. Such declarations did not, however, extend much beyond empty rhetoric. The performance of Italian forces in Spain had imbued the Spanish right with considerable scepticism about their goals and capabilities. Yet briefly, in the winter of 1939, Mussolini gained cult status in Spain. Not for reasons of which he would be proud, but for his hesitations and evasions. The Spanish admired his ability to run away from conflict, an ability that they hoped to emulate. Those suspected of wishing to entangle Spain in a new conflict, most notably the foreign minister and Franco's brother-in-law, Serrano Súñer, could expect a chilly welcome even amongst the most ardently Fascist Spaniards. Among the sullen remnants of the defeated left, on the other hand, at their strongest in the Mediterranean port cities, many hoped that the despised Italians would declare war and suffer humiliating defeat.[53] Franco had the intention of indulging neither his fire-breathing friends nor his hate-filled enemies. He would follow a policy of *hábil prudencia* – 'adroit prudence'.[54]

Each neutral was a study in ambivalence but the most ambivalent was undoubtedly Greece. Like Mussolini, its dictator, the so-called First Peasant, Ioannis Metaxas, co-habited contemptuously with a decrepit royal house. Greece was home to the classics beloved of the English; but those classics were no guarantee of a democratic temperament. The 1930s Mediterranean cocktail of sun, sea, classical literature and air travel was equally pleasing to others. Josef Goebbels's dreams came true in the airspace over Mount Olympus. 'Eternal Greece' made him warm and happy, perhaps the happiest he had ever been. Greece, after all, was the very homeland of the Gods: Zeus, he thought, was a Norwegian. The 'Fascist Frankenstein', Metaxas, reciprocated Nazi warmth. Neither was the liaison confined to tours of the Acropolis and oiled Aryan bodies. The Greeks turned to the Germans for a modern army and arms industry. These new arms were turned, however, not against the degenerate democracies, but against Fascist Italy, the hated ruler of the Dodecanese, molester of Corfu and, latterly, threatened ravager of Epirus.[55] Metaxas quite rightly feared that Mussolini would despoil Greece given half a chance. His fears had been exponentially increased by the Italian invasion of Albania. Metaxas found himself on the receiving end of a British promise of protection. He could hardly say no to such help – but it took him some days to say thank you, in the blandest terms possible.[56] He assured his German friends that he had not colluded in the offer.[57]

Mediterranean war planning reached a crescendo in the spring and early summer of 1939. Then the bubble of expectations burst. Faced with the real possibility of a land war in Europe, the three Mediterranean naval powers reached a tacit agreement that they would rather not fight each other at sea. By May 1939 Backhouse had worked himself into an early grave. His successor as First Sea Lord, Dudley Pound, arrived at the Admiralty fresh from commanding the Mediterranean Fleet. From his headquarters in Malta, Pound, the practical 'man on the spot', had regarded the stream of scenarios for a 'knock out' blow against Italy that had flowed from London with something akin to contempt. His own elevation meant that they were dumped unceremoniously in a filing cabinet as so much waste paper. Drax was shown the door. The Royal Navy performed a volte-face.[58] Darlan, bereft of further British support, was forced to abandon his own plans.[59]

A similar failure of minds to meet occurred between the Italians and the Germans. In late May 1939 Mussolini and Hitler consummated their formal alliance when the *Duce* travelled in pomp to Berlin in order to announce the Pact of Steel. At the heart of the alliance was Hitler's declaration that 'Mediterranean policy will be directed by Italy'.[60] Admiral Cavagnari was dispatched to the headquarters of his German opposite number, Admiral Raeder, in a bid to turn rhetoric into reality. Although the *Kriegsmarine* was by far the most 'Mediterranean-minded' of the German services, Cavagnari found little support for Italian ambitions. The German naval war staff, too, had taken part in the great Mediterranean war planning orgy of 1938–9. They had taken Italian policy at face value and had assumed that the *Kriegsmarine* and the *Regia Marina* would fight together. Predictably, however, the German sailors regarded Italy's struggle for the Mediterranean as merely a means to an end. If the Italians managed to close the Mediterranean, the British would have to use other 'oceanic' routes and by so doing leave themselves vulnerable to sinking by German raiders.[61] 'We must see to it', wrote the chief of the German naval operations division, that 'Italy does not go running after all sorts of prestige targets such as the Suez Canal.' Raeder wanted the Italians to fight a diversionary war. Cavagnari was horrified to find that the Germans had little aid to offer the Italians: they merely wished to use them as bait to draw out the British. What little enthusiasm he had had for war was snuffed out.[62]

On his return to Rome, Cavagnari told Mussolini, as baldly as one might in Fascist Italy, that his great plans were little more than a fantasy. Everyone had done much pointing at maps to demonstrate the absolute centrality of the Sicilian Narrows for mastery in the Mediterranean. Cavagnari did not want to fight for it. Naval communications were so poor that it was as much as he could do to speak to some of his ships some of the time. Combined naval-air operations were out of the question. He doubted whether Italian torpedoes worked well enough to sink any enemy ships. Attacks on the British and the French were entirely out of the question. At a pinch the navy might be able to run fast convoys between eastern Sicily and Libya, but he wasn't promising any good results.[63] Perhaps, Cavagnari suggested, there was an alternative. If the *Regia Marina* stuck close to its old bases like Genoa it could hope for safety in numbers, with the Spanish and the Germans nearby and the French too interested in their own convoy routes to attack them.[64]

Here lay the irony of 1939. The British accepted that the Mediterranean would be a 'closed sea' at the very moment that the Italians realized that they could not close the sea. The British had shocked themselves into a new way of thinking. In September 1939 they had a European war forced on them. Hitler's invasion of Poland made conflict in northern Europe inevitable. Despite the declaration of war on Germany, little in the way of immediate fighting in this theatre ensued. The Anglo-German war of 1939 was for the most part fought at sea. The most spectacular engagements were the sinking by a U-boat of the British battleship *Royal Oak* at Scapa Flow and the hunting to destruction of the German battleship *Graf Spee* off the coast of South America. In the Atlantic war zone the Germans formed the first wolf-packs, whilst the Royal Navy imposed a blockade on Germany. In the Mediterranean matters were quite different. Britain's commitment to Italian neutrality became so intense that the navy was willing to turn a blind eye to Italian ships busily transporting materiel through the Mediterranean to feed the German war economy.

The short breathing space offered by Italian non-belligerence – it was clear even to casual observers – rested on a contest between Mussolini's whim and his advisers' totting up of military capacity.[65] Mussolini had declared that Italy must never put itself in *Serie* B – a humiliation beyond contemplation for the dominant footballing nation of the 1930s. Stop complaining about lack of funds for the armed forces, he scolded the chiefs. It was an act of will to fight.[66] 'Are we in a position to do it?' demanded an agitated Ciano of the other major diarist of Italian Fascism, Giuseppe Bottai, on the last day of August 1939. 'No, no, no,' he screamed in answer to his own question. The head of the air force was 'shouting that he doesn't have fighters' – a recent inventory had shown only about ten per cent of *Regia Aeronautica*'s strength was fit for combat.[67] Cavagnari was wailing that the only result of a war would be that the Franco-British fleet would sink the Italian navy. With armed forces like ours, Ciano lamented, 'one can declare war only on Peru'.[68]

It is one of the great imponderables whether Mussolini would finally have acted in the Mediterranean if it had not been for Hitler's victories in Europe. Those who observed him closely noticed his consistent inconsistency.[69] Mussolini ordered the war machine to put into 'top gear' – even if no one quite knew what top gear was – at the end of January 1940. In March 1940 he fell into a paroxysm of rage when the Royal Navy finally got around, however hesitantly, to intercepting contraband coal shipments to Italy.[70] This act inspired his declaration that he was a 'prisoner within the Mediterranean'. He was certainly willing to take a meeting with Hitler at the Brenner Pass. The Führer knew how to play on the *Duce*'s insecurities. 'A German victory', he whispered, 'would be an Italian victory, but the defeat of Germany would also imply the end of the Italian empire.' On his return to Rome, Mussolini committed himself to paper. Yet his 'plan of action' revealed deep uncertainties. First, he wrote, that it was 'very improbable' that Germany would attack France. Then mulling over his conversation with Hitler he crossed out ~~very~~. Now it was merely 'improbable'. If the Germans did not go west soon, then the comfortable state of non-belligerence could be maintained 'as long as possible', Mussolini underlining as <u>long as possible</u>.[71]

But what happened if the Germans did attack France, and looked like winning? Then 'to believe that Italy can remain outside the conflict until its end is absurd and impossible'. If German victory was on the cards, Italy must launch a 'parallel war'. What was a 'parallel war'? Mussolini asked himself. His answer: it was Italy's war for the possession of 'the bars of its Mediterranean prison – Corsica, Bizerta, Malta and the walls of the same prison: Gibraltar and Suez'. The war would be a naval war, 'an offensive right down the line of the Mediterranean and outside it'.[72]

At the point of decision, the tensions in Mussolini's Mediterranean imagination were revealed more clearly than ever. That tension was visibly unhinging him. As Mussolini was writing his 'plan of action' others were writing character studies of him. 'Physically, Mussolini is not the man he was,' observed the British ambassador, Sir Percy Loraine, 'he is beginning to go down the hill.' He might boast endlessly about his running, riding, swimming, tennis, fencing, motoring, flying and, above all, his sexual athleticism. 'But', Sir Percy noted, 'this self-justification is a well known sign of senescence.' Mussolini was uneasy, fearing 'that great events are happening and there is no heroic role for Mussolini'; he was irritated 'that those muddle-headed English should have all the places of which Mussolini could make a really beautiful empire to the Greater Glory of Mussolini'. The ambassador concluded that what really drove Mussolini to distraction was that 'his principal advisers, both political and military, not only expect the Allies to win, but actually wish them to win'.[73]

Loraine was fooling himself that Mussolini's cronies were pro-British. He was right to believe that they were unenthused by Mussolini's plan. But they were either Mussolini's creatures or in the thrall of such creatures. If the *Duce* wanted a war they would never gainsay him: the only way to stop the dictator was to overthrow him, and they feared that conspiracy more than war. What they wanted to torpedo was his fantasy about fighting anywhere other than in the Mediterranean. They fell on the phrase 'an offensive right down the line of the Mediterranean and outside it'. There was no chance of the *Regia Marina* throwing itself against the Franco-British fleet, defeating them and then sailing elsewhere. What they would be doing would be waging a '*guerre de course* in the Mediterranean', trying to hinder movement between the eastern and western basins. Mussolini had given the navy the right of the line in his 'parallel war', but the man who had to lead it, Cavagnari, was almost beside himself with fear. Despite the prospect of the two new gleaming battleships he was about to commission into service, he did not believe that the naval balance had moved in Italy's favour since September 1939. He knew what would happen: one enemy fleet would assemble at Gibraltar, the other at Alexandria. Far from breaking the bars of the Mediterranean, Italy and her fleet would 'asphyxiate' within it.[74]

On 12 April 1940 Mussolini ordered the fleet to prepare for war. He mobilized the organs of Fascist propaganda to prepare the people for an offensive against Britain's 'tyranny of the seas'. On 21 April 1940 the Ministry of Popular Culture – the politically correct term for the propaganda machine – announced: 'the whole Mediterranean was under the control of Italy's naval and air forces; and if Britain dared to fight she would at once be driven out'. The spokesman who made the announcement confided to his diary that evening that he knew it to be nonsense.[75] The British could hardly do anything else but conclude that Italy was about to attack them. But even at his most belligerent Mussolini had inserted the caveat that 'Germany must defeat France first'. It was only on 13 May 1940, with the Maginot Line breached, and the Anglo-Belgian-French armies in disarray that he decided that Italy would go to war.[76] 'What can you say', he demanded of Ciano, 'to someone who doesn't dare risk a single soldier while his ally is winning a crushing victory, and that victory can give Italy back the remainder of its national territory and establish its supremacy in the Mediterranean?'[77] Mussolini had talked himself into a war. 'It's all over because the madman wants to make war,' a prescient Balbo warned his fellow Fascists, 'there won't enough lampposts to hang you all.'[78]

FOUR

Gog & Magog

The Mediterranean war lived up to the expectations of those who had planned it.[1] This correlation between ideas and execution owed much to the cold dose of reality forced on the Mediterranean dreamers by the war scare of the summer of 1939. Much of the wild talk of earlier years had ceased before the shooting began.[2]

Cavagnari's *Regia Marina* had abandoned grandiose plans for ruling the sea, much less sweeping out of it. They had instead set themselves realistic tasks on both the east–west and north–south axes. The Italians believed that they could erect a system of defence which would divide the Mediterranean into eastern and western basins. The lynchpin of that system was the central Mediterranean, and in particular the Sicilian Narrows. But they had no truck with the belief that the system of defence would be impermeable. With enough expenditure of effort it would still be possible, if difficult, for the British and the French to sail between the western and eastern basins.[3] The first naval mission of the war was minelaying in the Sicilian Narrows.[4] The British naval commander in the Mediterranean was soon to pay tribute to this Italian system of defence. Their arrangements were 'very efficient', 'first class' in fact. British submarine losses were so severe – nearly every boat that approached the Italian harbours was sunk – that they had to withdraw to safer waters.[5] Contact mines proved to be 'the primary menace in the Mediterranean'.[6] Although relatively few surface ships were sunk by mines in the first months of the war–the first, the destroyer *Hostile*, exploded catastrophically off Cap Bon at the end of August 1940 – the 'constant anxiety [about] what is to be done with a damaged capital ship' made 'minable water' virtually no-go areas 'without some *very* good reason'.[7]

Equally the *Regia Marina* believed that it could carry out the limited task of escorting convoys from north to south, setting off from Naples and arriving in the unlading ports of Tripoli, Benghazi and Tobruk. Although the relatively short distance favoured the Italian sailors, they were far from sanguine, realizing that they would have to rely on expedients, such as the use of submarines and destroyers as well as merchant ships. They had providently transported the bulk of the troops in the weeks before the war began.[8] Equally, the collapse of British enthusiasm for grand Mediterranean adventures, under the guiding hand of Dudley Pound, left the Royal Navy equally as sanguine as the *Regia Marina*. The British sailors believed that they could get through the Mediterranean, but with the greatest of difficulty. Heavily armed warships would have a chance; the average merchant was easy meat. The geography and distances were against them. Some officers even doubted whether the game was worth the candle. Such complete sceptics were, however, quickly shushed in both London and Alexandria.[9]

Even Mussolini might be given some credit for realism, on this issue at least. He had consistently railed against his Mediterranean prison, claiming that the British would stop up both ends and trap Italy within. And indeed that is exactly what the British did. Within weeks the Mediterranean had two gatekeepers, self-styled after the giant twin guardians of the underworld in English legend, Gog and Magog.[10] Magog was James Somerville, sent from Britain with a fleet – known as Force H – to secure the western exit at Gibraltar.[11] Gog was Andrew Cunningham who, on the eve of war, took the Mediterranean Fleet away from Malta and established it at the eastern exit, protecting the mouth of the Suez Canal from Alexandria. They were true naval twins, exact contemporaries, boys from the same class of the late-Victorian navy. Apart from that, the two gatekeepers were most unlike. Cunningham, the acknowledged star of the navy, was fierce to the point of over-confidence. Independent by temperament, now semi-marooned in the eastern basin, he felt himself to be the co-adjutor with London of the fate of the Mediterranean. Cunningham walked the fine line of insubordination – earning himself Churchill's dislike – with the arrogance of irreplaceability. Somerville was quite the opposite, a dug-out from the retired list, sent to Gibraltar mainly because of his immediate availability. In contrast to Cunningham's bursts of confidence, Somerville was perpetually gloomy, cavilling against, yet in thrall, to his masters, to whom he referred in terms of dread and contempt as Their Lordships. Somerville, unlike Cunningham, was kept on a tight leash, although that did not spare him

Churchill's similar dislike. His orders came directly from London; from London too – with a direct air link – came numerous senior officers enquiring into his conduct, some actively seeking his job.

The war developed much as the admirals had predicted. Indeed, the sea produced a conflict of curious symmetry. There were four major naval battles, two in the east, two in the west. There was one eastern and one western battle in July 1940, another eastern and another western battle in November 1940. None of these naval battles resembled the titanic and decisive fleet clashes that naval fantasists such as Churchill longed for. Two – Mers el-Kébir on 3 July 1940 and Taranto on 11 November 1940 – comprised not engagements at sea at all but attacks by one fleet at sea upon another riding at anchor. Both fleets at anchor suffered significant damage, but neither was destroyed. In both cases battleships were able to leave the port under attack and sail to safer ports. In the two battles at sea – Punta Stilo on 9 July 1940 and Cape Spartivento on 27 November 1940 – the two fleets followed engagement with evasion, privileging the survival of their ships. As a result, in neither battle were there heavy casualties. The fleets performed a delicate quadrille, living up to their own expectation that – barring disaster – the Mediterranean could be neither completely closed nor fully opened.[12]

If the hopes and fears of the cautious admirals, if not of their querulous masters, proved realistic, they did nevertheless suffer some unpleasant surprises. The Mediterranean lacked the wide expanses of the oceans, but it suddenly seemed a very empty sea. The opposing forces had great difficulty in finding each other. The Mediterranean in 1940 offered little proof that there had been a revolution in naval affairs. Cunningham saw the evidence of this within days. His newly installed naval interception service beautifully triangulated the Italian cruiser *Garibaldi*, lying off Derna, from stations at Alexandria, Malta and Gibraltar. No high-level codebreaking of the Ultra kind was involved, the location of the cruiser was derived from traffic analysis and call-sign recognition. It was a brilliant early achievement for communications intelligence. Cunningham had squadrons cruising off Tobruk, Benghazi and Crete. *Garibaldi* was neatly in the middle of a trap. Sadly, although the communications intelligence was a triumph, British communications were less so. Alexandria failed to raise Cunningham's flagship in time. By the time ABC knew what was happening, the *Garibaldi* had escaped.[13]

If the British had their difficulties, so too did the Italians. Italy had a good intelligence system. It had been used in the years of peace, however, as the means by which Mussolini had pulled diplomatic rabbits out of the hat. Mussolini and Ciano were past masters at this kind of trick. With the onset of war and the removal of embassies, many of their best sources dried up. In any case the bullying or cajoling tactics of the *Duce* – his so-called 'animal instinct' – were hardly a good foundation on which to base the careful consideration of military intelligence.[14] Nevertheless, Italian naval intelligence was certainly not without resources. Its crypt-analysts could read a fair proportion of Cunningham's signals. The Italian fleet at Punta Stilo was particularly well informed on his activities.[15] The listening war in the Mediterranean was roughly even in 1940, the successes and failures of each side mirroring each other. Both had a good idea of what the other was trying to achieve, both could read some signals traffic, neither had a complete enough picture to achieve a decisive advantage.

Both sides could hear each other, albeit fuzzily. They could see each other only intermittently. It was easy enough for the Italians to see Cunningham's fleet leaving Alexandria. Thereafter he and Somerville were too often swallowed up by the sea. This was not how it was supposed to be. The aeroplane was supposed to solve such problems. Ciano, for one, thought everything would be simple, and indeed enjoyable. 'I have tasted again in full the intoxication of being a flyer,' he boasted to his wife. On the third day of the war he bombed Toulon – 'magnificent, soothing, indescribable we carried out a real slaughter' – and then on his way home, crossing the stretch of sea between Corsica and Italy, he spotted the British. 'I saw a ship,' he confided in Edda immediately upon landing, 'I point my Zeiss: British flag. Imagine my orgasm.' Ciano's tumescence was perhaps premature. There is no proof that he actually saw anything. In any case he had no means of attacking a ship. Notably, other Italian pilots seemed to enjoy much less success than the multi-talented foreign minister.[16] The Italians had about one hundred planes out looking for British ships but most of them were 'incredibly antiquated' 'Gulls', a type of wooden flying boat, best known for long cruises. Somerville remarked on how often such aircraft were victims of 'summary destruction' as soon as they approached concentrations of British warships.[17] By the autumn of 1940, the *Regia Marina* and the *Regia Aeronautica* were involved in a vicious campaign of mutual discredit in the highest Fascist councils. The air force 'made fun of' the navy for failing ever to engage the British; the navy denounced the air force as liars, whose every claim to have found, much less damaged the British, was falsified.[18]

If Cavagnari did not rate the RAI's attempts at maritime reconnaissance

then neither did Cunningham admire the RAF's. He devoted much of
his prodigious energy to complaining about, or attempting to take over,
RAF activity in the Mediterranean. At the very least, Cunningham
argued, more use should be made of Malta. A silly idea, retorted his
air-force opposite number, Arthur Longmore; it was only a matter of
time before the Italians got their act together and bombed Malta into
impotence. In autumn 1940 Cunningham finally won the argument:
first flying boats and then, at the end of October 1940, land-based
reconnaissance aircraft were sent to Malta. These aircraft of uncertain
parentage – made by America for France, taken by Britain as stop-gap
– enjoyed an immediate and brilliant success, spotting the Italian fleet
at anchor in Taranto. But there was still a big difference between spotting a fleet at anchor – the Italians could spot the British in Alexandria
– and finding one at sea. The flyers lost sight of the Italian battleships
once they hauled anchor. The Royal Navy and the *Regia Marina*
complained about the same thing – the failure of air reconnaissance –
at exactly the same time.[19]

Whatever the details of Mediterranean operations, by far the most
unpleasant surprise – at least for the British – was who was fighting
whom. There were undoubtedly tensions between the British and the
French in the Mediterranean, but few on either side had believed before
June 1940 that they would end up killing each other. As it happened the
bitterest naval conflict in the Mediterranean turned out to be Anglo-
French, rather than Anglo-Italian. Because that conflict did not fit into
the grand narrative of 'total war' it tended to be underplayed – Britain
and France never declared war on each other – its main event, the sinking
of a French fleet at Mers el-Kébir, becoming an incident rather than a
battle. Yet at the time the shadow war against France was of equal importance to the 'real' war against Italy. Mussolini had often talked about
'breaking out' of the Mediterranean but there were never any realistic
plans for Italy to fight anything other than a Mediterranean war. France
too had had modest plans for the Mediterranean – the convoys between
North Africa and the metropole – but it had the genuine potential to
move in and out of the Mediterranean. France itself had both
Mediterranean and Atlantic coasts, but the Atlantic coast was occupied
by the Germans in June 1940. French North Africa also had Mediterranean

and Atlantic coasts, all of which remained in French hands. The French were willing and able to transfer warships between the two coasts.

Like the British, the French had deployed two powerful battle squadrons in the Mediterranean by the summer of 1940. In the western basin the *Force de Raid* was based in the Oran naval complex, including Mers el-Kébir. In the eastern basin Force X had come alongside Cunningham's fleet in Alexandria. The purpose of Force X was unclear. The French regarded it as a favour to the British, who had demanded reinforcement; the British suspected that it was a vehicle for demonstrating French power in the eastern Mediterranean.[20] What one can say for sure is that it completed only one mission in the entire war: the bombardment of the Libyan port of Bardia in June 1940.

Even before Force X sailed for Bardia, however, an Anglo-French *froideur* had set in. The pivotal figure was the great pre-war champion of the Mediterranean, Darlan. Not only was Darlan the head of the French navy by rank but he ran it through an informal closed shop, known as the friends of François, the *ADF*. Being Darlan's enemy was not the road to success. The only admiral to defect to Free France, Muselier, had been declared unfit as an officer – admittedly not without cause – and chased out of the service by Darlan. Darlan was undoubtedly master of the *Marine* but, to his chagrin, the *Marine* had not always been at the heart of France. As the French government fled south, towards the sea, the navy achieved the importance for which Darlan had longed, a force untainted by failure, the final bulwark of the nation. A prize so precious caused inevitable discord. British emissaries, including Churchill himself, rushed to Bordeaux to urge the French to fight on and, above all, for the fleet to abandon France. Darlan was repulsed. 'I was disgusted', he wrote after a meeting with Dudley Pound, 'by the attitude of these people who had no pity for defeated France and seemed to forget the heroic aid given them by the *Marine*.'[21] For Darlan, the fleet, alive in the empire, was the one bargaining chip that France had left, guaranteeing it against extinction. He understood British cupidity and loathed it. Darlan temporized, saying only that the fleet would never fall into enemy hands, German or British.

Promises given in bad faith fooled no one. The British ambassador to France dismissed Darlan's words as 'pathetic assurances'.[22] 'In a matter so vital to the safety of the whole British Empire,' in Churchill's fatal judgement, 'we could not afford to rely on the word of Admiral Darlan.'[23] By the time Churchill condemned Darlan, he had become much more than a mere admiral but rather the chief executive of the strong, if vague, will of France's new leader, Marshal Pétain. France had surrendered, the next order of business was the fate of the ships in the Mediterranean.

The British conducted a rapid poll of the French admirals and found little hope. The *Amiral Afrique* in Casablanca wearily dismissed the envoys, France was defeated but North Africa would remain indivisible from France; he awaited his orders from Darlan, whatever they might be. The *Amiral Atlantique*, commanding the *Force de Raid*, dismissed the idea that North Africa would fight on with its exiguous resources. The *Amiral Sud* in Bizerta said that the fleet was resigned to capitulation but was at least willing to ask Darlan whether he should continue the fight.[24] Darlan dismissed all such suggestions with contempt – those who asked were 'living in a dream world'. His mind was filled with the phantoms of German power. She and her allies, he believed, would soon control the whole coastline of western and central Europe from the Cap Nord to Trieste. Equally the southern coastline of the Mediterranean from Spanish Morocco to Cyrenaica would be theirs. If France decided to resist there could be only one result: the 'asphyxiation' – it is notable that he used Mussolini's favourite word for complaining about Mediterranean – of North Africa. Darlan imagined Casablanca, Oran, Algiers and Bizerta – and the ships hiding in their harbours – each reduced to rubble by German bombs. All that would be left would be for the navy to flee the Mediterranean, to eke out an impoverished and declining existence far to the south on the Atlantic coast of Africa. It was pointless to place any trust in the British: their men were mediocre, their leaders were stupid. Germany was going to win.[25] The Germans, too, believed that they would win with 'restraint and insight'. The key, Hitler assured Mussolini, was to offer France lenient terms on the fleet; then, the Führer correctly perceived, Darlan would castrate his own navy.[26]

When Somerville set sail for Gibraltar, his putative mission was to secure the Mediterranean approaches against the Italians; his real mission was to take on the French. Cunningham, too, was ordered to take out Force X. There the similarity between the two cases ended. The twins, issued with the same orders, effected very different results. Whereas Somerville attacked Mers el-Kébir, Cunningham refused to attack the French in Alexandria. The French at Oran were in the French empire; any damage caused would be to French or Algerian lives and property. The French at Alexandria were deep within British ground; any damage caused would be to British or Egyptian lives. The *Force de Raid* was much more powerful than Force X. At its core lay two of the most impressive vessels in any navy, the fast battleships *Dunkerque* and *Strasbourg*. These modern, rakish vessels, completed only in the late 1930s, had claim to be the most powerful warships in the Mediterranean. The key variable, however, was that Cunningham was in a position to say no, whereas Somerville had little choice.

It would have been hard to find a more reluctant warrior than Somerville. Upon reaching Gibraltar, all the senior officers on the Rock convened to agree that they did not wish to engage the French. Somerville was forced to admit, however, that no such sentiments existed on the lower decks of his ships, the killing didn't worry the sailors in the least, 'as "they never 'ad no use for them French bastards"'.[27] The gloom of the senior officers was lightened only by their firm conviction that 'the French collapse was so complete and the will to fight so entirely extinguished, that it seems highly improbable that the French would, in the last resort, resist by force'. In this ideal world the French would agree, if not to hand the ships over to Britain, then at least to flee to the West Indies or scuttle the things and have done with the whole affair. All that would be needed would be a British show of force off the coast of Algeria. The naval officers had seriously misread their new enemies. When Captain 'Hooky' Holland entered Mers el-Kébir harbour with British terms, he was barely able to persuade *Amiral Atlantique* to see him. His desperate pleas to avoid bloodshed were to no avail. His motorboat pulled away from the French flagship *Dunkerque* less than half an hour before the British opened fire and only thirty-two minutes before the old French battleship *Bretagne* exploded, killing nearly all the crew. Holland's small boat was picked up bobbing outside the harbour after the battle.[28]

As Somerville himself admitted, his assumption that he would not have to fight – that the French would abandon their vessels if he opened fire – led him to botch the battle. Although the British gunfire hit the *Dunkerque*, it missed the *Strasbourg* entirely. She was able to cast off from the middle of the harbour, escape from the anchorage and head off east before Somerville could react. By the time Force H swung around and gave chase, one of the fastest battleships in the world had a 25-mile head start and was beyond recall. *Strasbourg* made her way, unmolested, across the Mediterranean to berth with the rest of the French fleet in Toulon. 'I'm somewhat appalled by my apparent lack of foresight,' Somerville confided in his wife, 'I never expected for one single moment that they would attempt to take their ships out of harbour under such conditions.'[29]

The situation in Alexandria was very different. Cunningham had no intention of attacking his erstwhile allies. He and René Godfroy, the officer commanding Force X, had most cordial relations, Cunningham went so far as to describe them as 'exceptionally friendly'. The French had accepted Cunningham's refusal to allow Force X to sail for Beirut with good grace.[30] Cunningham even believed that he would be able to talk Godfroy away from his allegiance to Darlan.[31] That hope soon faded but Godfroy had enough trust in Cunningham that, on the same day as Somerville was sinking his compatriots in Algeria, he was willing to pinnace across the harbour to the British flagship, *Warspite*, to continue their conversation.[32] Their talks went on long into the night, as Cunningham tried to talk Godfroy into handing over his ships. Just past midnight on the day of Mers el-Kébir he conceded: 'I have failed.' Despite London's demands for action, however, he stuck to the view that a battle should be avoided, 'at almost any cost'.[33] If Godfroy discharged all his fuel into the harbour, thus rendering his ships unable to leave, Cunningham gave his word that his ships would remain unmolested.[34] Knowing that he could do no better, Godfroy accepted. It was a strange situation. The French squadron lay alongside the British, entirely reliant on them for water and provisions, but simmering with hostility. The officers adopted an attitude of super-patriotism. Each day the chaplains prayed for Pétain, equating him with the hammer of the English, Saint Joan. Officers prefaced all their remarks with reference to the Marshal's sayings, as if that ended any argument. Only one senior member of Force X defected to the British.[35]

The battle in the west, and the non-battle in the east, cast a pall over the Mediterranean for the rest of the year. Somerville's judgement that 'it was the biggest political blunder of modern times and I imagine will rouse the world against us' was too tinged with emotion to be entirely convincing.[36] The British action did, after all, win many admirers: Ciano and Cavagnari, for instance, were 'disturbed' at such proof that 'the fighting spirit of the Royal Navy is quite alive, and still has the aggressive ruthlessness of the captains and pirates of the seventeenth century'.[37]

The naval commanders in the Mediterranean had to be alive to the possibility that France could turn on them at any minute. In particular they feared that whilst they were engaged with the Italians, the French would run the Straits of Gibraltar. On 11 September 1940 their fears were realized when a French cruiser force sailed through the Straits heading for Casablanca.[38] French aircraft bombed Gibraltar from their

North African airfields. Darlan assembled naval officers in their newly established capital at Vichy to assure them that 'a state of war exists with Britain' and 'this is not finished'.[39] The Mediterranean cruiser force turned an Anglo-Gaullist attempt to seize Dakar in West Africa into a fiasco. The air raids continued in response to each new British 'outrage'. In September 1940 French bombers gave Force H 'an absolute plastering' in Gibraltar harbour.[40] The result, Somerville recorded, was that British warships were steaming around the Mediterranean in 'a ghastly muddle'. 'We simply don't know where we are or who we are supposed to be fighting.' The Germans and Italians, he feared, 'must be chuckling with joy'.[41]

The Germans were chuckling rather harder than the Italians. Mussolini had proved a master of twitting the British in peace time, but his skills were wasted in war. He had declared war on France expecting easy gains. None had been won on the battlefield – embarrassingly French troops had to maintain their supposed conquerors in the small area the Italians had occupied before the Armistice. The victorious Germans appeared to have a cosier relationship with their defeated enemies than their allies. If the French managed to slip into the 'anti-British camp', Italy might be 'defrauded of our booty'. Four days after Mers el-Kébir, with the crisis still smouldering, Ciano hung up his bomber boots and headed for Berlin. It was not a successful visit. There was an odd atmosphere, jovial to the point of edginess, not least because Ciano knew that the Germans had captured documents from the French in which he personally had described them most unflatteringly. Ciano spoke to Hitler, 'as if the war was already definitively won'. The Italian press was full of officially planted stories of his expected success. This was the meeting in which Italy would finally claim absolute dominance in the Mediterranean basin, its rightful 'living space'.[42] Ciano's demands tumbled out: 'Nice, Corsica and Malta would be annexed to Italy, which would also have assumed a protectorate over Tunisia and the better part of Algeria'. The Germans around Hitler shifted between embarrassment and amusement at the Italian's territorial incontinence. The Führer himself was simply unmoved; he ignored Ciano's great speech. The Italians had missed the bus. Now it was too late to discuss anything before England was defeated. Afterwards, Ribbentrop sidled up to tell his opposite number that he should not have eyes bigger than his belly.[43]

Mussolini's first gamble, that the war would be over within weeks, had failed. His second gamble, that Italy would be able to land a spectacular blow on Britain in the Mediterranean, failed whilst Ciano was still away. Mussolini's declaration that half of Britain's naval strength in the Mediterranean had been eliminated was a reflection of his political need, rather than military reality.[44] The two fleets clashed at Punta Stilo, off the south-east coast of Italy, on 9 July 1940. Punta Stilo was the classic Mediterranean battle, entirely based on movement around the basins. Cunningham was at sea to rendezvous with Somerville so that they could pass a convoy from west to east.[45] His Italian opposite number, Campioni, was at sea to prevent Cunningham intercepting a convoy that was swinging around the east of Sicily on its way from Naples to Benghazi. Both sides suspected that the other was there – they both had detailed signals intelligence – but the actual meeting was 'quite accidental'. The British were not too sure why the battle had occurred.[46] Militarily, as Cunningham conceded, the Italians probably had the better of it. He admired their 'impressive' use of smoke to obscure the battle space, and the accuracy of their guns. On his own side he conceded that his flagship had been lucky to achieve any hits, whilst his torpedo-bombers couldn't hit the side of a barn door, at least if it moved, which Italian battleships did, with rapidity. The Italian convoy reached Benghazi unscathed, whereas the British convoy suffered constant attack.[47]

The British and Italians had quite different perceptions of the performance of the *Regia Aeronautica*. Upon his return Ciano was 'incredulous' to find that 'the real controversy in naval affairs is not between us and the British but between our air force and our navy'. He was horrified to learn that 'our air force was completely absent during the first phase of the encounter, but that when it finally came it was directed against our own ships, which for six hours withstood bombing from our [own aircraft]'.[48] Cunningham on the other hand reported that his convoy had been bombed continuously from the Sicily coast, then from Cyrenaica, then from the Dodecanese, 'literally we have had to fight our way back to Alexandria'. He feared that the Italian airmen would only improve with practice, that 'the worst is yet to come' and doubted whether he would be able to overcome this formidable air power.[49] From the other side of the Sicilian Narrows, Somerville too concluded, that, 'as a result of this, our first contact with the Italian air force,' the risk to his capital ships was too great. He had turned them around and headed away to the west.[50] Churchill was livid with his admirals, thundering that 'warships are meant to go under fire'.[51]

He was only mildly propitiated when an Australian cruiser intercepted an Italian cruiser on its way from Tripoli to Leros and sank her with an outstanding display of gunnery.[52] Conversely, Mussolini was 'depressed on account of the loss of the *Colleoni*, not so much because of the sinking itself as because he feels the Italians did not fight well'.[53] The battle of Cape Spada, as the sinking of the *Colleoni* was called, made more of an impression than Punta Stilo. It occasioned another round of mutual denunciations between the *Regia Aeronautica* and the *Regia Marina* – Italian aircraft responded to the *Colleoni*'s demands for assistance only when it was too late. They instead bombed the British destroyers which were trying to pick up Italian survivors, provoking Cunningham's order that in future, 'difficult and distasteful as it is', shipwrecked sailors should be left to fend for themselves.[54]

Failure made Mussolini and Churchill gamblers. There were striking parallels between them. They both met their advisers on the same day in August 1940. They both demanded a new approach to Mediterranean conflict. The difference was that Churchill, although dictatorial, was not a dictator. His military chiefs fought back against his demands. Mussolini was a tyrant: when his military advisers displeased him, he found others who would agree with him. Churchill's gripe was the supposed impassability of the Mediterranean. In the debates of the 1930s he had been a partisan of battleships over aeroplanes. He was not minded to change his view. Somerville and Cunningham should stop pussyfooting around and force supplies through the central Mediterranean to Egypt.[55] In particular Churchill was fascinated with the possibilities of large merchant vessels converted to carry tanks. If, Churchill believed, he could send a rapid supply of tanks through the Mediterranean, he could force a reluctant Wavell to attack Libya. The admirals were 'unduly pessimistic' about the risks. The ships could pass 'without great difficulty'. The dangers of sending tank reinforcements to Egypt 'had been exaggerated.' It was lucky for Somerville and Cunningham – particularly lucky for Somerville who had sailed back to Britain to argue the case – that no one in the military hierarchy could be found to break ranks and endorse Churchill's belief.[56] In the end Churchill could not quite bring himself to overrule the admirals, generals and air marshals based solely on his own judgement – his political leadership would not have survived a slaughter in the central Mediterranean.[57] What he wanted was a merchant convoy – what he got, after a 'great battle', was 'Hands Across the Sea', a mission to send major warship reinforcements east to Cunningham.[58] Not that he conceded the point. Instead of congratulating Somerville and Cunningham for their excellent handling of the mission, he claimed that it showed that he had been right, they wrong.[59]

Mussolini's gamble was of a quite different order. Before the outbreak of war, troops had been rushed to Libya to defend it against the non-existent British legions that Italian intelligence estimated were present in Egypt. When the weakness of the British became apparent, Mussolini demanded that his army should attack. Churchill firmly believed that his generals and admirals were deliberately smothering his plans – they were, he complained, 'very wily when they don't want to do anything'.[60] Mussolini suspected the same. General Rodolfo Graziani, the chief of staff of the Army and the commander of forces in Libya, suggested that it was too hot to fight in Egypt and that it would be much better to wait until the next spring before any action was considered. He offered the poor compensation of a minor campaign, in the not notably cooler Somaliland instead.[61] Graziani used every wile at his disposal to avoid attacking Egypt. British intelligence had every right to be confused. There seemed to be endless orders for Graziani to attack, British forces braced themselves and then nothing happened.[62] Instead Graziani retired to his Mediterranean bungalow to be soothed by 'escapades'. In the first week of September 1940, Mussolini finally lost patience: he gave Graziani an ultimatum. If after a weekend of contemplation he could not bring himself to do anything, then he was to come home in dishonour – not a pleasant experience in the Fascist regime.[63] The fear of loss of emoluments, or worse, was too much for Graziani to bear.[64] Mussolini had given the world's most reluctant warrior little choice but to act. At the same time he consoled him with the thought that his campaign need be nothing more than a demonstration. It would be nice if he could sweep along the Mediterranean coast and capture the British fleet base at Alexandria. But Mussolini did not demand this. He did not even demand that Graziani should reach the first coastal town that the British held in strength. There were no 'fixed territorial objectives', he just had to do *something*.[65]

Mussolini's gamble was to twin his attack on Egypt with an attack on Greece. This was a course that the disgruntled viceroy of the Dodecanese, De Vecchi, had been urging almost since the war began. De Vecchi hated the Greeks – as indeed the Greeks hated him. From the beginning of the war Cunningham had gone 'so far as to say that we shall never be able to control the Central Mediterranean' until the fleet could operate from a base in the Greek islands. The location he desired above all others was Suda Bay on the north coast of Crete.[66] The Greeks had no intention of giving it to him. Indeed the Greeks protested vigorously on each occasion they believed that the British had entered their territorial waters. Metaxas held no brief for the British war effort, victory in the Mediterranean meant little to him, only the safety offered by neutrality. That was the reality, but De Vecchi worked himself up into such a rage against the Greeks, he would never believe it was so. His reports to Rome were stridently insistent that the Greeks were allowing the British to operate from Suda, and that all the denials they issued were nothing more than dirty lies. De Vecchi was unapologetic about the indiscriminate bombing of Greek ships in their own waters – Greeks, British were all the same in his eyes. 'To your fine diplomats who whine about me (who has had to amuse himself with Greeks here for four years),' he scolded Ciano, 'I can answer that in French "Greek" means "swindler".'[67]

Project G, the attack on Greece, was hatched in August 1940, after only a few days' discussion, with the hope of an easy victory. Its architects were Ciano and his henchmen in Albania. Their motives were opportunistic. Mussolini wanted something to happen. The Ciano équipe were sucking money out of Albania for their own enrichment and glory – Ciano had renamed an Albanian port Edda, after his wife. If Albania got bigger then there would be more money and fame to suck. They quickly cobbled together all the border disputes that existed between Albania and Greece in Epirus and claimed all the land for Albania. They threw in the island of Corsica for good measure. This done, Ciano wheeled his men in to see Mussolini. To Ciano's delight Mussolini thought the plan a good one. The first stage was his long-preferred method of intimidation. The movement of troops to the border and the use of terrorism might make 'the Greeks cave in'. If threats didn't work he was willing 'to go to the limit'.[68]

Mussolini may have thought the plan good; his military commanders were aghast. The happiest man was De Vecchi. If there was going to be a war, the Italians wanted a *casus belli*. De Vecchi already had the means of inflammation in his own hands. Mussolini and Ciano were mulling over a 'pirate submarine' campaign of the kind they had used against Spain. The very evening that the idea was suggested to De Vecchi, he ordered the submarine *Delfino* out of Rhodes. The captain was told that he was to strike the first blow in an inevitable, if undeclared, war.

De Vecchi's haste was dictated by local knowledge: the next day marked the Panayia, the great Cycladic religious festival held on the Lourdes of the Aegean, Tinos. Each 15 August since 1822, the wonder-working icon of Our Lady of Tinos had been paraded from her shrine. There to do her honour in 1940 was the Greek cruiser *Elli*. Predictably, given the nature of the occasion, the crew had given more thought to their decorations – the ship was bedecked with bunting – than their anti-submarine precautions. The *Delfino* slipped into the bay and torpedoed the *Elli* before sailing away, entirely unnoticed.[69]

Despite this spectacular violence to one of the Mediterranean's most famous festivals, Mussolini engaged in weeks of hand-wringing about his decision. Ships were loaded with stores at Brindisi and Bari, they were then unloaded and the stores dispersed. Men were mobilized for transfer to Albania, then the army high command rescinded the order and the men stood down. Then the men were remobilized on the proviso that when they reached Albania they were not to go to the Greek frontier until further consideration had been given to the issue. There the matter lay. Before Mussolini would do anything he wanted to know whether his instrument in Africa, Graziani, would act.

Graziani did not, in the end, disappoint. Given no option, he ordered his forces into Egypt. To say that he led them into Egypt would be too strong a statement. The Marshal had taken a great liking to the Greek tombs of Cyrene. Not because of their historical value, but because they gave excellent shelter from attacks by British aircraft. Nevertheless, in his own way, he conducted a model operation. Mussolini had given him no territorial objective, he himself had no wish to advance. The best answer was surely to advance for the shortest distance possible. Graziani took as his target not the first town across the frontier, Sollum, but the second town, Sidi Barrani, some twenty miles into Egypt. As an indefensible position that the British had no intention of holding, it couldn't be bettered. Six days of confusion saw it seized for Fascism. The Italian flag at last flew over a piece of Egyptian real estate. Sidi Barrani was the final stop, travelling east–west, on the British coast road. Sidi Barrani thus had some claims of being a point of moderate importance on the Mediterranean coast. Before 1940 the traveller heading west ate a great deal of dust until he could reach the *Balbia*. Graziani's men stopped and began the task of making the place habitable. They built themselves a proper road, 'the Victory Way', between Sollum and Sidi Barrani, considerably improving on previous British efforts. A tent city of most excellent quality was erected. History has not been kind to this operation, finding in it a means of mocking Italian martial virtues. But at the time it was enough. Mussolini was 'radiant' at the success of the operation. At last Italy had scored a 'success in Egypt which gives her the glory she has sought in vain for three centuries'.[70]

The 'triumph' of Sidi Barrani was useful to Mussolini because he had before him a difficult set of manoeuvres. Hitler had set aside October 1940 as the month in which he would consult with his friends in the Mediterranean and decide on whom he wished to bestow his favour. Punta Stilo and Sidi Barrani do not measure up well to 'total war' but in the context of the autumn of 1940 they were rather more impressive than the abject defeat of France or the inglorious inaction of Spain. It was in Mussolini's interest to belittle both. He had no reason to welcome a Hitler–Franco alliance, which would see the whole balance of the Mediterranean shift towards the struggle for Gibraltar.[71] Mussolini was confident, however, that Franco's caution would keep him out of the war. He was much less sanguine about Pétain or his henchmen Darlan and Laval. On the surface it would be a good thing if the French acted on their hatred of the British; the Mediterranean would undoubtedly become the centre of the war, 'which is good for us'. Looking deeper, however, Mussolini saw the French only as a problem. French arrogance would simply lead to one thing, 'a bill'. What was the point of fighting the British if, at the end of it all, an equally noxious French power would wax in the south?[72] An alliance with France was 'a cup of hemlock'.[73]

Mussolini and Hitler met twice in October 1940, on the Brenner at the beginning of the month and in Florence at the end. Mussolini had some difficulty in reading Hitler's mind. The Führer and his minions were studies in ambivalence. Historians have had little more success in deciding for certain on Hitler's intentions, even with access to diaries, documents and memoirs. Later writers divide into two schools of thought. Some believe that Hitler was content to let Mussolini fight a 'parallel war' in the Mediterranean – and strictly in the Mediterranean – and that there was a genuine alliance, if not of equals, then of partners. Others prefer the image of a 'brutal friendship' in which Hitler always intended to predate the Italians. The Germans certainly explored both options. The best that can be said is that Hitler himself had not made up his mind.

He was awaiting events on his whistlestop tour of the minor railway stations and major railway tunnels of Europe.[74] Waiting for Hitler to reveal his plans irked Mussolini, the twenty-four days between their two meetings being marked by fits of pique at not being privy to the Germans' plans. Mussolini talked of paying back Hitler 'in his own coin'; he could 'find out from the papers that I have occupied Greece'.[75]

Franco certainly lived up to Mussolini's billing. Hitler's intelligence chief and Spanish expert, Wilhelm Canaris, warned him that when he arrived at the pleasant French railway station of Hendaye he would find 'not a hero but a little pipsqueak'. So indeed it proved: the Führer was irritated by the *Caudillo*'s 'monotonous sing-song reminiscent of the muezzin calling the faithful to prayer'. He told Mussolini: 'rather than go through that again, I would prefer to have three or four teeth taken out'. Doubtless, the fat little Spanish dictator was without charm. At root, however, the Hendaye fiasco – reinforcing racial stereotypes, Franco's train was late, whereas Hitler's super-express, *Amerika*, was bang on time – was about the universal greed of the Fascists. Franco wanted something for nothing, massive German subsidies and a Mediterranean empire. *Amerika* had come from another small French station, Montoire, where Pierre Laval had been the guest, and shuttled back there the next day so that Hitler could interview Pétain. The Frenchmen both said the same thing, protect us from Spain. There was no grand Mediterranean alliance for the Germans to stitch together.[76] Britain's enemies, whether in Madrid or Vichy, each wanted to 'displace England from the Mediterranean', but would act only if Hitler gave them terms mutually damaging each to the other.[77]

On this note, Hitler and Mussolini greeted each other in Florence. That morning Italian forces crossed the Albanian border into Greece. Hitler warmly congratulated the *Duce* on his bold action. Unlike the scratchy meetings at Hendaye and Montoire, Florence was a triumph of Axis amity. 'German solidarity has not failed us,' declared a triumphant and relieved Ciano.[78] Mussolini had his 'parallel war'; he had sprung a surprise – although the preparations, if not the exact timing, of the invasion were apparent to the Germans.

28 October 1940 was Mussolini's best day in the Mediterranean. His armies were firmly encamped in Egypt, and on the move in Epirus. His ally was full of encouragement and compliments, his Mediterranean rivals had shown their weakness, the British were confused. In hindsight, of course, no one had much good to say for the day. It presaged an Italian

military disaster. The only people who remembered the date with any warmth were the Greeks. It gave them a rare opportunity for military glory, magnified years later when the victor of 1940, the army's commander-in-chief, Alexander Papagos, became dictator.

For a few hours it seemed that all would be well for the Italians. The Albanian-Greek border was divided into two sectors, and the Italians allocated an army to each. Epirus, the more southerly front, ran down to the Adriatic. The Italian goal in Epirus was the coastal city of Prevesa. Across a narrow seaway from Prevesa lay Corfu, Italy's key Mediterranean claim on Greece. The more northerly Pindus front was wholly inland. Both frontiers were mountainous, offering few goat tracks and even fewer roads. The Greeks recoiled at the first Italian assault, more so in the Pindus. For a moment it seemed that the Italian commander had achieved the holy grail of operational art, the encirclement battle, his army in the south pinning the Greeks, whilst his northern army swept behind them for a rear attack. Within days, however, the Greeks launched a counter-attack and did the unthinkable: they pushed all Italian troops off their soil and invaded Albania.[79] Prevesa and the Adriatic coast became a distant dream. Italian troops in Epirus may have been fighting mere tens of miles from the Mediterranean but they were in a different world. That difference was summed up by the fate of the *Siena* Division, comprising recruits from southern Italy. Tortured by blizzards and severe cold, slain as much by frostbite as by the Greeks, the *Siena* broke and fled before an exploratory mortar attack from Greek reconnaissance troops.[80]

The Greek campaign set in motion changes around the Mediterranean basin. Badoglio had been the Cassandra of the Greek operation. His constant predictions of disaster had irritated Mussolini and had allowed his enemies to deride his cowardice. Few had listened to his specific suggestions and warnings. In his last conversation with Ciano before the invasion, Italy's senior military leader had pointed out that if the British were operating freely from Greek waters then the fleet at Taranto 'would no longer be safe'.[81] No one listened to Badoglio. Taranto offered the huge sheltered expanse of the *Mar Grande*. As soon as the fleet sallied out of Taranto it was in the right place. The port had hummed with activity throughout 1940 as, one by one, *Caio Duilio*, *Vittorio Veneto*,

Andrea Doria, Italy's battleships were completed or completed modernization there. Along with the *Littorio*, the *Cavour* and the *Giulio Cesare* they comprised Italy's entire battleship fleet. When the invasion of Greece still seemed a glorious triumph, the fleet at Taranto was blessed with a visit from Mussolini and Ciano. It was a shining symbol of Italian power and modernity.[82]

Cunningham had harboured a plan to attack Taranto for months but it barely seemed practicable, 'the bridge between planning and execution' being a 'wide one'.[83] Five factors improved the chances of success in the autumn of 1940: the arrival of the modern aircraft-carrier *Illustrious* via the Suez Canal, the invention of long-range fuel tanks for the elderly torpedo-bombers used by the British, the upgraded detonation systems for British torpedoes, reconnaissance aircraft on Malta, and unseasonably good weather.[84] The operation was still a long shot. It was also a sideshow.[85] The main event was a combined Mediterranean Fleet and Force H operation to bridge the Mediterranean gap by passing a battleship, *Barham*, from west to east. The secondary objective was to run a major convoy from the eastern Mediterranean into Malta. The tertiary objective was linked with the Greek campaign. With Suda Bay now open to him, Cunningham intended to escort ships marooned in Malta out to Crete. It was only once he had achieved his central goal of temporarily opening the Mediterranean that Cunningham could afford to give his offensive instincts rein. Even then Taranto was but one of two subsidiary attacks. The other was a dash by cruisers and destroyers through the Straits of Otranto, between Italy and Greece, so that they might attack Italian supply convoys plying between Brindisi and Albania. Doubtless, this daring operation, which after all constituted the main element of the 'not very much' aid to Greece, would have attracted more attention if it had not got caught in the lee of Taranto.

The *Illustrious* and her escorts left the fleet after the main mission was completed on the evening of 11 November 1940, and sailed to Cephalonia, 170 miles away from Taranto. Twenty-one aircraft torpedo-bombers, bombers and flare-droppers, curved round to hit the *Mar Grande* in two waves from the west. Success was instantaneous: the lead aircraft of 'Hooch' Williamson and 'Blood' Scarlett, coming in so low that its wings touched the sea, scored the best hit – its torpedo sank the battleship *Cavour*. By the time both waves had passed through the harbour, three more torpedoes had hit the *Littorio*, the most powerful ship in the Italian fleet. Perhaps even more remarkably, the surviving aircraft were able to fly back to the *Illustrious* which in turn rejoined the Mediterranean Fleet. It was hard to know whether the Italians or the British were more surprised by their success. Early press reports attributed the attack to the RAF rather than the Fleet Air Arm; Cunningham was thought mealy-mouthed for not thinking to put Williamson up for the VC.

No one knew what effect Taranto would truly have.[86] The Italians had lost two battleships – but it was unclear for how long. Those assessing the raid were right to be cautious because despite the three holes in its hull, the *Littorio* did not sink; it was rapidly repaired. Even worse, the remaining battleships had fled Taranto. They headed for Naples. No aircraft spotted them, no intercepts revealed their whereabouts. A still formidable battlefleet was at sea and the British had no idea where it was or what it was doing. Somerville was cautious; faced with the possibility of the Italian fleet emerging unexpectedly from any fog bank, he argued that nothing had changed.[87]

Taranto momentarily divided the Cunningham–Somerville alliance in the Mediterranean. Having had time to consider his own triumph, Cunningham declared that it had opened the Mediterranean.[88] The time had come to embrace what they had both hitherto branded as madness: Churchill's plan to take a convoy, not only of warships, but slow-moving tank ships all the way through the Mediterranean, west to east from Gibraltar to Alexandria.[89]

Somerville had no hope of competing with a Churchill–Cunningham alliance. He was an unwilling cog in an inexorable post-Taranto wheel. The tank ships were to go from Gibraltar to Alexandria, the battleship *Ramillies* was to pass in the opposite direction back to Gibraltar, escort ships were to sail from the western to the eastern basin, convoys too would sail into Malta from both east and west. The Mediterranean would be free for the British to do as they wished. Somerville was far from convinced. The obvious strategy for the Italians, he believed, was to strike back against their setback in the eastern basin with an offensive in the west. What was he supposed to do, he enquired, if wallowing around south of Sardinia with a battleship, an aircraft-carrier useless at short range, a few light cruisers, and a convoy of slow supply ships, he was ambushed by all those battleships and heavy cruisers evicted from Taranto? He was told to stop complaining.[90]

Since the 1930s two opposing concepts of the Italian threat in the Mediterranean had butted up against each other in British thinking. Should one respect the modern ships, the concentration of the fleet, the good bases, the fine seamanship, or should one dismiss all these advantages because of an ill-defined but powerful feeling that the Italians were not 'up for it'? It was a big gamble to take, since nearly everyone who had argued for the superiority of morale over firepower in modern warfare had been proved catastrophically wrong. The battle of Cape Spartivento on 27 November 1940 resolved none of these arguments.[91]

It was a close-run thing. Somerville rendezvoused with his convoy just after half-past nine on the morning of 27 November 1940. He was in the 'danger zone' south of Sardinia that he had identified before sailing. Three-quarters of an hour later, a spotter aircraft landed on *Ark Royal*. Its report led to the conclusion that the Italian fleet was nearby. Further aircraft were flown off; they were able to report the Italian fleet turning south towards Somerville.[92] Force H was facing Admiral Campioni with the battleships *Vittorio Veneto* and *Giulio Cesare* escorted by a powerful cruiser force. For one and a quarter hours, Somerville was convinced he was in for a desperate capital-ship battle against superior forces. He, rightly, had no confidence that his torpedo-bombers, whatever their recently proved excellence against ships at anchor, could hit fast warships at sea.[93] His saving grace was the appearance of *Ramillies*, heading west as planned. Although the *Ramillies* was an old and slow warship, two battleships against two evened up the odds. That was most certainly Campioni's view: he turned his battleships round and they 'ran like stags' up the east coast of Sardinia.[94] Somerville gave chase but in less than half an hour, 'in view of our rapid approach to the enemy coast, now 30 miles distant, I had to decide whether a continuation of the chase justified'. In his view from the bridge, it was not. His primary mission was to escort the convoy, not to chance his warships. He turned away from Sardinia and headed back to the south.[95] Somerville's choice was undoubtedly correct: taking capital ships within easy range of a militarized enemy coast was potentially suicidal. The enemy would have had to have been Lilliputian rather than Italian. Not that he received any thanks for his good sense. Cunningham's lustre dimmed his own. The flags that met him in Gibraltar were quickly pulled down, Churchill accused him of cowardice; dismissal from the service was mooted. In the end Cunningham's support saved him.[96]

It was Cavagnari and Campioni who lost their jobs. De Vecchi and Badoglio too, were dismissed. In order to protect its leader, the revolution began to eat itself.[97] Days later, further humiliation was heaped on the Italians. Wavell, well equipped with supplies delivered from both the Mediterranean and the Red Sea, ordered an attack in North Africa. Wavell's idea was to secure Egypt by the recapture of Sidi Barrani. He did not believe that he was launching a great offensive, indeed his intention was to shift the main direction of operations against Mussolini's swollen east African empire, once he had secured the Libyan position. This was not quite what Churchill had in mind: that the Italians should be 'ripped off' the African shore. Wavell's operation was more in the nature of a raid. Whilst a diversionary force made its way along the coast road from Mersa Matruh towards Sidi Barrani, the main 'Western Desert Force' swung through the desert to the south. Their targets were the huge camps that Graziani had been happily building around Sidi Barrani. As the troops reached the target, they peeled off to the left and right, each unit taking its assigned camp. Although the movement of British forces was spotted by Italian aircraft, surprise was almost complete. The camp-dwellers either surrendered or fled back down the coast.

Within a few days all the settlements along the Egyptian coast were back in British hands. Sollum, 'the most distinctive spot in the Western Desert', where immense 600-foot-high cliffs falling from the desert plateau clipped the Mediterranean coast, was recaptured on 16 December 1940. From upper Sollum, the British once more surveyed the great curve of the bay to the Libyan frontier. They were as impressed by the Italian improvements to the comfort of life as they were disparaging about Italian efforts at fighting. Emboldened by this success Wavell met with Cunningham and Arthur Longmore in Cairo. They agreed that they could move part of the way with Churchill's demand for 'ripping the shore'. An advance into Cyrenaica would be possible in the New Year, its target Mediterranean ports, first Bardia, but ultimately Tobruk.[98]

On the day Sollum fell, Churchill lamented that the future was quite unclear. Hitler might involve himself with the Balkans, but Churchill thought that this was unlikely. He might take over the Italian war effort, unlikelier still since 'that would not be a victory for him'. Churchill's best guess was that the Germans would come to the Mediterranean to take over French North Africa.[99] In fact Hitler's mind was elsewhere: he was busy issuing the order for 'Barbarossa', the invasion of the Soviet Union.[100] Two days after the Barbarossa decision Mussolini reluctantly admitted to his confederates that, sooner or later, they were going to have to ask for Germany's help.[101]

FIVE

Mediterranean Eden

The Mediterranean image of early 1941 was columns of marching men. They wore Italian uniform and they were walking towards Egypt in great snakes of humanity. They did not come as victors but as the defeated. Hundreds of thousands of Italian soldiers trudged towards captivity, their journey immortalized by eager pressmen. Wavell's 'raid' just kept heading west. On 4 January 1941 Wavell's forces captured Bardia. Eighteen days later they reached Tobruk. Wavell had given his field commander, General O'Connor, two divisions for the campaign. They faced up to ten Italian divisions. The numbers of tanks possessed by each side was more even. Indeed the British and Italian tank forces were roughly equivalent both in terms of numbers and quality. The Italian tanks were grouped together in the elite *Brigata Corazzata Speciale* commanded by General Babini. At Tobruk O'Connor split his forces, sending the 7th Armoured Division towards Mechili, inland, where he believed that the main body of Italian tanks was deployed. His Australian infantry carried on along the coast towards the town of Derna. On 24 January 1941 the two tank forces ran into each other near Mechili. The battle itself was indecisive. The Italians lost nine tanks, the British seven. Some of the Italian tankers believed that they had done enough damage to start a counter-attack. Graziani, however, would not hear of it. The battle was no more than a delaying action. On 3 February he withdrew from Benghazi. He told Mussolini that they would have to abandon Cyrenaica altogether. His aim was to send his forces to the end of the *Balbia*. They would hold the Sirtean desert as the forward defence line for Tripoli. There were rumours of much greater (and non-existent) British tank forces on the way.

Accordingly, Babini disengaged his force and retreated to the west. He and O'Connor still had equal numbers of 'cruiser' tanks. It was thus with some trepidation that O'Connor put forward a daring plan for the next stage of the advance. Instead of reuniting his forces he would send the armoured division south-west on a short-cut across the desert. They would try to cut the *Balbia* far to the south of Benghazi, rather than following the coast, taking each town in turn. Wavell and O'Connor met at Tmimi on the road to Derna on 4 February 1941: Wavell approved the plan. Thereafter events moved with great speed.

The reconnaissance elements of the 7th Armoured Division spotted Graziani's 25,000-strong force retreating along the *Balbia* on 5 February. By the evening the tank forces themselves had reached the road near the small settlement of Beda Fomm. From a small hill by the roadside, known as 'the Pimple', they could survey a fourteen-mile stretch of road. They had reached 'the Pimple' before the Italians and thus cut off their line of retreat. It was up to Babini's tanks to force a way through. The Italian tank force advanced with elan only to run into the dug-in British tanks. The Italians took heavy casualties. Nevertheless, about thirty tanks managed to force their way onto the road south of 'the Pimple'. The Italian force was thus split. Most of the troops were stuck north of 'the Pimple'. A powerful independent force of tanks was to the south of the hill, their escape route blocked only by a battalion of the Rifle Brigade supported by a battery of the Royal Horse Artillery. The next day the Italian tanks tried to make their breakthrough. The British gunners held firm, however, continuing to fire until the last of the desperate tanks stopped short of their line. By nine o'clock in the morning of 7 February 1941 it was all over. The Italian main force, deprived of its tanks, and with the Australians coming up behind them on the *Balbia*, surrendered. 'Fox killed in the open,' the triumphant British field commander signalled Wavell.[1]

In Rome they could barely believe what was happening to the 'fourth shore'. The intelligence system that had once proved so adept at extracting juicy morsels from diplomats, failed to keep pace with the battle. The Fascist elite was reduced to listening to BBC radio broadcasts. First, news would arrive of defeat. Then garbled accounts of brave resistance would take its place. Mussolini made the final arrangements for his tryst with Hitler only when he had convinced himself that the defence of Bardia would restore honour to Italian arms. Surely, he would wail to his advisers, the generals would stop the English. The 'heroic infantryman' or the 'king of artillery' would find a way. If not the generals, then the fortifications would delay the advance. If the fortifications failed, then the very land would provide succour. The British could not fight their way through desert and along coast. The task of working up and down the cliffs would prove too much. Finally, the full scale of defeat would become clear and recrimination would follow. At that moment news would arrive of yet another humiliating defeat by the Greeks.[2]

To make matters worse, the British could not help crowing over their victories. It was not their fault that they were useless, Churchill told his Italian listeners. The disasters they were now enduring were the responsibility of one man, the *Duce*.[3] He had 'ranged the Italian people in deadly struggle against the British empire'. He alone had created defeat; if he were to be removed then the Italians would be absolved both of crime and cowardice. 'There stands', they should cry, 'the criminal who has brought the deed of folly on our land.' The message was in a sense well judged – there were plenty in Mussolini's own intimate circle who heard Churchill and agreed with him.[4] The cost of such barbs was nevertheless high. For years afterwards Churchill's words would provide the constant alibi for Fascists and their friends. Yet at the time there were no Italians with either the will or the power to overthrow Mussolini. The threat itself put Mussolini on his guard. It also resonated with Churchill's avid listeners in Germany. The idea that Mussolini must be 'saved' from the Italians entered the Führer's table talk.[5]

He had, Hitler told his courtiers at Berchtesgaden, reconsidered the situation. The previous month he had ordered the *Luftwaffe* to teach the Mediterranean Fleet a lesson.[6] At the beginning of January 1941 the first Stukas had touched down in western Sicily. As Hitler addressed his generals they were going into action for the first time. The Mediterranean Fleet played into German hands with a display of the very arrogance that Hitler was determined to humble. The victor of Taranto, *Illustrious*, was sent through the Sicilian Narrows so that it might cover a convoy bringing crated fighters from Gibraltar to Malta. Many officers had a bad feeling about the operation, but Cunningham waved aside their objections. *Illustrious* was the talisman of the fleet, everyone felt better when she was around. She proved, however, the perfect target for German bombs. The Italians, too, played their part.[7] Even though they had but a few days to prepare, the two air forces choreographed a complex aerial ruse. Italian torpedo-bombers flew a decoy mission to draw off the *Illustrious*'s fighters.

Once she was denuded of protection the dive-bombers attacked. 'The dive bombing attacks', Cunningham ruefully admitted, 'were most efficiently performed and came as a most unpleasant surprise.' The carrier was hit six times. The only consolation for the British was that there was no killer blow. The crippled ship was able to get into Malta harbour without being sunk. She brought with her the first concentrated German air raids over the island, as for days afterwards the Stuka crews tried to finish off their prey. As Cunningham said, a 'potent new factor in Mediterranean war' had arrived. No one doubted what had happened. Large British ships had been chased from the waters surrounding Sicily and Malta.[8] The passage of even smaller ships had become deeply problematic.[9]

The battle prompted another Mussolinian mood swing. This example of the two air forces working in such close harmony had cheered him to the extent that he was looking forward to his own visit to Berchtesgaden.[10] He would have been less cheerful if he could have heard what those already there were saying. The Italians had shown 'matchless amateurism' according to Hitler.[11] The war in Libya was a piddling and unimportant affair, but the Führer took seriously Churchill's words. Italy must be saved from itself. A small armoured force sent to Tripoli should do the trick.[12] The Italo-German effort on Sicily, the offer of forces for Tripoli, and Hitler's promise that the pesky Greeks would be humbled come the spring yielded a surprisingly cordial meeting of the two dictators. They toasted the 'absolute solidarity between the countries of the Axis'. It was time for them to 'march together'. Of course, many at the time and since doubted this togetherness. Italian diplomats warned that the Germans intended to displace Italian power rather than come to its aid. The contrast between the confident swagger of the German generals around Hitler and the cowed mien of Italian officers, small of stature and sporting hair dyed jet black, was palpable. Mussolini had come to Hitler as a supplicant and had left a client. Nevertheless, a deal of sorts was done that allowed for cooperation against mutual enemies over the next few months.[13]

Churchill might boom his voice in the Mediterranean, but in the inner councils of the British war machine he complained that no one seemed inclined to do much to counter this new threat. A formal decision was made in London to aid Greece against a new Italo-German invasion. The view from Alexandria, however, was that the Sicilian Narrows were now closed and that opening them, whilst defending Malta, should have the highest priority. The view from Cairo was that if any aggressive military operations were to take place in the Mediterranean – other than in Libya – they would best be directed against ill-defended small Italian islands in the far east of the Sea. No one appeared to be responding to the Prime Minister's ideas and demands. Each of the military commanders, Wavell, Cunningham and Longmore, had become used to the semi-independence granted by difficult communications. There was no instrument on the spot capable of enforcing Churchill's will.[14]

There was, as it happened, a member of Churchill's government travelling around the Mediterranean at the very moment of decision. But he was a man whom one would least like to see hove over the horizon in such circumstances. 'I adore Cairo,' Chips Channon wrote upon his arrival, 'it is everything I like, easy, elegant, pleasure-loving, trivial, worldly; me, in fact.'[15] The private secretary to the under-secretary of state was at the very bottom of the Foreign Office food chain. He had arrived in Cairo on a 'secret' mission in which no one in London had any faith. Chips's dearest friend, from their idyllic days as undergraduates, was Prince Paul of Yugoslavia. Since Mussolini had arranged the assassination of King Alexander in 1934, Paul had acted as Regent to his young nephew Peter. Mussolini had long wished to predate the Yugoslavians. As Hitler's interest in Greece rose, their role became pivotal. The Yugoslavs might join the Greeks as victims. Just as likely they could join with the Germans against the Greeks in return for territorial gain and protection from the Italians.[16] The lure of a Serbo-German alliance warred with Paul's natural Anglophilia.

In his moment of crisis Paul called out for Chips, and Chips came. As Hitler plotted in the Berchtesgaden, Chips crossed the Mediterranean from Cairo to Athens. He dropped in on another dear friend, King George of Greece. Paul and George, royal cousins, had last met at Chips's opulent house in Belgrave Square. Now they phoned each other each night, mainly it seemed to complain about the iniquities of their English friends. George warned Chips that beastliness was afoot. It was grim up north. 'I am already against the Balkans,' Chips lamented, 'and long for Cairo.'[17] Next day he hopped on the train from Athens to Belgrade, surrounded by kissing Greeks celebrating their victory over the Italians at Klisura.[18]

Chips's welcome in Belgrade was everything he might have wished. His familiar bedroom in the Palace of Beli Dvor awaited him. He was surrounded by the many precious *bibelots* with which he had showered the beloved Prince down the years. Then they were together, half-dressed, and Yugoslav prince and British politician cast aside the cares of office and 'fell into each other's arms'. Their joy was short lived. Barely had Paul had time to curse the entire German race, explain that no one gave the British any credence whilst they were so weak, and beg Chips to ensure that no aid should be sent to Greece, when the true voice of British officialdom arrived to inform the reunited friends that Chips had already been superseded. Wavell had been ordered to take time away from garnering victories in Africa to visit Athens. There he would exhort 'First Peasant' Metaxas to prepare to fight the Germans with British aid. 'Treachery and foolishness,' cried the two friends.[19]

Poor Paul, Chips had never had anything to offer other than love and diamond-encrusted knick-knacks. The British government had ignored his Mediterranean progress and had then brushed it aside. Chips's very pointlessness was not, however, without ultimate effect. 'This stinks', the Regent had shouted in a moment of rage, 'of Anthony.' The name of the villain that rang around the Palace was not Churchill but his newly appointed Foreign Secretary, their old undergraduate sparring partner Anthony Eden. Many in the Mediterranean attributed to Eden more power than perhaps he ever possessed. Eden was not unhappy to play upon this impression. He wanted to make a splash as soon as possible. Churchill was keen that his choice should have a chance to show his quality, and what better stage than the Mediterranean. Nothing could be achieved with an effete nobody like Chips, but perhaps an effete somebody could transform the situation. Eden, it was agreed, should not just issue instructions to the Mediterranean but should take himself there for as long as was necessary to enforce the government's will.

The mission was attractive. Eden would be greeted with the bouquets of victory. Somerville was ordered to take Force H and bombard the Italian mainland. He laid a bet. If the mission was a success Churchill and Eden would take the credit, if the Italians sunk one of his capital ships the fiasco would be blamed on the incompetence of the navy in the Mediterranean. It was a win-win bet. His unseen approach on Genoa was a masterpiece of naval operational art. The bombardment of the city was indeed claimed as triumph of political daring in London.[20] The impression was not much different in Rome and Berlin. The general whom Hitler had dispatched to lead his forces in Tripoli, Erwin Rommel, arrived in Rome as the British shells hit Genoa.[21] 'The

Duce's popularity is approaching zero level,' went back the word to Germany.[22]

At the same time as the navy landed a direct blow on Italy, the army maintained their extraordinary progress along the coast of Cyrenaica. Tobruk, Derna, Benghazi: in each of the fortified Italian coastal towns the pattern was the same. Imperial troops would breast a rise to see a neatly whitewashed settlement set against the sea. They would admire the skill of the Italian artillerists who opposed them, then the defence would crumble. Within the day the town would be in their hands, albeit thoroughly looted by the indigenous population. It was thus settled that Eden would 'stop at Benghazi and run over to the Balkans'. What he would do when he reached the Balkans was less clear. Some, such as his travelling companion, the CIGS, Sir John Dill, thought his mission was to persuade Turkey into the war. Others argued that the mission was all about Greece. The dictator Metaxas had listened sceptically to Wavell's blandishments but had then unexpectedly keeled over, dead. Greece's confused politicians might now be biddable. Eden was told to fly in, scout out the situation and try and make the best of it.[23]

In the end Eden didn't make it to Benghazi. Flying into a headwind his plane almost ran out of fuel. It landed on Malta in the middle of an air raid, diverted to Crete and finally touched down outside Cairo on 19 February 1941.[24] Despite the difficult journey, Eden came down the steps 'in his usual excellent form'. He had every right to feel cheerful – his timing seemed impeccable.[25]

As Churchill had suspected, the arrival of Eden in Cairo made it very difficult for the military commanders to object too vociferously to the idea of cashing in on the gains made in Cyrenaica. They signed up to the idea of projecting British power north across the Mediterranean. Wavell, Cunningham and Longmore each said a piece on the practical difficulties involved, but lodged no objection in principle. There was none of the outspokenness to which more junior visitors had been treated. When Channon had been in Cairo, Longmore had described Churchill as an adventurer, criticized his grasp of strategy and had ascribed their success up to that point to a mixture of luck and bluff.[26] Eden, on the other hand, was able to report a remarkable degree of unity amongst all the political, diplomatic and military leaders gathered in Cairo. They agreed that they would look north instead of south-east, towards Abyssinia, or west, towards Tripoli. They agreed that if they were looking north it should be towards Greece rather than towards Turkey. The dream of whipping up the Turks remained strong for some, but the consensus was that the Turks would do what they always did, make nice noises but play the sides off against one another. In any case there was a limit to the military aid that could be sent north and Greece, unlike Turkey, was under immediate threat. They signed up to the statement that if everything was thrown into assisting the Greeks as quickly as possible then there was a 'fair chance' of preventing the country being overrun.[27]

Armed with this assessment Eden left Cairo for Athens. There was, however, a difference between what appeared in formal statements and the private thoughts of those involved. The Greek decision was in one sense easy to make. Eden provided a very firm political steer. It was thus 'respectable' to sign up. At the same time the bullish statements emanating from Cairo, and the impression that the men on the ground were gung-ho for intervention stilled any qualms that might be felt in London. In their heart of hearts, however, most of those who discussed the problem feared that 'we must eventually be beaten there'.[28] There was for the moment, however, a conspiracy of optimism. In Athens, Eden and his entourage gave no sign of any doubts they might have felt about the enterprise – even though they concluded whilst they were there that Yugoslavia was likely to side with the Germans and that Salonika – the Aegean terminus of the railway line that ran from central Europe to the Mediterranean – was indefensible.

Immediately on his return from Athens, Eden flew out to Adana near Turkey's Mediterranean coast, boarding a train for Ankara. He reached the Turkish capital on 26 February. The Turks reacted just as expected. They said they would on no account aid Greece. They would fight only if attacked. Yet Eden sent home 'jaunty and self-satisfied' telegrams that talked of the 'frankness' and 'friendliness' and the 'realism' of the Turks. Had, some wondered, his head been turned by the welcome choreo-graphed by Ataturk's heirs? As his train pulled into Ankara, Eden had stood in the transparent observation car at the end of the train. The huge crowd assembled to meet him had climbed onto the railway lines and thronged round the carriage trying to catch sight of the visitor, cheering his triumphal entry.[29] The truth was that the Turks wouldn't do 'a damned thing'.[30] Having completed his mission in Turkey to his own – if no one else's – satisfaction, Eden returned to Athens on 2 March. There he presided over the signature of a formal military aid agreement by Dill and his Greek opposite number, Alexander Papagos. Whilst this document was finalized in Athens, Prince Paul of Yugoslavia was having a deeply disturbing meeting with Hitler in Austria. He was told that the day had come when he must openly ally with the Nazis.

There can be little doubt that Eden's mission in the Mediterranean achieved exactly what he and Churchill had intended from the outset. He had marshalled the military in such a way that no one could subsequently claim that either of them were dangerous adventurers – the charge of the 1930s, still heard *sotto voce*, amongst many Conservatives. He had ensured that Greece rather than Turkey would be the focus of British efforts on the northern shore. He had achieved a firm military agreement. All of this news was received with much tut-tutting in London. Eden had, it seemed, demonstrated that if you let a man off the leash in the Mediterranean, particularly in the east, he would soon be running his own show without regard for higher authority. In Greece as in Turkey, it was said, Eden's head had been turned by the obsequies of his hosts. British policy had become a vanity. 'He has', the Cabinet agreed, 'really run rather ahead of his instructions and *agreed* to things which the Greeks will take as commitments.'[31]

At the beginning of March 1941 Churchill sent a rather disingenuous message to Eden, suggesting that he might have overreached himself. They had agreed their joint aims before Eden had left. Whilst he had been away, however, the situation had changed. The Germans had demonstrated that the Suez Canal was vulnerable. At the end of January 1941 their bombers had started flying long-range missions out of Rhodes. The advanced magnetic mines they dropped into the Canal closed it for weeks at a time. The Canal defences had been revealed as weak and ill prepared.[32] The crippled *Illustrious* barely managed to escape the Mediterranean by this route. The Germans gloated over their success.[33] Projections based on the early success of the mining campaign suggested that less than half the supplies needed to keep the army in Africa active might arrive via this 'safe' route. With the southern windpipe constricted, it might not be wise to head north. The threat did not come from mainland Greece but from the Greek islands. Those islands had already yielded a warning about the dangers of a northern campaign. An attempt to seize the tiny island of Castelrizzo had been a farce, 'a rotten business and reflected little credit on anyone'. The expedition's naval commander had had a mental breakdown, and the troops landed proved incapable of defending themselves against the 'unbelievably enterprising' Italians.[34]

Neither Yugoslavia nor Turkey would fight. The Yugoslavs had 'sold their souls to the Devil'. All the Balkan peoples were 'trash'.[35] Vichyites and Francoists were hungrily eyeing British weakness. Franco and Mussolini had met, as had Franco and Pétain. Franco's men were becoming more flagrant in the aid they gave to German submarines operating from Spanish ports.[36] Somerville had complained that in seizing French ships his own men had been forced to kill 'harmless' civilians and children. 'It seems to me', he wrote, 'that we are just as much of a dictator country as either Germany or Italy and one day the great British public will wake up and ask what we are fighting for.'[37] Darlan could hardly improve on Somerville's formulation of the issue. He announced to the newly arrived American ambassador that he would 'first use his propaganda system to explain to the French people that Mr Churchill is responsible for their lack of food, and second, he will use his Navy to convoy French merchant ships and sink any British ships that interfere'. He had repeated the threat in a carefully staged conference with the international press, with Pétain present.[38] The management of the press was a triumph for the 'ambitious crook' Darlan. Churchill, fearful of his own reputation in America, effectively abandoned the blockade of French ports.[39] The result, as he himself said, was, 'convoys growing larger every day are passing in and out of the Straits . . . with only nominal escorts'.[40] Hitler decreed that Darlan should be regarded as 'trustworthy'.[41] These curs, Churchill wrote, would not act any more energetically merely because the Germans crushed the Greeks, but they would be emboldened if the Germans crushed the British in Greece.[42]

These thoughts were of course no help to Eden for, as became clear when the full text of the Dill–Papagos agreement reached London, he had committed Britain 'up to the hilt' with no get-out clauses. On 6 March 1941 Churchill announced that Eden's actions had settled the matter.[43] He had achieved his goal, a commitment to go to Greece's aid coupled with the 'secret satisfaction that if things went really wrong there was a good scapegoat handy'.[44] The next day British troops began arriving in the Piraeus.[45]

Churchill was predictably delighted with this arrangement. His reputation as an adventurer was by no means ill-won. But the scars of Gallipoli, twenty-five years earlier, ran deep. He preferred adventures from which no blame could attach to him. Hence appeasement in the western

Mediterranean, matched by wild advance in the east. He and his cronies agreed that it would be an excellent thing if Eden's Mediterranean sojourn should be extended indefinitely. Eden and Greece must be completely synonymous in the public eye.[46] No one in the Mediterranean could quite make up their minds whether they had been 'had'. They were told that it was their enthusiasm for the operation that had swung the vote in London in favour of intervention. They were not told of Churchill's private abusive outburst about their dithering. Their warning that, without reinforcement, disaster was likely was met with the rebuke that they had failed to 'appreciate what is going on outside the Mediterranean'.[47]

It was unclear who had talked whom into the Greek adventure. It seemed hard to criticize the decision on moral grounds. The Greeks had shown some ability at fighting; they were certainly under threat. The moral surety of the case might have seemed less secure if the British had been aware that, whilst British troops marched into the line with the Greek army in the north-east, the Greek army in the north-west was trying to cut a deal with the Germans.[48] Eden did not know any of this, but he most definitely had an inkling of his difficult position. In Cairo he pondered the situation. He had done all he could in the Mediterranean, he did not want to stay any longer.[49] The Greek decision had been made, the Yugoslavs had gone to the dark side: the only hope in Belgrade was the kind of deniable 'special operation' that Eden wanted nothing to do with. It was left to local diplomats and secret servicemen to 'play this difficult hand'.[50]

The only concession Eden would make was that he should have one more tilt at the Turkish problem. Perhaps it would be possible to pull a last-minute rabbit out of the hat. Wavell told him that this idea was pointless. There was little chance that the Turks might cooperate. If they did, it would be a disaster, yet another call on British resources to no military advantage. Eden was determined that his Mediterranean mission should end on a high note and persisted. Thus the penultimate leg of Eden's Mediterranean travels was a flight to Cyprus, unaccompanied by any military advisers, for a last meeting with the Turks.[51] Eden's encounter with his Turkish opposite number, Saracoglu, on 18 March 1941 proved a fitting postscript to the whole business. It caused a flurry of excitement but meant nothing. The Turkish foreign minister, convinced that it was advisable to encourage Eden more than his own colleagues thought wise, was unexpectedly accommodating about the idea of a last-minute appeal to Yugoslavia to stand up to the Germans. Eden reported home about his success, but when Saracoglu returned to Ankara the proposal was immediately buried.

In the event, weather delayed Eden in the Mediterranean long enough for the events to unfold in his presence. Whilst Eden had been making his way to Cyprus, Hitler had issued the final order for an attack on Greece. The aim, he said, was to conquer the entire country, and thus force the British permanently out of the Aegean. At the same time as Eden and Saracoglu were negotiating, Hitler was meeting Rommel to discuss his plans for operations on the southern shore. Rommel made a most favourable impression on the Nazi leadership. They lapped up the story that this 'magnificent officer' told. The German war machine was operating brilliantly. Any problems were the fault of the Italians. In the background Rommel's own colleagues grumbled about his inability to grasp either strategy or logistics. Regretfully, Hitler denied Rommel's request to be allowed to launch an all-out attack to recover Cyrenaica. That would have to wait a few months until victory over Russia. Rommel might make a limited advance to the first major Cyrenaican crossroads of the *Balbia* at Agedabia, but he could go no further. Rommel picked up the undertow in these conversations, however. He was a true Nazi hero, undervalued by his own colleagues in the *Wehrmacht*. If he could conjure something spectacular with existing resources it would not go ill for him. After all, the Führer himself had assured him that he would not turn away from Africa 'under any circumstances'. Immediately upon his return he ordered his one completed armoured division to lead the Italians forward. He would see how far they could take him.[52]

News of the first German probes filtered back to Cairo. Wavell hoped that they meant little. He had ordered his armoured forces back to Egypt to refit. He was 'anxious', but buoyed by the thought that the Germans had so few men in Africa. They could not, he guessed, do anything serious for another month. More immediately eye-catching was the announcement on 25 March 1941 that, in Hitler's presence in Vienna, the Yugoslavs had paid formal deference to the Nazis. On this rather sour note, Eden reached Malta.

Suddenly, however, the tide seemed to be turning. British cryptanalysts deciphered *Luftwaffe* signals that talked about some kind of Italian naval activity south of Crete. They could offer no real clue to its purpose.

The Italians might be thinking of attacking the ships bringing troops and supplies to Greece, they could be reinforcing the Italian garrisons in the eastern Aegean; more worryingly still, it was possible that an Italo-German expeditionary force was at sea, heading for Greece, Libya or even Malta. Cunningham was 'therefore faced with the problem of meeting a threat which he knew to exist, but whose nature he could not foretell'. He launched the Mediterranean Fleet into the unknown to try and find the Italians. The same fog that was keeping Eden trapped in the Mediterranean, helped Cunningham. Both sides had decrypts from the other and knew that their ships were heading towards a confrontation. Both sides had aircraft out looking and each spotted the other. Crucially, Admiral Iachino thought he was hunting a force of British cruisers with his battleships. Instead, on 28 March 1941, he found the full Mediterranean Fleet. Although the fast Italian battleships were able to outrun Cunningham's rustbuckets with ease, the unwary Italian cruiser division blundered into the British pursuit, to be destroyed by the heavy guns of the British battleships. The Mediterranean Fleet had been under a cloud for months and Cunningham's bravery had been questioned at the highest levels. With the one flourish off Cape Matapan the slate was wiped clean.[53]

Yugoslavia yielded an even more surprising turn of events. A coup carried out by elements of the Serbian military overthrew the government of the despised Prince 'Palsy' and proclaimed that they would govern in the name of King Peter. No one was sure whether the 'hidden hand' of the British was behind the coup.[54] Even the British themselves could not be quite sure of the role that they had played. At least three British intelligence agencies had had links with potential coup plotters. All had expressed enthusiasm for the demise of Paul. The long-time SIS resident in Belgrade, whose friends in the air force took a leading part in the final denouement, was nearest to events. The British were, however, by and large, spectators of a power struggle within the Serb elite.[55]

What the coup did not achieve was the emergence of a pro-British regime. As soon as they possibly could, the plotters were on the phone to Germany offering friendly relations. They were too late. A frothing Hitler had already gathered his generals and told them that the upstarts must be crushed.[56] Indeed he wanted Yugoslavia and its bastard multinationalism erased. 'This fair-weather nation will have to pay for its provocations against the Reich with its life,' Hitler decreed. It was essential that the civilian population of Belgrade should be bombed viciously and constantly.[57] Once destroyed, Yugoslavia would be replaced by a series of ethnically cleansed regimes. The Serbs would be purged of their leaders. As for the Croats, it was time to 'stroke them!'[58] The Ustasha – Insurgents – Croatian terrorists whom the Italians had financed and maintained in exile for many years were assembled at Pistoia.[59] Their leader Ante Pavelic was received by Mussolini with the promise of a new Fascist Croatia. The band was then dispatched to Trieste to await events.[60]

The potential fall-out of the coup held Eden in the Mediterranean. Churchill suggested that he return to Cairo to take control. In the end Eden chose to fly to Athens, passing directly over the battle of Cape Matapan.[61] From Athens there were hopes of moving on to Belgrade. Perhaps the north-east Mediterranean alliance that had eluded him for so many months was now in his grasp. It would then be possible to say 'when he finally does return to London' that he did so with '"Serbia in the bag" for which he has striven so tirelessly'.[62] Watching his progress, Hitler commented that 'the travelling warmonger' might be in Athens, 'but his activities are no longer a problem so far as his plans are concerned'.[63] Indeed, Eden soon found that the Yugoslavs had no desire for his presence. 'Belgrade is denying Eden's presence,' recorded Goebbels with satisfaction, 'he has not been invited and would not be received, even if he came privately. Strong words and dramatic evidence of the Jew-boy funk.'[64] Dill and the commander of the British forces in Greece, Jumbo Wilson, did hold secret meetings with the Yugoslav military, but they achieved nothing. The nearest that Eden got was a train journey to Florina at the end of March, where a Yugoslav general furtively crossed the border to meet him.[65] The Greeks and Yugoslavs refused to cooperate with each other in order to defeat the Germans.

By then it was clear that Eden had made a mistake by heading north. The German threat in the south revealed itself more clearly with each passing day. On 2 April 1941 Rommel's armoured forces took Agedabia, the limit of his authorized advance. On the same day, Bletchley Park reported that another German armoured division was in Sicily in the process of embarking for Tripoli. The intelligence intercepts still suggested that the German build-up would take over a month. The orders flowing from Germany to the battlefront did not give any real hint of reckless advance. Yet something was afoot. Rommel had little intention of obeying those orders.

The day after the fall of Agedabia, he browbeat his Italian opposite number, General Gariboldi, into submission. Gariboldi demanded that

Rommel should halt the advance. Rommel replied that his orders were not to advance unless the British were in headlong retreat. Then he had the authority to exploit the opportunity. As far as he could see, the British were fleeing. There were no armoured forces in front of him. Wavell was showing no appetite for the defence of Benghazi. It was his duty to chase him out of Cyrenaica. With Nelsonian arrogance Rommel seized for himself the triple initiative: over the British, over the Italians and over his own army high command.[66] Eden had to get back to Cairo. The idea was growing that 'we cannot face the Germans and their appearance is enough to drive us back many score of miles'. Such a suspicion would 'react most evilly throughout the Balkans'.[67] As he prepared to fly south again, Italian troops – effectively under Rommel's orders, whatever the formal command arrangements – occupied Benghazi. Rommel's patron, Goebbels, immediately flooded the airwaves with read-backs of all the gloating statements the British had issued when Benghazi fell into their hands. It was 'a dreadful humiliation for England'.[68]

In truth, there was little for Eden to do in Cairo. The dispositions had been made around the Mediterranean, and there was little that the Mediterranean-hopping representative of Britain could do to affect the outcome. The one substantive decision made during his final stay in Egypt was that Tobruk should be reinforced by an Australian division and held for as long as possible. The Mediterranean commanders urged this decision. Eden and Dill added their imprimatur. Eden's main task was to put a brave face on things, and to get his story straight for future consumption. When his Lockheed touched down at Heliopolis aerodrome on 5 April 1941, Eden himself cut a confident figure. His sartorial elegance had survived the journey, in contrast to his travelling companion who left the aircraft visibly 'travel stained'. The jaunty air that had marked both Eden's conversations and reports was still in place. This too was in contrast to the diplomats and officers who surrounded him. They were at the end of their tether, sunk in gloom at their repeated failures. A few hours in Cairo, however, was enough to bring Eden's mood into line with that of everyone else. For the first time he started showing signs of 'consider-able emotion and agitation'. The atmosphere became one of 'abysmal gloom'. As news from the battlefront trickled in, most notably that the British commanders in the Western Desert had been captured by the advancing Italo-Germans, there was a sense that people were cracking. They spent hours going over the same unprofitable ground, discussing ad nauseam how it had come to this. Out of these discussions came a

'line' about what had gone wrong. The whole scheme of sending assistance to Greece had been based on 'the definite and positive assurance
from the soldiers that they could easily hold the West'. It was the generals
who were to blame for this misjudgement. Eden had been let down by
the military.[69]

Eden was certainly wise to prepare such a cover story before he departed,
for a double-edged and doubly uncomfortable welcome was in preparation. 'The great trip', it was said in Whitehall, 'has been a failure.' Churchill
was 'saying he never wished to help Greece'. At the same time the Prime
Minister declared of Eden that he wished 'to exhibit him in triumph'.
Whether he liked it or not, Eden was to be yoked to events in the
Mediterranean and made to take responsibility for them. Eden delayed
his departure long enough to hear the news that the Germans had invaded
both Greece and Yugoslavia.[70]

Thus ended Eden's Mediterranean adventure. It took him three days
to reach home. By that time the news was even worse than when he had
left. The Greek army of the north-east, comprising 60,000 men – bigger
than the entire British expeditionary force – had surrendered. The
Germans had launched a second invasion of Yugoslavia from the southern
Reich itself. Zagreb had fallen and the independent Ustasha republic of
Croatia had been proclaimed. Rommel had captured Derna, prompting
renewed Nazi gloating. 'Wonderful! wonderful,' declared Goebbels, 'stunning blow for London; supplies excellent material for our propaganda.
We are on top of the world.'[71] The commanders in the Mediterranean
agreed, in part, with what the German propaganda chief said.[72] Arthur
Longmore, the RAF commander, was heard to say that 'it really didn't
matter' either way whether they held the Mediterranean. 'All we had to
do was to fall South [into Africa] and let the Mediterranean look after
itself.'[73] Longmore made the further mistake – ultimately fatal to his
career – of saying that Eden's tour of the Mediterranean had been a
disaster.[74] Such statements played into the narrative that the commanders
in the Mediterranean were 'windy', and it was only the unyielding will
of London that kept them up to the task.[75]

In fact, those commanders had formulated a highly risky 'island strategy'
for the Mediterranean. They would hold Crete, even though they doubted
it was really defensible with the Greek mainland in Italo-German hands,

and they would hold Tobruk despite the danger that it would become little more than a 'beleaguered garrison'.[76] They warned that Malta was *already* a 'beleaguered garrison'. There was finally a sufficiency of anti-aircraft guns. But by their very nature anti-aircraft guns were solely defensive. A few days previously Somerville's Force H had managed to fly Hurricanes onto Malta from the west. But short-range fighters were also solely defensive. What was really needed was that Malta should be reactivated as an offensive base, and for that to happen a much greater effort was needed. Malta needed bombers, reconnaissance aircraft, cruisers, destroyers and submarines. But there was no point sending ships and aircraft if they could not survive German air attacks for more than a few days. The Governor reported that this was unlikely. The Germans had established a moral and physical superiority over the island. Any aircraft that arrived were rapidly destroyed. The morale of the pilots was so low that some of them were combat-ineffective. The RAF commander on the island was having a nervous breakdown. Nevertheless, as a first step, Cunningham ordered a destroyer flotilla to the island.[77]

None of these ideas or actions saved the victor of Cape Matapan from the insistent insinuation that he was insufficiently bold. Just as Somerville had done previously, Cunningham argued that it was a misuse of naval power in the Mediterranean to take capital ships close inshore to bombard cities. The ships would be dangerously vulnerable to land-based aircraft. Whatever the psychological impact of their big guns, the bombardments produced few military results. At the moment of crisis it seemed to him futile to waste strength on high-risk, low-return adventures. He was told that this was simply not good enough. German reinforcements were arriving in Tripoli, he had to be seen to do something.[78] The 'whole situation', Churchill declared, was 'compromised' by Cunningham's inability or unwillingness 'to close the passage from Italy to Libya, or to break up the port facilities of Tripoli'.[79] What was required was a 'suicide' mission.[80] Cunningham's reputation was once again saved by another timely victory. He had consistently pointed out that Tripoli was not the only potential terminus for supply ships from Italy. Now that Darlan had thrown his lot in with the Nazis, there was always the possibility that a deal would be struck to allow the Germans to use Tunisian facilities. Already, the Axis convoys used the Tunisian coast as protection from the British. On 16 April 1941 the destroyers that Cunningham had sent to Malta were guided onto to a German convoy off the Tunisian port of Sfax by signals intelligence. The night-time interception combined elan with precise technical skill, winning universal praise. Five German transports were destroyed.[81]

Although such victories were to prove the key to the future of Mediterranean warfare, at the time the battle of the Kerkenah Bank seemed but a small ray of light.[82] Churchill described it as a 'skirmish'.[83] The high command of the German army might say in private that Rommel's failure to take Tobruk showed that they had been right all along: he was an over-rated Nazi stooge. The British, on the receiving end, could but notice the ferocity of his attacks.[84] The Yugoslavs were suing for peace, as were parts of the Greek army. King Peter of Yugoslavia had already arrived in Athens, fleeing into exile. Whilst the Greek forces in the east cooperated with Wilson's plan to hold the Germans at the Pass of Thermopylae, those on the west coast refused to withdraw to a new defensive line. The western officers maintained that the Italians were the enemy, the English were troublemakers and the Germans were potential friends. Hitler ruled that these 'brave soldiers' should be offered 'honourable surrender'. The generals of the Army of Epirus were a 'heaven-sent favour' who would lead Greece into the New Order.[85] Despairing of his country, the Greek Prime Minister committed suicide. In the confusion that followed the collapse of central authority in Athens, British officers, diplomats and secret agents all agreed that both the military and political will to resist had collapsed. Few Greek politicians viewed with favour a plan to carry on the fight from Crete. In the end the British stopped looking for a Greek leader to accompany the King into exile and found a Cretan banker, Emanuel Tsouderos, who might serve as politician. The British evacuated their second monarch, King George of the Hellenes, from Athens in a few days.[86]

For German aircraft in the Aegean it was a happy, killing time. In one 24-hour period they sank well over twenty ships which were trying to evacuate British troops. Over the same period the bombardment of Tripoli, albeit shorn of its suicidal aspects, proved, as Cunningham had predicted, a damp squib. The only redeeming feature of the operation was that the German air force, so successfully deployed elsewhere, missed the opportunity to sink a British battleship. He had, Cunningham wrote, got away with it by dint of good luck. The cost had been to tie up the Mediterranean Fleet for five days, 'at the expense of all other commitments and at a time when these commitments were at their most pressing'.[87] You have to understand, he signalled London, that 'the key which will decide the issue of our success or otherwise in holding the Mediterranean lies in air power'. Stop complaining, the reply came back; it was Cunningham's duty to establish control of the Mediterranean, not to try and slough it off on the air force.[88] In despair, Cunningham told Churchill that he understood nothing of what was happening in the Mediterranean.[89] He was 'blind to facts'.[90] Churchill's riposte was that he understood the failings of those in the Mediterranean only too well. He was providing the tools that they were too scared to use. It was he who had ordered a huge convoy of tanks to be sent from the UK to Egypt. It was he who had ordered Somerville to get the convoy through to Malta; it was he who had insisted that Cunningham pick it up on the other side and see it through to its destination. It was he who had overruled naval objections that 'their chances of getting through the Mediterranean were remote'.[91] Once more, Cunningham complained, Churchill misrepresented the situation. He was all for the single-minded pursuit of an essential goal, however dangerous, but his actual orders were to divert forces from the convoy. London insisted on another pointless coastal bombardment, this time of Benghazi.[92]

The mutual disillusion of Whitehall and Grey Pillars was the product of the collision of Cairo strategy with London politics. On the day that Force H sailed from Gibraltar with Churchill's prized tank convoy, and the Mediterranean Fleet sailed from Alexandria heading west towards Malta, Eden had to give an account of his Mediterranean mission to the House of Commons. Eden's explanation of the Mediterranean situation on 6 May 1941 was not a happy occasion. The speech was 'appallingly bad'. He rose to a hostile silence, 'gave a dim account of his travels and failures' and sat down to an even more hostile silence. Eden's enemies said that it was possibly the worst speech of the war. Everyone agreed that it was 'a complete flop'.[93] As Churchill had always intended, Eden carried the can for the crisis in the Mediterranean. The reviled Foreign Secretary stood as a bulwark for his leader. Churchill – taking a wider view of the war – was more warmly received, and the government survived a vote of confidence with ease. The Mediterranean had raised Eden up, the Mediterranean cast him down. But Eden could not be allowed to fall too far, lest the whole government be dragged down with him. The political strategy Eden had adumbrated in Cairo remained sound – blame the military. The fact had to be established that the government was 'completely hamstrung' by the 'sensational ineptitude of our commanders'.[94]

Wavell, holding out the hope of a counter-attack, was for the moment safe. Tobruk was a beacon of hope. Indeed in early May 1941 the German army high command had dispatched a mission to discipline Rommel for his failures in front of the town.[95] Cunningham could utter bitter truths because of his glorious victories: Taranto, Matapan and Kerkenah Bank were his shield. Their comrade-in-arms, Arthur Longmore, was less fortunate. He had no such spoils to show. Many in the RAF murmured that he had been too willing to kow-tow to Cunningham, too willing to spread his forces thin in order to support the navy and the army. Instead of trying to make the best of the situation, it should have been his task to celebrate the supremacy of the aeroplane over the ship. Longmore should have forced Cunningham to admit that disaster in the Mediterranean was the navy's fault. It was Cunningham, and before him Pound, who had padded their budgets with the ridiculous claim that warships could fight planes. If Longmore had few airmen friends, he had even fewer political allies. His pungently expressed pessimism had made him a marked man. Defeat in the Mediterranean was laid at his feet. He was the first Mediterranean commander-in-chief to be sacked.

In the days immediately after the debate it appeared that a 'very nervous' Churchill had been right. Italo-German forces attacked the great tank convoy but 'the scale was very much less than had been anticipated'. Indeed the attackers did not seem very good at their job. The formations were ill-coordinated, jettisoned their bombs too soon, or carried out brave but ineffective independent attacks. Only one of five big cargo ships was sunk. Observing, Somerville concluded that he had caught the Axis air forces by surprise. In addition, his forces were being helped by the heavy cloud over the Mediterranean. Full of praise for the skill of his captains and aircrews, Somerville concluded, nevertheless, that they had got through only because of the 'luck of the gods'. The German bomber units had been involved in a complex series of exchanges between Sicily, North Africa and Greece. Their base at Trapani was in confusion. The specialist anti-shipping strike aircraft were away. Cunningham took the convoy off Somerville's hands some fifty miles off Malta. Three days later he delivered its precious cargo into Alexandria. Like Somerville, Cunningham maintained that he too had been lucky. 'We got through all right,' he signalled London, 'but it mainly due to the extraordinary thick weather experienced off Malta and the whole way to Alexandria.'[96]

This luck soon ran out. At the end of April 1941 Hitler had agreed to a *Luftwaffe* plan to seize Crete, primarily through the use of air power and parachutists.[97] This was to be the last operation in the Mediterranean before the invasion of Russia. Operation *Merkur* was an air-force plan, to be carried out by air-force generals. Unsurprisingly, the *Luftwaffe* generals took air superiority very seriously. Whilst Cunningham was still at sea with the tank convoy, his air-force opposite number took the decision to withdraw RAF squadrons from Crete. Before his enforced departure Longmore had always been sceptical about the military logic of a German airborne invasion of Greece. He doubted whether, given the scale of likely casualties, they would try it, and believed that if they did try, ground troops could defeat the effort. In the meantime, however, he argued that the weight of German air attack from captured Greek bases made Cretan airfields too vulnerable to justify the waste of his resources. Thus when the German parachutists started landing, the RAF had largely vacated the island. Its aircraft fought at the edge of their range from Egyptian bases.

Naval forces sent north of Crete to prevent the Germans reinforcing their airborne troops from the sea proved desperately vulnerable to air attack. Crete was the perfect arena for *Stukawaffe*. The Stukas were feared by ground troops. If anything they proved even more effective in anti-shipping operations. Their main base on the island of Scarpanto was separated from Crete by the narrow Kaso Strait. The short-range aircraft could thus operate with comfort to the east of Crete. Another base in the Peloponnese was equally well placed for the sea lanes to the west of the island. Even Cyrenaican Stukas could reach ships to the south of Crete. Effectively, Crete was a killing zone. British cruisers and destroyers in particular proved frighteningly vulnerable to attack.

After three days Cunningham had had enough. He made the unilateral decision to recall his fleet to prevent its slaughter by the *Luftwaffe*. There had been 'nothing short of a trial of strength between Mediterranean Fleet and the German air force': the German air force had won. Not only was Cunningham losing ships, he was losing captains at an even quicker rate as they buckled under the accumulated strain of months of 'air fear'. 'I am afraid', Cunningham admitted, 'we have to admit defeat and accept the fact that losses are too great to justify us trying to prevent seaborne attacks on Crete. This is a melancholy conclusion but it must be faced.'

There was 'no hiding the fact' that 'the future out here does not look too good for the Fleet'. He persuaded his fellow Mediterranean commanders to defy London again and halt the evacuation of the defeated imperial forces even from the south coast of the island. Crete proved, he could not resist pointing out, what he had been saying for months. His ships had survived only because of the foul Mediterranean winter weather. The glorious Mediterranean spring was a death-bringer.[98]

SIX

Losing the Light

At the end of her semi-autobiographical novel *Friends and Heroes*, Olivia Manning tried to sum up what losing Greece meant for the British. She thought that they had lost the light. For refugees fleeing the débâcle, the play of light on the North African shore was 'too white'. 'They moved forward to look at the new land, reached thankfully if unwillingly.' In 'crossing the Mediterranean', 'they had life – a depleted fortune'.[1] That sense of survival – a life, but depleted fortune – permeated each of the Mediterranean powers. Britain, Italy, France, each survived but none could feel happy with their lot. All three wanted to fight for the Mediterranean, but their capacity to do so was sadly reduced. They could do little more than fall back on *mezzi insidiosi*, the Mediterranean guerrilla war that the Italians had feared might be their portion in the mid-1930s. The future of their reduced fortunes lay in German hands, and the Germans, established for the first time on the Mediterranean littoral as conquerors, were hard to read.

The Germans were such an unpredictable force in the Mediterranean world because of their own ambivalence. Combing through the records after the war, historians identified at least a dozen serious attempts by those gathered around Hitler to persuade him that the Mediterranean was the key to victory. Nothing in the Führer's past conduct suggested that he believed them. His eyes were cast ever eastwards.[2] This judgement took lapidary form on 11 June 1941 when the dictator uttered his directive on the future of the *Mittelmeer*. The future of the Mediterranean lay on the steppes, it was – as geopolitics had always insisted – a mere appendage of the Heartland.[3] The conquest of Russia would change everything. Turkey would have its twin fears – the Soviets and the Germans – unified into one terror. They would not resist as the forces of the Reich moved through the Straits by sea and Anatolia by land. The Spanish were timid, Franco had squirmed his way out of an attack on Gibraltar. With further proof of the Reich's invincibility, his courage would improve and the British would be swept off the Rock. The French would see that full collaboration was their only chance of survival: North Africa would be open to German forces. Then, the British Mediterranean would be choked to death, squeezed from east and west by what Hitler called a 'concentric' attack.[4]

Concentricity implied a number of important ideas. First, the Mediterranean could wait months, if not years, before the final reckoning. Second, that it was the three gates to the sea, Gibraltar, Suez and the Straits, which were important, not the actual battle for the central Mediterranean. Hitler's Mediterranean creatures were, in order of importance, Turkey, Spain and France. In the wider scheme of things, Italy was left out. Italy's main importance was its weakness. If Mussolini's regime collapsed before Germany had finished with Russia then the completion of the Mediterranean 'anaconda' would be much complicated. Hitler was quite prepared therefore to commit some resources to the Mediterranean, not least to fuel the efforts of his most photogenic general, Rommel.

The quality of Hitler's strategic reasoning has proved fertile ground for the 'what if' school of history. The most popular theory remains the claim that Hitler was wasting his time in the Mediterranean, that the victorious campaigns just completed were, in fact, a disaster because they delayed the invasion of Russia, placing the Germans at the mercy of 'general winter'. Running the argument the other way is almost as popular. The Germans squandered their Mediterranean victory – if only Hitler had listened to his Mediterraneanists and kept German power running at full blast after Crete then a world of opportunity would have opened up: the destruction of British power, the creation of a consolidated anti-Anglo-Saxon Euro-Asia, the benison of Arab oil. None of this, of course, is provable in any serious way. The Germans failed to break through Russia, so the Mediterranean anaconda was never attempted. What can be said for sure was that in the summer of 1941 Britain had more potential enemies in the Mediterranean than Germany. Few were confident enough to proclaim Germany as the new thalassocrat, but even fewer mourned British decline. As her representatives looked around for support they could expect vituperation from some, but silence from most.[5]

The expansive ideas about the Mediterranean came from those far distant from the sea. Those at work in the sea had a very limited horizon, their main aim was survival. The best they thought they might achieve was some damage to their enemies. It was time to face facts, Cunningham wrote home. 'We have lost our Northern flank and are unlikely to regain it.' The 'through Mediterranean route' was now 'virtually closed'. The Royal Navy could, with enormous effort, sail from Gibraltar to Malta but it couldn't get any further. Whilst the west–east route ground to a halt, the north–south route was, by the same token, made so much safer, since 'the attack on Libyan communications is made very hazardous'. Naturally, Cunningham did not countenance inaction but his proposals for remedy were modest.[6]

The best that might be done was some kind of ground offensive in Africa. This offensive would have no grand aims. It just needed to make some progress along the Cyrenaican coast. Cunningham's dream prize was the city of Derna. Cyrenaica's second 'city' was a pleasant enough place. European visitors praised it for being like the 'proper' Mediterranean, reminding them of Crete, rather than sub-standard North Africa. Rommel had a seaside villa nearby. Derna was the only place in eastern Libya where one could grow bananas. Charming Derna was not that far to travel – less than 200 miles by ship. Its position on the bulge of the Libyan plateau which pushed out into the Mediterranean, gave it its strategic attraction: not only a short flight from the Narrows but in range of Greece and the Aegean. In Cunningham's mind a string of airfields from Sollum to Derna could protect his fleet around Malta whilst attacking the northern shore.[7] Cunningham's military opposite number, Wavell, doubted whether even this modest plan was achievable. As Cunningham committed his thoughts to paper in Alexandria, Wavell recorded his in Cairo: he did not believe he could even get his troops over the Egyptian-Libyan border. The newly appointed air commander, the RAF's best Whitehall warrior, Arthur Tedder, used his own message home to gloat that 'the air has come into its own with a vengeance in the Mediterranean'. 'I need hardly say,' he toasted his fellow aviators in the *Luftwaffe*, 'I have refrained from saying, "I told you so".'[8]

The limited ambitions of Britain's Mediterranean leaders failed to take into account that enemies considerably less formidable than the Germans were now willing to twit them. Germany and France had agreed, even before the fall of Crete, that aid should flow to a pro-Nazi revolt in Iraq led by Rashid Ali. Rashid Ali had the enthusiastic assistance of Britain's old friend, the Mufti. Darlan had even been allowed into Berchtesgaden to see Hitler in order to seal the deal.[9] As they spoke, the first German aircraft were landing in Syria. Within days, supply trains were running along the railway from Aleppo to Mosul. The French were running a calculated risk. Darlan knew that such an act of aggression could well provoke a British attack on Syria. In preparation for this eventuality he had replaced the High Commissioner in Syria with a tough Alsatian general, Henri Dentz. Dentz preferred subterfuge – sadly undermined by British decryption of *Luftwaffe* signals – or deterrence to avoid war, but he was quite willing to fight the British if they came.[10]

If the British commanders in the Mediterranean had had their way, Darlan and Dentz's gamble would have paid off. They had no intention of invading Syria. Indeed they sought to maintain cordial relations with Dentz. The gamble was undone by Churchill, reading the Enigma traffic in London and demanding revenge. 'If the French Army in Syria will come over to us,' Churchill wrote, 'then Vichy would have a future as the colonial power in the Levant.' If, as it seemed, 'they are going against us, or maintaining an attitude of malevolent passivity' then the British should look elsewhere. Their new friends would be the 'Syrian Arabs'. 'I am not sufficiently acquainted with Syrian affairs to be able to formulate a plan,' the Prime Minister admitted, 'but I cannot doubt that our Islamic experts can easily do so.'[11]

Churchill's intelligence-fed take on Vichy was defensible enough, his faith in the 'wisdom' of Arab nationalism, or the competence of his own 'Islamic experts', less so. The leaders of Arab nationalism in Syria were most certainly looking for allies against the French, but had already found them elsewhere. One of the bargains Darlan made with Hitler was for the withdrawal of the Reich's premier orientalist, von Hentig, from Syria. His sin was his success with indigenous politicians. Von Hentig's successor, the equally dynamic Rudolf Rahn, was no less successful. It was not hard to see why. Despite the promises they had made in 1936, the French had delayed any transfer of power to indigenous politicians until the eve of war, when they suspended the constitution and appointed their own placemen to rule the country. The former Prime Minister, Jamil Mardam, was revealed, by the gleeful opening of the books by France's new placemen, to be corrupt on an almost industrial scale. Although the French delighted in his discomfiture, they regarded corruption as a venial sin. Mortal sin they attributed to Mardam's rival Dr Shahbandar, with his anti-fascist and secular principles. Thus the French colluded with

Mardam, first to have Shahbandar murdered as a British agent and an enemy of Islam, then to pervert his trial, and finally to whisk him across the border to a safe exile in Iraq. With Mardam having fled and Shahbandar dead, the field was left open for the other main leader of the National Bloc, Shukri al-Quwwatli, to emerge as the unchallenged spokesman of Syrian nationalism. Quwwatli used his new platform to celebrate openly the coming victory of the Axis and the great benefit to the Arabs thereof.[12] There was a notable increase in the number of German 'tourists' crossing into Syria from Turkey. The most visible *Abwehr* operative in the region, Paula Koch, was inevitably dubbed 'the Mata Hari of the Levant'. Lebanon's leading nationalist politician, Riad Solh, was closely linked to Koch.[13]

The choice between definitely anti-British and possibly pro-Nazi Frenchmen, or definitely anti-French but possibly pro-Nazi nationalists, was hardly appetizing. The means by which Britain might subvert such alignments were not in good repair when the point of crisis arrived. The man supposedly coordinating policy for Wavell was Colonel Illtyd Clayton. Clayton, by virtue of family connections – his older brother had been Lawrence of Arabia's boss – had spent his entire professional life enmeshed in the intrigues of the Arab world. He, if anyone, was the Islamic expert for whom Churchill sought. At the exact moment he was called upon, however, he was having little success in controlling the civil war that had broken out between the secret organizations in Cairo and the Levant. The long-time Middle East hand that he was, Clayton still preferred working with his old French contacts. 'Time and time again,' complained one SOE leader whom Clayton held in check, 'we have asked' to be allowed to to cooperate with anti-French heterodox sects, such as the Druze, disillusioned by Dentz's open favour towards orthodox Sunnis. 'The answer given by Clayton has always been', his interlocutor reported, '"No; nothing must be done to upset Dentz; we can always get the Arabs when we want them; we are staking everything on Dentz swinging over entirely to our side; or at any rate resisting any attempt by the Germans to occupy Syria".'[14]

In retrospect, it was clear that Clayton had misread Dentz, but he was not solely grasping for a shop-worn former amity. In his desire to bluff the British, Dentz had cast an indulgent eye on some cross-border contacts. Clayton and Dentz were fighting for the soul of Colonel Robert Collet. Collet's soul had both material and symbolic value, for he was by far the most famous Frenchman in the Levant. Everyone had to have their own Lawrence of Arabia; von Hentig was Germany's and Collet had been France's. In the inter-war period French governments and news-reels had made a cult of Collet, leading his highly colourful Circassian cavalry who, the propagandists had their audience believe, were his 'children', looking up to him as a 'father' if not a demi-god. The Circassians were not just there for show, although their fair-skinned women were undoubtedly a favourite of orientalist pornography. Collet's men had shown an enormous aptitude and appetite for butchering their racial and religious rivals in the massacres that had done so much to cement French rule. Dentz, however, was far from trusting his glamorous subordinate. Word reached him that the Circassians openly mocked the French for their wretched military performance against the Germans and the British. He had them confined to their barracks, and resorted to the low trick of having the carburettors removed from their lorries so that they could not decamp *en masse* to Palestine. Yet neither did Dentz wish to drive Collet into British hands. A ludicrous game developed between them. Each weekend Collet would announce that he was 'going to Beirut', pile a few Circassians into his car and then drive in the opposite direction across the Palestinian border to Haifa. The Circassians could then desert in safety and Collet would sit down and talk to Clayton's men. He would then drive to Beirut for the weekend, all under the eyes of Dentz's spies, who reported each move. It was not until the end of May 1941, when Collet finally took the momentous decision to desert, that Dentz ordered him to Damascus and court martial. One might call this game of shadows a draw between Dentz and Clayton since, when Collet finally fled to Transjordan, about half of his original Circassians came with him to fight with the British.[15]

Clayton viewed Arab politicians as tarts; they had been bought by the Nazis, but they would be happy to be bought by the British when the time came. It hardly helped the British cause that almost their only friends amongst the local population were 'the Friends'. 'The Friends' was the rather arch terminology used for militant Jews recruited to the British cause. Churchill, a believer in the wisdom of arming Zionists, should have been happy with these recruits. Most authorities in the Levant thought they were poison. Clayton at GHQ, the government of Palestine and the commander of British troops in Palestine all ordered Adrian Bishop, the champion of their use, to break off contact. Like any good secret operative he simply took pains to conceal his activities more carefully.

His critics objected not only to the fact of Jewish recruitment but to
the nature of the recruits. Bishop reasoned that it was no good having
intellectuals and politicians on one's side. Men of action were needed.
He found such men, 'toughs', among the Irgun. This was dangerous
ground. The Irgun were unreconstructed terrorists, tarred, not least, with
the brush of murdering fellow Zionists. The Irgun had been responsible
for blowing up a refugee ship in Haifa harbour, killing over two hundred
civilians and a number of policemen. The military wing of the Revisionists,
of which they were part, had in the mid-1930s been the clients of
Mussolini. Then they had accepted supplies and training from the Fascists;
now they were accepting them from the British.[16] It was only when the
call went out for 'special operations' in Iraq and Syria that Bishop was
able to reveal, triumphantly, that 'it is perhaps extremely fortunate that
we have a certain number of trained men at our disposal – trained, that
is to say, against the wishes of all the authorities'. The first mission for
which the 'toughs' were put up was the assassination of von Hentig, in
which they refused to participate.[17] Instead they were sent to Iraq with
orders to pose as Arab terrorists; their violence was to spread discord
amongst supporters of the revolt and aid British intervention propaganda. However, the leader of the Irgun 'was shot dead before they were
able to function'. As SOE's internal assessment concluded: 'the whole of
this undertaking was most dangerous and ill-conceived, and it is lucky
that the Iraqis never discovered that we employed Palestinian Jews against
them during their revolt'.[18]

As planning for the Syrian operation got under way, Wavell cabled
home that 'all senior officers on my staff who have dealings with [special
operations] are convinced that the organisation in the Mideast is a racket'.
He had decided to bring all special operations firmly under military
control through the creation of a 'Jerusalem bureau'.[19] As British power
teetered in the spring of 1941, many looked to the dark arts of propaganda to make right what had been lost on the battlefield. But those in
charge of black propaganda turned their weapons on each other, rather
than any external enemy; charges of sexual and financial misconduct
rebounded around the Middle East.[20] As one of the officers sent in to
clear up the mess remarked, 'nobody who did not experience it can
possibly imagine the atmosphere of jealousy, suspicion and intrigue that
embittered the relations between the various secret and semi-secret
departments in Cairo during the summer of 1941'.[21] In any case there
was little to suggest that the secret departments had anything to offer in

the way of expertise in manipulating Levantine politics to British advantage. They comprised a hotch-potch of military intelligence, Indian policemen, civilians who might speak Serbo-Croat, or were believed to be good at deception because they were, for example, lawyers. SOE's chief 'Islamic expert' was Heyworth Dunne, a tarbush-wearing English Muslim with an Egyptian wife. Dunne devoted his time mainly to 'astrologers, whom he used to prophesy the future and the outcome of the war'.[22] This is not what Churchill had in mind when he called for such experts to be consulted.

With so few friends, all that was left to Britain was the exercise of military power. Wavell was ordered to strike west along the Libyan littoral and north into Syria. He welcomed neither order, believing that he should be given more time to amass a critical weight of trained and equipped forces before taking on another major operation. Thus the stratagems emanating from Churchill's fertile and information-rich mind were contested at the time and have remained controversial since. There has remained, however, an odd imbalance in these controversies. Wavell ordered his forces to fight a battle and a war in June 1941. The battle – on the Egyptian-Libyan frontier – lasted for two days and changed very little. The war – against France in Syria and Lebanon – lasted for five weeks and led to the occupation of the Levant and the definitive joining of the Near East to the Mediterranean. It took British forces towards the Turkish border at a particularly vital moment. The Turks, always good bellwethers of military fortune, chose the moment when both the Syrian campaign and Libyan battle were in the balance to sign a Friendship treaty with the Nazis. At the same time they colluded with the Italians to subvert the Montreux Convention that banned warships from passing through the Straits in wartime. Churchill himself claimed that the 'prize is Turkey'. Yet the battle has been regarded as important, the war not. This imbalance was a product of propaganda as much as strategy.[23] The 'real' war, declared and open, was against the Italians and the Germans in Libya; Britain, through the Free French, still claimed France as a friend. The Syrian conflict had to be constructed as a scuffle with an illegitimate government. In fact, Wavell allocated roughly equal forces to each operation. The 'waste' of men against the French, according to his defenders, was the cause of his defeat by Rommel.

The invasion of Syria began exactly a week before the invasion of

Libya. The targets of the invasion force, a melange of British, Australian, Indian and French troops, were two great historic cities, Beirut on the Mediterranean coast and Damascus inland. The march up the coastal route from Haifa to Beirut brought the question of the war with the *Marine* to the fore once more. At the other end of the Mediterranean, Force H slipped its mooring in Gibraltar and took to sea, not to engage the Italians, but in expectation that the Rock would be once more 'plastered' by French aircraft.[24] In the event Darlan held his hand in the west, in part because he feared that the expansion of the war could destroy the whole French position in North Africa, but also because many of the aircraft from there had already been sent to reinforce Dentz. Cunningham agreed with Godfroy in Alexandria harbour that Syria 'alters nothing'. Some thought Cunningham ridiculously indulgent to his French friends given that the *Marine* outside the harbour battled with all their might against him.[25] The French flotilla in Beirut fought three fierce battles against the British. They were joined by the *Armée de l'Air* and the *Luftwaffe* in Syria to such good effect that, within days, Cunningham concluded that British casualties were unacceptable, that some British ships were 'bomb shy', and that the French ships 'well and boldly handled' showed standards 'considerably above' those of the British.[26] On land, too, the attack stalled against fierce resistance on the Litani River, the route by which the invasion commander 'Jumbo' Wilson intended to dogleg east towards Damascus. The columns further inland seemed to be racing towards Damascus. But as Rommel counter-attacked in Libya, Dentz did the same in Syria with the same result: British forces were routed and sent back to their start line.

As in Syria, so in Libya, the British attempted to move along the coast, whilst sending other columns inland in an attempt to outflank enemy positions. Unlike in Syria there was no clear objective other than a 'general advance'. There was no doubt what Churchill wanted, the relief of Tobruk. In fact, as Wavell had predicted, the battle was once more for that coastal speck, Sollum. One may recall that the town stood at the top and bottom of the great cliffs that divided the coastal plain from the desert plateau. The main route up the cliff was Halfaya – Hellfire – Pass. The British tried to enter the Pass from both coastal and desert ends with, especially at the latter, a brutal lack of success. The battle at Hellfire introduced them to the soon-demonized 88mm, few in number but formidable in efficacy: within hours British tanks, burnt out, littered the plain. First the field commanders and then Wavell himself declared the battle lost.

They had failed to get across the Egyptian border and were back where they had begun, Sidi Barrani.

The battle for Sollum fought between 15 and 17 June 1941 branded Wavell a loser, and within days cost him his job.[27] Whereas the British folded their hand in Libya, they persisted in Syria. The Rommel myth began at the Hellfire, but there was never a Dentz myth. Pointing to his success on land, sea and air, Dentz told Darlan that with reinforcements he could beat his opponents. The problem was that those reinforcements – 'Stukas' – would have to come from Germany. Darlan equivocated and then said no. He saw no value in small German forces aiding Dentz. A full-blown Franco-German alliance was only useful to him if German military intervention was 'quick, massive and continuous', a few squadrons of Ju-87s were simply of no use. He demanded that the Germans allow a French naval battlegroup to head east and that they would share with France the overlordship of Greece. Lighter forces had proved inadequate for the task. British bases on Cyprus, too far to the east to be useful in the usual run of Mediterranean operations, were perfectly placed for use against ships trying to make the run from Greece to Syria. A modern super-destroyer exploring the run was sunk by short-range torpedo-bombers. In the days following, the same aircraft hunted French troop and merchant ships around the north-eastern Mediterranean. The Germans talked, but offered few of the 'substantial, durable' advantages Darlan sought for fighting the British. He decided that Dentz was expendable.[28]

Dentz's isolation doomed him to defeat. The British inland columns returned to the attack and in late June 1941 captured Damascus. Another force invaded Syria from Iraq. The coastal route to Beirut, however, remained blocked by fierce resistance for a further three weeks. Indeed at the end of the first week in July 1941 Churchill reluctantly agreed to the assessment of Wavell's replacement, Claude Auchinleck, that the Syrian campaign must have priority over any plans to venture once more towards Libya.[29]

The observation that the Germans had the power to aid Syria, but chose not to, prompted some to rethink allegiances. The anti-British forces had been joined by another familiar face from the 1930s, Fawzi al-Kawokji, the leader of the foreign fighters during the Palestinian uprising. Fawzi, however, was badly wounded fighting the British in north-east Syria. The Germans thought highly enough of him to provide a special evacuation flight to Athens. Three days previously OKW had ordered that 'patient orientalist', air-force general Felmy to establish his unit *Sonderstab* F in Athens in preparation to receive anti-British elements from around the Mediterranean.[30] Like their British counterparts, the German high command saw an important role for propaganda and subversion amongst littoral populations; like the British, they were also hobbled by their allies. Hitler's directive that the Italians were to have the leading role in propaganda, pushing the theme of 'the Mediterranean for the Mediterranean peoples' had yet to be revoked. So too were his further orders to regard the Vichy French as true collaborators and that the Arabs were not to be turned against them with promises of independence. In any case, Germans on the ground did not admire their potential collaborators. Rudolf Rahn swore in Fawzi's band, stiffened by German deserters from the French Foreign Legion, as the defenders of Aleppo. Crowds cheered the raising of the Arab flag and declarations that Nazis and Arabs would stand side by side. In private, however, Rahn despaired. The only people he could trust were these 'professional bandits, smugglers and thieves' raised by Fawzi, himself 'half adventurer, half national hero'. As for the rest of Syrian nationalism, he could only agree with his English opposite number, Clayton. They would either run away or desert to the British. This was particularly true of the great beneficiary of *Abwehr* largesse, Shukri al-Quwwatli, who found it politic to leave for a cooling-off period in Baghdad. 'After long and difficult attempts,' Rahn reluctantly reported to his superiors, 'I had to resign from the co-operation with the old nationalist organisations.'[31]

The British might have rejoiced at this rare recent discomfiture of their German enemies, if they had not been so put upon by their own allies. The day before Rahn made his despairing last gesture in Aleppo, a new British political 'fixer' touched down by flying boat on the Nile. Wavell had maintained for months that the military were ill equipped to deal with the mounting political, organizational and diplomatic problems generated by his campaigns. Churchill did not pay him much regard, but the idea piqued his interest when it was suggested by his own son Randolph, a junior army officer, who drifted around the Mediterranean with no particularly well-defined duties. In July 1941 he dispatched his crony, Oliver Lyttelton, to Cairo with the very grand-sounding title of Minister Resident and backed his authority with membership of the London War Cabinet. The arrival of Lyttelton made some in the Mediterranean feel like 'poor whites'.[32]

The group that stood to benefit most from the British war with Vichy, and the discomfiture of the nationalists, were the so-called Free French.[33] Churchill had originally imagined that they might be sidelined as an unnecessary complication. 'Free French Forces', he wrote, 'should not be employed in Syria, but be moved to the Western Desert.' Such a suggestion was fantastical. The leader of the Free French in the Mediterranean, Georges Catroux, insinuated himself into every aspect of the Syrian project. He himself was another of the European orientalists who had played the intelligence game in the Levant since the 1920s. Catroux's slight frame may have disguised the heart of a voluptuary – it was said in Cairo that his luggage took up more space than a tank platoon – but he was a sinuous diplomatist. He had stoked up the pressure for the war by claiming that the *Abwehr* mission in Syria was, in fact, a division of German infantry. He raised expectations that the Syrian war would be a walk-over, as French troops flocked to his banner. The myth, sedulously propagated by Catroux, that Syria was ripe to fall, had driven Wavell to the brink of resignation. At root, however, Catroux was a realist. He did not, for one moment, believe his own claims about the love Syria bore his men. As a realist he understood that he must compromise with the British to their mutual advantage.

Such was not the view of his leader, Charles de Gaulle, who rushed to Cairo as soon as he realized that the invasion was imminent. De Gaulle lacked any Levantine guile. His experiences in London and West Africa had led him to different conclusions. He did not like the English, he did not trust the English. But he saw that they had invested a great deal in him as the symbol of an unsullied France. They were embarrassed that the sordid reality was so at odds with their own propaganda. Despite having no money, and precious few followers, de Gaulle realized that the psychology of the situation allowed him to bully his allies. It was a tactic that suited his *cassant* personality, just as compromise suited Catroux's. These very different approaches might have caused great bitterness between the two men, and there was indeed tension in private. But the very vulnerability of their position, allied to the temperamental willingness of Catroux, the more senior, to recognize de Gaulle's pre-eminence, bound them together. They were lucky to find in Lyttelton someone displaying the exact psychology that de Gaulle had identified as exploitable.

Almost as soon as he touched down, de Gaulle started making trouble. He tore up the propaganda plans claiming that the invasion was a peaceful Anglo-French occupation. The occupation was not Anglo-French, the British had no part in it. The legitimate government of France was merely confiscating territory from the usurper Dentz. Syria was an entirely French matter, the British were assisting under sufferance. Dentz would be removed and Catroux would become High Commissioner. The British would have no role in Syria. Even de Gaulle's most committed British advocate had to point out that this was taking things too far. Edward Spears, British army liaison specialist, Conservative MP, speaker of idiomatic French and, most importantly, friend of Churchill, had been with de Gaulle from the beginning. He had preceded his principal to Cairo in order to make sure that Free French interests were fully protected during the campaign. Invoking Churchill, he persuaded the Frenchmen that no British authority, civil, military or para-military, was willing to indulge the fantasy that Free France was doing the fighting whilst they provided minor logistical support. Catroux was instead given the ill-defined title of Delegate-General.

Compromise on the issue of titles did little to slow de Gaulle down. He next picked a fight with the British on the nature of any armistice to end the fighting. He did not want Dentz to be allowed to surrender, since the very act of negotiating would give the Vichyite recognition as a legitimate authority. Underlying the general principle was a particular issue. De Gaulle had been spectacularly unsuccessful in rallying Frenchmen to his cause – when given the choice, as they had been in Britain after Dunkirk, the vast majority chose to return to France. De Gaulle wanted to make sure that those in Syria did not have that choice. As soon as Damascus fell to Indian troops, he rushed there to claim the victory for France. To the British, who were actually fighting the war, such posturing seemed obscene. 'Everyone says: if only we had been without the Free French,' recorded Cunningham. He described de Gaulle as 'unbalanced', Auchinleck thought him 'mad and consumed with personal ambition'. Nevertheless, when Dentz appeared on the radio, admitting he could not fight on and asking for an Armistice, Auchinleck and Lyttelton agreed that it was only reasonable that the Gaullists should be given a chance to recruit as many troops as possible.[34]

In the event they had little say in the matter. 'Jumbo' Wilson had no intention of prolonging the war. He received Dentz's deputy, de Verdilhac, on the Mediterranean coast at Acre. Catroux, he said, could forget pretentious titles;

if he wanted to be present he could come as Wilson's staff officer, an offer that appealed to Catroux's supple logic. De Gaulle, always on the move to keep the plates of the delicate Free French enterprise spinning, had flown back to West Africa a few days before. The army telephone line connecting Acre with Cairo via Jerusalem barely worked. The Australians in Acre were partying so hard that they fused the lights in a three-mile radius. The deal was struck under the dim light of a dispatch rider's motorcycle. It was a straightforward deal between two regular armies to stop fighting. In the confusion, however, Wilson and de Verdilhac slipped in a secret protocol: the British would physically prevent the Gaullists from trying to recruit French troops – they would be allowed to sail home to France with full military honours.

When Lyttelton learned what Wilson had done he was 'incensed'. His irritation was as nothing to de Gaulle's white fury. Flying back to Cairo he stalked into Lyttelton's office, 'white with suppressed passion' and threatening to tell Free Frenchmen in Syria to regard the British as hostile invaders. 'There was nothing for it but what women call "a scene",' Lyttelton later recalled, 'and a scene we certainly had.' Such was de Gaulle's anger that Lyttelton instructed that he should not be allowed to use wireless or telegraph lest he issue orders to attack the British. For all the harsh words, however, both of them were bluffing. Despite British claims to the contrary, de Gaulle was no madman and perfectly capable of understanding that his forces were an isolated minority, ripe for massacre. Lyttelton had already ordered Spears to start unpicking the Acre agreement. After four days of negotiation Lyttelton and de Gaulle signed a new accord, mitigating the secret protocol and establishing the ground rules for Anglo-French cohabitation in Syria.[35]

In Cairo and London everyone slapped Lyttelton on the back for a difficult job well done. Few outside the higher echelons of command had any illusions that the deal was anything other than a sticking plaster. They had to live in the world of Catroux, the world of subtle subversion, rather than Gaullist posturing. The agreement stipulated that internal security was to be a matter for the French but that they were to cooperate with British officers attached to the *Sûreté Générale*. The first of these officers arrived in Beirut the day after the agreement was signed, to find that Catroux had already done deals that would reduce any British personnel to impotence. 'Unfriendly elements abound among the natives of the country and among Vichy Frenchmen, who have been retained because they were essential for administration or commerce,' he reported.

'The British security authorities cannot work directly, but only through the French administration, which does not favour the suggestion of British interference.' 'On the other side of a long frontier', he warned, 'is the nerve centre of German intelligence in the Middle East.' The *Sûreté Générale* maintained its close links with that network via the Swiss consulate, 'before and since the Allied occupation infested with pro-German personnel suspected of illicit correspondence, Axis propaganda and possible espionage'. When the British complained to Catroux that his security services were riddled with Nazi sympathizers, he temporized: some were sent to West Africa, many were allowed to remain in post. The group most targeted for dismissal were those who had shown any enthusiasm for working with the British.[36]

The accusations that the British made against the Free French were almost a mirror image of those made by the Free French. It was clear that the British were playing 'an anti-French game'. Like their Vichy counterparts at the time of Mers el-Kébir, the Gaullists complained that there was no 'fair play' – they used the English term in disdain. Indeed, Peter Fleming, brother of Ian, the creator of James Bond, and Bill Stirling, brother of David, the creator of the SAS, warned Lyttelton that the activities of Britain's secret services revealed a 'widespread delusion you can become a Lawrence of Arabia by sitting in offices and bars in Cairo and Jerusalem'. There were many secret organizations at work. As a result it was often the case that official protestations of innocence were not borne out in fact. Whereas SOE was trying to suborn tribal sheikhs to embrace new loyalties, SIME was keen to collaborate with the French on rolling up enemy agent networks.[37] The tactics of perfidious Albion were clear, junior officers were already travelling the countryside pretending that they could protect the villagers from the 'evil French'. Just as the French had 'divided and ruled' through their patronage of the martial minorities, so too now were the British trying to win those communities away from their allegiance. Lyttelton purged a number of senior spooks in the so-called 'August blood bath', but this did little to lessen inter-agency tension.

A fortnight after the Armistice, French troops moved into a position to attack a British post at Soueida, the chief town of the Druze. The situation was only defused by Lyttelton's order that the British should leave. 'Even the most Anglophile of us are seeing red,' wrote an officer whom the British themselves had identified as being on their side. The English were unbearable, hateful. It might be better to settle with them by violence.

Although Wilson's promise to keep Free French recruiters away from the troops had been overturned by Lyttelton, his officers stuck as close to the rule as they dared. Vichy officers did everything they could to stop their troops from going over. Pamphlets such as 'Why I am not a Gaullist' rolled off regimental presses. When enraged Gaullists showed this trash to their British counterparts, they shrugged and repeated the regulation – one Free French officer, closely supervised by a British minder, could speak to each unit with their own officers present. Only three in twenty men decided to stay. Although Lyttelton ordered that Dentz himself should be detained, his army was able to follow de Verdilhac to the sea. In a particularly crass piece of symbolism Lyttelton met de Gaulle in Beirut to the strains of an Australian military band playing the *Marseillaise* in de Verdilhac's honour. In high good spirits the Vichy commander kissed the pretty girls who had come to see him off, inspected the guard of honour provided by the British army, and boarded his ship for home.[38]

For all the allure of cloak-and-dagger intrigues, the most effective weapon in the eastern Mediterranean was much more mundane: food. The rural populations of the littoral had no say in the political manoeuvres or the military campaigns of the summer of 1941. That did not mean they were passive. Peasants and merchants began desperately to hoard food. The merchants knew that the Mediterranean was closed to the bulk containers which, until 1940, had shipped grain from the western to the eastern Mediterranean. The peasants could see that the 1941 harvest was one of the poorest on record. Hot winds in May were partly to blame. The war played its part as well; in the 1930s the eastern Mediterranean lands had benefited from German science which had provided mass-produced nitrate fertilizers for the first time. With the failure of supply, consumers scrambled for what there was. But there were now more, and more rapacious, consumers. Armies competed with civilians for food supplies and always won.

The problem of famine too arrived on the desk of the Minister of State. The British realized that they would have to buy food on world markets, bring it in to Egypt via the Suez Canal and then have some system for deciding who received it. They realized that they could never meet demand. The best they could do was live hand-to-mouth, ensuring neither that too many people starved to death, nor that the hoarders drove prices to such a level that social war would ensue. Yet another bureaucracy – the Middle East Supply Council – was brought into being to try and hold the line. Here too Lyttelton was faced with the jockeying of interests between colonial authorities, national governments, military commanders and private profiteers. As with SOE he had to purge the organization and bring in an outsider to run it. The centrality of this endeavour was indicated by Lyttelton's decision to pull the controller of supplies in besieged Malta off the island to run the MESC. Perversely, however, the more severe the food crisis, the more powerful the control of food made the British. And the crisis was at its severest in Syria and Lebanon. There, however well Catroux played the political game, he was hobbled by the reality that he could feed no one.[39]

The hot winds, the lack of fertilizer, the unproductive native agriculture, the dislocation of consuming armies and the uncertainties of war did not, of course, stop at the boundaries of the British-controlled Mediterranean. They had always planned to include Greece in the arrangements for Mediterranean relief; without the British, Greece starved. The Germans and Italians had few intentions of feeding the populace and the plans they did hatch were paralysed by their inability to agree on anything.[40] The 'food situation' was burdened, as even Ciano recognized, by 'too many heavy-eating and arrogant officers'.[41]

The 'food situation' had reverberations in the secret world as well. It set in train the fall of the 'old gang' of British Greek specialists who had escaped from the country in May 1941 and established themselves in Cairo. They believed that the Greek government housed in the city were, in the main, a bunch of crypto-Fascists. The old gang's goal was 'on M. Tsouderos' behalf, and without the knowledge of other members of the Greek government, to evacuate certain Greek politicians to broaden the Greek government with more liberal elements'.

In August 1941 representatives of the Greek political parties began to make their way to Turkey. Their main plea was that the British should allow food shipments to Greece, to be organized by overseas Greek communities and neutral countries. The British had little interest in allowing the food to flow in, knowing that it would be immediately diverted to feed German and Italian troops in the Balkans. On the other hand, the free passage of Greek food missions across the Aegean seemed to offer an opportunity to establish contact with the men the old gang wanted out.

Two factors complicated such plans. It soon became clear that the emissaries of the established parties had no interest in fighting the Germans. When they said they wanted food, they wanted food. As far as politics was concerned, they preferred that those who had fled overseas at the fall of Athens should return and make their peace with the Nazis. If the Greeks were a disappointment, then so too were the British. Sir Hughe Knatchbull-Hugessen, ambassador in Turkey, with London's authority energetically discouraged subversive operations across the Aegean. He argued that his job was to make sure that the Turco-German treaty would not blossom into a full-blooded alliance. He didn't want the Turks spooked by unlicensed agitators stirring up trouble in or for Turkey. In this he was supported by SIS and SIME, who did not want their good relations with the Turks disturbed either. The rival secret organizations 'took a close and not particularly friendly interest' in the old gang.

Seemingly thwarted in all directions the old gang were galvanized by the reappearance of an old friend, Gerasimos Alexatos, codenamed Odysseus. On 14 September 1941, Odysseus made landfall in Smyrna. Odysseus was a Macedonian tobacco-smuggler whom the old gang had recruited and trained at their special forces base on Crete. He had been lost during the evacuation. Returning to Athens he put his training to good use by contacting members of the pre-invasion organization to see whether they would be interested in forming an anti-German resistance. Possessing high-level evasion skills thanks to his former profession, Odysseus island-hopped over the Aegean to seek out his employers. His report merely confirmed what they had already concluded. There was not much taste for resistance to the Germans in Athenian political and military circles. The best that could be expected from the old elite was passive resistance; the worst, active cooperation with the Nazis. The reputation of the British, and those who had 'deserted' with them, was not high. The only group that Odysseus had found with any gumption was led by a former naval officer, Lieutenant-Commander Koutsoyannopoulos, 'a quiet type of man, energetic, silent and conscientious in his job', codenamed Prometheus II. Odysseus agreed to go back into Athens with a radio operator so that Prometheus II could tell them how to get supplies to his resistance group. The old gang had started off with the intention of supporting Tsouderos in liberalizing the royal government. Their primary aim was still to find politicians they could evacuate for this purpose. Some of the group had, however, come to the conclusion that this was not enough, that the attempt to 'reinstate an unpopular and unsuitable monarch and the rump of a totalitarian government is surely criminal'. As word leaked out what they were up to, the 'cunning' Tsouderos disowned them, demanding that the British authorities in Egypt should 'bell the cat'.[42]

These attempts and difficulties were not confined to the Cairo–Jerusalem–Istanbul–Athens quadrilateral. Days after Odysseus landed in Smyrna with news of a potential Greek resistance, Captain Hudson of SOE debarked from a submarine on the coast of Montenegro to look for Yugoslav resisters. He had some hope of finding Serbian army officers implicated in the Belgrade coup who might be willing to fight the Germans. Instead he ran into a small band of Montenegrin guerrillas. The guerrillas turned out to be Communists, and he was taken to their leader, who went by the nickname of Tito.[43] Tito showed little interest in his British guest – he wanted the Russians. On the run from the Germans, and finding himself in the lands of hostile Serb royalists, he had other things to worry about. Tito kicked Hudson on to meet Draza Mihailovich, the officer he had originally set out to find. Hudson realized that Tito's Partisans and Mihailovic's Chetniks were preparing to fight each other rather than the Germans. He was, however, in an awkward position. He had left his radios with Tito. Hudson was thus at the mercy of Mihailovic for a means of contacting the outside world. He was not able to radio Malta until November 1941, by which time his bosses back in Cairo had already decided that Mihailovic was exactly the sort of patriot to whom arms should be dropped. Then, a virtual prisoner, he was heard no more for the next seven months.

The Mediterranean in the high summer of 1941 presented an odd spectacle. British leaders in the sea were scrambling to stabilize Britain's fallen reputation and restore ruptured contacts, albeit with indeterminate success. Yet to outsiders nothing much appeared to be happening. Lyttelton became well known to the Cairo press corps for giving briefings of stultifying dullness. Of course, he had plenty of interesting things to say but he could hardly confide what he knew.[44] One British cabinet minister, a Cairene by birth, wrote that he was 'puzzled about the Middle East'. He had 'lots of friends out there', including Lyttelton, 'but he cannot make out what they are doing or going to do'. Were they, 'just sitting there waiting to be attacked?'[45] Most of the visible action was occurring at sea, rather than on land.

At first sight the fall of Greece heavily favoured the Axis. They now had the advantage of two major north–south routes across the Mediterranean. The more direct, but more dangerous, western route saw ships depart from Naples before taking formation under the lee of the north coast of Sicily, near Palermo. They would then dash across the central Mediterranean by the shortest route to Cape Bon. From there the ships would sail along the Libyan coast to unload at either Tripoli or Benghazi. Not only did Cape Bon offer a short route to North Africa, it took advantage of the usual British policy of respecting the sanctity of French territorial waters. British warships operated highly complex rules as to where they might sink the enemy. Ships on the eastern, or Ionian, route set out from Naples, from where they sailed along the northern coast of Sicily and through the Straits of Messina, the narrow seaway that separated Sicily from the toe of Italy. They were joined by ships already in the east, sailing from Taranto or Brindisi. They would continue east to Corfu and then turn for North Africa, docking at either Benghazi or Derna. Smaller ships sailed through the 'middle' of Greece, via the Corinth canal, then to Crete. The trip from Cape Krios to Derna was, at 180 miles, the shortest north–south crossing in the eastern Mediterranean. Churchill's summing up of Cunningham's situation was bleak: 'the Admiral has abandoned all hopes of blocking Tripoli and perhaps Benghazi also . . . Every single one of our plans has failed. The enemy has completely established himself in the Central Mediterranean. We are afraid of his dive bombers at every point. Our ships cannot enforce any blockade between Italy and Cyrenaica or Greece and Cyrenaica.'[46]

Conversely, British options for travel around the Mediterranean were severely limited. The only route they had left was the dangerous western Mediterranean run from Gibraltar to Malta. They could proceed no further than Malta, and no ships could reach Malta from the east. The best that Cunningham could do was to use his submarines to carry in fuel for Malta's aircraft, a contribution that he described as a 'flea bite'.[47] The balance was only redressed by some outstanding signals intelligence breakthroughs that came to fruition in summer of 1941. Towards the end of June 1941 the British codebreakers cracked the encoding machine used by the Italian navy. They were thus able to extract detailed information used about Mediterranean convoys. In September 1941 this breakthrough was supplemented by a partial success against the codes used by supply units in North Africa to communicate with their rear headquarters in Rome and Salonika. The code was also used for three-way conversations about supplies between North Africa, Rome and Berlin. The range and importance of this information was such that from August 1941, so-called special communications and liaison units began to be deployed in the Mediterranean. These units ran secure high-speed links between Bletchley Park and the very senior field commanders, greatly increasing the volume, quality and timeliness of the information they received. In the Mediterranean itself CBME had its successes, too, with lower-grade signals.[48]

The particularly rich intelligence banquet that lasted for the rest of 1941 gave the British a definite edge. The offensive potential of submarines, pre-warned of Mediterranean sailings, was massively enhanced. Hitherto, the Mediterranean had been regarded as a death-trap for submarines, forced to linger around ports on the off chance of a sailing and often picked off by the sophisticated Italian defences whilst doing so. 'Every submarine is worth its weight in gold,' Cunningham declared. Pound promised to send him every boat he could lay his hands on, and the number of British submarines operating in the Mediterranean doubled.

It is often argued, too, that the *Luftwaffe* and the *Regia Aeronautica* played into British hands. In mid-1941 the two air forces struck a deal whereby the Germans would continue to concentrate their forces in the eastern Mediterranean, operating from Crete and Greece, against the Suez Canal. The Italians were to operate from their Sicilian and Sardinian bases against British forces approaching Malta from the western Mediterranean. Some, although by no means all, *Luftwaffe* and *Kriegsmarine* officers were unhappy with the deal, and argued in vain that the Italians should concentrate their naval and air forces in the eastern Mediterranean whilst the Germans moved back to Sicily.[49] True, the *Luftwaffe* had enjoyed its most stunning Mediterranean success in the battle for Crete. But the proximity of German and Italian airfields to the island had given their aircraft a unique advantage in the battle. Aircraft operating from Sicily and Sardinia similarly had to cover rela-tively short distances in order to find naval targets. The German flyers, it was later claimed, had got a raw deal because only long-range aircraft could reach Egypt from Greece: they were never able to mount an attack of sufficient weight to choke off the Red Sea supply route. If they had gone to Sicily, they would have been able to stop convoy and warship movements between Gibraltar and Malta.

These arguments were based upon the assumption that the *Luftwaffe* was bound to be more effective than the *Regia Aeronautica*. This is not what the British, on the receiving end, believed. Cunningham argued that both the German *and* the Italian performances in the air were better than that of the RAF. In the west Somerville noticed that the Italians were much more skilled than they had been before the German spell in Sicily. The reconnaissance aircraft that it had once been possible to shoot down or chase off with relative ease, tenaciously shadowed his ships. Somerville was hit by a 'well synchronised torpedo-bomber and high-level bombing attack' whenever he ventured within range. The aircraft were fast and modern and the crews were 'a really gallant lot'.[50] The aircraft came in repeated waves. Supposedly obsolescent Italian biplane fighters out-performed the carrier-based British monoplanes. Finally a British battleship, *Nelson*, was torpedoed, leaving 'a bloody great hole' in its hull. Luckily the main damage was to the cold store, resulting in 'nineteen tons of rotting beef', but no sinking.[51] In the narrow seaways around Crete, dive-bombing had proved a particularly effective tactic. In the more open seas to the south of Sardinia, torpedoes were the most effective form of attack. As the British discovered from signals intelligence, it was unlikely that the Germans would have been any better at the all-important torpedo-bomber attacks than the Italians. The Italians had been slow off the mark with torpedo-bombers but the Germans had been even slower. They only began to improvise training for torpedo attacks in the autumn of 1941. A Mediterranean training centre at Grosseto was not established until 1942.[52] Neither was a German air-dropped torpedo, that could be used against moving ships, produced in large numbers until 1942. In the interim the German units had to borrow such torpedoes from the Italians.[53]

Neither, when the British were attacking and the Italians defending, was it immediately clear that the intelligence advantage was leading to overwhelming success. In their first few months back in control of the Libyan convoy route, the Italians held down the number of sinkings the British were able to achieve. 'What action will C-in-C Mediterranean take,' demanded Churchill, 'surely he cannot put up with this kind of thing?' Cunningham, Churchill wrote in disgust, should feel 'sorry' for his 'melancholy failure'.[54] The great British successes against the Libyan route had to wait until the autumn of 1941. In the summer of 1941 both British and Italians had had the same idea: the best ships to transport troops were big ocean-going liners. The problem was that such ships were vulnerable. The Cunard White Star liner *Georgic* was bombed and burnt out off Suez. Indeed the 'considerable stupidity' of the handling

ABOVE: Ingress: Gibraltar as seen from a *Luftwaffe* aircraft, August 1942.

BELOW: Egress: An Italian troopship sails through the Suez Canal on its way to Abyssinia, 1935.

The Sword of Islam: Mussolini drives along the Balbia greeted by his Muslim subjects, propaganda poster, March 1937.

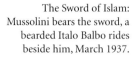

The Sword of Islam: Mussolini bears the sword, a bearded Italo Balbo rides beside him, March 1937.

The Spider: The Grand Mufti in Repose, October 1938.

ABOVE: The Brutal Friendship: Hitler, Mussolini and Ciano meet at the Brenner Pass, October 1940.

BELOW: The Dream and the Nightmare: Mussolini's dilemma as seen by David Low in the *Evening Standard*, 11 June 1940.

MUSSOLINI
THE EMPEROR OF
THE MEDITERRANEAN

MUSSOLINI
THE GHASTLY FLOP

WAIT!

ORDERS from BERLIN

ROOSEVELT

THE DREAM AND THE NIGHTMARE   (Copyright in All Countries.)

LOW

Gog: Andrew Cunningham saluting as morning colours are hoisted on board HMS *Queen Elizabeth* in Alexandria Harbour.

Mediterranean hero: Malta's great submarine ace Wanklyn, VC of the *Upholder* (bearded) with his first lieutenant, Drummond, May 1941.

Magog: Somerville addresses the crew of HMS *Sheffield* at Gibraltar.

The sinking of the Italian cruiser *Bartolemeo Colleoni* at the battle of Cape Spada, 20 July 1940.

A distant view of the Italian fleet as seen from HMS *Sheffield* during the battle of Cape Spartivento, 27 November 1940. The Italian ships are making smoke, visible at the junction of sea and sky.

Running the Narrows: An Italian SM.79 torpedo bomber attacks a British convoy, August 1942.

Lovely Derna: British troops stop to look at a portrait of Mussolini, February 1941.

The Coast Road: Stuart tanks drive along Benghazi waterfront, November 1942.

The Balbia: British troops pass through Balbo's Triumphal Arch, December 1942.

Two Mediterraneanists: Churchill and Darlan, November 1939.

BELOW: New Enemies: French sailors escape the British bombardment of Mers-el-Kébir, 3 July 1940.

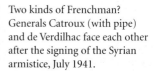

Two kinds of Frenchman? Generals Catroux (with pipe) and de Verdilhac face each other after the signing of the Syrian armistice, July 1941.

Eden in Cairo: Wavell (centre), Eden (covering his face) and Dill worry about the future, British Embassy, Cairo, March 1941.

Holding the East in Fee: Oliver Lyttelton presides over the MEWC – on the military side sit Commodore Norman (representing Cunningham), Tedder and Auchinleck; opposite them are the civilians, Arthur Rucker, Miles Lampson and Harold MacMichael, Cairo, February 1942.

The Face of Defeat: Sir William Dobbie after being relieved of the Governorship of Malta, May 1942.

of ships in the Gulf of Suez, the waterway that led up to the southern entrance of the Suez Canal, finally persuaded Cunningham to incorporate the Red Sea into the Mediterranean.[55]

It took some time for the British to recognize that the Italians were using liners as well. When they did, however, an ambush was laid for the ships off Tripoli. The sinking of the liners *Neptunia* and *Oceania* by the Malta-based submarine *Upholder* pushed Italian shipping losses for September 1941 off the chart.[56] It was the loss of the liners that made the Italians fear for 'the fate of Libya'. It also convinced Hitler that the Germans had to move into the Mediterranean in force to defend the north–south route. 'The fate of your and my troops fighting in Africa,' he wrote to Mussolini, 'and the continuation of the war against the British in Libya and the eastern Mediterranean depend on the supplies to Africa.' 'He is obviously concerned about us,' lamented Ciano, 'he fears English landings in Corsica, Sicily and Sardinia, and offers, beginning today, all his support like someone who does know what a successful blow by the English may do to us. Fundamentally the Germans don't trust us and in my opinion this letter is the proof.'[57]

Later commentators saw these decisions as yet more proof of Hitler's fatuity as a strategist; he was dispersing his efforts, guaranteeing failure everywhere. *Luftwaffe* units were transferred back from Russia to the Mediterranean. The *Kriegsmarine* was ordered to send the U-boats into the Mediterranean. In a reversal of roles, Admiral Raeder, formerly the most outspoken German Mediterraneanist, found himself trying to argue the Führer out of taking the Mediterranean too seriously. 'It is not possible to send U-boats into the Mediterranean,' he pleaded, 'as this would handicap operations in the Atlantic.' 'The clear water and the necessity of remaining submerged for prolonged periods make the situation in the Mediterranean unfavourable for submarine warfare,' he said. As a result, 'for operations in the Mediterranean only small boats manned by experienced crews can be considered, in view of the conditions under which they would have to operate'. If they were to fight in the Mediterranean he would have to dispatch the best and the brightest of the U-boat force in substantial wolfpacks. The journey was long, the passage of the Straits of Gibraltar was difficult: it was not worth the risk. As ever, Hitler ignored him. Raeder was ordered to get on with creating a Mediterranean flotilla, possibly to outnumber that in the Atlantic.[58]

Whatever the strategic demerits of Hitler's decision, he proved quite astute at reading Churchill. The operational reason that Raeder gave for keeping his U-boats out of the Mediterranean was that the 'British submarines and aircraft are the forces used in the Mediterranean to attack transports, and these cannot be combated by U-boats'.[59] Yet Churchill had finally managed to insist that surface ships should operate in the central Mediterranean, despite Cunningham's refusal to have anything to do with the business. If the army suffered any defeats in North Africa, Churchill assured naval leaders, with barely concealed menace, the Royal Navy would become the everlasting scapegoat for failure, 'because we had not made any attempt to cut communications to Africa'. Surface warships were exactly the kind of target that U-boats would be looking for.[60] They were offered up, knowingly, as a blood sacrifice for glittering short-term success.[61] Ciano's diary told the story. After the liner sinking the *Regia Marina* had stopped 'trying to get convoys through to Libya'. 'Tonight,' he wrote in despair, 'we tried again.' 'Seven ships left, accompanied by two 10,000 ton cruisers and 10 destroyers, because we knew at Malta the British had two warships ready to act as wolves amongst the sheep.' 'An engagement occurred,' the results of which, to Ciano, were 'inexplicable'. 'All, I mean *all*, our ships were sunk, and one or maybe two or three of our destroyers. The British returned to their ports after having slaughtered us.' The Malta force had, in fact, executed a textbook cruiser, destroyer and submarine attack with spectacular results. Few doubted the importance of this humiliating defeat. The Germans accused the Italians of an 'inexcusable blunder'. They insisted that a German commander must now be installed in the central Mediterranean to take over the conduct of the war. A deflated Mussolini could only agree. 'Clowns, tragic clowns,' Ciano said of the air force and navy, 'who have brought our country to the current condition of accepting, in fact, of requesting outside protection to be protected and defended!'[62]

A few days later Hitler appeared to have been further vindicated in ordering forces to the Mediterranean. The first wolfpack had run through the Straits of Gibraltar in September 1941. This second wolfpack proved very lucky. As it emerged from the Straits it ran into Somerville's Force H.[63] On 13 November on a return run from Malta, only thirty miles out from Gibraltar, Force H's aircraft-carrier *Ark Royal* was torpedoed by a U-boat. The shock was immense. The British knew that the U-boats were there but none of the *Ark*'s escorts detected the submarine, no one even saw the track of the torpedo. The hit was so heavy that aircraft parked on the *Ark*'s flight deck visibly jumped into the air. At first it seemed the carrier would brush off the impact. Then a fire in the boiler room disabled the pumps. Bulkheads started to explode under the pressure of the inrushing water. The crippled ship took on a 'terrible list'. The crew struggled long into the night to save her but watchers on the helping ships realized that she was doomed. At the end she was just a 'blur in the dark' lying on her side. 'Then slowly, slowly she turned over like a tired and wounded ship going to sleep.' 'It was', Somerville said, one of 'the blackest of days when I saw my poor *Ark* sink'.[64]

SEVEN

Italy Victorious

In the winter of 1941 and the spring of 1942 the British spent much of their time arguing about propaganda. They argued over who should make the propaganda. They argued about what the propaganda should say. The only thing that they could agree on was that their propaganda was not much good. After the bloodbath of August 1941, Oliver Lyttelton had insisted that London should send him a director of propaganda. The candidate offered was the Duke of Windsor's former lawyer, Walter Monckton, a man of such noted emollience that he was nicknamed 'the oil can'. Monckton spent some months trying to understand what was going on in Cairo. His findings were not encouraging. Britain had many outlets for propaganda, covert and overt: SOE, the BBC, the Ministry of Information. Each guarded their patch rather too zealously. It emerged, for instance, that far from being an organization committed to derring-do and dirty fighting, SOE employed more than half its staff in the Mediterranean as propagandists.[1] The newly created body that was supposed to coordinate propaganda, the Political Warfare Executive, had no real presence.[2] Its attempt to take control of propaganda in North Africa via a radio service broadcasting from Gibraltar ended in embarrassment when the transmitter failed to function.[3]

In any case few of Britain's propagandists had a clear idea of the message they should be putting across. As far as politics was concerned, they were 'restricted to the negative task of explaining the horrors which are in store for those who do not resist the Nazis'. Sadly there appeared to be little audience response to this message. The British repeated it on their radio stations, in their leaflets and through their rumour mills. But they could point to 'nothing in [the] way of an alternative future'. When faced with any political equation more complex than 'the Nazis are evil', the propagandists floundered. When Vichy, for instance, replaced their overlord in North Africa, Maxime Weygand, no one knew whether this was a good or a bad thing. In very few places was it possible to find unalloyed hatred of the Nazis; the Mediterranean peoples were too caught up in their own parochial concerns to be anything other than ambivalent. With regard to military affairs, too, the propagandists had the knack of mistiming things, optimistic when there was a need for quiet caution, querulous when it was appropriate to set a firm course.[4]

The trouble with bad propaganda was that it was hard to keep secret. The week Monckton finished his top-secret report, war correspondents in Cairo openly expressed their disdain for the efforts of 'the amateurs controlling propaganda . . . unskilled men who were and are bewildered by events'. Before the battle for the Libyan littoral had begun, they had boasted of Britain's might, its tanks and its guns, 'so any future victory of ours had been discounted in advance'. Then they had continued to proclaim, for too long, that Rommel was on the brink of defeat, without tangible proof. 'People all over the world were beginning to suspect' that something was amiss.[5]

The British propaganda apparatus in the Mediterranean was in poor repair. Its fundamental problem, however, was not amateurism, lack of communication or personal rivalry. The propagandists did not have a good tale to tell. The British Mediterranean was collapsing in front of them, sometimes too quickly for their broadcasts and presses to keep pace. The growing tendency to fetishize small pockets of resistance, in particular Malta and Tobruk, told its own story. The Mediterranean had been disarticulated. British propaganda was poor because Britain's writ ran only where its armies continued to hold territory. Its navy was being reduced to a husk.

The unachieved victory, discounted before it was won, went down in British lore as Operation *Crusader*. The Axis called it the Battle of Marmarica, the eastern region of Cyrenaica. The Axis definition had the benefit of clarity. Once again the British plan called for imperial forces to move along coast and desert as far to the west as possible. Although these battles are remembered as part of the desert war, there was little in the desert valued by anyone except a few explorers. All the prizes lay on the Mediterranean coast: Derna, Benghazi and, hoping against hope, Tripoli. Just as the battle for Cyrenaica was known as *Crusader*, a future Tripolitanian adventure was *Acrobat*. Summing up the true state of private British incertitude, Churchill remarked, 'we may not win *Crusader*; we may not decide to embark on *Acrobat*; we may fail in *Acrobat*'.[6] An imperial army just shy of 120,000 men fought an Italo-German army of much the same size. When two such evenly matched forces met it was impossible to predict the outcome.

The public confusion surrounding the nature of the Marmarican battle was not simply the product of poor propaganda. The British had done all they could to deceive their enemies, suggesting that they might attack much earlier; that this was a probe, not the big push, that they would wait until the spring of 1942. In one sense they had a great success. Rommel was indeed caught by surprise. But they deceived so much that they confused themselves. Imperial forces were strung out on a wide front, from the coast near Sollum deep into the desert reaching as far south as the Oasis of Jarabub, the holy city of the Senussi.[7] Those who observed the battle had to work hard to make sense of what was happening. The American military attaché in Cairo, Bonner Fellers, was a determined fellow, with excellent contacts amongst the British.[8] As soon as the offensive was announced he made his way into the desert, towards a previously unnoticed speck on the map, Sidi Rezegh. Once there he ran into a pack of British war correspondents. They 'called across to him, "What's happening?" He just had time to answer, "Damned if I know".'[9]

Sidi Rezegh became the pivotal point of the battle, symbolically as much as militarily. 'One desert airfield was apt to look very much like another,' wrote a squadron sergeant-major in the 4th Armoured Brigade with disfavour.

> Someone would select a likely place, iron out any bumps, erect a windsock and a few tents and with the arrival of fuel tankers and a couple of wire-less lorries, he was in business. . . . Sidi Rezegh was no real exception. It only seemed worse because of our obsession with it that winter. It was probably chosen because it was near the Trigh el Abd, the broad beaten track which ran from the frontier and passed south of Tobruk. About five miles from it was a white marabout, or tomb . . . Only a hermit would have wanted to live on that plateau which must have been a forbidding place at any time . . . the ferocious battle raging for its possession had turned it into a giant ashtray full of glowing embers and smouldering stubs.[10]

Although each of the belligerent capitals had excellent sources of intelligence, understanding tended to cease at the borders of Cyrenaica. Commanders even had trouble communicating with one another. Rommel, fighting with his mobile forces in the desert, was out of contact for long periods with the coast. He reported what he saw in front of him, victory, not always with good cause.

The mobile spearhead of the British attack was its three armoured brigades, the 4th, 7th and 22nd. On 19 November 1941 the initial British advances had mixed success. The 7th Armoured Brigade seized Sidi Rezegh. The 22nd Armoured Brigade on the other hand attacked the well-dug-in Italian *Ariete* armoured division at Bir Gubi and were beaten off with high tank casualties. The Germans were initially unsure what to make of this assault of their allies. Rommel persisted in belief that the British were merely testing the defences. The commander of the *Afrika Korps*, Ludwig Crüwell, on the other hand, correctly concluded that they were facing the main offensive. He dispatched elements of the 21st Panzer Division forward to find out what was happening. They encountered and mauled the 4th Armoured Brigade. Crüwell thereupon set both of his tank divisions, the 21st and the 15th, in motion to the east.

On 20 November the unlucky 4th Armoured Brigade was hit again, this time by the 15th Panzer Division. 'There was nothing very clever about the enemy tactics', wrote a tank commander in the brigade, 'which were simply common sense. They had recently introduced a 50-mm high-velocity towed anti-tank gun . . . it was mounted on a low carriage and easily concealed. The German tanks engaged the British at extreme range. They would then fall back, drawing the British tanks onto their anti-tank guns. The Paks having laid about . . . would withdraw in their turn covered by a few 88s . . . while the tanks took up their new positions. When the 88s went back the whole began all over again.'[11] The British armoured brigades spent the rest of the battle trying to evolve counter-measures with only limited success.

The effectiveness of the German armoured divisions in mobile operations, and of Italian armour in defensive positions, were far from being the only operational problems for the British. On 21 November, the garrison of Tobruk sallied out to take the Axis in the rear. As a result the battlefield had no clear front line. In the 'twenty miles or so of country from the front of Tobruk sorties to the open desert south-east of Sidi Rezegh the forces of both sides were sandwiched like layers of a Neapolitan ice'.[12] One Italo-German force was facing north to meet the attack from

Tobruk. Other Axis troops were facing south towards Sidi Rezegh. The British at Sidi Rezegh were themselves facing south to oppose the 15th and 21st Panzer Divisions who were driving north, followed in turn by the British 4th and 22nd Armoured Brigades. It was the 21st Panzer Division that struck the crucial blow at Sidi Rezegh on 22 November. Their attack on the airfield was so fierce that the British commanders decided that they would have to withdraw eastwards, away from Tobruk and towards their own starting positions. In doing so the 4th Armoured Brigade was once again hit by the 15th Panzer Division, the brigade HQ was captured and the formation dispersed, ceasing to operate as a coherent body.

The rampaging 15th Panzer Division kept up the pressure. On 23 November Crüwell ordered the panzers to head east and relieve the *Ariete*, which had remained dug in since its defensive victory on the 19th. In doing so the German tanks ran over a South African brigade in their way. Although the South African infantry put up a brave resistance they were crushed in the open, losing nearly four thousand men and ceasing to exist as a fighting force. The battle of *Totensonntag* – Remembrance Day – sparked something close to panic in the British high command. Auchinleck was forced to fly in from Cairo to try to steady nerves. After five days of fighting Rommel reported home that, 'the battle seems to have passed its crisis – two hundred enemy tanks shot up so far. Our fronts have held.'[13] Then he disappeared from view.

Up to that point the battle had been fought with great success by Crüwell. But Rommel was determined that he should take over in person. When the two German generals met, they disagreed about what to do next. Crüwell wanted to pursue the imperial troops he had just defeated, east. He believed that he could rout them. Rommel said no. He was going to lead the *Afrika Korps* south, away from the immediate battle. Only then would he turn east along the Trigh al Abd and head for the Libyan-Egyptian frontier. His first goal was to relieve all those units near the frontier, isolated when the initial British attack bypassed them. Then he would sweep round behind the British, force the Hellfire Pass and take Sollum. The British force in Libya would be cut off from Egypt. Rommel would create the 'cauldron battle' that would destroy all British mobile forces, creating a great strategic victory. Crüwell objected that this was a bad operational plan. They risked splitting up and confusing their own forces. The likely result was defeat in detail, rather than a great victory.

Rommel had no patience with these arguments. At 10.00 on 24 November he personally led the 21st Panzer Division south. They reached the frontier as planned at 16.00 on the same day. But as Rommel disappeared over the horizon with the two victorious German tank divisions, those Axis forces left behind fared less well. The infantry of the New Zealand division launched a series of attacks to recover Sidi Rezegh. Crüwell was constantly looking over his shoulder, urging that they needed to get back to the real battle around Sidi Rezegh and Tobruk. Rommel still demanded that they push on to Sollum; 'Rommel's advance to the Sollum front', remarked the chief of staff of the 15th Panzer Division, was 'an evil dream'. Nevertheless, by the evening of 26 November Rommel acknowledged that he needed to get the tanks back to the fight around Tobruk. He headed west with the comment that, 'I've just spent four days in a desert counter-attack with nothing to wash with.' Despite the hygiene problems he was satisfied that, 'we had a splendid success, the battle will be of decisive importance to the whole war situation'.[14]

The optimism and timing of Rommel's claims were important. On the day after he returned from the desert, unwashed but triumphant, a grand Fascist jamboree convened in Berlin. Perceived victory suffused the week-long proceeding. Ciano observed that he had left Rome in some gloom, gripped by confused reports of battles in which the Italians were heavily engaged. He arrived in Berlin to find a mood of gaiety. The Germans could not have been more complimentary about the blood sacrifice of the hard-fighting Italian forces. The Battle of *Totensonntag* had seen Italian tanks fighting alongside German armour with similar elan. '"Fire! Fire!" Side by side, the two columns penetrate the enemy lines and steamroller inexorably through them,' wrote an officer of the *Ariete* armoured division. 'Grenades eat up the ground furiously, armour piercing shells throw up plumes of smoke, outgoing and incoming fire mingle into one great pounding. Our tanks advance irresistibly, firing with their usual precision. In front of them and on their left flank the enemy tanks vainly improvise an attack. Some of them are immediately set on fire, and others are forced to flee. . . . There is not a moment of indecision in their irresistible advance and when the first shadows of evening fall on the plain, the battle reaches its conclusion. The first white rockets go up from the Italian and German side. They say: "Cease Fire!"'[15] 'The battle of Marmarica has raised us in the esteem of the Germans,' Ciano reported back to Mussolini, 'for the first time they speak of Italian bravery and our military contribution.' The Germans were formidably optimistic, 'if we win this battle, the English position may become very insecure, perhaps untenable'.[16]

These cheerful prognostications were in contrast to the gloom caused by the ravages of Force K a few weeks before. In anger, Ciano had said that the 'clowns' who led the Italian armed forces deserved to be subordinated to a German. That German, 'Smiling Albert' Kesselring, arrived at the very moment Ciano was in Berlin enjoying the plaudits of Marmarica. Kesselring brought with him his HQ from the Russian front, *Luftflotte* II, as precursor to the doubling of German air strength in the Mediterranean, *Fliegerkorps* II being added to *Fliegerkorps* X.[17] Kesselring himself bore an exceptionally grand title, *Oberbefehlshaber Süd*, commander-in-chief of the South. When it had come to the crunch of handing over Italian forces to the Germans, however, Mussolini had cavilled. Kesselring's power had been whittled down until he commanded only the German air force in the Mediterranean.

Some, in particular Rommel, dismissed Kesselring as little more than an overrated shipping coordinator. Kesselring, however, possessed a number of important qualities, which meant his authority outran his power. He was one of Germany's most successful air marshals, enjoyed the favour of Hitler and Göring, commanded a formidable air fleet and got his way with ruthless charm. He was also the first German commander in the Mediterranean who thought much about the Mediterranean. Waiving impossible 'claims to overall command', Kesselring opted for 'confidential co-operation' with the chief of the *Comando Supremo* in Rome, Ugo Cavallero. His declared aim was to overcome 'the salient feature of the military operations, the inadequacy of the communications system across the Mediterranean'. To do this Kesselring was willing to subordinate everything to the protection of the north–south convoys, even if this meant his aircraft and crews flying unpalatable missions.[18]

Rather more profound forces were at work in the Mediterranean than a new commander, albeit one pursuing ambitious reforms. The moment of Rommel's success and Kesselring's arrival brought into play other interested parties keen to pick over the bones of Britain's defeat in the Mediterranean. On 28 November 1941, as part of his Berlin festivities, Hitler received the Grand Mufti, finally arrived safely in Germany after his Near Eastern odyssey. Their one-and-a-half-hour meeting was in many ways a true meeting of minds. *Der Grossmufti* was a man whose hatred of Jews matched even that of Hitler. That underlying, visceral bond underpinned all their transactions. Second only to the Jews, the *Grossmufti* loathed his English oppressors. He painted for Hitler an ambitious picture of a Great Arab State stretching from the shores of the Mediterranean to the Persian Gulf. Palestine, Syria, Lebanon, Jordan and Iraq would be united under German tutelage. The Arabs would owe their freedom to the Germans and would be aligned with the Nazis in all things. Hitler admitted that this was a most attractive vision, there was no doubt that the *Grossmufti* deserved to be in due course, the Führer of the Arabs. Regrettably, he warned his Arab guest, he had competition: there were others equally hostile to Judaism or England in the Mediterranean whom Hitler must satisfy. The *Grossmufti*'s vision of a Nazified Arab state worried his Italian friends. Although it was true that the Mufti had said nothing against the interests of his erstwhile patrons, they feared that ideas of a 'total' Arab federation might spread along the shores of the Mediterranean, threatening control of their own colonies and blocking their expansion into new areas. The Führer's advisers assured him, too, that the Mufti would create problems for his former protectors in Beirut. The English and the Gaullists had had little success in winning the hearts and minds of Vichyites in the Lebanon, but if they were told that the Germans were backing an Arab state they would be forced into the arms of their enemies. Regretfully, therefore, Hitler had to refuse the Mufti's request for the immediate and public proclamation of a Nazi-Arab alliance.[19]

The golden moment did not last. A couple of days after the Berlin festivities broke up, the British – having replaced their failing field commander – renewed their pressure in Marmarica. They were able to bring up significant reinforcements, not least elements of the 1st Armoured Division, sent from the UK, which had started disembarking at Port Suez in the second half of November 1941. Auchinleck also stripped other parts of the Mediterranean, such as Cyprus, to replace casualties. On 1 December orders were issued to restart *Crusader*. Once again the British would attack at Bir Gubi. 'The Libyan situation has crystallised somewhat,' Cavallero reported. It was 'difficult but logical'. 'God only knows what he means,' lamented Ciano, 'experience teaches me that when generals hide behind unintelligible jargon they have a guilty conscience.'[20] In this case it meant that Crüwell had fallen out with his Italian opposite number and was accusing him of failing to support the *Afrika Korps*'s defence of Bir Gubi.

Italian-German relations had soon moved away from mutual admiration to mutual recriminations. On 5 December Rommel ordered a westwards retreat. 'I've had to break off the action outside Tobruk on account of the Italian formations,' he complained. 'I'm hoping we'll succeed in escaping enemy encirclement and hold onto Cyrenaica.' In fact he left mainly Italian garrisons at Bardia and Sollum stranded, though still fighting 'magnificently'. As the German and the Italian mobile forces pulled back, the road to Tobruk opened.[21] The siege was lifted by imperial forces on 10 December. 'It was a memorable event driving into Tobruk,' wrote one observer. 'Coming from the east, you do not see the town until you are right upon it. Then as you wind down, the scarred white village breaks suddenly into view.' There was remarkably little triumph at the relief of the town of which Churchill had 'blathered' for so long. All anyone could see was a wasteland of 'utter dreariness and monotony as if the earth itself was tired'.[22]

Rommel was still not far away. He had withdrawn twenty-five miles to Gazala on the Gulf of Bomba. There the cliffs 'came so close to the seashore that the road had barely room to squeeze past'. From the top of those cliffs there was a 'superb view along the sweep of coast back to Tobruk'. The new Axis headquarters was the scene of a massive row between Rommel and his titular Italian superior, Bastico. Bastico suggested that the time had come to create a fall-back position far to the west at Agedabia where the *Balbia* kinked inland. Rommel grew angry at the very suggestion. If Bastico had no faith in his ability to turn the tide of battle in Marmarica, then he would quit Cyrenaica altogether. He would take all his Germans and motor back all the way to Tripoli, abandoning the Italian ingrates to their fate. Bastico had little choice but to back down to the incensed German.[23] But his judgement was superior to Rommel's. A few days later the Desert Fox himself decided that 'we're pulling out', 'I hope we get back to the line – Agedabia – we've chosen.'[24] Just as Kesselring was pulling the Italians and Germans together on the northern shore, Rommel was driving them apart on the southern. When the two shores came together it was not a happy meeting. Kesselring and Cavallero flew over the Mediterranean to confront Rommel; he told them that they were 'too late to alter my decision' to flee. He was going to Agedabia whatever they thought, 'the orders had already been issued and were in some cases being executed'.

It was sometimes said that war in the desert was like war at sea, as at sea there was surface, space and no people, except those who chose to fight. Anybody who read correspondents' reports of the fighting with any care knew this to be untrue. Coastal Cyrenaica was not a desert: the irrigated coastal towns and the terraces of the Green Mountain were fertile if delicate ecosystems.[25] It was through those ecosystems that the benighted Italian infantry fled, marking as they did the death of the 'fourth shore'. Behind them they left desolation and social conflict. British troops scrambled down the thousand-foot cliffs into 'lovely' Derna. They found that the indigenous population had fallen upon all signs of the civilization built by the Italian colonists. The gap between defeat and occupation had led to an orgy of looting and destruction. Everything that had made Derna beautiful, except its supply of 'good clean spring water', had been lost. Even the famous banana groves 'seemed to have gone sterile'. The road from Derna led into the Vale of Barce. There the 'barren moorlands had been made to give out flowers and fruit and all the rich things of modern farming'. The valley was dotted with 'white homesteads and creameries'. Now most of the farms were broken down, prey to the weather. This was not a desert of sand and heat but of mud and rain. The crops grew rank in the field and fell back into the morass of mud. It was wet and cold and the 'red mud stretched interminably across the dreary landscape'. Benghazi was 'liberated' on Christmas Day 1941. It proved no great prize. Within an hour of its evacuation Axis aeroplanes flew over from Sicily, bombing and mining. At no point in the British occupation did it operate as a port.[26]

In between Rommel's decision to retreat to Gazala and his decision to retreat to Agedabia, Japan attacked Pearl Harbor, the Germans and Italians declared war on the USA, and the British Pacific battlefleet was sunk off the coast of Malaya. These profound events, although noted and discussed, had remarkably little salience for the short-term balance of power in North Africa. The main impact the outbreak of 'world war' had on the wider Mediterranean was in ending any possibility that Britain might send major naval reinforcements into the sea to offset their losses. Any plans for replacing the carriers sunk earlier in the year were abandoned. The immediate problem was not outside the Mediterranean but within. In December 1941 Britain's Mediterranean Fleet lost the naval war. The Mediterranean's own 'day of infamy' was not 7 December but 19 December 1941.

Whatever the confusions of the land war, the British could read the north–south convoy war with almost complete clarity. The routines of sea transports, bills of lading, ports of embarkation, sailing routes, ports of unlading were almost designed for signals intelligence. The British knew what was being sent, where from and where to. November 1941 proved the perfect month for cutting the trans-Mediterranean route. Nearly every gallon of the Axis's most precious cargo, fuel, was lost during the month. Force K on Malta showed such preternatural ability to intercept ships that the skilled Italian codebreakers almost twigged what was going on. They guessed that the British were breaking German codes. The head of Italian military intelligence made a presentation on the subject to Kesselring, but he was ignored. Aware that many officers in the *Regia Marina* were outspokenly anti-German, Kesselring was convinced that traitors were leaking information to the British. Understandably the Italians – in reality blameless – were indignant at the accusation. They were equally indignant at German aspersions – in this case accurate – about their own signals security. Both Italians and Germans continued to provide the British with a near-perfect picture of their convoy arrangements.[27]

Beautifully constructed intelligence assessments were, however, as much of a danger as a boon. Overriding all voices of caution, London ordered the Mediterranean Fleet to reinforce Force K.[28] During the mission to put more cruisers into Malta, one of Cunningham's three battleships, *Barham*, was sunk by a German U-boat, with great loss of life. After the initial shock, Cunningham's assessment was that he could survive with his two remaining battleships, *Barham* being the least capable of the trio, 'but I must keep them rather in cotton wool as it won't do to get another put out of action'. 'It is all right', he signalled, 'if the *Littorios* can be kept facing west.'[29] From Gibraltar, however, Somerville signalled back, 'we can't do anything at this end to draw off some of the stuff from your end'.[30] Since the *Ark Royal* had been sunk, his anti-submarine ships had devoted themselves to patrolling the Straits of Gibraltar to try and intercept the U-boats. Whilst they were doing this they could not escort the fleet. Both fleets were in cotton wool; neither was keen to venture out of harbour. Somerville even suggested that Force H's days in the Mediterranean were done and that it should become an Atlantic force.[31]

For their part the Italians were growing in confidence. On 13 December 1941 Ciano had recorded, 'the usual naval woes'. 'I wonder', he went so far as to ask, 'whether the war won't outlast our navy.'[32] To try and avoid such a possibility the navy decided to escort convoys with a battlefleet too strong for the British to dare attack. 'Today the entire fleet is at sea,' Ciano recorded in hope and trepidation, 'Riccardi believes a clash with the British is inevitable. He says that we are definitely superior in quantity and quality, and he promises success – the success that we have been waiting for so long in vain. Can it be our luck will change?'[33] Italian expectations were tolerably accurate. The British only had cruisers at sea. When they collided with the battleships in the Gulf of Sirte, the British squadrons were hopelessly outmatched. Faced with the big guns of the Italian fleet, their shells sounding 'like motor buses going overhead', they had little choice other than to flee. Avoiding destruction in the Gulf of Sirte did not save the British. Signals intelligence told Force K that the Italian battlefleet had left the convoy near the coast of Libya. It set off again from Malta in an attempt to sink the ships before they were able to enter Tripoli. But the British had underestimated Italian technical ingenuity. They had no idea that the Italians had developed a method of tethering mines in very deep water. On 19 December Force K ran at full tilt into an unsuspected minefield and was destroyed as a fighting force within minutes. All four cruisers hit mines. Two were sunk instantly, the other two were damaged, only one with a reasonable hope of timely repair on Malta.[34]

If Force K was destroyed by one kind of *mezzi insidiosi*, then the Mediterranean Fleet fell victim to an even more spectacular version on the same day. Over the course of 1941 *Decima Mas*, Italian underwater special forces, had attacked the British in each major harbour in which they had anchored: Suda Bay, Malta and Gibraltar. Their masterpiece, however, was the attack on Alexandria where Britain's two remaining battleships were supposedly wrapped in cotton wool. Their assault force sailed from the Italian submarine base on Leros. A mother submarine carried three 'pigs', two-man human torpedoes. The Italians carefully looped under the French warships that occupied the western side of the naval harbour. The 'pigs' attached charges to the *Queen Elizabeth* and the *Valiant* at the eastern end of the harbour. The charges exploded just after daybreak, sinking the *Queen Elizabeth* and crippling the *Valiant*.[35] Force K had hit the minefield off Tripoli at 05.30; the battleships in Alexandria started to explode at 06.06.[36] British naval power in the Mediterranean was thus humbled in two separate *Regia Marina* operations in the space of minutes. The convoy that Force K had been hunting entered Tripoli harbour without loss. Thereafter the Italians began a regular series of successful 'battleship convoys' across the Mediterranean. The British were no less aware of these shipments than before; they simply lacked the strength to do anything about them.

When Hitler had met the Mufti, German hopes of Vichy collusion had hampered the emergence of an open alliance between Nazism and radical Arab nationalism. Much of the mood for that meeting had been generated by Italo-German military success, balanced by aero-naval failure. By the time the Germans opened formal negotiations with Vichy, the whole aero-naval balance in the Mediterranean had altered. The British tried desperately to bluff the world into believing that they still had a Mediterranean battlefleet. All of the 'pig' operators had been captured, depriving the Italians of after-action reports. There was a news blackout on events in Alexandria. The Royal Navy even righted the useless hulk of the *Queen Elizabeth* in an attempt to fool air reconnaissance. In doing so they bought themselves a few weeks of uncertainty about the extent of the damage the Italians had done. The one power it was impossible to deceive was Vichy since the sunken ship shared an anchorage with the French. Vichy warships could communicate by radio, albeit intermittently, with Darlan. He had no particular reason, however, to tell the Italians the whole story.

In December 1941 delicate lines of negotiation had opened about the Mediterranean future. Ciano and Darlan had met in Turin to discuss Italo-French cooperation. Ciano's impression of Darlan was 'rather good', not least because 'he hates the British'.[37] At the same time Cavallero was telling Mussolini that the best way to solve the convoy problem was to send the ships to Bizerta, making them virtually impossible for the British to intercept. If the French were not willing to hand over Bizerta it should be seized by force. 'I would rather take my divisions to Tunisia, than see them sent to the bottom of the sea en route to Tripoli,' Mussolini wrote to Hitler.

There was a rather more subtle approach to the problem. Göring delivered two 'requests' to the Vichy military authorities. First, the Germans and Italians should be allowed to smuggle supplies to Libya via French territory. Such equipment would be shipped from French Mediterranean ports to Tunisia disguised as French civil cargo. Once in Tunisia, the French railway network would deliver it safely to neighbouring Tripolitania. Göring's second request was that if things in North Africa went completely wrong, Rommel would be welcomed as an ally into Tunisia and that the Franco-German armies would together fight the British. The answer to both demands was a – provisional – yes.[38]

Darlan, as had been the case over Syria six months previously, was reluctant to declare war on Britain without first having France's military strength rebuilt by the Germans. His aim was to become a full partner in the 'New Order'; not to sink to the level of – always his measure of ultimate degradation – Belgium. He was much more willing to engage in the kind of hostile operations, short of war, embodied in Göring's first suggestion. As Darlan put it, it was better to agree to a request than to face an ultimatum backed by force. In his view a British defeat in Cyrenaica was most desirable. It would take at least a year for American strength to be deployed in the Mediterranean. If, in the interim, the British were chased out of the Mediterranean, the Axis would have complete freedom of movement from the Black Sea to Gibraltar. From such a position they might achieve Darlan's desired outcome, a negotiated peace from which France might profit. The position was 'delicate but could be fruitful'.[39]

The Franco-German negotiations for the full military use of Tunisia dragged on for some months and ended in failure, despite 'very cordial' meetings between Göring and Pétain, Darlan and Raeder. Plans for the smuggling operation that Darlan had always favoured went ahead apace, however. Darlan, Ciano and Göring, whatever their high political disagreements, agreed to proceed with the technical arrangement. 'Now the pendulum is swinging in our favour and against the British,' Ciano noted, 'the Vichy government is anxious to smile on us.'[40] The Vichyites held out against specifically military supplies, so the centrepiece of the plan became the transport of hundreds of lorries per month into Libya. Rommel's retreat had graphically illustrated the need to motorize the Italian forces. Whilst he fled by the quickest route across the desert, the foot-bound infantry was forced to march around the coast, leading to the loss of many units. The arrangement was only undone by the openness of all Mediterranean traffic to British prying. The Minister of Economic Warfare, Hugh Dalton, told the House of Commons what Vichy was up to. The Americans threatened to cancel food shipments to France.[41] Darlan declared that 'the risk to France now outweighed the advantages to the Axis' and the supplies petered out.[42]

In truth, the brief efflorescence of the Tunisian option had been over-taken by events elsewhere in the central Mediterranean. A few days after the British fleet had been crippled, Kesselring began the serious attempt to pummel Malta into impotence. With *Fliegerkorps* II fully deployed in Sicily, he was able to send over raids of over two hundred aircraft at a time. Within a fortnight the naval commander on the island had concluded that 'the enemy is definitely trying to neutralise Malta's effort and I hate to say so but gradually are doing so'.[43] There were half a dozen good airfields on Sicily. The German planes took off and climbed at their leisure over the island, confident that no one could molest them. 'Within a few minutes of riding over the tops of the last of the Sicilian moun-tains,' Malta was in sight. The flight took less than half an hour. The pattern of each raid was much the same. The British defenders took off from their three airfields, but their Hawker Hurricanes struggled to reach the bombers' altitude before the attackers dropped their bombs. In any case, the climbing British would inevitably be met – 'bounced' – by German fighters. They fought at a perpetual disadvantage, unable to reach the attackers, vulnerable to their escorts. Although Malta's air strength was increased rather than decreased in December 1941, without higher-performance aircraft there was little that they could do.

Neither were Malta's bombers able to fill the gap caused by the demise of the Mediterranean Fleet.[44] The newly appointed Malta air commander, Hugh Lloyd, described attempts to send his Bristol Blenheim torpedo-bombers against properly defended ships as 'sheer murder'. Lloyd let it be known on the grapevine that, whatever his formal orders, he was not using 'my Blenheims constantly in low-level attacks on heavily-escorted merchant ships'.[45] The Italians were fully aware that their situation had been transformed by the victories of 19 December 1941. 'The enemy have learnt', Cunningham wrote after a large tank convoy had docked unmolested in Tripoli, 'the utter futility of our air forces over the sea and I fear he will run convoys to Tripoli without worrying himself about our air.'[46] He admitted that 'in face of enemy's strength existing surface forces are powerless to intervene'. 'I cannot see', Britain's Mediterranean commander concluded, 'how Malta can be maintained far less the enemy's supplies to Tripoli stopped.'[47]

Even Rommel, who moaned constantly about the failure of his colleagues to supply him properly, conceded that 'we're gradually getting more stuff across'. Kesselring was 'doing very good work over Malta'. His troops had made their planned stand at Agedabia, defeating the British vanguard. He himself had continued the retreat to the last town in Cyrenaica, El Agheila. In front of him was the Mersa Brega position, even more defensible than Agedabia. The gap between sea and desert narrowed, the Italo-Germans were protected by impassable salt marshes, soft sand and camel-hump dunes: the British made little attempt to displace them. Beyond Mersa Brega, the *Balbia* wound round the southern and western shore of the Gulf of Sirte, six hundred kilometres of desert, before reaching the first town in Tripolitania, Misurata. Even if the Mersa Brega position could have been turned there was no immediately achievable objective beyond it. The British came to a halt.[48]

Signals intelligence was good at measuring the supplies flowing into Tripolitania, but it offered little insight into the emotional state of Germany's commander, semi-detached from the Mediterranean world around him. Rommel's paranoid egotism made him well-suited to subverting modern methods of warfare. As he himself remarked: 'I'm full of plans that I daren't say anything about round here. They'd think me crazy.'[49] His crazy plan was to take the newly arrived stores and counter-attack. Although his first target was Agedabia, he chose not to confide in anyone that he intended to keep going until he was stopped. He 'maintained secrecy over the Panzer Group's forthcoming attack eastwards from Mersa el Brega and informed neither the Italian nor the German High Command'.[50] His distrust of Italian signals security actually protected him from poor German signals security. Everyone was caught by surprise. On D-day – 21 January 1942 – Auchinleck was in Palestine, and the commander of the 8th Army was in Cairo. Just as he had presented Kesselring and Cavallero with a *fait accompli* when they flew in to argue the toss about the retreat from Gazala, he presented them with another *fait accompli* when they flew in to protest against the return to Gazala. For Rommel, 'the theatre' was Cyrenaica, not the Mediterranean. Those outside Africa merely spent their time 'sitting in Rome'. He was simply going to 'keep at the enemy just as long as my troops and supplies would allow'.[51]

No one could argue with the results. On 25 January German tanks attacked the ill-prepared and strung-out 1st British Armoured Division. They 'broke into the enemy at tearing speed and threw him into complete confusion'. Orders were issued for the evacuation of Benghazi; the orders were countermanded; the orders were reinstated. The British fell prey to 'panzer terror', the fear that Rommel would get behind their lines and cut off their lines of retreat as they had once done to the Italians. On 29

January the Germans captured Benghazi, suffering a mere fifteen casualties. Although the British casualties were more severe, they were by no means crippling. British troops withdrew without fighting a serious battle. Within a fortnight of setting out on his 'crazy adventure' Rommel was back near Gazala, delighting in the fact that 'the foreign press opinion about me is improving again'.[52] A few days later he could boast: 'we have got Cyrenaica back. It went like greased lightning.'[53] In the immortal words of a British rifleman: 'we had a go at them, or they had a go at us. Then one of us fucked off! You fucked off about five hundred miles without stopping.'[54]

If British power had little resonance around the Mediterranean in November 1941, it had even less by 1942. Control was imposed through the barrel of the gun, albeit barely.[55] When Rommel was retreating in disorder, the Egyptian government had cast around for some painless measure by which they might curry favour with the British. Their internal target was the Muslim fanatic, Hassan Banna. SIME had long regarded Banna's Muslim Brotherhood as a seditious menace, a suspicion only strengthened by the move of radical Islam towards a Nazi alliance.[56] The external target was Vichy France. Sir Miles Lampson had bellowed his condemnation of the French and his distaste for those, like the admirals, who preferred appeasement. The day Rommel abandoned Agedabia, the safe length of Cyrenaica away, the Egyptian Prime Minister broke off diplomatic relations with the French. His timing was poor. What was unpopular, but achievable, when Rommel was retreating was political poison when the Italo-German forces were advancing again. The shadowy forces of palace and mosque were mobilized against him. He was forced to release Banna. Ali Maher and the sheikhs orchestrated demonstrations at Cairo University and the main mosques. The demonstrations became riots, the mobs on the street calling Rommel's name and welcoming his forthcoming cleansing of Egypt.

Auchinleck and his commanders were understandably 'grumpy' that, as their forces were desperately digging in at Gazala, insurrection threatened in their rear area. They blamed the political and security authorities for gross mismanagement. The politicos – Lyttelton and Lampson – thought that the soldiers were unnecessarily hysterical. The troubles were as much opportunity as crisis. A moment when there were so many well-armed troops in Egypt was the perfect time to put the 'frighteners' on the 'absolute coward' boy-king Farouk.[57] Their solution was to put the secular republican nationalists of Nahas Pasha's Wafd back into power. Nahas had after all been the signatory of the 1936 Anglo-Egyptian treaty that had guaranteed the Suez Canal against Fascist aggression. Not without difficulty Lampson and Lyttelton secured a promise from the military that any threats they made could be backed by force as necessary.[58] A delighted Lampson told Farouk's emissary that either he must appoint Nahas prime minister or face dethronement. There followed a day of tension with students running through the streets shouting once more: 'Long live Rommel', 'Long live Farouk' and 'Down with the English'. At nine o'clock in the evening Lampson arrived at the Abdin Palace with his promised military escort, a general and 'an impressive array of specially picked stalwart military officers'. Everyone in the Palace could hear the 'rumble of tanks and armoured cars taking up position'. To Lampson's profound disappointment, Farouk preferred to appoint Nahas prime minister rather than sign the instrument of his own abdication.[59] 'We are still faced', he wrote the morning after the night before, 'with the fact that we have a rotter on the throne and if things go badly with us he will be likely to stab us in the back.'[60]

British tanks reduced the Egyptian elite to the 'resistance of daily life'. Their topsy-turvy world of collusion and subversion was brought to public attention by the 'Borsa incident'. Prince Abbas Halim, the patron of fast cars and aeroplanes in Cairo, made little secret of his desire for an Axis victory. As a result he had a large number of adherents amongst the officers of the Egyptian air force. His wife's birthday party was gatecrashed by a group of British officers and their female companions. They believed that they were going to a high society jolly, only to walk into a gathering of the 'New Order elite'. In this case the female relations of the politician Sidky Pasha led the barracking of the unwelcome British and their 'Jewesses'. One of the Sidky girls was married to Signor Borsa, an Italian whose presence around Farouk constantly worried the British. As SIME concluded, 'the Borsa incident is in fact merely a striking public instance of the spirit that Abbas Halim has fostered among his considerable following in high Egyptian society'.[61]

The exact degree of support the Nazis enjoyed in Egypt in royal, military and religious circles remains unclear, as a result of contemporary confusion as much as subsequent obfuscation. Farouk's circle had certainly made a number of contacts with German representatives during 1941.

German radio broadcasts initially celebrated Nahas's appointment as a victory for anti-British Egyptian nationalism. The Italians had to show them intercepted American dispatches to convince them of the true position, that Nahas had colluded with the British to seize power. It was hard to coordinate information about, or contacts to, potential resistance movements, despite British fears to the contrary. SIME's wireless monitoring revealed that there was at least one German transmitter on air from Egypt during January 1942. A security audit noted that although ports such as Alexandria were well guarded, even more so after the disaster of 19 December 1941, smaller ports such as Rosetta and Damietta had little security and it was 'entirely possible for agents to slip in'. Various suspects were picked up and shipped out of Egypt, including an 'extremely dangerous pro-German Jew of Greek nationality', a Polish Jew counterfeiter working for the *Abwehr* in Athens, and a German cabaret artiste travelling on a forged Egyptian passport.[62] The Germans thought it worthwhile to take the risk of flying an aircraft from Greece to the Pyramids to pick up the former chief of staff of the Egyptian army, Masri Pasha. The mission failed, Masri had already been detained by the British, but the aircraft was able to make it back across the Mediterranean in perfect safety.[63] The Axis's deep-desert-penetration expert Count Almasy, 'the English Patient', put *Abwehr* agents across the border to make contact with Egyptian army officers. Eventually the agents and their Egyptian army contacts were arrested in Cairo, broken at CSDIC, and handed back to SIME and 'very useful they were in identifying newly-arrived German suspects'.[64]

The British inoculated Egypt against Nazi contamination by a mixture of crude and subtle methods. Their subtle efforts to win support on the northern shore were almost entirely without success.[65] There was no word of any kind emanating from Yugoslavia. The Yugoslav armed forces in Egypt amounted to one battalion raised from Slovenes who had been captured serving in the Italian army. They refused to fight against their former comrades. In January 1942 the bloated officer corps in Cairo 'mutinied' against the government in exile in London, a condition that lasted for the next eleven months.[66] The only word from Italy came from front organizations loyal to the Fascist secret services. The only audible signals of resistance that went back and forth across the Mediterranean came from Greece and they caused as much concern as hope.

Over the days when the Egyptian crisis was at its height, Cairo became aware that they had a Greek crisis on their hands as well. In their attempts to derail the 'Frankenstein's monster' that was the Greek government in exile, the eye of the old gang had fallen on a charismatic university professor, Panyiotis Kanellopoulos, codenamed Cuthbert, a Venizelist dynast whose family had for long been at the heart of the Republican movement. The problem with 'plan Cuthbert' was that its target appeared unreachable. A number of agents had been sent in to find him, none had been heard from since. There was, in fact, only one secure radio link in and out of Greece. SIS had procured a caique in Alexandria and it had sailed to Smyrna. Under the captaincy of Odysseus the small ship had reached the Piraeus, smuggling radio parts and a codebook to Prometheus II. As soon as the *Crusader* offensive was announced, 'wireless set 333' came on air. Cairo thus had contact not with 'moderates' such as Cuthbert, but with dissident 'red' officers serviced by Odysseus the smuggler. When *Crusader* reached the height of its success and Rommel fled to Agedabia, Radio 333 asked for arms to be parachuted in to the monastery of Kymi on Euboea, so that Prometheus and his friends might start fighting the Axis.

When *Crusader* was declared a failure, Radio 333 informed Cairo that its attempts to contact other opposition groups via courier had been a disaster. Following the failure of Greek agents, an officer working for MI9, the organization that helped British servicemen escape from occupied Europe, had agreed to do some political warfare work 'on the side'. He was provided with a complete briefing on pro-British Greek politicians, including Cuthbert. The unfortunate officer headed for Antiparos, a tiny Cycladic islet which served as a good transit stop for the Piraeus. There he was captured by the Italians with all of his documents. The Antiparos 'incident' blew the cover of virtually every Greek who had had contact with the British. 'In other words,' SOE's history concluded, 'this affair had effectively knocked on the head the only party, that of Kanellopoulos, whose programme in the least degree met the wishes of the Foreign Office or which had any chance of acting as a bridge between the King and the exiled government and the resistance.'[67]

Radio 333's report was not the only bad news on the wireless that week. SOE had hoped to make up for the lack of a real Greek resistance by creating a pretend *maquis*. It had created the 'Voice of Free Greece'. The 'Free Voice' purported to be transmitting from an undisclosed location in Greece where a resistance movement was taking shape under the noses of the Germans and Italians. It told the Greeks to prepare for liberation as popular action would sweep away the hated occupiers. The Free Voice actually emanated from an office in Jerusalem. It was staffed by a group of exiles, certainly anti-Axis, but resisting in word rather than deed. Jerusalem proved a magnet for anti-royalists.[68] On 8 February 1942 the *ersatz* 'resistance' in Jerusalem/free Greece drew attention to the fact that the government in exile was still staffed by ministers appointed by Metaxas, suggesting in so many words that royalism could be equated with Fascism. A few days later the real resistance, gathered around wireless 333 in Athens/occupied Greece, responded with a statement that it was 'astonished' and 'angry' at British support for the King. It announced a petition against the monarch ever returning to Greece. These exchanges galvanized the loyalists in exile, focusing 'a powerful and malignant Royalist spot-light that proved itself possessed of the lethal qualities of a Death Ray' on the British representatives in the Mediterranean. More broadcasts from Radio 333 did nothing to cool the temperature. With the desert fighting having reached a stalemate, and the weather over Greece improving, the RAF finally attempted to drop arms to Kymi. Nearly all of the equipment was gratefully salvaged by the Italian garrison of Euboea. 333 was loud in its complaints, informing Cairo that, disgusted by British incompetence, not even 'red' officers of the regular army would now collaborate. The only resistance that was left was the even 'redder' irregulars.

To everyone's surprise a new factor was added to the war of words. At the beginning of April 1942 Kanellopoulos suddenly appeared in Smyrna. Betrayed by Antiparos, he had gone on the run, helped by one of the agents sent in to find him. The two men had finally found a caique on which they could make their escape. Cuthbert's long-desired escape was soured by the circumstances. As he tried to make his way from Turkey via Syria he was 'put on ice' in Aleppo. Fearing his popularity, the King and Tsouderos insisted that they should be allowed to establish themselves in Cairo. In Aleppo, Kanellopoulos was 'scathing' about the cack-handed British attempts to influence Greek opinion. When he was finally brought to Cairo, it was made clear to Kanellopoulos that he had fled Greece virtually alone and that he was still alone. As a symbol of Free Greece he had value, but that value was slight. The King refused to promise a referendum on the future of the monarchy once Greece was liberated. Finally, Kanellopoulos agreed to join a 'united front' government without such a promise. Wireless 333 radioed the message,

'Kanellopoulos and all people round the traitor King are themselves traitors.'[69]

The efforts of Britain's secret agencies to project themselves across the Mediterranean, begun on the eve of *Crusader* and stretching to the end of the stalemate in Libya that followed it, had ended in the same disconnection between the two shores as there had been before. The commander of the Italian occupation forces could report with satisfaction that 'throughout Greek territory during one year of occupation public order has never been disturbed by events which could be seriously regarded as threatening the security of the troops and the population'.[70] All that could be heard with any clarity was a single radio signal. What lay behind it was uncertain.

As was usual with knotty political problems, attempts to sort out the various confusions and turf wars landed on the desk of the Minister of State in Cairo. With the failure of *Crusader* and all its attendant political hopes, Lyttelton had been summoned home in February 1942, feeling 'rather *dégonflé*'. The seat had been kept warm by Monckton but just after Kanellopoulos signed his deal with Tsouderos a more permanent representative arrived. In order to acknowledge that the war in the Mediterranean was an imperial as much as a British affair, Churchill chose an Australian diplomat and politician, Richard Casey, to replace Lyttelton. Prolonged exposure to Cairo rarely enhanced anyone's reputation, and Casey was to prove no different. Like Lyttelton before him, however, he arrived with a fair head of steam. Alan Brooke, the acerbic head of the British army, dismissive of nearly all political appointees, 'was very much impressed by him and his grasp of things'.[71]

Greece would take up much of Casey's time, but it was far from his most pressing concern. His first task was to sort out the position of Malta in Mediterranean affairs. The meetings of the Mediterranean supremos, who had been regularized by Lyttelton into the three bodies, the MEWC, the MEDC and the MEC-in-Cs, were dominated by an inability to agree on the importance of Malta. 'I do not find the attitude of the soldiers to the Malta situation much to my liking,' recorded Cunningham. 'I pointed out that we can't gamble on the convoys getting through.' They replied: 'it is better to lose Malta than Egypt'.[72] On the eve of leaving his command, Cunningham had come to believe that the Middle Eastern tail was wagging the Mediterranean dog. 'The strategic reason for our presence in Gibraltar, Malta and the Middle East', he wrote in his valedictory report, 'is in order that we may have control of the Mediterranean Sea.' For Cunningham the 'logical outcome' was that 'the controlling voice' in 'strategical direction' should 'lie with those trained to the exercise of sea power'. The time had now come to create an admiral as a Mediterranean *generalissimo*.[73]

The flaw in his logic, as Cunningham acknowledged, was that whilst the navy might understand what to do *with* the Mediterranean, they had failed in what needed to be done *in* the Mediterranean. He had the largest command in the Royal Navy but 'there is now no fleet to go to sea in'. As soon as the Egyptian crisis had been resolved, he had ordered a convoy from Alexandria to Malta. Air attacks had turned it back. In a 'desperate measure', an outmatched British cruiser force took on the Italian battleships at the second battle of Sirte on 22 March 1942, saving another convoy, through a mixture of pluck, luck, bad weather and smoke. The next day Kesselring's forces sank the convoy in Malta harbour. Declaring that surface ships could no longer operate in the central Mediterranean, Cunningham ordered the withdrawal of the ineffectual remnant of Force K from Malta.[74] Both friends and enemies realized the enormity of what had happened. 'The most significant factor at this time is that not a single heavy British ship in the Mediterranean is fully seaworthy,' Admiral Raeder crowed in Berlin, 'the Axis rules both the sea and the air in the Central Mediterranean.'[75] Reading Cunningham's reports back in London, Alan Brooke felt that failure presaged further disaster: 'I do not think Malta will be able to hold out as it will no longer be possible to run convoys in from East or from West.'[76]

A few days later Churchill was forced to go cap in hand to President Roosevelt. He explained that the only chance he could see of saving Malta was by equipping the island with modern fighters capable of holding off Kesselring. To get sufficient numbers onto Malta, a proper fleet-carrier was needed and Britain had run out. The first major appearance of American forces in the Mediterranean thus resulted from a plea of impotence. The mission of the USS *Wasp* had other symbolic elements. The *Wasp* task force sailed to and from Scotland. It had as little to do with the Mediterranean as possible. The escort force was drawn from the Atlantic, with no reference to any Mediterranean command. The entry of the carrier into the danger zone was strictly controlled by high-level agreements. The fleet went only as far east as Algiers, refusing to even come near the Sardinian air bases. Its cargo of Spitfires barely made it to Malta on extra fuel tanks; as they landed, the *Luftwaffe*, with plenty of time to track their coming, were already flying off Sicily, catching the desperately refuelling aircraft on the ground and destroying them.[77]

The loss of the convoy from Alexandria and the destruction of the Spitfires was too much for Malta. Stories began to circulate that the Governor and commander of the island, General William Dobbie, was starting to crack. He appeared to be showing too much concern for the suffering of the people of Malta even though, hardliners pointed out, 'only' three hundred had been actually killed. Dobbie himself wanted to sack the air commander, Hugh Lloyd, because he was not a 'team player'; Lloyd wanted the head of the naval commander for failing to force the Maltese dock workers to labour twenty-four hours a day. Richard Casey's first job was to make an assessment of this poisonous situation. He sided with Lloyd. Dobbie was flown off the island and, as Casey had previously arranged, Lord 'Fat Boy' Gort was flown in from Gibraltar.[78] A byword for courage if not intelligence, Gort was, in this case, a lucky general: following in his wake, the *Wasp* task force, learning from its mistakes, managed to fly in a large consignment of Spitfires. Although the Malta Spitfires were later to take on a mythical quality, at the time their arrival was regarded as a minor tactical setback for the Axis. On 10 May 1942, two days into Gort's governorship, Kesselring declared his task over Malta 'accomplished'. *Fliegerkorps* II had flown 11,000 sorties over the island. Now it began to withdraw. 'Thanks to its success,' Kesselring wrote, 'our ascendancy at sea and in the air in the supply lanes from Italy to Africa was assured.'[79]

Wise after the event, some claimed that the reappearance of the Italians over Malta was the moment of salvation. This is not how it appeared at the time. The chief civilian 'character' on Malta, Mabel Strickland, termagant daughter of a former governor, editor of the island's newspaper and bane of Dobbie, said: 'It was in June 1942 that the siege settled down in Malta good and proper, grim and cruel, and the German wireless announced that as the island was made of rock other means would be found for dealing with the 300,000 whose Navy would never reach them.'[80]

The Nazi propagandists' crack about the Navy never again reaching Malta seemed all too likely. All the ships left, the submarines the last to go. The great Mediterranean submarine ace, Wanklyn of the *Upholder*, was sunk by an Italian sub-hunter on that last mission. When a small flotilla of destroyers tried to return a symbolic naval presence, the result was disaster. Over a one-and-a-half-hour period in the late afternoon of

11 May 1942, two Ju-88 *Gruppen*, flying from Eleusis in Greece and Heraklion in Crete, performed a series of textbook attacks on the ships. Three of the four destroyers were sunk; only the flotilla leader was able to flee back to Alexandria to tell the tale. The Mediterranean Fleet had been stripped of each of its ship classes in turn: they had started with aircraft-carriers but they had been lost; there were no more battleships; the cruisers were sunk or were overmatched; even the sprightly destroyers could not evade their hunters. Kesselring's boasts seemed sound. The route from Italy to Libya was indeed open, east–west passage by sea was impossible. Their beautifully constructed signals intelligence net allowed the British to listen to their own defeat.[81]

EIGHT

The Last Summer

The final summer of the old Mediterranean can be dated with extreme accuracy. It lasted from 26 May 1942, when Rommel set off to capture Tobruk, until 23 October 1942, when Montgomery started to chase his Axis adversary out of Egypt. Historians of the Second World War have, in recent years, tended to downplay the importance of the Italo-German invasion of Egypt. They depict the battles of the summer of 1942 as a doubly forlorn hope. Forlorn because the ineluctable logic of 'total war', the productive and manpower capacity of the combatants, was grinding against the Axis. No amount of tactical expertise could offset the steadily building materiel superiority of the 'grand alliance'. Forlorn, too, because Rommel's final advance was an operational nonsense. It led him to a worthless patch of desert, dependent on a misfiring and vulnerable supply line, comprising one coastal road and some desperate coast-hugging ships.[1]

The inevitability of Rommel's defeat was not, however, so clear to his contemporaries. They said that there was a 'coming decisive four months'.[2] The British collected and analysed every snippet of intelligence about Rommel they could. Their knowledge of his supplies was encyclopaedic. Their understanding of his operations was growing at an exponential rate. The first two weeks in June 1942 were labelled as 'revolutionary' by the collectors and readers of intelligence. As Rommel advanced, he had to use his wireless rather than land lines. His communications were entirely insecure. The system for dealing with them had been perfected. Within twenty-four hours the messages had been deciphered – sometimes at Bletchley, often at Heliopolis – translated, re-encrypted and the flimsies placed in the hands of Claude Auchinleck. Possessed of all this information, the British had no idea as to whether they could beat the

Panzerarmee Afrika.[3] If the initiates of Ultra could not be confident, how little could the broad mass of politicians, soldiers and onlookers hope to guess the eventual outcome of the struggle. Each side filled the airwaves with boasts about their military prowess, yet in Britain there was talk of mismanagement, incompetence, possibly cowardice, in short a 'proper balls of it'.[4]

What had not been a secret was that Rommel was coming. In Rome Ciano was able to learn much about the forthcoming offensive from listening to the BBC.[5] There was no doubt about the direction he would travel – east – and his final destination – the Nile Delta. At the beginning of the summer there was still some confusion about his route. Whilst the Desert Fox still used the telephone, his mind was unknown. The British could hear the sea and the air but not the land. They guessed that he would come straight along the *Balbia* heading for Tobruk. In fact he headed south, deep into the desert. Both sides talked about the Gazala line, beginning on the coast at Gazala, but there was no line as such. The British were arrayed in a series of strongpoints, known as 'boxes'. The sense that the boxes were not anywhere in particular, was reflected by the fact that many of them lacked recognizable local names. The most famous box was called Knightsbridge.

Rommel's target did, however, have a name: Bir Hacheim. Its importance as one of the great battles for the Mediterranean world, however, rested less on what the crossroads was called and more on who was there. The Bir Hacheim box was held by a French general, Pierre Koenig, leading a force of 'French, Italians, Germans and Jews convinced that there would be no pity for them'.[6] For some months discussions had been taking place about rebranding France. The term 'Free French' was becoming rather ripe, given that 'free' tended to mean freedom to quarrel with their British paymasters. The new name agreed upon for use in the media was 'Fighting French', the 'fighting' being against the Germans rather than the British. It was particularly lucky for the rebranders that Rommel should have headed for Koenig. *Le vieux lapin* had been entrusted with a pivotal box because he was the one French general that the British trusted. Koenig was the model of what the British thought the French should be, but rarely were. He had come to their notice for his efforts in the thankless task of persuading French escapees in Britain to fight. At Bir Hacheim they did fight, for a long, bitter week. In the end the legion was defeated but its stubborn defence of Bir Hacheim became a symbol for a longed-for, but fictional, Anglo-French amity. An RAF wit replied to a message from the garrison thanking the flyers for air support with the signal, *merci pour le sport*. The Germans played their part, too, in declaring those they had captured 'illegal combatants', not covered by the laws of war. After the war the memory of the Bir Hacheim desert crossroads faded, whilst that of the coastal towns Tobruk and El Alamein remained fresh for a generation. The atmosphere created by Bir Hacheim nevertheless proved a powerful counter-balance both to the pro-Vichy conduct of the Royal Navy in Alexandria and to the mutual detestation of British and French leaders in Syria.

The political advantages of Bir Hacheim were, in the short term, scant recompense for its disastrous military implications. With the fall of Bir Hacheim, Rommel boomeranged north, heading for the coast and the flank of the surprised imperial forces in his way.

Five days later German troops crossed the *Balbia* from the south, completing the encirclement of Tobruk. His supply difficulties were already apparent, but far from insuperable. Rommel's wide southern arc into the desert, followed by his northern march back to the coast meant that – as the crow flies – he had moved only a short distance along the coast. Although Rommel himself neglected the wider problem of Mediterranean supply, others were working hard to make that struggle a hard-fought battle. The British problem remained the same. In order to slow down Rommel, they had to interrupt the north–south route. In order to interrupt the north–south route, Malta had to be effective. At the moment of Rommel's advance it was impotent. No one knew whether this situation could be reversed.[7]

On the day that Bir Hacheim fell, 11 June 1942, *Abwehr* observers based at Ceuta in Spanish Morocco spotted a large convoy heading east for Malta. The spotting was notable because it was achieved with a bolometer, an amazingly advanced thermal-imaging device, designed to overcome British use of the night and bad weather to disguise their naval movements. By June 1942 the Germans had assembled an impressive network of such devices on the northern and southern shores of the Straits. Their innovations included parallel infra-red beams emitted from infra-red searchlights on either shore. The system was worrying enough for Sir Samuel Hoare to bother protesting to Franco. The *Caudillo* brushed him off with bland lies and carried on his hand-in-glove cooperation with the Germans. All this was known to the British from their decryption of *Abwehr* communications, but there was little they could do as long as Franco's confidence in German success continued. SOE blew up an observation post in Tangier to little effect. The political and technical sophistication of the so-called *Bodden* operation was cited by the British secret services as evidence that German opposite numbers were greatly to be feared.[8]

Although *Bodden* was a new and worrying element, the battle of convoys followed much the same pattern as earlier battles, albeit with even worse results for the British. At the same time as the Gibraltar convoy was launched, British cruisers led out another Alexandria convoy from the east. American involvement in the convoy ensured that Bonner Fellers in Cairo had a last hurrah as a prime Italian source. Soon afterwards his carelessness with ciphers was discovered and he was sacked. In a neat reversal German intelligence from Morocco allowed the Italians to make a good job of attacking the western convoy, whereas the Italian intelligence from Egypt gave *Fliegerkorps* X the chance to do an even better job on the eastern convoy. On the day that Rommel's forces crossed the *Balbia*, the British cruiser leader in the east signalled that it was impossible for him to keep his convoy heading towards Malta; to do so would lead to the sinking of all the merchant and warships alike. He ordered his charges to reverse course and run back to Alexandria. In the west an Italian cruiser squadron caught the convoy near Pantelleria. In a confused battle four of the six merchant ships were sunk, including the all-important oil tanker.[9]

These intense battles had some, albeit limited, resonance on the north shore. In the week of Bir Hacheim and the convoy battle, there were signs of life in both Greece and Yugoslavia. It would be wrong to think that merely because the most spectacular action was taking place to the south, less attention was paid to the north. The main occupying power in Greece and Mediterranean Yugoslavia was Italy. In the summer of 1942 Italian forces in Yugoslavia peaked at a strength of twenty-three divisions. Eight divisions garrisoned mainland Greece and another three were spread out across the Aegean. Italian forces in North Africa also reached their peak in the summer of 1942 at a strength of ten divisions. Admittedly many of the northern divisions were 'hollow', under-strength infantry units; meanwhile every effort was made to bring the African divisions up to strength, and they included all the elite armoured and motorized formations.[10] These deployments nevertheless made the point about the salience of the north.

The *Regio Esercito* took some care over the morale of its men. Its studies revealed that information did filter across the Mediterranean. The men knew that the Fascist propaganda that they were fed was doctored, and set little store by it. Neither did they believe much they heard from the British. They knew that the English had a track record of boasting about victories that later proved illusory. The main source of news on the northern shore was the 'bush telegraph', what the Italians called *Radio Fante*, gossip gleaned from comrades arriving from Italy or North Africa.[11] These studies showed that aside from the kind of griping about women and families found in all armies, the soldiers were relatively happy with their lot. This was particularly so in Greece. The commanding general in Athens sent back a string of reports to Rome complaining that life was so quiet that his soldiers were happily settling down into a 'peace-time mentality'. Whilst the Greeks starved, their occupiers were so well fed that exercise programmes had to be devised to slim them down. The threat faced by the fat Italians was minimal. Misled by false reports of British victories, the Prometheus II organization carried out its first act of sabotage at the very moment when Rommel was driving along the *Balbia* surveying with satisfaction 'the evidence of the British defeat'. The group sent a swimmer to plant a limpet mine on an Italian ship docked in the Piraeus *en route* to North Africa. The attack was no more than an isolated incident. The magnitude of Prometheus' mistake soon became apparent as members of his organization were arrested and executed.

The situation across the border in Yugoslavia was less comfortable for the Axis, but it was unclear whether this discomfort had anything to do with events on the southern shore. June 1942 saw a complex series of realignments, military, political and geographical. In Greece Britain had a secure radio link, wireless 333, but no man. In Yugoslavia Britain had a man, the unlucky Captain Hudson, but no radio. In June 1942 Hudson came back on the air. Since November 1941 he had been the prisoner of Draza Mihailovic, the Chetnik leader. He was carried around almost as one of Mihailovic's possessions, never allowed to come to the Chetnik headquarters or allowed to talk to their leadership. All the missions sent in after Hudson – something of the order of nine – had disappeared, through desertion, capture or murder.[12] Unlike Hudson, Mihailovic was not completely isolated. He had a radio link with the outside world, albeit without proper codes and thus insecure. He was able to send couriers on missions to Istanbul for meetings with representatives of King Peter's government. As the seemingly endless schism between the officers of the royal armed forces in Egypt continued, Mihailovic's stock rose with the Yugoslav government in exile. In 1941 he had been a mere colonel. In June 1942 he was appointed as head of the Yugoslav armed forces.[13] Mihailovic was moving nearer to the Mediterranean, both physically and mentally. Not only was he promoted in the summer of 1942, he was also relocating. His home range in German-occupied Serbia had become much too dangerous. The German commander in Serbia, General Alexander Löhr, calculated that his troops had executed over 20,000 Serbian hostages over the winter of 1941–2. Italian-occupied Montenegro provided a much safer base.

When Hudson had arrived the previous year, he had found Communist partisans operating on the Montenegrin coast. By the summer of 1942 they had been cleared out by a new Italian commander waging war in a different manner. Under the post-invasion settlement of 1941 Italy had, in one way or another, seized most of Yugoslavia's Mediterranean coastline. The longest stretches had simply been annexed as the province of Dalmatia, its largest city, Split, joining the existing Italian enclave of Zara as the main population centre. Montenegro was under military occupation. Mussolini's former terrorist clients, Ante Pavelic and his Ustasha, were the overlords of an Independent Republic of Croatia. Smarting from the years 'on ice', when the Ustasha had been prisoners in Italy, Pavelic rapidly concluded that he preferred Nazis to Fascists. He won Hitler's approval for his total commitment to finding Jews and shipping them to concentration camps. Nevertheless, half of the Croatian republic, including all the coastal areas, was under Italian military occupation. Dalmatia, Croatia and Montenegro all suffered from a terrorist problem. Dalmatia suffered a spectacular coup at the end of May 1942 when the prefect of Zara was 'riddled' with machine-gun bullets in a roadside ambush.[14]

Ousted from the *Comando Supremo* in a power struggle with Ugo Cavallero, Mario Roatta, characterized by Ciano as 'not a very pleasant person, but the most intelligent general I know', arrived in Yugoslavia with a point to prove.[15] He had three main ideas all of which had a profound impact on the war in the Adriatic littoral. It was time, he told his commanders, to get rid of the *italiani brava gente* – the Italians are nice guys – myth. The Italians should stop trying to get on with the local population and start massacring innocents, as the Germans had done to such good effect in Serbia. The violence of Roatta's conduct earned him his nickname – 'the Black Beast'. Second, it was time to recruit the Chetniks as allies rather than enemies. He wanted to see Chetnik and Partisan 'slaughtering each other'. As a result of a series of deals between the Italians, the Chetniks, and the Ustasha during the spring of 1942, the Partisans were driven out of Montenegro and eastern Bosnia and forced to flee north-westwards and inland. The Partisan 'long march' lasted for the rest of the summer and autumn. The Communists were aided in their potentially disastrous flight by the third of Roatta's policies. He decreed that his newly brutalized Italian forces should stop sitting around in penny packets across Croatia. Instead they would concentrate only on major communications centres inland, whilst doing a proper job of holding the coast. A few days after Mihailovic became titular head of the Yugoslav resistance, Roatta signed a deal with the Ustasha for the withdrawal of his garrisons from Croatia. The Partisans moved north-west, the Italians moved south-west and out of the way. The Italians would later pay for this mistake. In the summer of 1942, however, Roatta could pat himself on the back for a job seemingly well done. The Partisans had been cleared from Montenegro and eastern Bosnia, the Chetniks were allies of a kind, and he had safely redeployed his forces into Dalmatia and its borderlands. It was the Germans who took on the Partisans in west Bosnia.[16]

June 1942 can hardly be said to have yielded a good haul for the British, defeat in Libya offset by the merest and most ambivalent signals coming across the Mediterranean. The month would be remembered above all for Rommel's capture of Tobruk. Tobruk had defied him for so long that it had become part of the landscape. The Germans had even built a ring-road, the *Axen*, so that they could drive to and fro along the *Balbia* without passing dangerously close to the British guns. The gap between propaganda and reality hurt the British. Churchill had fetishized Tobruk as the unbreachable fortress. The fetish was adopted by his enemies: 'to every man of us,' wrote Rommel, 'Tobruk was a symbol of British resistance'.[17]

The trouble was that Auchinleck did not see 'greater' Tobruk as anything other than a supply base. Its defences had been allowed to deteriorate; it was filled with second-line troops. The Auk had put his trust in the 'boxes' of the Gazala line and once that had been destroyed, Tobruk stood little chance. It took but five days for the Italo-German army to force the surrender of the South African garrison. German propaganda had a field day with the death of a symbol. Broadcasts from Berlin were divided into two parts. In the first part the Germans rejoiced in the elimination of Tobruk, 'for so long a thorn in the flesh of German troops on the road to Egypt'. Then the German broadcasters luxuriated in the speeches and declarations made about the town by British politicians, 'a damning revelation of British propaganda methods'. All this, British commentators concluded, showed that Axis diplomacy 'marched together' with 'Rommel's strength and determination in attack' and would now stretch its net from 'one end to the other' of the Mediterranean.[18]

In reality there was no Axis master plan. There was little more than immediate extemporization. As usual, the German and Italian military professionals counselled caution, the need to consolidate gains, rest the men, refit and resupply; 'these beggars never change', moaned the Desert Fox.[19] Rommel, in this instance egged on by Mussolini, was determined to advance. The day after the fall of Tobruk, the *Duce* declared that he himself would go to Africa. 'In reality', he claimed, 'he was the man behind the decisive attack, even against the opinion of the *Comando Supremo*.' 'Now', he feared, 'they might not realise the magnitude of the success and therefore fail to take full advantage of it.' Mussolini trusted 'only Rommel'.[20] Kesselring complained that the newly promoted Field Marshal had an 'hypnotic influence' over both Mussolini and Hitler. They did not 'originate or follow any clear-cut plan', instead they allowed their hand to be forced 'by fits and starts'.[21]

Rommel raced along the coast, brushing aside opposition, spewing ever more optimistic reports in his wake. The Egyptian coastal towns that had punctuated reports of previous campaigns fell in rapid succession: Sollum, Sidi Barrani, Mersa Matruh. He wrote home at the end of June 1942, 'the battle has been won and our leading units are only 125 miles from Alexandria'. 'There'll be a few more battles to fight before we reach our goal', he went on optimistically, 'but I think the worst is well behind us.' 'We're already 300 miles east of Tobruk', he concluded gleefully, 'British road and rail system in first-class order!'[22]

The arrivals and departures that occurred at the moment he wrote, suggested that many of those most closely concerned with the Mediterranean conflict believed that matters were teetering on the brink. Mussolini left Italy to take up residence in Libya. He brought with him all the paraphernalia necessary for a full-scale victory parade in Cairo, including the obligatory white horse as seen when he had last unsheathed the sword of Islam. Much more furtively, the leader of the Green Shirts and his German minders slipped out of Berlin bound for Istanbul. Their mission was to get a message to Farouk: fly now to Rommel and your throne is guaranteed under the new order.[23] Churchill, too, decided that he would have to go to Cairo.[24] The Mediterranean had been left semi-detached for exactly two years of war. The expedient of having a member of the War Cabinet permanently based in Cairo was no longer sufficient. He needed to impose his will directly and in person.

The remnants of the British fleet abandoned Alexandria. All that remained was France's Force X. It was entirely plausible that the only battleships left in the eastern Mediterranean would ally themselves with the Nazis.[25] Panic gripped Cairo the next day, christened 'Ash Wednesday'. The war correspondent Alan Moorehead, married to the secretary of a senior officer, described how 'a thin mist hung over the British Embassy by the Nile and over the sprawling blocks of GHQ – huge quantities of secret documents were being burnt'. Moorehead observed 'all day a group of privates shovelled piles of maps, lists of figures, reports, estimates, codes and messages into four blazing bonfires in a vacant square between the GHQ buildings'.[26] The head of SIME, Raymond Maunsell, who himself stayed in the city, noted contemptuously that, 'it is among the Europeans, Levantines and Jews that panic has reared its head'.[27] Attempts to prepare a resistance movement for Axis Egypt foundered when the officials in charge 'insisted on being evacuated from Egypt with the general exodus'.[28]

The Egyptians themselves stayed firmly put. They had no need to commit themselves. Two pilots of the Egyptian air force did fly over to the Axis lines, although one was killed by German flak. The Germans had been told to expect two pilots as emissaries of Farouk. They were thus surprised and disappointed when the survivor denounced the King as a 'Turk' who cared only for his own self-enrichment and demanded that they should assist in the creation of a 'new order' in Egypt. Both British and Egyptians were alarmed enough by this 'extraordinary incident' that they drained the fuel from all the aeroplanes of the Egyptian air force and finally interned Abbas Halim, the speed-machine-obsessed prince of the Borsa incident. King Farouk himself turned a deaf ear to British suggestions of refuge in the Sudan. His reply to German messages was that he would hide in his own country, avoid capture and await Rommel. Farouk said to the British that he intended to emulate the King of the Belgians. That monarch had abruptly surrendered his country once the Germans had arrived and then remained to collaborate in the occupation. Such was the seriousness of the situation that this stance was regarded as not too bad for the British cause.[29]

Farouk's caution proved wise, just as Mussolini's burst of enthusiasm was premature. Rommel reached the final British defensive line and stalled. As he himself said, 'one loses all idea of time here'. The Alamein position emphasized the importance of the Mediterranean coast like no other place on the littoral. All who came to Alamein, itself a flyblown railway station, remarked on the beauty of the landscape. The Mediterranean there was a special colour of turquoise blue, the beach was startlingly snow white. The pristine beauty of the coastline, almost a parody of the imagined Mediterranean, was mocked by the ugliness inland. Beyond the dunes of the beach, the fine sand was replaced by grey salt flats so cratered that they 'looked as the surface of the moon might be'. The flats in turn were succeeded by ultramarine salt lakes and then by the yellow hogsback of Alamein ridge itself. Beyond the ridge was desert, then the second ridge of Ruweisat, then desert and then the Depression, where stark cliffs descended to the soft sand bed of a long-lost prehistoric sea. The Depression made impossible the kind of desert dash that had undone the Gazala line. The result was a straight slugging match on a limited front.

The previous two years had been marked by spectacular coups, as either side rushed hundreds of miles forward and hundreds of miles back along the Libyo-Egyptian coast. Much happened but little moved in July 1942. The Axis attacked six times, the British counter-attacked six times, neither moved anywhere. After two weeks, Auchinleck's intelligence chief concluded that 'Rommel has shot his bolt by coming so far across the desert'.[30] The Italian generals, too, began to mutter that 'whoever stops in the desert is truly lost'.[31] Rommel came to the same conclusion a week later. On 18 July 1942 he signalled, in a message read with some gratitude by the codebreakers, that he could go no further because British attacks on coastal traffic had starved him of the necessary supplies. Mussolini left Africa immediately, cursing his lying generals, his Rommel-philia cured for good.

In the three weeks between Mussolini's departure from Libya and Churchill's arrival in Egypt the whole definition of the Mediterranean world changed. Mussolini and Churchill had conceived their journeys within a few days of one another in late June 1942. Then they had been of one mind. The war in the Mediterranean, they believed, had reached its tipping point. What the Germans called the *schwerpunkt* was to be found in the Libyan-Egyptian borderlands. There was a good chance that the Italo-Germans might win. Churchill's grand conclave in Cairo no longer believed in any of these propositions. The very manner of his arrival suggested the difference between past and future. For Mussolini, little changed between 1937 and 1942: same route, same aircraft, same white horse. Churchill came in much grander style. He was conveyed by the most sophisticated type of American aircraft, the Consolidated B-24, known to the British as the Liberator. This remarkable aeroplane had no need of the old Mediterranean stop-overs. It did not even bother to fly over the Mediterranean. It took off from Gibraltar and flew at high level, and at high speed, across North Africa, depositing its distinguished passenger, 'in excellent form having apparently had a very comfortable and easy journey', in Cairo.[32]

The best known and most public decision Churchill took in Cairo was to dismiss Auchinleck for not being up to the job. He imported a successor, Harold Alexander, the defender of Dunkirk and Burma, previously untouched by Mediterranean warfare. A simple change in personnel was not necessarily the nub of the matter. Immediately on arrival, Alan Brooke recorded: 'we discussed the relative importance of Egypt as opposed to Abadan and all agreed that the latter's importance was paramount'.[33] Abadan was the great Anglo-Iranian oil-refining complex on the Persian Gulf. As a result of its products, easily tankered around Arabia to Egypt, the British forces were awash with fuel. They could even afford to regard the pipeline that ran from the northern Iraqi oil fields to Haifa as little more than a convenience for refuelling the fleet. Those gathered in Cairo knew full well, on the other hand, that the long-predicted fuel crisis of the Third Reich had arrived in the summer of 1942. Until then fuel problems in the Mediterranean had meant the difficulty of shipping petrol from Italy to North Africa. From June 1942 onwards, the Axis suffered not only a crisis of transportation but a crisis of supply. The most obvious Mediterranean manifestation of this crisis was that the *Regia Marina* ran out of fuel for its battleships. There was no problem getting fuel oil to their bases; Germany had simply stopped supplying any, pleading more pressing commitments. The Mediterranean Fleet was still devoid of battle-ships but so too now were the Italians.[34]

At the end of July 1942 the Germans began their 'oil offensive', the drive for the Caucasian oil centres of Maikop and Grozny. As the British discussed future developments in early August, it seemed that the 'oil offensive' was likely to succeed. German forces were brushing aside Soviet opposition. Once the Germans were over the Caucasus mountains, they could fight for Iranian and Iraqi oil, whatever happened in the Mediterranean.[35] One did not have to be in possession of secret intelligence to understand the threat. The press carried interviews with German POWs who made much the same point. 'We are not going to attempt to conquer all Russia,' boasted a captured *Luftwaffe* flyer in perfect English, but 'come through the Caucasus and take Iraq, Iran, and probably Egypt. Then we will offer you peace.'[36] Such an alternative strategic future made the British question where the Mediterranean war began and ended. Churchill's answer was the Suez Canal. Everyone to the east of the Canal could ignore the Mediterranean and turn their eyes north, either to the Caucasus or to Turkey. Commanders west of the line – the Near East in Churchill's unique definition – could continue to concentrate on the Mediterranean littoral. He was talked out of such a drastic division of responsibilities. The eastern shore of the Mediterranean had been organized as just that, not as some kind of heartland bulwark. In the end Churchill confined himself to lopping Iran and Iraq out of Middle East Command, confirming rather than reversing the essential unity of the affairs of the littoral.[37]

It is indicative of Churchill's priorities that once he had settled matters in Cairo, the next destinations for his Liberator were Teheran, and then Moscow. Even before he left Cairo, however, the hand of the Mediterranean traditionalists had been strengthened by the reassertion of the old certainty that the war hinged on the east–west and north–south passage on the sea. As Churchill conferred in Cairo, another major convoy, authorized before he had left London, set sail for Malta. 'All attention', wrote Ciano in Rome, 'is concentrated on the battle in the Mediterranean. It appears that things are developing rather well for us.'[38] The convoy's organization made clear that the Royal Navy in the Mediterranean was now little more than a husk. An incredibly powerful escort, including two battleships and four aircraft-carriers, was assembled, but this was a one-off task force made up of ships seconded from the Home Fleet, and even the Far East, specifically for this one mission. The experiences of the Mediterranean Fleet's cruisers in June 1942 made any thought of a convoy from the east unrealistic. The Mediterranean's cruiser ace, Philip Vian, was reduced to assembling a few ships from Haifa and Port Said and leading them out, empty, solely as a decoy. Even with this diversion, and deprived of their battleships, the Axis commanders could deploy formidable forces against the true convoy.

On their map of the Mediterranean they drew four lines. Line one ran between Algiers and Majorca. Submarines would attack the convoy along that line. On line two, the Skerki channel, between Bizerta and the Skerki bank, a force of Italian submarines deployed. Line three was drawn between Cape Bon and Pantelleria, where squadrons of torpedo boats would attack. The final line lay beyond Pantelleria; there a squadron of cruisers was to ambush and finish off the survivors. All along the route the *Luftwaffe* and the *Regia Aeronautica* would attack the convoy, first from Sardinia, then from Italy. The Italians also threw a 'secret weapon' into the mix: a radio-controlled bomber packed with explosives, designed to crash into the decks of aircraft-carriers. Lines one and two worked almost to perfection. On line one a German submarine torpedoed and sank the aircraft-carrier *Eagle*. Just before the capital ship escort turned back at the entrance to the Skerki channel, the last Sardinian mission of the day, flown by German Stukas, crippled the flight deck of a second aircraft-carrier. The 'secret weapon' malfunctioned and crashed in Algeria. On the second line, nine ships were hit by submarines and aircraft. The commander of the Italian submarines accurately reported 'a line of burning ships'. At midnight the convoy hit the third line. Only ten miles off the Tunisian coast it was illuminated by the French lighthouse on Cape Bon. The waves of Italian and German torpedo boats sank a further five ships. The last victim, a tanker, exploded in a 500-foot pillar of flame. It was only on the fourth line that the Axis plans misfired. The cruisers, fearing a night battle, withdrew without engaging; two were sunk on their way home by a British submarine. The failure of the Italian cruisers to finish the job, it is argued, spared Malta. Five of the original fourteen merchant ships reached Malta between 13 and 15 August 1942, including crucially an oil tanker dragged in by two destroyers with an Italian Stuka still impaled on its deck.[39]

The military commanders whom Churchill left behind in Cairo pointed out that the grand strategies discussed during the Prime Minister's visit were not necessarily relevant: the future lay not in great imagined sweeps across the Caucasus in months to come but in what happened in the Mediterranean in days to come. 'Jumbo' Wilson, although appointed to head the Persia–Iraq command, headed west rather than east, taking command of the force that would fight on in Egypt if Rommel destroyed the field army at Alamein.[40] The Malta convoy, the Chiefs of Staff admitted, had failed. The best that could be achieved would be for the island to go down fighting. It was of 'supreme importance' that Malta should use all its remaining fuel in a 'bee sting' even if it meant that the island could no longer survive.[41]

The British commanders in the Mediterranean were not the only ones unhappy at a new conception of their region. In Rome, relations between the Axis's Arab allies broke down on the same issue. The Grand Mufti and Rashid Ali, the former leader of pro-Nazi forces in Iraq, had been glowering at each other for some time. The Mufti used his inside track with the Nazi hierarchy to peddle the myth, found in the pages of Lawrence of Arabia and John Buchan, that there was a secret Arab network controlling Islam. In the Mufti's version the network was organized on the Führer principle, and he was that Führer. Rashid Ali, he told the Germans, was merely an unthinking tool used by the grand conspiracy. To Rashid Ali's chagrin the story stuck. The money which the Mufti extracted from both Germans and Italians allowed him to disburse gratuities to the exile community in Istanbul, the watching post for those hoping to take advantage of British collapse, winning them to his side. The Nazis became so keen on the Mufti that they sought to change his racial profile. He could not be an Arab, 'since pure Arab blood could not have been so consistent and systematic in the struggle against the English and the Jews'. Various racial identities were suggested before Hitler settled the matter by declaring that he was a blond and blue-eyed Aryan, spoilt only slightly by Arab miscegenation, whose ancestors had come to Palestine in Roman times. All was going well for the Mufti, until the strategic calculations of high summer allowed Rashid Ali to turn the tables on him, albeit temporarily.[42]

The Germans announced that the Arabs training in Greece would be transferred to the Caucasus to pave the way through their co-religionists, eventually all the way to Iraq. Rashid Ali was happy to acquiesce to the scheme and was rewarded by a summons to Berlin. The Mufti was horrified and was left in Rome. Needing to shift the emphasis back to the Mediterranean – where he had hopes of North Africa as well as his traditional stamping ground in the Levant – he was forced to oppose German plans and back those of the Italians, for a *Centro Militare Arabia*. Although he willingly visited the training camp near Rome to enthuse its members for the Axis cause, it did not really meet his needs. The Mufti wanted an Arab Legion, Arabic in language, Muslim in religion, operating from Italy into the Levant. The Italians envisaged a composite of Arabs and the children of committed Italian Fascist 'fourth shore' residents sent home for indoctrination. When these recruits were parachuted into Syria later in the year the British were impressed with their quality in contrast to the 'unintelligents' previously used. Such Christian half-breeds were of no use to the Mufti. He had to wait impatiently for months before the Germans reconsidered their enthusiasm for the Caucasus.[43]

The Mufti, the Italians, the *Abwehr* and their clients in Istanbul still had their eyes firmly on the Levant, whatever the dictates of grand strategy. The balance of power in Syria and Lebanon was visibly on the cusp. According to an American appreciation, 'situation in Middle East Command seriously deteriorated due to long-continued Axis success, efficacy Axis propaganda, conflict between Jewish and Arabic aspirations, extent of fifth column activities, acute lack of foodstuffs, contributing to instability of puppet governments, native hostility to French (whether Vichy or Free), native distrust of British, and, finally acute crisis in Syria and Lebanon in relations between British and French military authorities.'[44] Churchill was pursued to Cairo by Charles de Gaulle. Pausing but briefly to celebrate the heroism of Bir Hacheim, de Gaulle soon injected himself – to the Prime Minister's visible annoyance – into the discussions. His main message was a bitter denunciation of Sir Edward Spears. Spears had returned to the Levant, setting up shop in Beirut, in the spring of 1942. He had a complex mandate. He was a diplomat, holding the position of minister to Syria and Lebanon. As head of the 'Spears Mission' he was the representative of the Minister of State in Cairo in the Levant. His informal influence stemmed from his personal relationship with Churchill. His visible power emerged as the franchisee of the Middle East Supply Centre: as such he was the arbiter of food supplies.[45] His real mission, according to de Gaulle, was to destroy French power in the Levant. De Gaulle's allegations against Spears were true. Spears had started out as a champion of the Free French. Prolonged acquaintance had made him hate them. He had concluded that they had no intention of fighting the Germans; only of sucking the life blood from the British. As one of his staff wrote home, 'he had never known what was meant by animals eating their young until he had seen Sir Edward Spears devouring the Free French movement'.[46]

The particular issue that strained relations the most in the summer of 1942 was the attempt to create a force that might defend Syria if victorious German armies poured into the Levant from south or north. The British proposed that Syria should have its own native 'Home Guard'. Catroux and Collet agreed that this was a splendid idea; indeed, they were 'unusually co-operative'. The reason for their accommodating attitude gradually became clearer. The Frenchmen insisted that the British should hand over funds and allow them to raise indigenous troops as they saw fit. The Free French intended, Jumbo Wilson wrote on the eve of his departure from the Levant, 'to make as much political propaganda as possible out of the scheme by putting about that the whole idea is Free French, that they wish to arm the country against the invaders, and that they are responsible for bringing the benefits to the towns and villages, and, in fact, belittling the British altogether'. The whole scheme foundered in the face of such obstructionism. 'I despair', Clayton said, 'of ever achieving anything in Syria in face of the ridiculous and obstructive vanity and *amour propre* of the French.'[47]

The distrustful atmosphere created by Catroux was as nothing to that left in de Gaulle's wake. Failing to achieve satisfaction from Churchill in Cairo, de Gaulle descended on the Levant with a message of defiance. He spent a month touring every major town in Syria and Lebanon. At each stop on his grand tour he gave much the same speech. Whatever the people may have heard, whatever promises Catroux had made, the notables should get used to one thing: the French were staying. De Gaulle issued vitriolic denunciations of the British in private: they were saboteurs whose actions benefited only the Axis. He made no criticism in public. He did not have to. His speeches were notable for the fact that they did not mention the British at all. The fact that they had defeated Vichy, insisted upon national independence and were the current occupying power was airbrushed out of de Gaulle's account. Both by his words and his silences, de Gaulle made it clear that Britain was nothing, France was everything.

De Gaulle was pursued by increasingly urgent requests, turning into orders, that he should leave Syria. Sensing his time was short, he made his claims explicit in an ultimatum. Britain, he declared, had no military power left in the Levant. Their 9th Army was not any army at all, but merely office boys, incapable of fighting; or, even worse, anti-French agitators hiding behind their uniforms. The true military power in the Levant was France. It was time for the British to leave. He would give them ten days to do so. The army had become used to subtle taunts and insults from the French, but this was a bit rich. Britain had 44,000 troops in Syria. These troops were supported by heavy equipment and air power. The Free French could boast some lightly equipped native levies. The British did not think that, if it came to a fight, there would be much of a contest. Met with refusal verging on derision, de Gaulle was finally persuaded to leave the country. The Free French movement had much to lose, some of his advisers argued. They might push the British so far that they would attack French influence throughout the eastern Mediterranean; cooperation was much more fruitful. De Gaulle dismissed those who gave such advice. All the good done by Koenig at Bir Hacheim was undone by de Gaulle in Beirut.[48]

De Gaulle's most ardent supporters lamented that he had played into Spears's hands.[49] Even Spears deprecated the idea of turning the British military on their French opposite numbers. The external threat of the Axis still bound them together in some kind of community of interest. Faced with Rommel, the last thing the British military wanted was a crisis in Syria. Spears sought other instruments to do his work. The most effective way of destroying French influence that he could find was to turn to indigenous nationalist politicians. Those he found in place disappointed him. Even those who indulged in nationalist rhetoric were bound into the French system.[50] In the end they would be bought and sold by French gold. Spears needed politicians who genuinely wanted to be rid of the French. The trouble was that those politicians of influence, with truly Francophobe credentials, were those who had most enthusiastically embraced the coming of the Nazis. This problem gave him little pause. In the summer of 1942 he instructed his political officers to recruit former *Abwehr* agents of influence to the British cause. He found willing collaborators. In Lebanon, Spears formed a close relationship with Riad Solh.[51] In September 1942 Shukri al-Quwwatli returned from exile.[52] A minor by-blow of these Levantine machinations was yet another crisis in secret operations. Spears saw SOE as a useful adjunct to his plans to subvert the French. The army in the Levant saw them as dangerously unpredictable.[53] The head of SOE in Syria and Palestine was removed at military insistence.[54]

SOE's plots against the French might have been forgiven, but when added to charges of plots against other allies they added up to a significant charge sheet. With Churchill in Cairo, the Greek government in exile issued a denunciation of British conduct in the city. Having spent three months in Egypt himself, Emanuel Tsouderos claimed that he had had the opportunity to make a thorough investigation of British conduct. He found it disgraceful. Incidents such as the 'Free Voice of Greece' broadcasts were customarily blamed on 'rogue' Greeks, leftists whose skills and contacts had allowed them to slip through the security net. Such explanations, Tsouderos claimed, were mere cover stories.[55] Foreigners making accusations against British officials usually received short shrift. Tsouderos, however, was heard sympathetically in London. There was general agreement that the Cairo special forces mission had gone seriously awry, indeed that the conditions in the Mediterranean had come close to creating a 'rogue' operation.[56]

At the same time as Churchill was in Cairo, publicly sacking generals and replacing them with men from outside the Mediterranean, the secret services were surreptitiously doing the same. The 'old gang' were deployed to posts as far from the Mediterranean as their superiors could find. The new head of SOE, flown in from London, said that it was his ambition to organize a system so orderly that the Mediterranean would come to resemble Scandinavia.[57] Without the old gang, their clients had little chance of finding favour. Kanellopoulos, for instance, was presented as a potential leader to a reluctant Churchill in Cairo but had failed to impress. The seriousness with which Churchill regarded him can be gauged from his bath-time reaction to entreaties to meet the senior Greek politician in the Mediterranean. 'Winston,' recorded the head of the Foreign Office, 'who had a sponge in his hand, tossed it into the air saying: Canellopoulos – can't-ellopoulos – can-ellopoulos – can't-ellopoulos (on the principle of blowing petals off a daisy), ending up Canellopoulos, so Canellopoulos was asked to lunch today.'[58] The post-prandial verdict was that he was a 'not very inspiring specimen'.[59]

In August 1942 arguments, however bitter, about the nature of Britain's 'hidden hand' in Greece, or indeed anywhere else around the Mediterranean, were fairly academic. Towards the end of the month, Axis forces did begin to detect opposition to their rule, but they attributed little or any of it to British action. As in the previous year, the main problem was starvation around the Mediterranean basin. In 1941 the Germans and Italians had done nothing to prevent famine, whereas the British sought to lessen its impact in their areas. The pattern repeated itself in 1942. The spring of 1942 was cold, pushing back the harvest to the end of June.[60] Instead of aiding supply the Germans demanded 'astronomical indemnities'.[61] On his way back from Libya, Mussolini had stopped over in Athens; even he had been convinced that German rapacity was building up trouble for the future. The most forceful of the quisling Greek leaders, Gotzamanis, wailed that 'Greece can no longer yield anything for the simple and clear reason it has nothing to offer'. The government in Athens was desperate for control of the harvest; food was their last remaining asset.[62] Rural populations had no desire to disgorge their harvest for the convenience of the cities. Violence ensued between purchasing agents and farmers, *gendarmes* and 'brigands'. At the end of August, Italian troops intervened for the first time. If the countryside was not ripe with food, it was fertile for mischief-makers and preachers of social revolution. The military-political class whom the British had attempted to court by radio and courier, however, was supine. Only the truly desperate took to the road. Odysseus told the story of a Venizelist officer and adventurer called Napoleon Zervas who had attempted to extort money from Prometheus II, flush with British sovereigns, at gunpoint.[63] The naval officer coolly replied that if he did not flee to the bands in the hills within ten days he would be denounced to the Gestapo.[64] There were armed bands but there was no resistance. Only the prospect of Axis defeat would make sense of anything other than local and defensive violence.

The tipping point was the failure of Rommel's final attack on Egypt. The military events at the end of August 1942 were later written off as a minor prelude for what came after. For observers around the contemporary Mediterranean, however, the decisive battle of the war was Alam Halfa. On the eve of the battle there had been a heightened air of expectancy. Rommel had been confident. The tanks, aircraft and reinforcements that he had demanded had been ferried across the Mediterranean. He was able to fit out, and rest, both his German and Italian units. By the end of August 1942, Rommel had the most powerful force he had ever commanded, raring to go. He was happy with his own plans for fighting the battle. As usual he intended to decoy the British into defending the coast, whilst looping into the desert with the *Afrika Korps* and the Italian armoured divisions to take the British defensive position on Alam Halfa ridge from the south. The only fly in the ointment was the enemy's preternatural ability to sink oil tankers. During the battle of Alam Halfa, sinking reached a crescendo. But as Kesselring later pointed out, the battle was lost at the tactical, not the Mediterranean level: the *Panzerarmee* had enough fuel to fight the battle, the problem would have come in exploiting the breakthrough. Since Rommel did not break through, the point became moot.

Thanks to their codebreakers the British knew that he was coming. As Rommel's shock troops prepared their speciality, the surprise night attack, on 30 August 1942 they were immediately illuminated by flares, 'the whole valley with its mass of the *Afrika Korps* stationary was lit up like a huge orange fairyland'. In his first, and possibly most important, command decision, Britain's new leader at the battlefront, Bernard Montgomery, installed as part of the shake-up ordered by Churchill, told his commanders to dig in their tanks in protected reverse slope positions. On no account were they to venture out into 'a wild goose chase on to the muzzles of the waiting 88 mm guns as Rommel had so often managed to make his enemy do in the past'. Fighting a defensive battle from their entrenched positions the imperial forces reduced Rommel's assault to a bloody ruin.[65]

Those close to the action had no doubts about Alam Halfa's importance. Ciano declared that defeat was now inevitable. They knew that it had been Rommel's best chance to break through. The British were going to complete the conquest of North Africa and then come after Italy. Italy had to 'find a way out' through agreement with the British.[66] Such views eventually cost Ciano dismissal and, ultimately, execution. His opposite number at the other end of the Mediterranean, Serrano Súñer, paid more immediately. Franco sacked the brother-in-law who had treated him like a 'moronic servant'. When an Italian submarine made it to Spain full of dead and wounded it was 'for all practical purposes interned'. Under Serrano such 'submarines could come and go into Spanish ports as if they were public parks'.[67]

The tocsin sounded elsewhere around the basin too. Prometheus II began transmitting requests for the British to parachute special forces into Greece. Similar radio traffic also hummed to, from and around Yugoslavia. Mihailovic had, unwittingly, been broadcasting the Chetniks' Mediterranean vision for some time. The Chetniks were Serb nationalists. Serbia's most notable feature was its lack of a Mediterranean coastline.

The news of Alam Halfa was causing mass desertions from the Ustasha Croatian army. The real prize would be the land between the Dalmatian coast and the Serbian border. Whenever the British landed in Dalmatia their Chetnik allies should be there to welcome them, and claim the territory.[68] The problem was the godless Partisans. But Tito was in the wilds of north-west Bosnia, uncontactable from anywhere in the Mediterranean. The best way to deal with this situation, Mihailovic believed, was a short-term alliance with the Germans and the Italians who, in turn, could be betrayed when the British drew near. The recipients of these musings were not the British, but rather the Germans and the Italians, whose radio interception units were busily decoding Mihailovic's messages to his sub-commanders. Each responded differently to Mihailovic's vision. The *Wehrmacht*'s south-eastern commanders were constrained by Hitler's partiality to Pavelic. They declared that previous flirtations with the Chetniks were nothing more than 'weakness'. They were to be crushed with the same vigour as the Partisans. Mihailovic would be hunted down and executed. Roatta's *Supersloda*, by contrast, met with Chetnik commanders to offer an alliance: fight the Partisans together, and discuss what to do about the British if they ever arrived.[69] German accusations against Roatta were heard widely around the Mediterranean. 'Roatta is an arch-enemy of Germany,' General von Thoma, a recently captured *Afrika Korps* commander, said to a CSDIC bug.[70] At a loss to make up their mind about the situation, the British decided to parachute missions into Yugoslavia as they had already parachuted them into Greece.

NINE

Of Worms and Frenchmen

When the Americans started to discuss the possibility of invading North Africa, some people within the bowels of the War Department concluded that a more scientific approach to Mediterranean warfare would be needed than had been hitherto imagined. Casting around for such an approach, they fell on the new discipline of opinion polling, developed in the 1930s mainly so that the popularity of Hollywood's movies could be assessed.[1] The scientific soldiers consulted the leading experts in the field. The experts pointed out that little could be done in terms of quantitative polls. There were no pollsters in North Africa, and suspicious regimes, perched on the shores of a war zone, were hardly likely to endorse a large-scale experiment with unpredictable results. On the other hand a smaller-scale effort involving qualitative methods might be possible. One would need to identify a 'focus group'. These individuals could then be taken through a detailed questionnaire about the war and its likely, or desirable, outcomes.

There still remained the obstacle of finding pollsters, but that did not prove to be insuperable. The American government had taken a considerable interest in the fate of France. That interest reached to the highest levels of the American government. America's former ambassador to Vichy, Admiral Leahy, whilst retaining his interest, had recently been given an even more important task, as the personal representative of the President, to be the first chairman of the newly created Joint Chiefs of Staff. Leahy's erstwhile deputy with specific responsibility for French North Africa, Robert Murphy, now became the senior American representative on French territory. Although a professional diplomat, Murphy had for long been associated with the seedier, spying end of his calling. As the arbiter of food supplies from America to France, Murphy was only a phonecall away from the great men of Vichy. As time went by, Murphy became less concerned with comestibles and more interested in conspiracies. In 1942 he was reinforced by a group of amateur spies, appointed as 'vice-consuls'.[2]

It fell to the vice-consuls, and their contacts, to carry out the polling. Those questioned lived in French and Spanish Morocco, including the international city of Tangier. The interviewees in French Morocco declared themselves anti-German, anti-British and pro-American. Most believed that an American-led coalition would win the war. The results in Spanish Morocco were quite different. Only a 'small minority – twenty per cent – think that the Allies will win', the pollsters discovered. A larger group, thirty per cent, believed that the Germans were still on course to win the war, and 'about half the population doesn't know what to think'. It was argued at the time that Spanish Morocco, the Francoist heartland, was not a particularly representative territory. The American analysts concluded that French Morocco was a much better gauge of North African opinion. They convinced themselves that the Americans would be welcomed ashore with garlands. Yet if the tests captured anything for posterity, it was a deep sense of ambivalence.

Another means of testing popular opinion produced similar results. The village of Thibar lay in the Medjerda valley, in the hill region of the Tunisian-Algerian border. The main road to Tunis ran along the valley. As a result Thibar became, by chance, the subject of an *ad hoc* oral history project when Allied war correspondents settled there for some months at the beginning of 1943. The settlers told of their own mixed feelings when they heard that Algeria had been invaded. On the one hand they hated the Italians, 'the macaronis', and worried that the Germans might be a little too keen on the Arabs. On the other hand they were happy with their lot. Their land was beautiful, well kept and fertile. Their produce and livestock commanded excellent prices. They had no desire to see a war ruin things. They doubted that the Germans would be defeated, even if they suffered setbacks. In their mind, the north–south link across the Mediterranean remained indissoluble; they found it hard to imagine any situation other than the Germans controlling the northern shore. All along the littoral, people referred back rather than looking forwards. Their points of reference were the Anglo-Gaullist fiasco at Dakar in 1940 and Syrian war of 1941 rather than the brilliant series of amphibious assaults that subsequently came to characterize the Anglo-American way in war.[3]

The design of the American opinion poll was a reflection of how they regarded the problem of North Africa. They started off from the point of view that North Africa was not in the Mediterranean, and that the Mediterranean was not very important to them. The exercise was confined to the two Moroccos because Morocco had the important coastline, running from the Straits of Gibraltar, not east into the Mediterranean, but west and south down the Atlantic seaboard, the coastline that faced America. The Americans were willing to be convinced that there should be a North African operation to divert attention from British defeat in the Mediterranean – the US general Dwight Eisenhower was appointed to command the mission whilst Churchill was in Cairo sacking failed British commanders – but they wanted to capture something worthwhile, with the least possible effort. The British, in part because they accepted that they were more unpopular in North Africa than the Nazis, were willing to let the Americans take the lead in an invasion, acting, as Churchill put it, as their 'handmaids'. They were not willing to concede, however, that an invasion of North Africa was only indirectly connected with the Mediterranean. Their purpose was to seize the southern littoral, in particular Bizerta, 'the key', and thus reopen the Mediterranean once more to through traffic. The two sides bickered about the question throughout August 1942. Alam Halfa was once more the turning point: as soon as the 8th Army had won its victory, Churchill and Roosevelt struck a deal. There would be three main landings: Casablanca on the Atlantic; Oran and Algiers in the Mediterranean.

The British had dealt with the French for long enough to be convinced that they would have to fight for North Africa at the same time as they were fighting Rommel: Tunisia would be the next Syria. The Americans thought that they might have North Africa without fighting. Murphy had a string of supposedly useful contacts in Algiers. But the true loyalty of these contacts was hard for the Americans to understand. The most promising 'robin hood' was General Charles Mast, chief of staff of the army in Algiers. Mast, however, wished to have nothing to do with the 'traitor' de Gaulle and his Fighting French. Instead the general's *éminence grise*, the businessman Jacques Lemaigre Dubreuil, unearthed an alternative leader, General Henri Giraud. Giraud had been captured by the Germans in 1940, escaped and now lived in open 'hiding' near Lyons. Apart from the fact that Giraud was brave, tall and distinguished, he was an almost entirely unknown quantity to non-Frenchmen. Neither were the 'robin hoods' themselves particularly knowable. Some kept in contact with Laval, others with Darlan. Some of the civilians working with Mast, on the other hand, particularly the Aboulker family, were strong for de Gaulle. Their Gaullism earned them suspicion; their Judaism made them even more suspect. As one of the vice-consuls observed, they had, 'God knows', set out to look for liberal-minded, pro-democratic Frenchmen; but they had found anti-Semitic reactionaries bound up in an alliance of convenience with desperate Vichy-hating Jews.[4]

It became clear that Darlan himself wanted to talk to the Americans, but his purpose was obscure. He flew into Oran in October 1942 in the friendly company of a German general. His purpose was to make a thorough inspection of coastal defences to ensure that an invasion was thrown back into the sea. Darlan's intermediaries told the Americans that he feared the *growth* of German power. The consolidation of their position in southern Russia had allowed them to send Kesselring significant reinforcements, accurately charted by Vichy intelligence. Perhaps, his messengers suggested, the Germans had their eye on expansion in Tunisia. Darlan himself told the Germans that he feared the *growth* of American ambitions. Perhaps, he said, they had their eye on expansion in Africa. Murphy himself was convinced that he could 'deliver' North Africa; many British observers doubted whether it was possible to trust the reliability, or indeed the authenticity, of any statements made by Frenchmen. They knew, for instance, that much of the tittle-tattle the Americans picked up was spread by a Polish intelligence agency, posing as porridge exporters, based in London.[5]

A few weeks after the invasion plan was finalized, and on the eve of the Alamein offensive, Murphy came up with a concrete offer. Mast wished to meet a senior American officer. Within days the remarkable decision to send in an undercover mission headed by Eisenhower's deputy, Mark Clark, was taken. Clark, one of nature's conspirators, was desperate for the *gloire* such an exploit would bring. The brilliant stories he brought back of the daring landing by submarine, the dangers of discovery, the risky escape back to sea, won him admirers, from Churchill to the journalists who wrote up his legend. The fact that an officer with a complete knowledge of all planning, including the invaluable hold the British had over German and Italian communications, was put in very great danger of capture was seemingly ignored. Clark crept ashore in Algeria on the night that Montgomery attacked at Alamein. The meeting with Mast, although interrupted by suspicious police, was cordial. The two men were, however, talking to cross-purposes. Clark implied that the landings were not imminent, but rather lay some months in the future. Mast imagined a prolonged period in which to suborn his fellow officers. Mast thought, too, that the invasion would be a Franco-American affair, with Giraud in command. Knowing the real situation but keen to please, Clark spoke glibly of a French 'supreme command' at the appropriate time.[6]

Even as the convoys sailed at the beginning of November 1942, however, their purpose was ambiguous. The broad-brush Churchill–Roosevelt agreement on landing sites left open the question of where the actual *schwerpunkt* of the operation lay. 'The essence of the operation', for the British, 'was the early capture of Tunisia', for the possession of Bizerta 'would threaten the Mediterranean position of the enemy'. British intelligence predicted that Spain would play little part in the unfolding of events. The most one might expect from the Francoists was an attempt to nibble away at disputed points of the border between the two Moroccos. The Spaniards would only move against Gibraltar if the Germans insisted, and backed their insistence with an army, air force and navy. Since Ultra-powered British intelligence had an excellent grasp of German deployment they predicted, accurately, that the Germans were not preparing for such an operation. The American Atlanticists would not let the matter rest; the supposed Spanish threat was a means of keeping the operation focused on the Straits of Gibraltar rather than Bizerta. The final plan for *Torch*, as the invasion was codenamed, implied that the most important target for the operation was French Morocco, which possessed no significant coastline on the Mediterranean.

The ambiguities of *Torch* were not confined to the relative importance of the Atlantic and Mediterranean coastlines. They spread out to sea as well. The commander of the naval operation was that old Mediterranean hand, ABC Cunningham, swapping the cap of Gog for that of Magog, hailed by Eisenhower as 'one of the finest men I have had the privilege of meeting'.[7] Cunningham came fresh from negotiations in Washington, to become, in the new Americanized terminology, NCXF, Naval Commander Expeditionary Force. Cunningham's new command stretched far out into the Atlantic, for the American assault force was coming straight across the ocean onto the Moroccan coast. As a result of his appointment, the planners had to decide where the western Mediterranean ended. A line was drawn from Cape Bon across to the islet of Marittimo, with a short dog-leg to Trapani, the westernmost Axis air base on Sicily. The infamous Skerki Bank, beyond which no British capital ships had dared sail for years, was included. The chosen line split Tunisia in two: the northern coast, including Bizerta and Tunis, lay within the western Mediterranean, whereas the east coast was placed within the eastern Mediterranean. Also firmly in the eastern Mediterranean was Malta.

There were elements of both calculation and accident as to the degree that the two halves of the Mediterranean were divided from each other. The British were reluctant to see American influence too far to the east. Alan Brooke had a furious row with Churchill on the eve of El Alamein when he 'discovered that Winston, after giving me a solemn undertaking that he would not tell anybody what I had told him about details of impending Middle East attack, had calmly told Eisenhower'. Brooke argued that 'he had no reason whatever to tell Eisenhower, this attack did not concern him in the least'. El Alamein and *Torch* were concerted by little more than the 'newspaper reporter' in Churchill.[8] Even when the British sought close cooperation things did not go as planned. A few days before *Torch* was due to begin on 8 November 1942, Bletchley Park switched on its link to Gibraltar. Eisenhower's headquarters was to receive all the Ultra intelligence from around the Mediterranean. Within minutes the link started to spew out decrypts on Mediterranean shipping and air movement. This priceless information had been systematized to the highest degree in Cairo, Alexandria and Heliopolis. It had not been systematized at all in Gibraltar. Eisenhower's staff could not cope. For *Torch*, rumour and conspiracy triumphed over scientific intelligence.[9]

Brooke claimed that he did not want Eisehhower informed about the attack at El Alamein because he did not trust the Americans to keep the information safe. Distrust ran deeper than details of operational security, however. The very same ideas that had led to 'handmaiden' status in the western Mediterranean, the supposed distinction between disinterested, popular Americans and discredited imperialistic Britons, were floated in the east as well. 'The people of the area', the Americans told the British, 'seem to realise that the United States has no territorial or political interest there, and, due largely to a century of American missionary, educational and philanthropic efforts, there is widespread goodwill towards the United States.' Regretfully, their British opposite numbers conceded that these claims were probably true.[10] Cairo and

Beirut saw an influx of Americans. American bombers operated from Egyptian airfields, and an American military mission oversaw supplies both to them and the British forces. American officials joined the Middle East Supply Council and started to take an interest in where and how civil aid was delivered.

In mid-1942, 'Wild Bill' Donovan finally succeeded in his campaign to create an American central intelligence agency, the Office of Strategic Services.[11] Donovan, aware of the suspicion with which the military, diplomats and politicians regarded OSS, was desperate for quick success to demonstrate OSS's mettle. He had already written that the eastern Mediterranean was 'wide open and ripe for plucking'. OSS opened its Cairo office in September 1942. Although Donovan signed a 'treaty' with his opposite numbers in SOE, ceding leadership in the eastern Mediterranean in return for leadership in the west, he had no intention of holding to it once American agents arrived in force. In the interim the spies and diplomats agreed that they needed a figurehead to compete with the British Minister of State in Cairo. They suggested to Roosevelt that one his personal friends, Harold Hoskins, would be most suitable for the posting. Hoskins represented exactly that class of men whom the Americans assumed the people of the Levant would love. The son of Christian missionaries, he had been born in Beirut. In adulthood he made his fortune as a cotton trader, a calling that had taken him around the Mediterranean basin.[12]

As it turned out, Hoskins disappointed some of Donovan's expectations.[13] He proved unexpectedly sympathetic to the British. Hoskins's view of the eastern Mediterranean, as might have been expected from one with his 'colonial' background, chimed closely with the old practitioners of the 'hidden hand' such as Illtyd Clayton, with whom he got along famously. The first American take on how they might become a power in the Levant thus concluded that the best way forward was to use the same methods as the British and the French.[14]

Old-style thinking about the Mediterranean dominated German actions as well. The response of littoral populations showed how confusing a place the Mediterranean could be. The British made their biggest effort thus far to muddy the waters. Cunningham and his commanders were confident that they could get the convoys, comprising hundreds of ships, to the Mediterranean; however they were less sanguine about getting them to their targets once they entered the Mediterranean. Colonel Dudley Clarke, in charge of deception operations within the Mediterranean, was ordered to give *Torch* a great deal more thought than Alamein. In the east everyone knew that the British would attack and where they would go. The trick was tactical surprise. In the west more imagination was necessary for, as Clarke put it, 'the scene in Gibraltar [was like] the flying-deck of some gigantic carrier'. 'It seemed amazing', he worried, 'that German agents across the frontier line in Spain could not give Berlin a proper account of what was in store.'

The British could not disguise the fact that there was a super-convoy on its way into the Mediterranean. Instead they bent every effort into convincing the Germans that that convoy had some purpose in the east. All the deception agents Britain had set up over the previous two years started broadcasting that the convoy was heading first for Malta and then another, unspecified, target.[15] Hitler was particularly taken by the rumour of a landing in Crete, for he ordered Kesselring to pay as much attention to escorting supplies there as to Africa. Once, as expected, the *Luftwaffe* spotted the convoy, the Germans attempted to guess its destination. Their eventual assessment of its destination took Malta to be a certainty, a piece of coast between Benghazi and Tripoli as a probability, and Sicily and Sardinia as a possibility. The most important decision that resulted was an order to move the U-boats further east.[16] Indeed, *Torch* demonstrated the growing inconsequentiality of the still-feared German submarines. In August 1942 they had sunk the British aircraft-carrier *Eagle*. But their numbers were not increasing. Without a major influx of new craft from the Atlantic it was clear that a 'knockout blow' was beyond the submarines. The creator of the wolfpacks, Admiral Dönitz, newly promoted to head the German navy, shocked the Italians by announcing that U-boats 'have only a nuisance value'. Under orders from Hitler he would maintain the Mediterranean flotilla but, he said, it was more useful for carrying supplies than sinking ships.[17]

Despite the lack of detailed coordination, the chances of battle meant that military operations in east and west ended up dovetailing beautifully. The first phase of the El Alamein battle lasted a fortnight. British historians have shown an endless appetite for refighting it since. Subsequent accounts divide the battle into three parts: the initial attack, or 'break-in'; a period of confused fighting known as the 'dog fight'; and the 'break-out', as the battle moved from the desert to the Mediterranean coast, and the Axis line finally gave way. The assumption is often made that Montgomery's superiority in numbers – nearly 200,000 imperial troops faced just over 100,000 Germans and Italians – made victory inevitable. Such neat divisions obscure the confusion that participants themselves felt. Montgomery 'confessed in conversation afterwards that the confident and assured way in which he talked during the first week of the battle had been assumed, and that towards the end of the first week he had actually felt that the battle might have been broken off, in face of stiff resistance he was meeting'. He believed that he, like many of his predecessors, was being lined up for the sack when Richard Casey travelled to his headquarters from Cairo. As in previous battles, the beautiful intelligence picture in the Mediterranean was obscured by the terrain away from the coast. 'Smoke and dust covered the battlefield,' observed one German report of the battle, 'and visibility became so bad that the general picture was of one immense cloud.'[18]

It was by no means clear who was winning until 4 November 1942, when the extent of Montgomery's 'vast victory' began to emerge. The previous day, Rommel received one of Hitler's notorious 'fight to the death' orders. Kesselring and Rommel had one of their tense conferences on the morning of 4 November. Both subsequently claimed that they had told the other that the Führer's order had to be disobeyed. Through the personal animus there was meeting of minds that the *Afrika Korps* would have to run for it, abandoning in large part their Italian allies in the *Panzerarmee Afrika*.[19] Stories began to spread of Germans and Italians fighting each other over trucks; the Italian infantry divisions were left 'in the middle of the desert, where masses of men are literally dying of hunger and thirst'.[20] The four days before *Torch*, comprised a pell-mell German flight to Mersa Matruh so rapid that the pursuing British forces were unable to catch them. At the moment of the *Torch* landings the Germans were getting their motor-cade across the Libyan border onto the *Balbia* and, they hoped, escape.

The major victim of British success, Italy, was quick to realize its significance. The Italians, unlike the Germans, had correctly predicted that the convoys that entered the Mediterranean were heading for North Africa. Indeed SIM actually overrated the Allies' capacity for concerted action. The resulting situation, they thought, would be 'extremely serious', with Italy becoming the 'centre of attack by the Allies in the offensive against

the Axis'. Only Mussolini saw the invasion of North Africa as an opportunity to indulge his long-held ambition of seizing Corsica. Tiredly, his
advisers explained that they had no capacity for an amphibious landing.
The *Duce*, however, insisted and a 'crazy' flotilla of light cutters was organized to take Italian troops over the short sea crossing – some thirty-five
miles across the Piombino Strait. Given the gimcrack nature of the enterprise they were relieved to find not even a 'gesture of opposition, at least
for the honour of the flag'.[21]

Corsica was notoriously inward-looking with, for an island, few
communities who looked to the sea, concentrating rather on its own
disputes and hatreds. In November 1942 the island seemed symbolic of
the French malaise. The Anglo-Americans struggled to understand
why the Frenchmen whom they encountered acted in the way they
did. On the Atlantic coast the Americans were unpleasantly surprised by
raging surf and French troops who tried to throw the invaders back into
the sea. In the Mediterranean the opaque politics of Algiers soon over-
took the military operations. A day into the invasion Eisenhower had
already concluded that 'all these Frogs have a single thought – ME'. 'It
isn't', he lamented from deep inside his Gibraltarian bunker, 'the operation that's wearing me down – it's the petty intrigue and the necessity
of dealing with little, selfish, conceited worms that call themselves men.'[22]

The 'worm' with whom Eisenhower had had to deal directly was
Giraud. The operation to smuggle him from Lyons to Gibraltar had gone
smoothly. Not so his arrival on the Rock. Giraud had informed his host
that he, Giraud, would be taking charge of military operations. Not only
was the liberation of France a task pre-eminently for a Frenchman but
he was superior in every way to Eisenhower. The 'junior' man should
give way to the senior. With his assault troops in the Mediterranean
and approaching their debarkation points, Eisenhower was locked in
a room for seven hours, disillusioning a man whom he concluded was a
fantasist.[23]

The Mediterranean *Torch* landings on 8 November 1942 provided a
study in contrasts. Anglo-American forces seized both of Algeria's main
ports, Algiers and Oran, in a two-day battle. In both places it was possible
to witness the almost casual landing of troops whilst, only a few miles
away, bloody and intense fighting was in progress. *Torch* was the first
major test of a new form of warfare: the use of landing craft in large
numbers to get ashore from specialist landing ships. Four hundred landing
craft were used in the landings at Algiers and Oran. 'We clambered down

the side,' wrote one American war correspondent of the experience, 'and down the landing nets into the landing craft, our way lighted by gun flashes as British battleships shelled the coastal batteries west of Algiers. When the landing craft left the transport there was a curious sensation of being alone.'[24]

A British infantry officer, clambering into the landing craft, noted that he was not really equipped for a hard assault landing:

There was the normal Field Service marching order, then the partially inflated 'Mae West' lifejacket, 48 hour rations in the two halves of my mess tins in the small pack, respirator, gas cape, ground sheet, full water bottle, binocular, compass, revolver and ammunition, two 36 grenades, maps, message pads and air photographs . . . my ash walking stick, spare pipes and about a pound of pipe tobacco. Worse was to follow, for when we were at sea we were told to carry a few extra things: a 'toggle' rope about six feet long to be draped over the shoulders for use should we have to climb cliffs; a 75 anti-tank mine to attach to my belt; then maps and silhouettes [of the beach]; some spare field dressings and, finally, a machete draped from my belt. Just before we were due to disembark, the CSM [asked] . . . 'Whether I could hang the wire cutters somewhere?' . . . Michelin Man was off to war![25]

Most of the landing craft cast off from their ships at about one o'clock in the morning. Many veered off course in the dark, getting stuck on shoals rather than their allotted beaches. They were lucky that the winter Mediterranean was benign that morning. By the evening of 8 November the wind and the swell off the North African coast had increased alarmingly, with over a quarter of landing craft, manned by inexperienced crews, being swamped and lost.[26] In the morning, however, 'Michelin man' and his followers, 'slithered off the bow and up to our shoulders into the warm water . . . the sea became shallower and after about 100 yards we hauled ourselves ashore with several gallons of unwanted sea water to contend with. We all flopped down unable to move. . . . One German or Vichy French soldier with a rifle could have picked off the lot of us.' The soldiers landing on the half dozen beaches selected for the assault had a similar experience. Thirty-three thousand men got ashore around Algiers with minimal casualties during the first twenty-four hours of the landing.

The same was not true of the forces ordered to head straight into the ports themselves. These commandos, loaded on small warships, faced bloody ruin. At Algiers two destroyers tried to get American infantry into the harbour. In the dark they failed to find the harbour entrance. Once the French detected the ships outside the harbour wall they opened fire. One of the destroyers was so heavily hit that it had to withdraw. With dawn, the second destroyer could see the harbour entrance. It ran down the harbour boom. The troops were disembarked. But in the light the ship was vulnerable to French fire. Just after nine in the morning the French heavy artillery got the range. The sailors reluctantly decided to abandon the landing party and make for the open sea. But in doing so the ship was repeatedly hit by shells. It managed to fight its way out of the harbour but was so badly damaged that it sank in the open sea. The isolated and pinned-down landing party was forced to surrender a few hours later.

At Oran the experience was similar. In the case of the western port two converted US Coast Guard cutters carrying US Rangers were deployed. They had more luck in finding the harbour entrance, breaking the boom just after three in the morning. Having done so, the ships faced the awful danger of the light warships of the *Marine* stationed at Oran. Both Allied assault ships were attacked at pointblank range by French ships. One of the Coast Guard cutters had her engines smashed in the initial engagement. She drifted helplessly around the harbour, raked by French crossfire. At about nine in the morning she rolled over and sank, taking her crew and the embarked troops with her. Her sister ship did not fare any better. Not long after entering the harbour she was engaged by a French destroyer. So great was the damage that she was immediately abandoned. Those men who dragged themselves ashore were captured by the French. The cutter itself exploded and sank, also around nine in the morning.

The only saving grace of the operation was that another force of Rangers landed in the much smaller port of Arzeu to the east of Oran, capturing it in the face of much lighter opposition. Nevertheless, the French at Oran, emboldened by their success, went on the offensive. The warships that had destroyed the cutters issued out of Oran harbour to give battle. Outside the port, however, the odds were reversed. The French destroyers were engaged and badly damaged by a British cruiser. Meanwhile the French shore batteries tried to engage the heaviest warships lying offshore. The British battleship *Rodney* was surprised when 'Fort Santon opened fire at us, and came as near to hitting us as anyone has been in this war, the *Bismarck* included'. The British had carefully stationed their battleship just beyond the range of the French coastal guns, but the French willingness to engage in a shore-to-ship duel with the pride of the Allied fleet was a powerful signal of hostile intent. Eisenhower 'was in the depths of despair because Oran did not fall at once'.[27] In the event, the safe landing of the bulk of both the Oran and Algiers forces over the beaches proved more significant than the bloody failure of the direct attacks on the ports themselves. The troops who landed were able to push out to secure their objectives, most importantly the military airfields near the two cities. Once the air bases were secured, close air support could be flown in to cow any further French resistance. When a general assault on Oran by land, air bombardment and heavy naval gunfire was declared, the garrison surrendered. This happy outcome was, however, still unclear to senior commanders as 8 November drew to a close.

The pre-invasion plots that had looked so promising when the Americans believed that most Frenchmen would welcome Yankee liberation rapidly unravelled.[28] Giraud's *amour propre* proved to be the least of the problems the invaders faced. Mast to some extent requited his promises. His position in the hierarchy gave him many opportunities for mischief through the issuing of false orders. His 'fighting' forces were, however, pitiful. He had boasted that he would lead an 800-strong force of resisters. When it came to the moment for action, fewer than half turned up to fight. The overwhelming majority of the active resistance was made up of Jewish volunteers. The volunteers enjoyed some early spectacular success. They captured not only the Resident General in Algeria, Alphonse Juin, but François Darlan himself, resisted the urge to murder them and summoned Murphy to a meeting.

From the moment Murphy arrived to interview the French leaders matters went badly awry for the American. Juin quickly repaired the damage done by his treacherous subordinate, Mast. Orders not to act were countermanded, strongpoints were recovered by their legitimate defenders. The unlucky volunteers were arrested. At Murphy's request that he should declare his allegiance to Giraud, Juin simply laughed. 'Apparently,' Darlan told the American, 'you have the same capacity as the British for making blunders.' Exactly what Juin and Darlan said to each other is unknown but it is clear that neither of them was convinced that the game was up for the Axis. They played for time, giving orders not to attack the main Allied force when it arrived in Algiers.[29] The orders infuriated Hitler, who rang Kesselring personally to order intervention in Tunisia. His decision was 'the total occupation of France, landing in Corsica, bridgehead in Tunisia'. Hitler, recorded Ciano, summoned to Munich, 'did not underrate the American initiative'.[30]

The Germans were, perhaps, a little harsh on Darlan. He had, in fact, committed himself to little more than a local Algiers ceasefire. The war in Morocco and Oran went on. The French Resident General in Tunisia, Admiral Estéva, immediately struck an agreement with Kesselring's emissaries to allow in German forces. Darlan was still playing for time when first Giraud, then Clark, flew in from Gibraltar. Like any good con artist, Darlan intuited what his audience wanted and gave it to them – a promise of a ceasefire. Murphy and Clark had staked their reputation on pulling off a spectacular deal. Because they wanted to be, Clark and Murphy were taken in by the Admiral's 'aura of command', when he, in fact, had little power. With Juin's support he had some control in Algeria. The French forces in Morocco, under the command of Auguste Noguès, fought on. Estéva in Tunisia had already been ordered to resist the Americans and had welcomed the arriving Germans.[31] Pétain announced Darlan's dismissal. In order to bolster his shaky claim that he had something to offer in North Africa, Darlan appealed to his famed dominance over the *Marine*.

The French battlefleet still lay at anchor in Toulon, as yet unmolested by the Germans. If he gave the order, Darlan boasted, the fleet would sail for Gibraltar. Just as the promise to deliver a bloodless victory in North Africa whetted American appetites, Darlan knew that in offering the fleet he was saying exactly what the British wished to hear. It was not just 'inexperienced' Americans who longed for a deal with Darlan but the experienced 'old East Meds'. The most powerful voice at Gibraltar was Cunningham, not only NCXF, but the Mediterranean commander with an unblemished record of indulging the Vichy navy, keen to test Darlan's claim that he was 'the only British admiral that he would shake hands with'.[32] Cunningham's old Alexandrine policy was still active. At the time of *Torch*, Alexandria was still abuzz with the *Anadyr* incident, the British seizure of a Free French ship at Port Said believed to be harbouring sailors who had deserted to the Gaullists from Force X.[33] As Darlan predicted, Cunningham was ever willing to give the *Marine* another chance. 'I think he is genuine,' the Admiral declared.[34] The Frenchman was more than happy to requite the promise of his handshake, if not the French fleet. Their meeting was 'embarrassingly cordial'.

Darlan, though, was trading on his own myth. The *Marine* disowned him as a traitor. The admiral commanding the fleet in Toulon, who had loathed Darlan for decades, said but one word in reply to his messages: '*Merde!*'[35] Alexandria followed the lead of Toulon.[36] Darlan neglected to mention to the Allies that his vaunted negotiations comprised an exchange of expletives. He improvised brilliantly, claiming that he was in secret communication with Pétain. He rushed the story to the press, who published the claim that the Marshal endorsed Darlan. The Admiral soon constructed an even more ambitious back story to the exchange: 'Darlan also said that he Darlan was looked upon generally as the natural successor to the Marshal.'[37] Eisenhower and Cunningham flew into Algiers on 13 November 1942 to give their imprimatur to the deal.[38]

Darlan's bravura performance had an unexpected resonance. He brought the conditional and temporary nature of all allegiances in the Mediterranean to a wider audience. The nature of that world came as no surprise to the old lags such as Cunningham. It came as a very grave surprise to an Anglo-American public thoroughly propagandized that the war was a fight between good and evil. In that war there were defined heroes and villains. Darlan was neither. Within days Roosevelt and Churchill were trying to stuff his genie back in its bottle. The deal was expedient, temporary, they said. It was not even 'political', but rather a simple military arrangement. Darlan, it might be said, was the true begetter of the rhetoric of 'unconditional surrender', as the President and the Prime Minister sought to distance themselves from distasteful Mediterranean morality. Anglo-American propaganda for the rest of the war comprised a denial of Algiers. Atlantic Morocco surrendered on 11 November 1942 because General Noguès was desperate to avoid the renewed American assault that was due later that day. Atlantic West Africa would later accept that with Morocco gone, they too needed to throw themselves on the mercy of the Americans. The one place where Darlan's coup had little impact was in the Mediterranean itself. Toulon, Bizerta, Alexandria and Beirut rejected him.[39]

No one knew how far the *Panzerarmee Afrika* would retreat. Montgomery concluded that Rommel would revert to his old ways, retreat to the end of the Cyrenaican littoral and there make a stand. On this assumption he vetoed hot-headed plans to take short-cuts across the desert in order to seize the *Balbia* west of Benghazi. Instead he followed along behind

Rommel until he stopped. It was only when Rommel reached and passed right through Benghazi that the pursuers realized that he had no intention of stopping. Kesselring, personally acquainted with Rommel's psychology, later commented: 'neither arguments nor orders had any influence on Rommel: he wanted to get back to Tunis; if possible still further away, to Italy and the Alps'. Another reason for Montgomery's slow advance was his belief in the pivotal importance of Derna. 'My final objective', Montgomery recorded in his 'pursuit diary', 'was to establish the RAF in the [Derna] triangle of aerodromes; from this area the RAF could dominate the Mediterranean, and could see the Malta convoys on their way.' This decision was later reviled as one of the series that allowed Rommel to 'get away'. Montgomery was particularly irritated when Air Marshal Tedder, ever a man to score a cheap point, the commander for whom he had secured the airfields, criticized him in those very terms. The Derna operation showed, at the very least, that Montgomery, for all his fierce and selfish consideration of his own needs, had a broader Mediterranean imagination.[40] With the airfield complex safely secured, the convoys could launch eastwards. In the event, however, Kesselring's own decision to shift his squadrons away from Crete meant that the air cover provided from Derna was scarcely necessary against the Germans. Merchant ships from the east sailed unmolested into Malta harbour.

Just as the capture of Derna was less helpful than imagined, so too was the resupply of Malta. The shallow waters around Cape Bon and the Tunisian ports were heavily mined. Just as in 1940 the Italians proved to be formidable foes in the Narrows. The route was, according to one veteran submarine commander, 'quite the nastiest patrol area I have ever endured'. Over thirty Axis supply ships crossed to Tunisia in November 1942. Malta aircraft managed to sight half of them but sunk very few.[41] Virtually no effort was forthcoming from the North African coast. 'It may not be realised,' Cunningham wrote, 'but we have at present no anti-ship striking force at all.' He blamed his old rival Tedder for the situation, claiming that 'when *Torch* was planned we pressed hard on this subject but all we could obtain was a nebulous promise'. Whoever was to blame, the result was failure, 'the Axis [was] running supplies at this critical moment into Tunisia by day by sea virtually unhindered'.[42]

Cunningham's pointed remarks had an immediate effect, if not on the air effort, then on Mediterranean command politics. The experienced air commanders at work in the Mediterranean had much in common. Kesselring and Tedder both believed that the Mediterranean was an airman's sea, and that their vision stretched further than anyone else's. They were both masters of protecting their own backs. Just as Kesselring had the political measure of Rommel, Tedder had a similar measure of Montgomery. Just as Kesselring detected the unexpectedly swift shift of military and political power to the west, so too did Tedder. Tedder had spent most of November 1942 trying to stay in Cairo. Within days of Cunningham voicing his criticisms, and as soon as the new AFHQ (Allied Forces Headquarters) permanently transferred from Gibraltar to Algiers, Tedder flew west to 'hook' Eisenhower on the idea of a new pan-Mediterranean air command, with Tedder at its helm.[43]

As it turned out, however, Kesselring was able to redefine the Mediterranean more quickly, even though the opposite seemed more likely as Tedder landed in Algiers. For a brief moment it seemed that Tunisia was about to fall to the Allies. Allied forces advanced in two columns, taking advantage of the two available west–east roads, one on the coast towards Bizerta, one inland, through the low Atlas, towards Tunis. Although Bizerta was the most important prize, the coast was the least promising route, the road so windy as to be unsuitable for anything other than infantry and light vehicles. The inland road was a tarmac-surfaced dual carriageway, alongside which ran the main railway line, and thus constituted the main line of advance. Kesselring attempted his own deal with the French. Alongside the arriving *Luftwaffe* squadrons, a familiar face appeared to conduct political negotiations. Rudolf Rahn believed that the parallels between Tunisia in November 1942 and Syria in July 1941 were so strong, that his first request was for the vacillating Admiral Estéva to be replaced by his old partner, Henri Dentz. His request denied, Rahn did his best with what was there. The problem with Estéva was that he was 'constantly trying to assure himself a way out in case of an American advance'. These equivocations saved Estéva's life, if not his reputation, when he was put on trial in 1945. In practice, however, cooperation with the French in Tunisia ran smoothly. Although Estéva showed no initiative, he carried out all tasks as instructed. The Germans had a potential problem in Bizerta because the French forces in the city were so much more powerful than their own. There was, however, not a hint of trouble. The ports of Bizerta and Tunis worked at full capacity, unloading German and Italian divisions from mid-November 1942 onwards. The remaining symbol of French military power in Tunisia, the great Bizerta–Ferryville naval base, with its 10,000-man garrison, was handed over, in perfect working order, to the Germans in December 1942.[44]

On 25 November 1942 'Blade Force', a third column, taking neither of the two main roads but dispatched to try and find a back-country route to Tunis, had a small success which reverberated widely. Blade Force's tank element was an American unit led by Patton's son-in-law. It drove forty-five miles ahead of the main force, until, in the late afternoon, it was surprised to see German aircraft taking off from behind a hill. The tankers had discovered the German airfield at Djejeida. With admirable presence of mind the seventeen tanks formed up and drove onto the airstrip, shooting up every plane and building they could see. Satisfied with a job well done they then retreated. The 'Deedahdeedah goose shoot' – Anglo-Saxon tongues struggled with the pronunciation – briefly loomed as large as the contemporaneous Russian encirclement of Stalingrad, to which history would later accord more significance. In Rome the Italian military predicted that it presaged the fall of Tunisia. The German commander in Tunisia rang up Kesselring in a 'state of understandable excitement and drew the blackest conclusion from the raid'. Ultra picked up his statement that it was 'doubtful if Tunis can be held for long if the enemy continues his attack with the same superiority'. Rahn started evacuating his newly arrived political team from Tunis, believing that their mission was over before it had begun. In fact a German tank column reached the unoccupied airfield the next day and went on to defeat Blade Force's light tanks in the first German-American tank battle of the Second World War. British forces on the main road to the south saw the *Luftwaffe* landing its aeroplanes back onto the airfield. Beyond it they could see the minarets of Tunis in the haze. That brief sighting marked the end of the advance.[45]

Another small, but equally symbolic, engagement had taken place a few hours before the Deedahdeedah goose shoot. Eddie Myers, the leader of the party parachuted into Greece after Alam Halfa, had spent the best part of two months trawling around the country looking for a resistance he might aid. The first people that his party met were some non-aligned brigands who were surprised to see them. The best that could be done was to send a runner to Prometheus II. He had a radio which could talk to Cairo and Istanbul. He also had useful contacts. Cairo was excited by news that there was a 'Military Centre' run by a group known as the 'Six Colonels' and wanted Myers to link up with these regular officers. There was, however, no sign of any such resistance group. The two groups that did seek him out were those with whom Prometheus II had close contact. One band was led by Napoleon Zervas, the other by Thanassos Klaras, known as Ares, a Communist revolutionary with a reputation for cruelty and perversion. Zervas had a band of about two hundred men, hiding out in western Greece. Ares claimed that the Communists had an armed force of six hundred, of whom he brought a hundred with him. Zervas was willing to help Myers in an act of sabotage. Ares refused. It was no part of the Communist plan to risk their organization by provoking the Germans and the Italians. Only a few weeks previously they had started their main campaign, which was the replacement of traditional village authorities in mountainous rural Greece with soviets.[46]

Myers made a convincing case that such equivocation would not serve. He had an immediate mission; the resistance group that helped him could expect British money and arms. Only timely action against the Salonika–Piraeus railway would demonstrate worthiness. Greece's only major railroad ran the length of eastern Greece. Salonika was the main rail hub linking the eastern Mediterranean with central Europe. The railway was monitored with interest by British codebreakers who read the frustrated complaints of its German users. Two major viaducts, the Gorgopotomos and the Asopus, carried the line across treacherous gorges. The Salonika–Piraeus line was a saboteur's dream. Myers's arguments carried the day. He, Zervas and Ares attacked Gorgopotamos on the night of 24/25 November 1942, Ares proving a much cannier leader than his rival.[47] Myers himself dropped out of sight after the attack, but special operations in the Mediterranean was able to live off the sole, if spectacular, success at Gorgopotamos for months to come.

Despite Gorgopotamos, the whole concept of special operations reaching across the eastern Mediterranean was under challenge. At the time of the operation Christopher Glenconner of SOE was in Jerusalem locked in an argument with Paul Vellacott, the head of the Political Warfare Executive. Glenconner had a particular view of special operations. They did not mean commandos like Myers running about blowing up bridges. He thought that the 'old gang' had put their trust in too many rogues, but he shared their view that the secret services' job was to project British power around the Mediterranean basin. He wanted to purge his organization of its 'military' taint.[48] This commitment to subversion and political warfare was exactly what SOE's critics deprecated.[49] Some of his own subordinates were also opposed. Glenconner's chief of staff, Brigadier

'Bolo' Keble for instance, denounced political operations and advocated daring sabotage missions. His enthusiasm for such dangerous activities moved one of SOE's bravest officers to write that Keble was a 'globe-shaped and choleric little militarist'.[50] Glenconner was accused of having 'gone native', becoming like others before him, 'semi-detached' in the Mediterranean. Vellacott of PWE was one of those dispatched to reassert London control. He described Glenconner as being 'more interested in departmental quarrels than defeating the enemy'. Indeed Glenconner said that his rivals, rather than the Axis, were SOE's 'main enemies' in the Mediterranean.[51]

The travails of Cairo and Jerusalem were nothing to events in Algiers. The prominence of political warfare was greater, and more public, in the west than it had ever been in the east. As it had been for the navies and armies, the opening assumption of special warfare was that the western Mediterranean should be kept strictly separate from the eastern Mediterranean. Not only did the British hope that the Americans could be corralled in North Africa, but London was determined to avoid any more semi-independent Mediterranean operators. 'We shall need', said Colin Gubbins, SOE's rising star, 'a microcosm of what we have here in London.' The Algerian operation would be untainted by existing Mediterranean connections. Indeed its main mission was European, not Mediterranean. SOE and OSS were charged with finding, training and inserting operatives to encourage resistance in France. Almost immediately, however, the 'freelancing' habits that had made Cairo so unpopular resurfaced. There was no rush of recruits wishing to fight for the freedom of France. 'Massingham', as the joint Anglo-American operation was code-named, opened for business at a formerly upmarket beach club along the coast from Algiers. Its few French members preferred to fight each other rather than the Italians or the Germans. Massingham hoovered up the disenchanted remnants of Mast's rising, alienated by the deal with Darlan. Within days, plans to assassinate Darlan were being hatched at one of Massingham's training camps. Massingham's senior British officer, like many of the British irregulars, was disgusted with the Darlan deal. He was not particularly discreet with his opinions and was formally warned in 'pretty strong language' by the Americans that 'if SOE afford any assistance to anti-Darlan or pro-Gaullist elements in North Africa

General Eisenhower will order the removal of the mission'. SOE promised that 'we shall of course be careful not to burn our fingers'.

Less than a fortnight later, on Christmas Eve 1942, a beneficiary of special forces training shot and killed Darlan in his Algiers HQ. It is still unclear whether anyone other than a small group of monarchist fanatics was involved. No one wanted an investigation. Giraudist, Darlanist and Vicyhite leaders met in immediate conclave. Careful to make no contact with the Allies, they had the killer executed. The most senior figure ever directly connected to the conspiracy was the head of the Algiers police, brother of de Gaulle's representative in the city. There was nothing to suggest that Massingham knowingly commissioned the assassination. Nevertheless, many were the voices calling for the 'hidden hand' to be purged in the west as well as in the east.[52]

Darlan's death merely confirmed that Algiers, supposedly so closely controlled, was not so dissimilar to Cairo. Already Allied Headquarters at the Hôtel St. George, 'a white rambling building decorated with hideous statues and paintings', was becoming a proconsular building, adding more and more non-military functions just as GHQ at Grey Pillars had done before it. Indeed the British commanders in Cairo seemed positively monastic when compared to Eisenhower, gambolling at his country hideaway with his mistress on an Arabian stallion. 'I found myself hating the place soon after I landed,' Alan Moorehead, so recently the observer of Ash Wednesday in Cairo, wrote, 'it was not so much the weather, which was wet and cold, it was the overriding atmosphere of suspicion and bickering argument, the feeling that the intrigues of Algiers were a mean and petty betrayal.'[53] British councils were 'filled up' with the gloomy thought that Algiers was all about 'jaw, jaw' rather than 'war, war'.[54]

TEN

The Deceivers

~~~~~

The Mediterranean had always been a gimcrack idea. Its most ardent advocates were cranks like Mussolini, Darlan and Churchill. The real battle for the north–south, west–east routes leavened fantasy with some hard military logic. Something more than fantasy came in with New Year, 1943. The Mediterranean story became a conscious set of lies, dreamt up in Cairo and Algiers. The Allies, the deceivers proclaimed, had a grand Mediterranean project. One might expect them to arrive anywhere and everywhere, any day soon. It was best to be prepared, they implied, lest one's soul was demanded that very night. An armada could appear over the horizon in Crete, the Dodecanese, the Aegean, Sardinia or Corsica.

Dudley Clarke of A Force, 'quite small, brilliantly clever and imaginative', the leader of Britain's deception apparatus, was determined that the Mediterranean fantasy should be adorned with all the curlicues that his teams of fake agents, wireless operators, builders and painters had at their fingertips.[1] The fantasy was good because the Axis believed in it. It was even better because it served the purposes of Colonel Clarke and his ilk as well. The acute careerists had heard the call of the west. The American view, that the Mediterranean became less and less interesting the further one journeyed from the Straits of Gibraltar, might well prevail. Clarke would have spent years building his balsa-wood empire in the east to no purpose. He might end up in a back office of AFHQ. Clarke's answer was that of a professional deceiver. The Mediterranean had to remain united because the Germans had to believe in that unity. He had to command it from Cairo for the very reason that east was less important than west.

Clarke's double bluff worked exceptionally well. He managed to subordinate the Americans to his will more successfully than any other British commander. He succeeded in thoroughly confusing the Axis. Self-evidently the war was being fought in Tunisia; Tunisia commanded the narrowest sea crossing of the Mediterranean to Sicily; Sicily was but a mere hop across the Strait of Messina to Italy. The Italians were obsessed by these simple geographical facts, but even they circulated reports from the 'most reliable sources' that the invasion of Crete or Rhodes was imminent. Hitler himself declared that Allied invasions of Crete, the Aegean and the Balkans, supported by indigenous risings, were 'foreseeable'.[2]

The sheer torrent of lies that Clarke and co. produced about the Mediterranean was, if anything, too much. German intelligence agencies began to doubt even old friends. Deception agents received a string of unwelcome *Abwehr* visitors. The army's intelligence assessment staff in Berlin had a finely calibrated idea of how much shipping was available in the Mediterranean. They knew that there were not enough ships for all the invasions of which their 'reliable sources' warned. In February 1943 OKW issued a formal warning. There were so many reports of imminent landings around the Mediterranean that commanders had to assume that the Allies were practising deception on an industrial scale. Clarke's very ambition undermined the possibility of manipulating the Germans, sending them west and east like a ping-pong. But the Axis was still left with the problem of seeing the whole Mediterranean as a potential war zone. 'At times,' Ciano wrote, 'I have the impression that the Axis is like a man who is trying to cover himself with a bedspread that is too small. His head is cold if he warms his feet, and his feet freeze if he wants to keep his head warm.'[3]

Enemies were not the only victims of the 'big lie': potential friends had to be deceived as well. Deception plans needed souls emboldened by the promise of imminent liberation to start resisting. Since liberation was far from imminent, the bravest were likely to be slaughtered for their false hope. Equally, those for whom the Axis yoke was bearable might hesitate to throw off a burden when others would do it for them at less risk.

However illusory was the idea of a 'whole Mediterranean', both sides were at pains to work out new structures to control it. Self-aggrandizers on a rather larger scale than Clarke got to work. Kesselring carried off the most spectacular coup. For months he had chafed at the limitations of his power. *Oberbefehlshaber Süd* in name, he commanded only the *Luftwaffe*, smarting each time Rommel ignored him. Now Rommel's star was waning. His constant complaining about supplies, his strongly expressed view that Libya was lost and the *Panzerarmee Afrika* should make all haste to Tunisia, his own faltering health, all played into Kesselring's hands. As Eisenhower's first offensive in Tunisia petered out, 'Smiling Albert' was at Hitler's elbow in the Wolf's Lair at Rastenberg.

Their first idea, that Kesselring should become the Mediterranean *Generalissimo*, faltered on Italian refusal meekly to hand over their armed forces to German command. Kesselring set about achieving his goals by more subtle means. Whilst conceding that Rommel was right about Tripolitania, he shifted the blame for its imminent loss entirely onto his rival. Mussolini was propitiated by the offer of Rommel's head and his replacement by an Italian officer. He was also persuaded that the *Comando Supremo* needed an infusion of German talent. As Kesselring intended, the German officers on the so-called 'Africa Staff' attached to *Comando Supremo* were a cuckoo in the nest. Their numbers soon outstripped those of the Italian members of a supposedly Italian supreme command. Orders for Tunisia were drafted by Kesselring at his base in Frascati but were rubber-stamped at the *Comando Supremo* in Rome. Kesselring well understood the needs of tyrants and danced attendance on Mussolini each day. With the *Duce* eating out of his hand, griping Italian generals could do little to get in his way. Their only means of revenge was to make Ugo Cavallero, Kesselring's lap-dog, the scapegoat for defeat.[4]

Kesselring's Rastenberg coup had knock-on effects elsewhere. He had already stripped the eastern Mediterranean of *Luftwaffe* units. Now that his attention was focused on the battle in the central and western basins, others would have to pick up the slack in the east. Yet thanks to the efforts of Dudley Clarke, the eastern Mediterranean could not be written off as a backwater by the Germans. Allied landings were supposed to be imminent and, in Yugoslavia at least, the indigenous rising that was held to herald their coming was already apparent. For months the Führer had turned a deaf ear to the diagnosis offered by his commanders in the Balkans; that they were hobbled by the incompetent brutality of native Fascists as well as by the willingness of the Italians to indulge native anti-Nazis. Having conceded Kesselring a supra-Mediterranean command, Hitler offered a similar facility to Alexander Löhr, whose powers as *Oberbefehlshaber Süd-Ost* were enhanced, albeit with the proviso that Kesselring could continue to intervene in the area when he so chose.[5]

The low motives that underlay the Nazi redefinition of the Mediterranean are, plausibly, seen as evidence of the increasing dysfunctionality of their command arrangements. The Allied redefinition of the Mediterranean that took place a few weeks later is seen, plausibly, as proof of their increasing mastery of coalition warfare. As the case of A Force suggests, however, low motives could march hand in hand with sensible strategy. Both sides were responding to the demands of Mediterranean warfare. Both sides fudged the reorganization, blurring responsibilities, as a result of personal rivalries, national pride and turf wars. If anything, the Allied version took longer, was equally confusing and produced more Byzantine results.

On 13 January 1943 Churchill and Roosevelt drew near the Mediterranean. They did not enter because the Mediterranean was cold and disagreeable. At Churchill's suggestion they met on the Atlantic coast of Morocco, where he had often retreated from political failure in the 1930s. There the nights were clear and cold, the days wonderfully sunny. The bougainvillaea and flowering shrubs were in full bloom. In this 'superbly beautiful' setting the two men conducted a fortnight-long 'mixture between a cruise, a summer school and a conference'. Not that the thousands of attendees saw much of the two principals. The military had located a hotel surrounded by a group of luxury villas at Anfa five miles south of Casablanca. 'Like a meeting of the late period of the Roman Empire the two Emperors met usually late at night and disported themselves and discussed matters with their own generals and each other's generals.'[6] All was lubricated by the prodigious ingestion of highballs.

Well trained in Churchill's bibulous work habits, the British ran rings around the possibly befuddled Americans. The British side was brilliantly marshalled by Alan Brooke, a birdwatcher rather than a boozer. Brooke was a Mediterranean 'crank' of the highest water, believing what the Americans always suspected the British believed: that the Mediterranean littoral was the real prize. Yankee plans for the invasion of north-west Europe should be avoided at all costs. As Brooke said to his staff officer and fellow birder John Kennedy, before they set off for Anfa, he was 'quite determined to go flat out in the Mediterranean: if we can get near enough to bomb the Rumanian oil fields and cut the Aegean and Turkish traffic there is a real probability that the Germans may collapse within a year'.[7]

Since such a statement, if made in conclave, would have wrecked the conference immediately, Brooke, like Kesselring, had to proceed by stealth. He played fully on the successes that the deceivers had achieved. In France, he told his audience, the Germans had a compact army, quite strong enough to defeat any cross-channel invasion without recourse to their forces in the east. The beauty of the Mediterranean was that it forced dispersal rather than concentration. Ably supported by the head of the RAF, Peter Portal, Brooke banged away on this theme for days, until the American military conceded that the next operation after Tunisia should be the invasion of Sicily.[8]

Brooke worked equally hard to quell dissidence in his own ranks. The staff papers which he kept carefully hidden from the Americans doubted that the conquest of Sicily would make much difference to the war. Nobody could be a more enthusiastic Mediterraneanist than ABC Cunningham, but he nearly let the cat out of the bag at a meeting of the Combined Chiefs of Staff. He boasted that he could command the Mediterranean without the possession of Sicily. He openly doubted whether possession of the island 'would add very greatly to the security of the sea route through the Mediterranean'. 'If we were in Sicily,' Cunningham observed, 'he would estimate the route as being 90% or more secure, without Sicily it would be 85% secure once we held the whole of the North African coast.' An inwardly raging Brooke insisted that anyone who was not going to espouse the party line should shut up.[9]

The real butt of Brooke's contempt, however, was Dwight Eisenhower. He was a 'hopeless' general who knew 'little if anything about military matters'. He tried to hide his military incompetence by 'submerging' himself in politics.[10] The British insisted that Alexander should be transferred from Cairo to Algiers to take over operational control of the campaign. Jumbo Wilson took his place in the east. Defeat – and it was hard to find a better description for Eisenhower's performance – did not enhance reputations. Brooke's regard for Eisenhower was on a par with Kesselring's for Rommel. They were both generals for whom inflated reputations had brought political protection. One had to wait until the political protection wavered before eviscerating such incompetents. That point had not yet quite arrived for Eisenhower, although as he conceded in his own diary, as the conference began, he had presided over a 'succession of disappointments'.[11] As Churchill and Roosevelt talked blithely at Anfa about what they would do after victory in Tunisia, Eisenhower was being mauled at press conferences in Algiers. What was he going to do about the fact that the *Luftwaffe* was shooting the shoddily equipped Allied air forces out of the sky? He didn't have an answer. What was the Allied response to the new German super-mortar? There wasn't one.[12] Eisenhower's attempt at a public defence of his operations was not helped by the aftermath of Hitler and Kesselring's summit at Rastenberg. The conferees had accepted that Tripoli was forfeit. Rommel was ordered to sacrifice his army, and his reputation, to buy time for the defenders of Tunisia. He was told to make his stand at Buerat, where the long haul of the *Balbia* through the Sirtean desert ended in coastal salt flats. Rommel complained so much about this order that he was allowed to retain his tank forces alone at Buerat. One of the best qualities of the tank was its ability to run away at speed. As the Anfa conference moved into full session, Rommel, as he had always intended, withdrew his tanks as soon as Montgomery essayed an attack. The entire Anfa conference was punctuated by daily briefings of how far and fast Rommel could flee in the face of the oncoming British. On the penultimate day of the conference, 23 January 1943, the 8th Army took Tripoli without a fight. Prepared for the blow, Axis propaganda diverted attention from British victories with constant references to Allied incompetence in Tunisia.[13]

With his standing at an all-time low, Eisenhower lost a series of arguments about the Mediterranean. He had tried to head off Air Marshal Tedder's scheme for a unified Mediterranean Air Command by appointing the American 'bomber baron', Tooey Spaatz, as his air commander. This new arrangement came into operation just as the Anfa conference began. By the end of the conference it had been overturned. The attraction of Spaatz for Eisenhower, apart from the fact that he was American, was his single-minded belief that the USAAF could bomb the Reich into submission, without any help from armies. The application of American bombs to the 'choke points', from ball-bearings to oil, would bring the German war economy to its knees. Spaatz only cared about bomber bases, and since some of his chosen targets were in southern Germany or in Nazi satellites like Rumania, bomber bases in North Africa were useful to him. In the short term Spaatz and Eisenhower shared a vision of a great strategic base stretching from the UK to North Africa. As Eisenhower himself admitted, that shared vision did not admit of the best use of air power in the Mediterranean. But he did not want to be a Mediterranean commander, he wanted to be a European commander. There would be a London–Algiers axis, not an Algiers–Cairo connection.[14]

The public humiliations of the Allied air forces in Tunisia, being enacted as their overlords sat in Morocco, made a nonsense of this vision. It was encapsulated in a bitter little British Army ditty, sung to the tune of 'The White Cliffs of Dover':

> There'll be Stukas over the vale of Tébourba
> Tomorrow when I'm having tea.
> There'll be Spitfires over, ten minutes after,
> When they're no bloody use to me.[15]

Even sceptics, such as Brooke, who had previously described the RAF plan as a 'quite impossible' claim for an air empire 'from Gibraltar to India', were won over.[16] The Anfa military chiefs agreed that there had to be a Mediterranean Air Command, stretching from the Atlantic approaches to the Red Sea. Tedder was nominated as the new air supremo in Algiers. Under him would be Spaatz and the North-West African Air Forces; Tedder's old overarching Middle East Command was reduced to a subsidiary formation under MAC. When he had been in Cairo, Tedder had always insisted that Malta should be under Cairo's control. As soon as he left Cairo he cut the links and made Malta a separate air command directly answerable to Algiers. Military failure in Tunisia had provided Tedder with the Mediterranean empire of the air for which he had long schemed. The French, and by inheritance American, idea that North Africa was part of Europe was, by the end of the Anfa meeting, rapidly losing ground. The British contention that the Mediterranean was a discrete space had reasserted itself.

The second beneficiary of this reassertion was ABC Cunningham, who 'assumed the old title again'. 'It's funny,' he wrote, 'coming in through the back door so to speak.' Cunningham became Commander-in-Chief, Mediterranean. Whereas he had once shunned the company of his fellow Britons in Cairo, he gladly kept ashore in Algiers with the Americans. He fled the garden he shared with Eisenhower only when Churchill hove over the horizon. Cunningham did not aspire to such a great empire as Tedder. His Mediterranean was anchored on the Tripolitanian-Tunisian border, went east to encompass Malta and found its northern tip on Cape Spartivento, confusingly not the Sardinian Cape Spartivento of 1940 memory but its Calabrian namesake. To his bitter fury, Cunningham's successor and predecessor, Henry Harwood, was penned into the eastern Mediterranean but not even given a Mediterranean title – he had to make do with 'the Levant'.[17]

Apart from the details of command and plans, the second week at Anfa was dominated by Roosevelt's attempt to distance himself and America from the Darlan deal, whilst insisting that it had been the right thing to do all along. The results, revealed to the world on 24 January 1943, were predictably gnomic. Amongst those confused by Roosevelt was the Sultan of Morocco. Unexpectedly invited to an Anfa dinner, he found himself made much of by the President. Perhaps, Roosevelt hinted, Morocco would not simply revert to the French. The Americans would offer the hand of friendship to the Arabs. Puzzled by Roosevelt's high-flown but ill-defined rhetoric, the Sultan dispatched his Vizier to see the President's vizier, Harry Hopkins. Could Mr Hopkins, asked the Vizier, explain what the President had been getting at? Mr Hopkins could not. His own take was that the Americans would not 'exploit' Morocco; they wanted Moroccans to have their fair share of 'life's good things'. The best that the Sultan could make of these exchanges was that America both encouraged and deprecated disloyalty to the French, whomsoever the French might be.[18]

The fluid loyalties of the Mediterranean did not align with a Manichaean Atlantic morality any more closely because Darlan had been eliminated. If Darlan's successor, Giraud, was personally more palatable, the Darlanist system and its personnel were untouched. The main victims of the post-assassination *épuration* were, predictably, Jews.[19] The heroes, to Allied soldiers at least, of 8 November 1942 were rounded up and sent to Laghouat. Laghouat was one of the series of nine well-established desert camps the French maintained for potential dissidents – mainly Jews and Spanish Republicans.[20] When challenged, Giraud's right-hand man insisted that it was no business of the Allies who was in the camps. He refused even to reveal how many detainees there were. Investigations by Allied officials came up with an approximate figure of 7,500, nearly all of whom were labelled as 'Communists'.[21] It took months for a 'joint commission' staffed by Allied intelligence organizations to gain access to the prisoners for screening.[22] Whilst the traditionally pro-Vichy Allied commanders such as Cunningham were ready to believe assurances that no one was detained simply because they had Allied sympathies, the investigators concluded that such was indeed the case.[23] Both in private and public, Giraud was hostile to anyone who suggested that Vichy laws stripping Jews of their civil rights might be suspended.[24] He appointed a former Vichy Minister of the Interior, the architect of its programme of anti-Semitic persecution, to govern Algeria. Eisenhower's first appointment on returning to Algiers from his grilling at Anfa was to greet the new governor warmly. He was at a loss to explain why the same journalists who taxed him for military incompetence, next wanted to move on to discuss his support for Jew-baiting.[25]

Giraud himself was a fixture throughout Anfa, irritating President and Prime Minister alike with his mantra that they should keep their noses out of French domestic issues. Instead, he demanded, they should endorse his plans for a rainbow army of French, Africans, Arabs and Berbers, which they would equip with the finest *matériel*. Such an army could liberate France. Since Eisenhower's briefings contained a daily statement of the inadequacy of French martial spirit, Giraud's claims were met with some scepticism. So, too, was his assumption that his position as Darlan's heir needed no further discussion. Roosevelt wanted to establish a less politically damaging 'narrative' for subsequent consumption; Churchill was embarrassed by the indissoluble public tie between his government and Charles de Gaulle – the Fighting French were, after all, still recognized by Britain as the legitimate government of France. Churchill promised he would get de Gaulle to Anfa for a grand reconciliation. The Americans hurried the old *éminence grise* of the Giraudists, Jacques Lemaigre-Dubreuil, back across the Atlantic to try and formulate some kind of coherent political platform for Giraud. The British and Americans can hardly be said to have been working to common purpose, since Lemaigre-Dubreuil was the most passionate anti-Gaullist of a group that, to a man, regarded de Gaulle as fit only for Laghouat.

An excited Lemaigre-Dubreuil and a glowering de Gaulle arrived at Anfa within a few hours of each other. De Gaulle described Anfa as Berchtesgaden: Churchill and Roosevelt were no better than Hitler. He described himself as a prisoner; he had been told that unless he presented himself, Giraud would be recognized as the sole legitimate leader of France. Lemaigre-Dubreuil was keen to bring about such a result. To his horror, however, he found that Giraud had done nothing more than discuss tables of equipment for his imaginary army. In a day Lemaigre-Dubreuil wrote him a political testament, going back to all the promises of support he had received from the Americans since Murphy's contacts with the 'robin hoods'. Presented with the testament Roosevelt signed it with a flourish.[26]

Unfortunately Roosevelt's signature ran directly contra to the other approach he had agreed with Churchill: to bang the heads of Giraud and de Gaulle until they agreed that a unified government of free Frenchmen was the best way forward. The most that could be achieved was a scrap of paper, produced by Catroux: it acknowledged the two generals had met each other, that they had talked to one another, and that they had agreed that the liberation of France would be a good thing. The only thing that Roosevelt cared about was the photo call. He had himself wheeled out as Giraud and 'Lady de Gaulle' were bundled into a handshake.

Roosevelt had more ambitious plans for lancing the boil of collaboration than a handclasp between two despised Frenchmen. He wanted the press to stop asking their pernickety questions about his warm embrace of Fascists, anti-Semites and opponents of democracy. He thus addressed the assembled journalists about how the war would be fought. Roosevelt later claimed that he had extemporized. This was untrue, since Churchill had argued with the Cabinet back in London about the statement for days beforehand. The internal British argument centred on the nature of the war in the Mediterranean. The Cabinet were surprised to learn that Churchill and Roosevelt were going to declare their intention 'to continue the war relentlessly until we have brought about the "unconditional surrender" of Germany and Japan'. No one had even intimated that Anfa would produce a major public statement on war aims. Churchill's colleagues were even less pleased to hear that he had pleaded that Italy should be excluded from the formula, 'to encourage a break up there'. All the information available in Britain pointed to the extraordinary effectiveness of the Fascist state in cowing its own people and the absence of any effective opposition. The only threat to Mussolini's regime came from a royalist-military coup, bringing to power men as tainted as Darlan. At Anfa itself Brooke went out of his way to deny the military usefulness of such a coup, warning that 'we should be very careful of accepting any invitation to support an anti-Fascist insurrection – to do so might only immobilise a considerable force to no useful purpose'.[27] The best Churchill's colleagues could do was to urge that, if there was to be 'unconditional surrender', it must apply in the Mediterranean as well.

Roosevelt solved the problem by making a statement that contradicted itself over Italy. 'I think we all had [something] in our hearts and heads before,' he told the pressmen, 'but I don't think it has ever been put down on paper by the Prime Minister and myself, and that is the determination that peace can now come to the world only by the elimination of German and Japanese war power.' As originally planned he excluded Italy. He then went on to say, however, that 'the elimination of German, Japanese and Italian war power means the unconditional surrender of Germany, Japan, and Italy'. Having muddied the waters Roosevelt gave the press an unambiguous headline: 'this meeting may be called the "Unconditional Surrender" meeting'. Anfa thus ended both with a promise that things would be done differently in the future and an intimation that, in the Mediterranean at least, the past would be a model for the future.[28]

For Roosevelt, Anfa ended with the political fix. The Mediterranean itself held no interest for him, beyond its play in middle America. For Churchill, however, a Mediterranean 'crank', Anfa was but the starting point for a grand spree. Just as he had given London little warning of 'unconditional surrender', he had not shared his plans for onward travel with colleagues. The whole point of the exercise was that he should be in the Mediterranean, unfettered, and they should be in London, impotent. Churchill envisioned a veritable *periplus*. He would fly from Marrakesh, from where he had waved off Roosevelt and taken a short holiday, to Cairo to sort out bothersome eastern Mediterranean issues. In his mind Cairo would be merely a jumping-off point for an entirely new set of destinations. First he would fly up the coast of Palestine, Lebanon and Syria into Turkey. Churchill, if few others, believed that the time had come to make good on the most ambitious plans of 1939 for an active alliance with the Turks. The professional deceivers routinely lied about the centrality of Turkey to the Mediterranean, in order to worry the Germans. In January 1943 their line was that the British were so worried about a German invasion of Turkey from Bulgaria that they were rushing forces into the area for a pre-emptive strike. Churchill wanted the lies to become reality. From Turkey, Churchill would visit Cyprus, an important British possession, although a military backwater since the end of the Syrian campaign. Then it was back to Cairo and a cruise along the littoral, first to Tripoli, to take the applause for the victory against Rommel, and finally to Algiers and a return to the problems started at Anfa. Churchill carried the spirit of Anfa with him on his journey: his converted Liberator included a cocktail bar amongst its amenities. The party's second Liberator was not so lucky. 'I won't be dragged around the world again in these conditions, which are filthy,' screeched Britain's senior diplomat at the end of the journey, 'I don't think the PM has ever looked into our 'plane, or realises how beastly it is.'[29]

If one leaves aside Jacqueline Lampson, surprised by Churchill's demand for a liquid breakfast as soon as he arrived at the Embassy, the Prime Minister discovered two victims in Cairo: Henry Harwood and Draza Mihailovic. Churchill wanted to know why Harwood had not solved the problem of Force X. Vichy had been definitively buried with Darlan. There was nothing to stop Godfroy pledging his loyalty to Giraud. He was deeply dissatisfied with Harwood's standard navy reply: Godfroy needed to be treated delicately, any attempt to make life less comfortable for him was to be avoided. It was quite simple, Churchill insisted: stop pay and rations and the gutless wonders would fold in a few days. Not so, Harwood replied, these would be interpreted as 'hostile acts', potentially leading to violence. What really sunk the naval hero, however, was the arrival of a letter from Montgomery complaining that the navy was failing to get on with the clearance of Tripoli harbour. The Mediterranean naval command was already slated to move from Cairo to Algiers. Churchill's meetings with Harwood not only made this decision irreversible but denied Harwood even the rump Levant command.[30]

Churchill also rootled around in Cairo's plans for the hidden hand. His interest was both timely and personal. In the second week at Anfa, news had come through of major military activity in Yugoslavia. The newly empowered Löhr lashed out at the insurgents who, the Germans imagined, were plotting to welcome the British onto Balkan coasts. The senior German commanders who gathered at Löhr's HQ outside Salonika did not make nice distinctions between the various flavours of insurgent. The German generals were initially interested in Partisan offers of a *modus vivendi*. Tito's proposal that the Germans should recognize his Bosnian 'Republic of Bihac' had to be rejected because Hitler forbade deals with Communist 'bandits'. The Führer directive that had preceded the elevation of South-East command had ordered 'an intensified fight against the plague of banditry'. A 'sharp order' to murder any captured 'sabotage troops of the British and their hirelings' soon followed. The plan the German commanders drew up – codenamed *Weiss* – had three parts. First the Germans would attack the Republic of Bihac.

Second, Partisan forces fleeing south into Croatia would be ambushed and destroyed. Third, the Axis would turn on the Chetniks. They had little sympathy with the Italian view that the Chetniks made better allies than enemies.

Churchill granted an audience to Bolo Keble in Cairo nine days after the Germans had launched *Weiss*. *Weiss* had the effect of temporarily clarifying the Partisan position, whilst adding further layers of ambiguity to that of the Chetniks. The Partisans were in a desperate fight for survival. As Churchill turned his mind to the north-east Mediterranean, the Republic of Bihac was going down in bloody ruin. At the same time, however, Löhr was angrily claiming that he had been betrayed by Roatta. Roatta had no intention of implementing Löhr's plan to ambush the fleeing Partisans. He carefully deployed Italian units away from the Partisan escape routes. The armed men he did leave along those routes were the very Chetniks he was supposed to be disarming. Mussolini was forced to sack Roatta to propitiate German ire. The removal of a notorious anti-German did Löhr little good. No Italian generals had much appetite for *Weiss*.[31]

Despite the difficulties of the Axis in Yugoslavia, Keble did not have a very appetizing tale to tell Churchill in Cairo, either. Since he held many members of his own organization in contempt – venal, hot-headed, irresponsible, pseudo-soldiers, were the words he used – he made no attempt to put a positive spin on their achievements. Keble had a vision of British saboteurs fanning out across the northern Mediterranean littoral. They and their commanders in Cairo would be disciplined, patriotic military men, 'who hold with pride His Majesty's Commission', obeying orders and eschewing politics.[32] What he had at that moment in Yugoslavia was Bailey's mission, sitting in Montenegro, wholly political, carrying out no sabotage and engaged with a group that was enthusiastically collaborating with the Italians.

Keble was, however, willing to give 'politically-minded young men', whom he affected to despise, his approval when they were well connected. His brief on Yugoslavia was written by the civilian in uniform most likely to appeal to Churchill. A young Oxford history don, Bill Deakin, had recently arrived in Cairo. In the 1930s Deakin had been one of the team Churchill had employed to write the books that were published under his name. Deakin had thrown his lot in with the self-christened 'Children of Light', SOE leftists who denounced Mihailovic as a Fascist and exalted Tito. Even if one took the view of the SOE rightists, 'the Children of

Darkness', Keble told Churchill, and supported the Chetniks, it was 'useless' trying to turn Mihailovic into the 'hireling of British saboteurs', 'when we lack almost entirely means of supporting him'. They would soon have a bespoke special forces airfield near Derna, putting the Balkans in easy range of specially-converted long-range bombers. But the secret warfare organizations, SOE, ISLD, PWE were reluctantly sharing a grand total of five clapped-out long-range aircraft. With such an air force, plans for an arc of sabotage were laughable.[33]

Keble's message certainly got through. An enthused Churchill thereafter took a 'particular interest' in the question of special forces aeroplanes in the Mediterranean.[34] Soon afterwards Keble was able to realize his dream of parachuting small 'non-political' sabotage teams, directly under his command from Cairo, into eastern Serbia. As Churchill knew, and Deakin suspected, however, Keble's reductive military vision was utterly irrelevant, except as an unwitting part of the deception plan. It was the politics he despised that really counted.

Five months previously, Churchill's visit had put Cairo at the centre of the universe, his dismissal of Auchinleck the desperate last throw of the dice. Harwood's demise caused barely a ripple. Churchill's energies were already focused elsewhere. His Liberator touched down on the wretched, impoverished mud-bath that was the plain of Tarsus after the three-hour flight from Cairo. It was indeed a strange venture. The British could legitimately claim ignorance and confusion about events in some parts of the Mediterranean littoral. Their information about Turkey, on the other hand, was without equal. The full range of diplomatic, military and secret service representatives reported on the country. British codebreakers read not only Turkey's own diplomatic traffic, but that of all the other diplomats based in the country. The country's ruling triumvirate – President Inonu, Prime Minister Saracoglu, the moving force behind the Turkish-German alliance, 'a trustworthy friend to the Nazis', and foreign minister Menemcioglu, 'that snake Numan' – were well known. They headed a government of landowners, wealthy businessmen and war profiteers. Their main domestic policy was the imposition of a 'wealth tax', allowing corrupt Muslim officials to despoil Jewish and Greek property and send its owners to concentration camps.

Every one of the many indicators of Turkish policy that Britain possessed yielded the same conclusions about the Turks: they were wedded to a policy of neutrality, 'the one fixed point in Turkish policy'. Whatever Inonu might say to Churchill, they saw no danger from the Germans and they did not particularly welcome Allied success in North Africa since it upset a Mediterranean balance of power from which they profited. The triumvirate certainly received Churchill with warmth, whatever their private perturbation about such a provocative presence on their soil. But he was received as one part of the balance, not as an inevitable victor. As Churchill arrived, Turkey's prized strategic mineral, chrome, was made available to the Germans. The Prime Minister's offer to equip the Turkish armed forces was the only thing that truly interested Inonu and his companions. They said in private – the British soon decrypted the Turkish minutes – that Churchill's visit had been a success for two reasons. First, because, unasked, he had promised that 'our country must be equipped with the most modern mechanised armaments' and, secondly, because they themselves had avoided entering 'into any engagement on any point'. As a MEIC study concluded, 'the Turks hope they will get great profit out of both sides without entering the war'.

Adana was such an odd meeting that it was subjected to furious speculation from the moment Churchill flew away to Cyprus. Only fellow 'cranks' saw it as part of a Mediterranean master plan. Although the deceivers took the opportunity to elaborate their rumours further – the British would seize Crete and the Dodecanese in order to hand them over to the Turks as bases for Mediterranean operations – they seemed too far-fetched to most hearers. Admittedly, Ciano followed the obvious flight path to conclude that 'it is the Casablanca plan that is finding its application, and Turkey is too important a base not to be exploited. I am not sure that the Turks have been neutralised as Berlin believes or says.'[35] No one else in Rome agreed with him. He was in any case sacked a few days later. Mussolini claimed that 'this proved the weakness of the English if Churchill must go to the trouble of begging for Turkish help'. The more measured analysis of Italian officials mirrored the conclusions of their British counterparts. Lamentable Turkish signals security made them as vulnerable to the Axis as the Allies; 'intercepted diplomatic reports from Ankara', noted Goebbels, 'proved that Turkey intended to hang grimly on to her neutral position until the end of the war'.

Goebbels was the author of an entirely different line of interpretation that caught post-war imaginations. Churchill could not be as stupid as he seemed. His main purpose in supplying the Turks with arms had nothing to do with the Mediterranean: he was preparing for war with the Soviet Union. In fact, Churchill had flown the length of the sea in a genuine attempt, however delusional, to rekindle an Anglo-Turkish alliance.

In his view, Turkey 'measured herself with Italy in the Mediterranean'. Once the Anglo-Americans had removed Italy from the scene, Turkey 'could hardly fail' to come rushing forward with offers of aid in the Mediterranean. It took him a further six months to come to the same conclusion as everyone else: Allied Mediterranean victories would make the suspicious Turks favour them less not more, that neutrality did indeed mean equal favour to Britain and Germany, and that the Turks would never fight.[36]

Churchill longed for the fulfilment of the aborted 1939 alliance. That alliance had, of course, had a third partner, France. Indeed after the brief stop-over in Cyprus, where everyone complained about the bitter cold, Churchill swept back into the French question in the eastern Mediterranean. Edward Spears was waiting for him in Cairo. Over lunch in the Blue House – 'very millionary, wonderful rugs and parquet floors' – Spears reported how events in Anfa and Algiers had gummed up movement in the Levant. Ever since Catroux had promised Syria and Lebanon independence, he had engaged in endless delaying tactics to avoid making good on his pledge. At least Catroux had been able to exert control over the various French factions. Once he had been called to Anfa, Levantine politics had been paralysed. His replacement as Delegate-General, the former Vichyite Jean Helleu, had none of Catroux's authority. The Arab side of Levantine politics was much rosier. In Damascus the two leading National Bloc politicians, Shukri al-Quwwatli and Jamil Mardam, had been 'reconciled'. Spears's Political Officer in Beirut was in almost daily talks with Riad Solh. He was convinced that, although SIME had tagged Solh as a Nazi sympathizer, the Lebanese leader was now confident enough of an ultimate Allied victory to become a loyal collaborator. Even better, Solh had formed an alliance with a Maronite faction doubtful of the unquestioning alignment of Maronite and French interests. The only fly in Spears's ointment was the constant whining of Foreign Office officials, who disloyally supported de Gaulle rather than the interests of his own nation. At this point Spears halted himself to interject the lie that 'in spite of everything my fundamental feelings towards the French nation had not altered'. To Spears's enormous gratification, Churchill shot back that 'his had, that he found them either defeatist or arrogant and De Gaulle was the worst of the lot'.[37]

The next leg of Churchill's journey offered a brief respite from France. A 1,200-mile flight brought Tripoli, and a cathartic triumph. Reviewing the Highland Division, Churchill and Brooke wept openly; 'it was only after having stared utter perdition in the face', Brooke wrote, 'that one could sense the fathomless depth of relief caused by a realisation that victory had now become a practical proposition. I felt no shame that tears should have betrayed my feelings, only a deep relief.'[38] That relief was mingled with trepidation about re-entering the Algiers cesspool. Whilst the party was in Cairo, intercepts reported the existence of a German plot to have Churchill killed in Algiers. The plot was not a figment: the designated assassins were Islamic extremists from groups collaborating with both the SD and the *Abwehr*, who had already tried to kill Giraud. Surrounded by troops laid on by Eisenhower, Churchill was safe enough, but the threat did not improve the atmosphere. Churchill disembowelled the Anfa memorandum, removing all suggestions that the Allies were beholden to Giraud. That final stroke of the pen marked the end of the great Mediterranean circumnavigation. Even Churchill's prodigious energy was waning. Coming down with a nasty dose of pneumonia, he finally flew back to Britain on 7 February 1943. The Mediterranean that Churchill left behind contained as many unconvinced by the Allies as when he had arrived.

Had Rudolf Rahn known about Edward Spears's enthusiasm for the Nazi discards in Syria he would have laughed. Rahn's own experience of the Syrian nationalists had bred a deep contempt for the Arabs. They were, in his view, untrustworthy and cowardly. 'The Arabs have no fighting value,' he declared. In Tunisia he was faced with a range of potential collaborators: on the French side Darlanists and Pétainists, on the Arab side the traditional elite, led by the Bey of Tunis, and the radical hotheads of the pre-war anti-French movement, the Néo-Destour. His general approach was to allow a head of steam to the Arabs only sufficient to terrify the French into cooperating in the interests of European civilization. He had little doubt that if Arab forces were allowed to grow too strong, the most likely outcome would be the massacre of French and Italian settlers. Indeed even his limited encouragement for Tunisian nationalism stirred up trouble. A new nationalist government appointed by the Bey over French objections galvanized the east coast, as men wearing the banned red-on-blue crescent regalia of the Néo-Destour turned on the settlers.

Elements of the SS were, however, keen to use the leader of the

Néo-Destour, Habib Bourguiba, in concert with the Mufti. Bourguiba and other leaders of the movement had been liberated by the SS intelligence organization, the SD, upon the fall of Toulon. Their return to Tunisia had, however, been held up by the Italians, whom they hated as much as the French. Bourguiba was accordingly delayed in Rome. The Mufti had rushed back to Berlin, from Rome, to urge his paymasters to raise an army of half a million Maghrebis for, as he declared in a major address to the Central Islamic Institute, there was a complete alignment between Islam and Nazism in their fight against the Jewish-Bolshevik-Anglo-Saxon enemy. The Mufti was rather strong meat even for the Nazis. One could not have a true Arab uprising without him, but such an uprising was likely to precipitate a holocaust, not only of Jews but all Europeans. The Italians remained adamantly opposed to unleashing the Mufti anywhere near their own people. Nevertheless, he did get his way in the return of his Arabs from Russia – in which he had never had any interest – to the Mediterranean.[39]

The *Abwehr* ran a highly effective counter-subversion operation in Tunisia. Numerous Allied secret missions sent to find an anti-German 'Tunisian resistance', whether French or Arab, were betrayed and captured. It was only after the conquest of Tunisia that the intelligence agencies discovered that active support for the Allied cause was a fantasy. The hostility of the indigenous population was, however, painfully apparent to troops near the battlefront. Eisenhower worried that the French units he had withdrawn from the front line, because they could not face the Germans, could no longer be relied on even to maintain internal order, 'where the native population is known to be disaffected'. Certain areas of Tunisia, he warned, offered 'a golden opportunity for some German Lawrence of Arabia'.[40] The SOE mission in Tunisia became paramilitary field police dealing with the threat of Arab treachery. They attracted complaints of thuggery.[41] Indeed the levels of casual violence – murder, rape and the burning of 'woggeries' – perpetrated by the British, French and Americans against the native population did much to establish German claims for support. By the time Churchill left Algiers, Rahn had received orders to throw more weight into supporting Arab interests by getting Bourguiba out of Rome and on a plane to Tunis.[42]

Whilst the Germans were able to maintain their military position in Tunisia, it was far from clear that the Allies were winning the battle for 'hearts and minds' around the Mediterranean. 'Unconditional Surrender' had no resonance whatsoever. The organizations which made reference to Roosevelt's statements tended to be Communist fronts.[43] There was, for instance, a rapid deterioration in the anti-German credentials of non-Communist Greeks. In Athens, Prometheus II was betrayed to the Italians. Captain Chris Woodhouse, Myers's political officer, barely escaped capture. He was in Athens looking for the non-existent 'military centre' run by the Six Colonels. He might have been spared the trouble since intercepted messages from the Colonels to Cairo via Smyrna revealed their plans. Any money received from the British was to be used to maintain the lifestyles of Metaxist officers. These officers were to take no action against the Axis, their purpose was to prepare for the day when the Germans might leave and the King's rule would be reimposed by force. Beyond the indication that the officer corps of the regular army in Greece believed that one day the Germans would leave, as a result of Allied action elsewhere in the Mediterranean, these messages offered little hope.[44]

Woodhouse had more reason to be grateful to the Communists since he was rescued by one of their leaders. Although the Communists maintained armed bands, KKE's Central Committee in Athens had a similar outlook to that of the Colonels: conflict was best avoided. Commissars were dispatched to hold Ares and the more belligerent *kapetans* in check. The armed bands were merely a tool in the campaign to insert a shadow government of soviets. The main targets of violence were the Greek police. The hated Italians were also fair game if isolated forces could be outnumbered and ambushed by a sudden gathering of the bands. The Communist goal was a monopoly of legitimate violence. One of the main engagements of February 1943 was an attack on the guerrillas of Colonel Sarafis, who had formed a band in Zervas's name. Sarafis found this demonstration of Communist power most convincing. He promptly renounced his previous allegiance and became the most prominent front man for the KKE-controlled 'national front', the EAM. Myers and Woodhouse signalled Cairo with the news that the most likely development in Greece was a civil war. Such a war could only be avoided if the Greeks believed that the British were about to invade. In the meantime, if Cairo wanted any significant resistance they would have to strike a deal with the Communists.[45]

At the same time as the reports of the British missions in Greece reached Cairo in February 1943, the British-equipped and -financed Greek army, stationed in Palestine, mutinied. The troubles stemmed from a poisonous combination of politics and place-hunting. The soldier-refugees who made their way out of Greece to Turkey and thence to the Levant, comprised a disproportionate number of officers. With too many chiefs and not enough indians, meaningful and remunerative positions were in short supply. The new arrivals rapidly devolved into competing guilds, divided along political lines. A rightist guild planned to paralyse the army by withdrawing royalist officers until they were given all the plum jobs. The rival leftist guild was well prepared for the coup. As the royalists handed in their resignations they were arrested and denounced to the British as mutineers. The main victim of the failed coup was Panyiotis Kanellopoulos. Once touted as a charismatic figure who could reconcile Greek factions around the Mediterranean, his mission in Cairo was revealed as having influence with no one.[46] Kanellopoulos resigned. Although the mutiny itself was physically contained with relative ease, it caused the political warfare and security agencies to start reimagining the eastern Mediterranean. They had been caught completely by surprise. They were unsure whether rightists were the real villains of the piece or whether they, and the British, had been caught in a sophisticated Communist sting. King George was told that he would be returning to the Mediterranean; his seat of government forthwith would be Cairo.[47]

The Adriatic coast looked no more rosy than the Aegean. Just as the problems of Greece and the Levant brought inspectors hurrying to Cairo from London, so another set of inquisitors arrived to examine the failure of the Balkans to fit into the Casablanca narrative. At the same moment as major combat operations restarted in Tunisia, so too did the battles between the Italo-Chetnik alliance and the Partisans in Yugoslavia. 'Now', Mihailovic told the Chetnik captains, 'is the unique moment to square all our accounts with the Communists once and for all.'[48] Serious fighting began on the crossings of the Neretva River. The Partisans needed to cross the river in order to escape from German Bosnia into Italian Bosnia. The Chetniks held the crossings against them.

The battle was accompanied by a complex Chetnik *pas de deux* with the Germans, involving both collaboration and conflict. The Chetniks cut a series of deals with German commanders on the ground. The Germans agreed not to cross the Neretva. At the same time a Nazi delegation, led by foreign minister Ribbentrop and OKW operations chief Walter Warlimont, was in Rome urging the Italians to conform to an Axis strategy predicated on the imminent arrival of Allied forces on Balkan coasts. The lies of the Allied deceivers had made the Chetniks as bad as the Communists in German eyes. 'If we do not succeed in disarming the Communists and the Chetniks in the same measure,' read the letter from Hitler to Mussolini, carried by the delegation, 'and in pacifying the land completely the German divisions will be busy fighting the Communists and the Chetniks [in Yugoslavia], and Italian troops will no longer be able to prevent the invasion [of Greece].' The Italian response was procrastination. Mussolini's reply to Hitler said that the Italians would only consider action against the Chetniks 'when the Partisans ceased to be a dangerous armed movement'. He offered pointed congratulations for the deals made between German and Chetnik commanders.[49]

A mixture of exaltation about the Neretva battles, fear of the Germans and satisfaction with the Italians provoked Mihailovic into a vitriolic anti-British outburst. At a wedding party held at the end of February 1943 he turned on his British liaison officer, Colonel Bailey. At his moment of need the English had done nothing for him. It was the Italians that 'remained his sole adequate source of benefit and assistance generally'. 'We work', he told his men, 'for ourselves alone and for no one else; we are concerned only with the interests of the Serbs.' He broke off all contact with Bailey and left Montenegro, heading for the Neretva killing zone. Mihailovic had no intention of allowing the captains of the loose-knit armed bands to take the glory of victory for themselves.[50]

That ringing declaration of 'ourselves alone' was, subsequently, to damn Mihailovic. Partisan partisans later used it to prove that he was a Fascist. At the time many in Cairo were more indulgent. The senior officer sent by London to try to resolve the struggle of the Children of Light and Darkness concluded that Mihailovic's complaints about the British were fair. He could hardly be blamed for working with the Italians. His critics were indulging in 'ignorant twaddle' based on 'half-baked and unintelligent pink opinion'.[51] The Partisans were just as likely to collaborate with the Germans. Tito had decreed that the Chetniks, rather than the Nazis, were now the main enemy, and German-Partisan negotiations began in the second week in March 1943.[52] The Chetniks, the negotiators claimed, were of no use to the Germans, for they would never fight an English invasion. The Partisans, on the other hand, would most certainly 'take up combat against the English, if the latter were to land'.[53]

Through luck as much as judgement, the Partisans' attempts at collaboration escaped the notice of the Allies. The Germans, bound by Hitler's orders, were unable to make the deal. At the same time the tide of the fighting on the Neretva turned. At the moment Mihailovic arrived to claim victory, the Chetniks were defeated. The Partisans crossed the river and fled eastwards. By so doing they escaped not only destruction but the taint of collaboration. Mihailovic had gone to the Neretva to seize the glory; it brought him only opprobrium.

By the time the Neretva battles had played out, the risks of a long drawn-out Tunisian war were fading. Most accounts agree that the Germans effectively lost the battle for Tunisia in February and March 1943. Allied dominance over Mediterranean travel and information was finally put to good use. The coordination of intelligence, aeroplanes and ships allowed the tactics used against Tripoli and Benghazi to be transferred to Bizerta and Tunis. The Germans were once more left blaming non-existent Italian traitors for the loss of their petrol, as Allied aircraft and submarines repeatedly found their targets. Of more immediate import was the resumption of major combat operations on land. Kesselring's attempt to rid himself of the incubus of Rommel proved more difficult to enact in practice than in theory. Showing some of his old skill in appealing to Hitler, Rommel portrayed himself as the victim of an Italian plot. It would be a betrayal of German troops if they were sacrificed to the command of an Italian general. The result was constant delay in Rommel's removal. Kesselring was forced to give Rommel one last chance. There was to be a German offensive in Tunisia, but it would comprise two separate fronts, Rommel fighting in the interior, General von Arnim further to the north. Once the Germans attacked on 14 February, Rommel's superior panache in the handling of operations soon shifted the balance in his favour. The *Comando Supremo* approved his ambitious plan to go beyond resistance in Tunisia, fight through the Kasserine Pass and invade Algeria from the south-east. Having captured the major American supply base at Tebessa, he could strike northwards towards the Mediterranean coast.

The Battle of Kasserine certainly frightened Rommel's opponents. The initial attack on 19 February pitted the *Afrika Korps* against inexperienced American engineers and light armour. These forces dissolved under attack. Eisenhower was worried enough to cast around for scapegoats other than himself. The battle revealed the mediocrity of Allied field command. Neither Kenneth Anderson, the British army commander in Tunisia, nor Lloyd Fredenhall, the American general on the Kasserine Front, impressed. Anderson was competent but uncharismatic. Fredenhall had been a protégé of George C. Marshall, the head of the US Army. Currying favour, Eisenhower praised him to the skies. Unfortunately he turned out to be both a bully and a coward. Eisenhower claimed, too, that his British intelligence chief, Eric Mockler-Ferryman, was incompetent for failing to warn him of the attack.[54] But it could hardly be claimed that either high command in Tunisia was the acme of military professionalism. Although Rommel caused panic amongst the low-quality American forces in southern Tunisia, he came nowhere near breaking through to Tebessa, let alone launching a *blitzkrieg* towards the Mediterranean coast. Kesselring flew into the Desert Fox's tactical headquarters near Kasserine on 22 February. His verdict on his rival was, as usual, damning. Rommel had neither the courage of conviction nor the necessary awareness of strategy to lead.[55] Later that evening the *Comando Supremo* issued the formal order for Rommel to halt his attack. In one of the few successes of the week, British codebreakers had a decrypt of the order in the hands of their superiors within five hours. The Kasserine crisis evaporated as quickly as it had arisen.[56]

Kasserine was an important moment. The battle ended in a clear defeat of the Germans. Any rational analysis suggested that it presaged an Allied victory. Yet it bred an attitude of deep-bitten pessimism. As late as the beginning of April 1943, Harold Macmillan, the British Minister Resident at AFHQ, lamented that 'the trouble is that no one really has any idea as to the future course of the war'. 'The experts', he noted, 'cannot give any guidance. The better they are, the less willing I find them (I mean men like Cunningham, Tedder and Alexander) to express a view.' 'Certainly,' he concluded, 'there is no sign of any break in German morale on this front. They are fighting fiercely and valiantly.'[57] In particular Macmillan found: 'there are still many hesitant Frenchmen, oppressed with the sense of defeat and almost mesmerised by German power'.[58] A few days later Eisenhower made the opposite complaint, that 'so many people are considering the war already won and are concerning themselves with considerations of "after the war" jockeying for position'. His conclusion, however, was the same as Macmillan's: 'the toughness and skill of the Germans, both in offensive and defensive battle'.[59]

Kasserine unleashed frenzied political manoeuvres around the Mediterranean. At the height of the Kasserine battle, Harold Macmillan, for instance, was almost immolated when he tried to fly from Algiers to Cairo in an ageing Lockheed Hudson. The centrepiece of these manoeuvres was the so-called 'New Deal', an attempt to hammer the ill-fitting French Mediterranean into a shape.[60] The hamfistedness of American dealings with the French had led Churchill to insist that the presence of a senior politician in Cairo should be mirrored by a similar appointment in Algiers. The two minister residencies were to follow a similar trajectory. Just as Oliver Lyttelton had arrived in Cairo in 1941 with an ill-defined brief and a staff of three, so too had Harold Macmillan arrived in Algiers in 1943. As the Cairo mission had done before it, the Algiers mission took on responsibilities around the Mediterranean like topsy. In the matter of France these two missions flowed into each other. Until Kasserine, Giraud could argue that 'with German forces threatening Algeria' the Allies needed him more than 'liberalism'.[61] After Kasserine, the last vestiges of that fear were allayed. Everyone had to adjust accordingly. The point was best made by Georges Catroux in Beirut. He had had, Catroux acknowledged, a good run. Despite all the promises of 1941, a careful mixture of collaboration and obstructionism had thwarted any political reform in the Levant. Now he was 'fed up' with this game. The fate of France would be decided in Algiers. There they needed help against the Americans. He had come to Beirut to strike a deal. If the British wanted constitutions restored, provisional governments appointed, election dates set, so be it.[62] Catroux was followed east by Harold Macmillan.[63]

By the time Macmillan had returned from Cairo, via Alexandria and Malta, Giraud's new adviser Jean Monnet had convinced him that, now that the Allies were likely to win, he had to ditch his tainted followers. In a 'painful' first interview Monnet told Giraud that he was an authoritarian, reactionary, anti-Semite whose only chance of survival in the new world order was to throw a bone to the Jews. The 'Gaullist plotters' at Laghouat were released. Once Monnet had convinced Giraud that his own survival was at stake, he was slowly but surely persuaded to sacrifice others. On Sunday, 14 March 1943, the victors gathered to hear Giraud deliver their carefully scripted ideas to an audience from Alsace-Lorraine. Giraud offered three things: an end to the persecution of Jews, the dismissal of his 'evil' advisers, whose chairs had been removed from the stage before he began speaking, and the offer to talk to Catroux about a union of all Frenchmen. The most important feature of the 'New Deal' was the expectation that when Catroux returned from the East, Giraud would treat with him.[64]

As the New Deal was being hammered out, Montgomery was invading Tunisia from the east. In the week before it was promulgated, he opened the battle for the Mareth Line. The Mareth Line was the fortified position created by the French in the 1930s to protect Tunisia from Italian aggression. Now it was occupied by those selfsame Italians and their German allies: three German and four Italian divisions. The two armoured divisions of the *Afrika Korps* provided a reserve. The Mareth position was as strong for the Axis as the Alamein position had been for the British a few months before. Those who saw it described the countryside as 'unpleasant'. From the Mediterranean coast a plain tilted up into the Matmata hills. The surface was covered with gravel and sand. Hidden in the sandy areas were salt pans which, with a little rain, became impass-able for wheeled vehicles. The plain was scarred by wadis – seasonal river valleys – which ran west–east, from hills to sea. Inland, the wadis were steep and rocky. Nearer the sea they opened out but were often filled with water or swamp. The main such river valley, the Wadi Zigzaou, had felt the heavy hand of military engineers. It had been fashioned into a formidable anti-tank ditch, its sides deliberately scarped to prevent passage by armoured vehicles. Behind this formidable obstacle lay the small town of Mareth. The country between Mareth and the coast had been heavily fortified. Belts of thick barbed wire ran along a length of nineteen miles. The French had built 'nests' of pill boxes, joined together by deep, narrow trenches. Up to 400 men could defend each of these interlocking strong-points. In front of the permanent fortifications the Germans and Italians had sown nearly 200,000 mines of every type.

Approaching Mareth, Montgomery had four infantry divisions, two armoured divisions and a large range of odds and sods. There were two ways for them to deal with the Mareth Line. One could either go through it, or one could go around it. Either journey began in Medenine, the last town on the main road south of Mareth. From Medenine it would be possible to take a short direct drive across the Wadi Zigzaou. The problem was that the coast road also took an invading force straight to the strongest point of the Mareth fortifications. The long route around would take Allied forces west of the Matmata hills. The first waypoint on this journey was Ksar Rhilane, fifty miles south-west of Medenine. A relatively flat route then led up the western edge of the hills to the Tebaga Gap. A west–east road ran through the gap leading to the coastal town of Gabes. If an army reached Gabes it would cut off the Mareth Line from the rest of Tunisia. Any enemy troops left in the Mareth Line would be unable to retreat.

The Germans and Italians were more than aware of this possibility. They had constructed a 'second defence line' in the north of the Matmata hills to prevent a hostile army forcing the Tebaga Gap. Nevertheless, in turn, each of the commanders in Tunisia argued for a withdrawal to prevent encirclement. Some argued that they should take up position on the Wadi Akarit, a valley crossing the coast road to the north of Gabes. Others demanded a more drastic manoeuvre: a 200-mile retreat to the town of Enfiladeville. They maintained that the best strategy was to create 'fortress Tunisia', a small enclave around Tunis and Bizerta. Such a pocket would be defensible for many months: keeping forces on the Mareth Line risked a swift defeat in the south and the rapid collapse of the whole Tunisian front. Their views got nowhere. Kesselring, Mussolini and Hitler all ordered them to fight where they were. 'Fortress Tunisia' would be an open admission of inevitable defeat, albeit long drawn out. Not least, it would allow Eisenhower's army, so recently given a bloody nose, to join hands with Montgomery without further fighting.

A countervailing risk haunted the Allies. Montgomery's 8th Army had been called forward to the Mareth Line to 'save' the Americans from their defeat at Kasserine. Kasserine had demonstrated that the Axis generals were still more than capable of the aggressive deployment of armoured forces. Both Ksar Rhilane and Medenine were highly vulnerable to such an attack launched from the west. Ksar Rhilane was on the west of the Matmata hills, on the extreme of the Allied line, with no easy access to reinforcements from the coastal plain. Medenine was to the east of the Matmata hills, on the coastal plain, but a west–east road ran through the hills making it easy to reach from the west. The march to Medenine on 25 February 1943 was thus described by a British corps commander as, 'one of the weirdest advances . . . there was very little opposition . . . yet no one had any confidence in the manoeuvre and many of us got a stiff neck through looking nervously at the mountains over our left shoulders. For the mountains stood up clearly across the plain . . . our left flank was completely exposed to the German threat from the mountains.' His leader was more sanguine. Axis aggression, Montgomery wrote, was 'exactly what we would like . . . it would give us a great opportunity to take a heavy toll on the enemy as a first step and then to put in our own heavy attack when he was disorganized'.[65]

The Germans and Italians did not disappoint. They were indeed planning to take on the British. Ultra revealed their intent, if not the exact details of the attack. For the Axis commanders were divided amongst themselves. The disagreement was not between Germans and Italians but between Rommel and his subordinates of both nationalities. They argued for the attack from the west, which caused the British to so crick their necks. He wanted to do the unexpected and come at Medenine from the coast, from the north and east. They argued that such a manoeuvre would take them into the main concentration of Allied forces, across the difficult terrain: the idea behind the Mareth Line was that it should resist attack, not that it should be the start line for an attack. In his last major command decision, Rommel gave way and let his subordinates get on with their preferred plan.

The Battle of Medenine on 6 March 1943 was a crushing Allied victory but a misunderstood and underreported engagement. Many spoke of Kasserine, few of Medenine. Recognizing this mistake the war correspondent Alan Moorehead, like most of his comrades attached to the Anglo-American 'Torch' forces who had entered Tunisia from Algeria, wrote that, 'this action, which could not be assessed at its true value at the time, was, I believe, the turning point of the Tunisian campaign. The Germans lost the offensive on that day, and they never again recovered it. It is not too much to say that the battle of Mareth was won in this preliminary tank action, and from Mareth flowed all the rest.'[66] For the first and last time, three German tank divisions swept forward in unison. Waiting for them, expecting them, were the British and the New Zealanders, dug in. Montgomery had reinforced them. 'So,' he wrote on the day before the battle, 'my position today is that I have with me up forward: three veteran divisions; a great mass of artillery; nearly four hundred tanks; about five hundred six-pounder anti-tank guns. I am in fact sitting "very pretty" and Rommel can go to hell . . . he will get an extremely bloody nose.' To British watchers the German tanks seemed to be wandering 'rather vaguely' towards Medenine. As a result they 'got shot'. Only the 15th Panzer Division got close to the British lines: their reward was a textbook display of anti-tank gunnery which left many of their vehicles burning wrecks. The Germans lost fifty tanks. It was, wrote a New Zealand observer, a 'truly grand victory for the Tommy gunners . . . the way in which they held their fire was an example to us all'. At nightfall Rommel acknowledged defeat and ordered the cream of German forces in Africa to retreat. It was the end for him. 'The Marshal has made a balls of it,' a British general recorded Montgomery as observing. Three days later Rommel boarded an aircraft at Sfax and flew to Italy: he never returned to the 'fourth shore'.[67]

The successes of Monty and his veterans caused some embarrassment. The press pack swirled with reports that Americans were fit for little else beyond cleaning up the battlefield after the British had finished. The full might of the American public relations machinery was enlisted to celebrate the performance of US troops.[68] The argument attracted fascinated partisans for either side, then and since. The Anglo-American slanging match, which had serious consequences for later campaigns, tended to obscure the political importance of Kasserine and Medenine. It was in the aftermath of Kasserine-Medenine that the process of winnowing Mediterranean wheat from chaff began in earnest. Giraud survived, de Gaulle was resurrected, Kanellopoulos remained discarded, Mihailovic was compromised, Tito was anointed.

As ever, all things in the Mediterranean were tied together by the deceivers. From London and from Cairo they converged on Algiers at the moment of the New Deal. Whilst Montgomery attacked, A Force revealed its new version of the Mediterranean lie. In the summer of 1943, the 'Twelfth Army' – an entirely fictional formation – would embark at Egyptian ports for an invasion of the Balkans, via Greece. The first landing would go ashore in the Peloponnese. At the same time there would be a landing in western Crete to convince the Turks that the time had come to fulfil their Adana promises. In order to prevent German forces rushing to contain the Balkan bridgehead, which was the true 'Second Front', secondary operations would be launched in the western Mediterranean. The 8th Army, reinforced by the newly unified French Army, would storm ashore in southern France. General Patton would lead the Americans into Sardinia and Corsica. One major Mediterranean target was 'firmly rejected'. It was 'the prospect of a long and laborious advance through the mountainous terrain of Italy's mainland with the formidable barrier of the Alps at the far end'. The story was told by radio double-cross agents and corpses washed up on the Spanish coast. Greek troops, recently mutinous, found themselves practising amphibious landings, as did French troops, recently withdrawn from the Tunisian battlefield.[69]

Deception required instant action. Instant action required immediate allies, however unpalatable.[70] Cairo made a decision in favour of the Communists of Yugoslavia. On the day the A Force agreed on their deception plan, the Partisans defeated the Chetniks on the River Drina, thus forcing their way into Montenegro. At the same time *Wehrmacht* commanders reasoned that, since the main threat was British invasion, they would pursue the leader who would work with the Allies most effectively: Mihailovic. Pursued by both sides Mihailovic fled the Montenegrin death trap. Meanwhile his enemies on the other side of the Mediterranean, 'the Children of Light', sedulously used his wedding party outburst against him. A formal apology to Churchill did him little good. By the beginning of April 1943 the secret services had decided to aid the Partisans. Mihailovic's enforced return to Serbia undid the Chetniks' Mediterranean plan. Their intention of being the force waiting on the coast for the British to arrive was nullified. In February 1943 Mihailovic had felt confident in abusing Bailey. Now he had to endure the humiliation of Bailey reading him his instructions. Mihailovic had gone east to survive; he was never to return. To remain an ally he must remain in Serbia. The coast was strictly an affair between the British and the Partisans.[71] When the Germans attacked in Montenegro, their blow fell not, as intended, on Mihailovic but on the Partisans. The British officers who parachuted into Montenegro were already predisposed in favour of the Communists. They found an uncompromising battlefield on which Partisans fought Germans. They reported what they saw. The Partisans were a formidable anti-Nazi fighting force.[72]

In Greece Myers and Woodhouse similarly concluded that only the Communist bands could 'create the utmost havoc in the enemy's communications throughout the length and breadth of Greece, in order to deceive the enemy into thinking that this was the preliminary to the invasion of Greece'. Since January 1943 they had heard of a string of violent encounters caused by the Communist strategy of destroying the authority of the Axis-backed Greek government. At the beginning of April 1943 that government collapsed. Although the Communists were attacking Greeks rather than enemy troops, they were causing *stasis*.[73]

The collapse of the Greek government was a welcome sign, the potential collapse of the French government less so. With him into Tunisia, Montgomery had brought the idol of North African Gaullism, *nom de guerre* Leclerc. Leclerc had charisma. In order to fight the Germans he had led a small force of Frenchmen and Africans across the Sahara from central Africa to Tripoli.

Leclerc's longed-for 'day of initiation' came as an appendix to Medenine. Montgomery had sent him to occupy Ksar Rhilane. The German tank divisions had ignored Ksar Rhilane as insignificant: it was not on their route to Medenine. After their defeat, however, the fear of an Allied outflanking manoeuvre became even starker. On 10 March 1943 a powerful German reconnaissance battlegroup with about fifty vehicles arrived to find out if Allied forces were massing in the lee of Ksar Rhilane. They were not: only the French and a small force of Greek royalists were there. What followed was a microcosm of Medenine. The Germans attacked the dug-in French all day. The French hung on. In their rather hyperventilated prose it was not only a 'day of initiation' but of 'anguish', 'exaltation and fear' but in the end victory, even triumph. As at Medenine, the Germans retreated leaving many of their vehicles burning on the field. Montgomery was terse in his congratulations for a well-handled minor skirmish. 'Good show,' he told Leclerc: given his previously expressed view that French soldiers were good for nothing more onerous than guarding aerodromes, this was high praise.[74]

In fact Leclerc was more fortunate in his victory than Montgomery was to be with his own. Medenine was soon overshadowed by the 8th Army's supposed failure to end the fighting in Tunisia by turning the Mareth Line into a 'cauldron battle'. With Rommel's departure, his Italian replacement, Giovanni Messe, and indeed Messe's titular German subordinates, were more determined than ever not to be encircled. Rommel's German replacement, Colonel-General von Arnim, had always been a champion of 'fortress Tunisia'. There followed a confused debate as to where the Axis forces might retreat.

Whilst the Axis argued, Montgomery attacked. He did indeed send an outflanking force, led by the New Zealanders, via Ksar Rhilane. Their target was the Tebaga Gap. But this western task force, which gathered up Leclerc's men for the advance, was really a decoy. Montgomery's main blow fell near the coast on the Mareth Line itself. The attack which opened on 20 March 1943 did not go well. Montgomery predicted it would be a 'dog fight' and the Mareth Line lived up to its sinister reputation. By dint of a major engineering achievement some tanks got across the Wadi Zigzaou, but when the crossing collapsed they were isolated. Instead of attacking well-dug-in anti-tank guns as had been their fate at Medenine, the 15th Panzer Division counter-attacked an inferior and isolated tank force on the north bank of the Wadi Zigzaou. 'It was', the senior operations officer at Montgomery's HQ admitted, 'a very, very serious setback, undoubtedly. We weren't used to this sort of failure – so it was a considerable shock.'[75]

As a result of this 'shock' Montgomery was forced to transform the

Tebaga Gap decoy force into his main offensive formation. Reorganization caused delay. When the New Zealanders reached the Gap on 26 March 1943, they found an Axis rearguard. The Germans and Italians on the ground had agreed that whatever the orders coming from on high demanding that the Mareth Line be defended to the death, they would move out. With relief they recorded that, 'the enemy does not follow, although he sees that the Mareth Line is being evacuated'. The forcing of the Tebaga Gap unhinged the formidable Mareth Line. On one level it was a brilliant victory. As Moorehead came to understand, and Kesselring feared, the Battle of Mareth had finished not only the Italians but the Germans in Tunisia as a force capable of anything other than grudging defence. As Kesselring said, the offensive 'sealed the fate of Axis forces in Tunisia'.[76] They had become 'retreat minded'. But the fact that Axis forces were engaged in a slow fighting withdrawal did nothing to endear Montgomery to his bosses, hungry for spectacular advances. With the fall in Montgomery's stock went the chance that the conquest of Tunisia would be seen as a mainly British victory.

Eisenhower ruled that no American forces would be sent to the south to assist in making the 8th Army's advance the main offensive. Instead the 8th Army would become the diversionary force for his plan to capture Tunis and Bizerta from the west. That offensive was finally launched on 22 April 1943. By 27 April the British 78th Division had captured Long Stop Hill, 'critical because it covered the direct approach to Tunis'. They found that, 'generally speaking the Boche stayed put and fired until we were right on their positions. They then packed it in and tried to surrender.' British troops, angry at the casualties they had taken, refused to accept German surrenders, 'and in most cases they died pretty rapidly'.[77] 'With the capture of these heights,' Kesselring wrote, 'the gateway to the Tunisian plain had been smashed open; through it from 5 to 8 May four and a half divisions, shoulder to shoulder and supported by an un-precedented artillery bombardment and a rolling carpet of bombs, drove their irresistible assault.'[78] Tunis and Bizerta were captured on 8 May 1943. In Tunisia the Axis ground commanders could give ground despite orders from outside. What they could not organize, without Hitler and Mussolini's blessing, was an escape across the Mediterranean. That blessing never came. The escape never happened. The result was 'Tunisgrad', the forced surrender of a quarter of a million Axis troops. The Italian army, in particular, lost irreplaceable components of its fighting strength. The last of its armoured divisions, the *Centauro*, for instance, was lost in Tunisia, never to be replaced. Very few, perhaps 2,000, Axis troops crossed the Mediterranean. A British warship captain reported that he had rammed boats trying to escape, killing their occupants. 'I shook him warmly by the hand and left him without enquiring further,' remarked ABC Cunningham, 'I trust there were more like him.'[79] Tunisia was not a 'war without hate'. It was also a campaign of uncertain glory. Kesselring said that Tunisia had been a victory for 'the classical Mediterranean power', Britain, 'with the aid of the Americans'.[80] This remark was, literally, accurate. The British Empire had contributed about two-thirds of the forces that had some hand in the Tunisian campaign. But at the moment of victory it felt that an enormous amount of the credit had to be shared.

An advance force of the 8th Army reached Tunis at about the same moment as the main force arrived from the west. By then, however, there was no disguising the fact that the 8th Army had not been the main show for some weeks. In lieu of the great prizes, Montgomery's forces were relegated to a series of subsidiary battles, first at Wadi Akarit and subsequently at Enfiladeville. Their main claim to glory was the liberation of the port towns of Tunisia's eastern – Sahilian – coast. This was but minor recompense for the British, but manna for the Fighting French. The towns, rivers and hills of southern Tunisia possessed none of the wider resonance that had become attached to the long-fought-for towns of the Libyan littoral: Tobruk, Derna, Benghazi and Tripoli. Few had heard of Medenine or Mareth, the Matmata hills or Wadi Zigzaou. Little was said about them afterwards. The eventual prize of the battle, the coastal towns of Gabes, Sfax and Sousse, were hardly better known. The question that had dogged Montgomery since the pursuit from El Alamein – did he have the wit to conduct anything other than a battle of attrition? – persisted. Leclerc, however, emerged from the Battle of Mareth with glory both immediate and memorable. Not only had he beaten the Boche in a straight fight but he had been unapologetic about whom he had been fighting for. *VIVE LE GÉNÉRAL DE GAULLE*, Leclerc had cried in victory.

Ksar Rhilane joined Bir Hakeim as the second battle honour of the Fighting French. Leclerc's undoubted heroism did not, however, make him a comfortable political companion. Meeting Giraud, under whom he had served as a junior officer, he told him bluntly that it was not for him to dicker with Catroux, but to bend the knee to de Gaulle. The Germans had hoped that the import of Bourguiba would help them in the Sahilian stronghold of the Néo-Destour. Instead of the planned parade of the independence fighter, Bourguiba, rallying the Arabs to Germany, however, those coastal towns saw the forces of Leclerc rallying the settlers to de Gaulle. Enraged that an official welcoming ceremony at Sousse failed to mention de Gaulle, Leclerc took over the platform and whipped the crowd into Gaullist frenzy. Even the notoriously dense Giraud could feel the ground shifting under his feet. If he lost the Army he had nothing. When Montgomery's armoured forces entered Tunis the city was draped in the Cross of Lorraine, de Gaulle's emblem. Giraud finally, reluctantly, agreed to receive de Gaulle in Algiers. The Gaullist soldiers had ensured that although Giraud stood on the Tunis victory rostrum with the Americans and the British, it was de Gaulle who came to Algiers bathed in reflected military glory.[81]

ELEVEN

The Good Italians

Despite a few American attempts to introduce polling and focus groups to the Mediterranean, gauging public opinion in the lands around the sea remained an inexact and imprecise science. Propaganda and political warfare specialists argued endlessly amongst themselves in Cairo and Algiers.[1] Notwithstanding the overall fuddle, one point upon which most contemporary authorities could agree, but which was lost to later commentators, was the identity of the most reviled Mediterranean power: Italy. Soon apologists for Italy would claim, with a straight face, that 'it never could have been the Italian infantrymen, alpinists, or *bersaglieri* who obeyed the order to burn a village or shoot women or children: these were actions only the Germans and Fascists could have carried out'. The Italians may have committed some questionable acts, but they had been 'forced' 'to imitate, against all custom and the Italian temperament, German practices'.[2]

The bad German, good Italian contrast seemed ridiculous at the start of 1943. Wherever the Italians went they were loathed. Few lamented the despoliation of the Libyan Fourth Shore. When General Pariani was sent to rule Albania in the spring of 1943, he reported that the one stable factor in a 'chaotic' land was 'hatred of Italy'.[3] In Greece the Italians were regarded with infinitely more bile than the Germans. The most notorious massacre of civilians had been perpetrated by Italian troops in Thessaly. Not only did the Italians murder civilians but they combined such violence with a 'mania for plunder'. Italian troops were famously fond of raping very young girls. The despoliation of villages, beyond hope of recovery, was later characterized by Mario Roatta as the theft of 'a few chickens'. Equally, the most notorious concentration camp in Greece was also an Italian facility. Larissa housed civilian 'hostages' for the good behaviour of the population. The camp commander conducted a regular series of executions. The deaths were complemented by an imaginative programme of torture, including the removal of eyeballs without anaesthesia and the inflation of intestines with air pumps. Lower-grade humiliations included enforced public masturbation by Orthodox priests. Such Italian concentration camps were certainly not imitations of a German model. They had been developed in Cyrenaica in the 1920s and had then crossed the Mediterranean.[4] The Allied liberators of such camps found them full of the tell-tale 'living skeletons'.[5]

Even in Yugoslavia, where murderous German brutality had come into play earlier than elsewhere in the Mediterranean, the Italians were a match for their allies. Mario Roatta, now head of the Italian Army, had instituted a policy of being as brutal as the Germans, whilst not being with the Germans.[6] What the Italians lacked was a determined commitment to the extermination of the Jews. Failure to murder Jews was not, however, necessarily a popular alibi around the Mediterranean littoral in 1943. In some territories, such as Tunisia, the Germans had been able to offer the local population an attractive cocktail of anti-Semitism, anti-imperialism, well-disciplined troops and a sympathetic choice of imported and indigenous militias. That these efforts came to nothing was, often as not, the result of being shackled to the reviled Italian.

The most remarkable change that occurred in the Mediterranean world over the course of 1943 was the transformation of Italy, not only from Axis power to Allied cobelligerent, but from reviled oppressor to innocent 'victim' of Nazi oppression. This transformation was made much easier by a fortunate confluence of events. Those shorn of empire have no one to oppress. The Germans quickly demonstrated that they needed no lessons from their erstwhile allies in the application of barbarity. The various organs of the SS state, *Waffen*-SS, SD, Gestapo, *Sonderkommandos*, present but not of overwhelming importance to the Mediterranean world before 1943, began to uncoil themselves. The *Wehrmacht* sought to demonstrate the 'proper' application of counter-insurgency technique.[7]

Although the Germans replaced and outdid the Italians on the northern shore, they had no similar pretensions to Mediterranean empire. The only major figure who still articulated such ideas was the Grand Mufti. Even though his personal stock in Berlin rose with that of his patron,

Heinrich Himmler, there was little time to waste on such fancies. The redefinition of 'the South' was the subject of six months of vicious infighting amongst the Nazi elite. Kesselring, who had once aspired to a great pan-Mediterranean command, spent those months on the brink of dismissal. In the end his combination of military skill and political savvy saved him from eclipse, or worse. What did not survive was any unity of command. Kesselring lost any control over the *Luftwaffe* in the eastern Mediterranean. In the western Mediterranean he was removed from the command of *Luftflotte* II. His replacement, *Freiherr* Wolfram von Richthofen, arrived from Russia and sacked those with 'Mediterranean experience'.[8]

Subsequently, the *Wehrmacht* further reorganized the Balkans, the South-East, into a self-contained area. There too a senior 'Easterner', the 'praying Field Marshal' Maximilian von Weichs, arrived to take command.[9] The former *Oberbefehlshaber Süd-Ost*, Alexander Löhr, was 'reduced' to the Greek command. To further stress that the Balkans was now a self-contained area, the changes in military command were paralleled by the appointment of a 'Supreme Representative of the Foreign Office in the South-East'. Although the star of Foreign Minister Ribbentrop was waning rapidly, his appointee in Belgrade, the well-connected Austrian Nazi Hermann Neubacher, was quite strong enough to defend his own patch; he even dismissed the head of the SS in Greece, a 'hero' of the extermination of the Warsaw Ghetto, when the latter crossed him. Von Weichs's primary mission was formally Mediterranean-oriented. He was supposed to defend the Balkans against a British invasion. Like Neubacher, however, he was based well away from the littoral, in Belgrade. Their most pressing concern was the elimination of 'Communist bandits'. The anti-bandit campaign was supposed to be a means to the end of preventing invasion from the Mediterranean; it became an end in itself. The 'bandits' became the vanguard of the Bolshevik-Asiatic horde.[10] The one figure touted as unifying the South was Rommel, backed heavily by Goebbels. The idea never came to anything, however, and Rommel was finally dispatched to north-west Europe. With the final disappearance of his old rival, Kesselring's position was formalized by his appointment as Commander-in-Chief, South-West, essentially a job confined to what he was already doing, leading the army in Italy.[11]

Italy – in reputation at least – was equally fortunate in having Britain as its enemy. The only power that retained a vision of the unified Mediterranean was the British. As with the Germans, the question of command in the Mediterranean was the subject of vicious infighting amongst the Allies. But whereas the Germans were pulling east and west apart, the British were grappling with the problem of how to push the Mediterranean back together. Formerly neat geographical divisions fell apart. Although the shortness of the sea crossing made Tunisia the most logical launching point for operations against Italy, it was by no means impossible to control some functions from Alexandria or Cairo. This was particularly true if Apulia, the Heel of Italy, was regarded as important, as it indeed became.[12]

The other side of the problem was the alliance with the Americans. It was not that the Americans offered a competing vision of the Mediterranean, it was that they had little interest in the Mediterranean *per se*. American agencies, moreover, began to show, for the British, a disturbing interest in individual territories. Many troubles were exacerbated by the nature of the people whom the Americans held up as their Mediterranean specialists. The British maintained a fairly strict distinction between their *dragomen*, British interpreters of native custom, and their *compradores*, Anglicized native collaborators. Those who crossed the line, either way, were treated with a pinch of salt.[13] By contrast the wave of Americans interested in political warfare who arrived in numbers during 1943 tended to be first-generation Mediterranean immigrants. They had excellent language skills – an officer was found to liase with Mussolini's successor, Badoglio, in the absolutely correct Piedmontese dialect favoured by the Marshal – but were obsessed by the domestic political factionalism of their own country of origin, to the exclusion of wider interests. Some, such as OSS's Italian specialist in Algiers, the Sicilian Max Corvo, or their Greek specialist in Cairo, Ulius Amoss, were violent Anglophobes.[14]

The Italo-British rivalry that Mussolini had launched in 1935 was drawing to an end. The evident superiority of the British Mediterranean over the Italian Mediterranean should have been a moment to gloat, to take advantage of Italian crimes for the greater glory of 'enlightened' British dominance. The British did indulge themselves in one highly symbolic act of Mediterranean supremacy. 'The Mediterranean route to the East', they declared, 'was again open.' By this they meant that 'super convoys' of well over a hundred ships at a time could sail west through the Sicilian

Narrows, passing beyond Malta to points in the eastern Mediterranean. Due to their size these super convoys had a relatively low proportion of escorts to merchant ships. Their composition was thus in stark contrast to the old convoys in which a few merchant ships were fought through the Mediterranean by a much larger flotilla of warships. A ship sailing from Liverpool to Egypt now had its journey time shortened by forty-five days as a result of cutting through the Mediterranean instead of having to sail around South Africa. As it happened, the 'opening' of the Mediterranean actually increased ship casualties in the short term. The Germans and the Italians had to fly a long way to find them, but there were now many more merchant ships to sink.[15] Still, as a proportion of the whole, such losses were annoying rather than fatal. They were not enough to dim the festivities. By the summer of 1944 well over 800 convoys, comprising 12,000 ships, were to pass through the Mediterranean.[16]

On Trinity Sunday, 20 June 1943, King George VI sailed in triumph from Tripoli to Valletta. 'I thought', Cunningham wrote, 'a visit to Malta would have a great effect all over the British Empire.' 'We entered the Grand Harbour shortly after eight', the commander of the Mediterranean Fleet continued jubilantly, 'and it was a fine sight to see the old walls and battlements black with cheering people as he stepped ashore all the bells on the island started ringing his reception was wildly enthusiastic everywhere.'[17] 'I do hope', confirmed Harold Macmillan, who was accompanying the King, 'the pictures and the account of the trip will do justice to its success and its profound moral effect.' 'Mussolini', Macmillan crowed upon his return to Algiers, 'called the Mediterranean *Mare Nostrum*. The King, in a cruiser with four destroyers, has crossed it twice in 36 hours.'[18] The point was certainly taken on Malta's sometime tormentor and neighbour, Sicily. The *Carabinieri* on the island reported that Mussolini's Mediterranean propaganda theme, the sacred duty to defend the shoreline, 'the first line, the front of the fatherland', left the public indifferent 'because they no longer have any faith in him'.[19] Even Edda Mussolini noticed on a visit to Palermo that 'civilians feel themselves abandoned'.[20]

Macmillan could not resist adding parenthetically at the end of his account of the Malta visit: 'it was the first day [in the Mediterranean] that I have spent entirely in the company of British people, it is quite a relief'.[21] As a man fully attuned to the needs of coalition warfare, Macmillan knew that his relief was not practical politics. A few days before the King reached the Mediterranean, he had been one of the Anglo-American authors of a draft proclamation to the Italian people. The Allies, it claimed, were not 'enemies of the Italian people', they were not fighting in the Mediterranean for mastery of the sea but merely 'as an inevitable part of their war to destroy the German overlordship of Europe'. The Italians would be the 'beneficiaries' of German defeat. The proclamation originally concluded that the Italians could become part of a great crusade to lift 'the Nazi and Fascist yoke from Europe by quick and total victory'. On the day the King visited Malta, the words 'and Fascist' were quietly scored out. There was no need to be unnecessarily hard on Fascism when the sole enemy was German Nazism.[22]

The British ended up rooting for the Italians, portraying their demise as a European tragedy rather than a Mediterranean triumph. Likewise the Italian collapse forced the British to take a stand on issues of collaboration and resistance in the Mediterranean basin. The problems they had in sorting out the 'good guys' from the 'bad' showed how poorly the idea of a war with two sides transferred to the Mediterranean reality.

Although the Allies had agreed in January 1943 that they would invade Sicily, it was only in May 1943, with the final resolution in Tunisia, that they were able to finalize a serious plan for doing so. Within days, Churchill himself arrived in Algiers to broker an agreement with the Americans that the seizure of a bridgehead in southern Italy should become part of the operation.[23] Faced with such a prospect, both enthusiastic Britons and reluctant Americans had to admit that they actually knew very little about Italy. In intelligence terms the Germans were old friends. The British had read so many of their signals that even the personalities of nicknamed cipher-machine operators could be imputed. The Italians were much less knowable. 'The cryptographic position is as follows,' Bletchley Park conceded, 'German strong, Italian weak.' A great deal of information was derived indirectly from the Germans, but the best single direct line into the Italians, the convoy signals, dried up with the convoys themselves. Attempts to crack Italian codes relevant to the Balkans and eastern Mediterranean from Heliopolis had always been spasmodic, and the Italian section broke up completely in the spring of 1943.[24] The tendency to downgrade Mediterranean cryptology in favour of centralization in the UK was undoubtedly a wise decision in terms of successful code-breaking, but it had led to Italian traffic being given a consistently low priority.[25] When a team of naval codebreakers arrived in Algiers at the end of May 1943, they proved ineffective. Lacking the necessary preparatory work on Italian codes, they were unable to read any traffic. The kind of work that could be done in the Mediterranean, traffic analysis and direction finding, was tactically useful but offered little insight into how the Italians thought.[26]

Sources of human intelligence were equally lacking. A great deal was known about Italians in areas already controlled by the Allies. There were many thousands of POWs in Allied hands and counter-intelligence had rolled up and captured an array of agent networks.[27] The reports on such groups hardly suggested high morale: as one captured colonel was heard to say to his second-in-command, 'four years of war and no satisfaction, we've lost everything, it's enough to get drunk on'.[28] What was lacking was any real insight into what might be expected in Italy itself. The Allies had very few agents in Italy. Attempts to recruit either anti-Fascist exiles or internees in the Middle East had ended in failure: both groups politely declined the opportunity to 'risk their necks' by entering Italy, preferring 'propaganda and intrigue'. The operations that were conducted with exiles willing to enter Italian territory had not engendered much confidence. Italians sent to Sardinia in the spring of 1943 were captured and turned, betraying the French groups on Corsica with whom they had been trained. There appeared to be a small resistance movement on the mainland. Agents, both Italian and British, were sent in to make contact, but nothing of much use seemed to come out. The reasons for this later became apparent. The resistance movement was not small, it was non-existent. The groups which the British tried to contact were in fact front organizations run either by SIM or the Fascist secret police, OVRA.[29]

The result was a shake the tree and see attitude. As the commander of the Sicilian expedition, Harold Alexander, said to the political and military leaders that gathered in the Villa Eisenhower at the beginning of June 1943, 'none repeat none of the possibilities he had discussed could be accurately foreseen. In war the incredible often happened.'[30] Without any specific knowledge, rather a lot rode on what the Italians might do. As Eisenhower admitted, 'the thing that I am really counting on more than anything else is that the Italians really have no stomach for fighting'.[31] Although this supposition proved to be true, at the time there was little feedback to confirm it. A significant effort was put into propagandizing the Italian population. That effort was later regarded as a triumph for psychological warfare.[32] The 'psywar' campaign was guided, however, by little more than a series of assumptions not much different from those championed and then discarded in 1939.

What was needed to transform the prognostications of the 'psychological warfare boys' into an executable plan of action was some tangible sign of Italian willingness to change sides. There were no such signs for two reasons. The organs of the Fascist state still had a firm grip on the populace. Although Fascism might have been a 'rotten pear' there was no chance of that state being overthrown by popular action. Its enemies were within. Those enemies were, however, committed procrastinators. There were two groups of potential *frondeurs*. Fascist bosses with a grudge against Mussolini were led in July 1943 by the former foreign minister, Dino Grandi. They had grumbled in their villas for months, monitored by the secret police, without any threat of action. Generals with a grudge against the Germans were legion, but they could not agree on a leader. With or without the war, the higher reaches of the Italian military elite were a cesspool of personal rivalry and hatreds. Vittorio Ambrosio, the chief of the *Comando Supremo*, did not trust the leading military figure of pre-war Italy, Pietro Badoglio; neither man trusted the head of the army, Mario Roatta. Badoglio talked to the unofficial leader of the 'pre-Fascist' political parties, Ivanoe Bonomi, but the two old men regarded each other with suspicion. Everyone vaguely looked to the King for legitimacy, but Victor Emmanuel III had not survived so long on his throne by trusting anyone. They were all deeply committed to inaction, until diminishing chances of their own survival left them without a choice. They would be moved only by incontestable proof of Allied power and intent in their own backyard. As Ambrosio's deputy, Giuseppe Castellano, put it, 'we should remain at our ally's side as in the past [but] if the battle in the summer fails, the argument is the exact opposite'.[33]

The two Allied invasion forces that went ashore in south-eastern Sicily on 10 July 1943 had no real idea of what they might expect, beyond fierce German opposition to the attack, but neither had the Fascist-military leadership. Before the Battle of Sicily the military performance of the Italian armed forces had been mixed. There had been many defeats but some units of the Italian forces had always fought well. When General Montgomery saw the initial planning for the invasion of Sicily he said that it 'breaks every common sense rule of practical battle-fighting and is completely theoretical. It has no hope of success and should be completely recast.' According to Monty, 'planning so far has been based on assumption that opposition will be slight and that Sicily will be captured relatively easily. Never was there a greater error. Germans *and also Italians* are fighting desperately now in Tunisia and will do so in Sicily. . . . We must plan the operation on assumption that resistance will be fierce and that a prolonged dogfight battle will follow the initial assault.' At his insistence the Sicilian landings were concentrated in the south-east of the island. The key goal was to establish a beachhead, not to take a pleasure drive to victory.[34]

The most recent Italian military failure had been the surrender of the 12,000-strong garrison of the island of Pantelleria on 11 June 1943 after a pummelling from the air and from naval gunfire, but before any Allied troops could land. The surrender of Pantelleria, strongly fortified at Mussolini's personal insistence in the 1930s, could be taken as a sign of the collapse of Italian will. Air Marshal Tedder, often willing to deride Montgomery, joined him in worrying that such a dangerous assumption might gain ground. 'Even Eisenhower', he complained, 'has begun to say, can't we possibly do something like this for Husky [Sicily]. In short, I can see Pantelleria becoming a perfect curse for us in this manner.' The sixteen formidable batteries that protected the only landing site at Porto di Pantelleria on the north coast of the island barely fired a shot. 'The effects on morale were so striking', an official report noted, 'that it has stimulated a fairly widespread view that the fall of island was due almost entirely to the collapse of morale on a poor-spirited garrison, and little to the damage of fixed defences.' But the operational researchers who crawled over Pantelleria after its capture warned:

> So far as morale is concerned, it has been demanded of few people to stand up to bombing of the intensity experienced by the batteries. Perhaps only those who have experienced it are competent to judge whether any troops, of whatever nationality, would have succeeded where the Italians failed . . . the Germans do not appear to have believed that a few deter-mined men could have manned light defences and prevented our assault forces coming ashore, or alternatively that they could have made an assault very expensive for us; they withdrew all but fifty of the six hundred men whom they had on the island at the start of the air offensive.[35]

Indeed, having witnessed the impact of naval gunfire on German troops on the south coast of Sicily on 10 and 11 July 1943, their commanding general lamented that, 'I had the bitter experience to watch scenes, during these last few days, which are not worthy of the German soldier, particularly not a soldier of the Panzer Division *Hermann Göring*. Persons come running to the rear, hysterically crying, because they have heard the detonation of a single shot fired somewhere in the landscape. Others, believing in false rumours, moved whole columns to the rear ... these acts were committed not only by the youngest soldiers but by NCOs and warrant officers.'[36]

On Sicily everyone, Americans, British, Germans and above all the Italians themselves, finally concurred that few Italians any longer had the will to fight.[37] Nine divisions of the Italian army defended Sicily, supported by only two German divisions. They faced a landing by three British, three American and one Canadian division. 'One disappointment followed another,' Kesselring complained in the context of his first visit to Sicily after the invasion on 12 July 1943. 'The Italian coastal divisions were an utter failure, not one of their counter-attack divisions reaching the enemy in time or even at all. The *Napoli* Division in the south-west corner of the island melted into thin air. The commandant of the fortress of Augusta meanwhile surrendered without even waiting to be attacked. . . . Whether or not the court-martial promised me by Mussolini was ever held I never discovered.'[38] A diarist for a British infantry battalion wrote, 'the myth that the Italians would fight with great fortitude in defence of their own country was exploded'. In the days to come the Americans, who faced the bulk of the Italian troops, were to conclude that 'there is no question that Italian resistance is negligible'.[39] The commander of Italian armed forces on the island agreed: he reported 'the shameful phenomenon of disintegration which casts deep discredit on the Italian soldier'.[40] It was the collapse on Sicily, rather than any long-planned change, that forced the factions to consider real action. As Mussolini himself commented, 'the military crisis could not fail to bring on a political crisis, which was directed against the Fascist regime in the person of its leader'.[41]

'The actual landings on the shores of Sicily' that had so worried the best military minds on the Allied side 'were, as far as fighting goes, rather an anti-climax'. Reports from each of the twenty-six beaches spoke of perfunctory opposition from the Italian 206th Coastal Division and 18th Coastal Brigade. Large landing ships were able to come right up to the beach to deposit their loads. '"Stand by your vehicles" had come the order,' wrote an artillerist of the British 5th Division of his arrival in Sicily:

as at last [16.00] our LST [Landing Ship Tank] was signalled to the beach and slowly she slid forward to the absurdly small stretch of yellow sand.

Truck motors were started up & the roar filled the great space of the hold. The chains holding them were released. As the big doors in the bows were lowered we crowded forward between the lines of Sherman tanks, which were to go off before us . . . Slowly the LST's bows slipped down the coast within yards of the land. The sand shelved steeply and looked soft and treacherous. Would the vehicles make it? At last we grounded and held firm. There was a bare stretch of twenty yards between the lowered prow door and where small waves lapped the beach. The first of the Shermans rumbled out of the hold, through the water with a great cloud of steam and fumes and without pausing, clambered up the beach and was away . . . the warm water reached only to the thighs of my khaki drill trousers and I squelched ashore.

A British commando attached to the Canadian 1st Division made a wetter entry to the island. 'We had', he wrote, 'a choppy sea and wet landing up to our chests in water. There were holes everywhere and when my section waded ashore in the beautiful warm water the chap in front of me disappeared and then came up spluttering and cursing.' The opposition on his beach was only slightly more formidable and included the flora. 'When we got among the sand dunes,' the commando reported, 'where we could smell the wild garlic (this causes blindness if eaten) machine gun tracers were just passing over our heads. The Italians were putting up token resistance but we moved fast and took all our objectives . . . we captured umpteen prisoners . . . a friend of mine . . . lost an eye from an Italian Red Devil grenade. The Italian who threw it died quickly.'[42]

The British were able to occupy the main town in south-eastern Sicily, Siracusa, and the Italian naval base of Augusta, with barely any fighting. Within four days of the landing they were fully operational. By the end of July 1943 nearly 10,000 military vehicles had been unloaded across Siracusa's docks. The Americans near the southern coastal town of Gela had to face more formidable opposition in the form of a counter-attack by elements of the German *Hermann Göring* tank division and the Italian *Livorno* Division. That battle, although intense and much memorialized, was over by the early afternoon of 11 July. At 16.00 the Germans concluded that 'the counterattack against enemy landings has failed. Support by Italian forces can no longer be counted on, nor can Italian orders be expected. The enemy is continually being reinforced and is beginning to surround *Hermann Göring* Panzer Division from the west and east. Continued defence in present positions would result in the annihilation of the division. Effective resistance is possible only in a shorter continuous defence position of all German units in Sicily in terrain favourable to defence.'[43]

The German decision to concentrate their units on a national rather than on an Axis basis, in terrain that they could defend, had the effect of decoupling the strategic and tactical battles for Sicily. By the time the Allies faced their first military reverses, everyone had come to the conclusion that the outcome of the battle was merely a matter of time. The Germans rapidly improvised an operational plan that they described as the 'swinging door'. They would send two more divisions into Sicily, one panzer grenadier, one parachute, to create a bloc of forces capable of fighting its own battle. They would abandon southern and western Sicily, and the Italian troops stationed there, in attempt to defend northern and eastern Sicily. The 'hinge' of the door would be the port city of Catania on the east coast. The city would be vigorously defended by a detached battlegroup of the *Hermann Göring*, reinforced by men of the 1st Parachute Division, flown in from the south of France. Inland, the 'door' of German troops would make a fighting retreat, 'swinging' north and east. The 'favourable terrain' they would use was the mountains of northeastern Sicily and in particular the huge volcanic mass of Mount Etna. 'Christ! What a steep hill this is,' wrote a British intelligence officer, summing up the feelings of many.[44] The asset that they were really defending was the port of Messina in the far north-east of the island. The two-mile-wide Strait of Messina was all that separated Sicily from the mainland. As long as Messina was safe it would be possible to escape from Sicily. Kesselring had no intention of repeating the Tunisian débâcle, from where the troops had been unable to flee.

The initial 'victims' of the German plan to mount a convincing defence of Sicily were the British divisions advancing up the east coast from Siracusa to Catania. 'I can still vividly recall the view that greeted us,' wrote an officer of the 5th Division:

[looking] down for the first time on the Catania Plain. The panorama before us was magnificent. Thirty miles to the north, dominating the horizon, was the huge, misty, snow-capped conical mass, 10,000 feet high of Mount Etna. On the plain itself we could see through our binoculars the Simeto river curling irregularly from the west down to the sea . . . Along the coast, past the Simeto, the city of Catania was dimly visible, shimmering in the heat. All this would have constituted a picture of great

beauty and tranquillity, had it not been for the thud of shells, with their tell-tale puffs of black smoke, exploding near the river.

The Germans had identified the Simeto as the outer bulwark of their defence of Catania. This became clear when the British 50th Division tried to cross the river at 'Plimsole Bridge' on 15 July.

'They started to cross the river when all hell broke loose,' wrote a private in the Durham Light Infantry. 'On the other side of the river suddenly a row of heads, machine guns and rifles popped up. Soon the river ran red, literally, with the blood of the Durhams. Some did reach the other side, scamper up the bank and engage the enemy in hand-to-hand fighting, but there were not enough to hang on to what they had gained. We in the HQ company went down to see what we could do to help, there wasn't a lot. We stopped just short of the river and fired at anything that looked Tedescish [German].' 'The Germans were Paras,' the DLI private concluded his account, 'well armed and they knew what to do with them. With both sides it was hand-to-hand, rifles, bayonets and plenty of Spandaus.'

The whole battalion moved silently in single file to the attack [recalled an officer of another DLI unit further along the bank], sliding down the bank into chest high water, again in single file, guiding ourselves by hanging onto a wire stretched between the banks for this purpose. Below the far bank the battalion bore left then turned to face the enemy, the three assaulting companies in line. So far all had gone well, our objective a sunken road, was some 500 yard away through the vineyards . . . recollections of what happened after that are confused. Firing began at isolated Germans seen running away, then from the direction of the road came a murderous fire from the Spandaus located there. The gunners were firing on 'fixed lines', they could not see us in the dark. Bursts of tracer swept past at knee height. The line of infantry kept going on in spite of the men being hit until we were struck by heavy concentrations of artillery. Some of this was probably enemy DF (defensive fire) but in the opinion of those who had been shelled by our own gunners on previous occasions we were on our own [firing line] . . . then it stopped, lifted, and groups of men got up, moved on through the cactus hedge into the sunken road. There was a lot of shooting, suddenly it was over . . . the place was littered with German equipment, Spandau machine guns, belts of ammunition and corpses.

By the next day, 'there had been no time for burial parties and there were dead bodies everywhere. A sunken road was paved with them . . . the Brigade lost 600 men. When you realise that no battalion had more than three hundred men to start with, it meant that one in three had gone.'[45] To their horror the men who had fought in the battle of Primesole Bridge discovered that it was but the first German line they had taken at such cost. Yet it was such actions that forced the Germans to articulate what had been implicit in their defence plan: they were fighting to lose, not to win. 'During the night of 15–16 July,' Kesselring recalled, 'I flew to Milazzo, in north Sicily, by flying boat, as it was now impossible for aircraft to make a landing, and gave General Hube detailed instructions on the spot. His mission was to dig in on a solid line even at the cost of initially giving ground . . . I also told him that I was reckoning with the evacuation of Sicily, which it was his job to postpone for as long as possible.'[46]

Within the Allied high command the prospect of victory soon degenerated into an unseemly squabble about who would get the credit. As the Primesole bridge was secured, American commanders were crossing the Mediterranean with accusations of a British plot to dun them. The commander of the American troops in Sicily, George Patton, confronted his British superior officer, Harold Alexander, in Tunis. Alexander was wasting Patton's time, Patton said. Messina – which the Germans had just decided was their greatest prize – was unimportant. What was vital was that he, Patton, should be allowed to drive all around the coast road from his present position on the south coast, up the west coast of the island, and onto the north coast. There he would seize the capital of Sicily, Palermo. Patton's subordinate, John Lucas, flew to Algiers to make the same points to Alexander's superior, Eisenhower. 'I think the British have a bear by the tail in the Messina peninsula,' Patton wrote, 'Alex has no idea of either the power or speed of American armies. We can go twice as fast as the British and hit harder . . . our method of attacking all the time is better than the British system.' 'Future students', he boasted, 'will study the campaign as a classic example of the use of tanks.'[47] Patton's own officers had little doubt about his true motivation, or the quality of his military reasoning. 'As to Palermo as a port,' Lucian Truscott, the commander of the US 3rd Division on Sicily later said, 'we could have been supported from the beaches and ports we already had for two months. . . . It was the glamour of capturing Palermo . . . that attracted Georgie Patton . . . the glamour of the big city was the chief thing that attracted General Patton.'[48]

On 17 July, however, Patton disarticulated the Allied armies. He set off on his wild coastal dash. Of course he enjoyed rapid and spectacular success since his army was heading for those very parts of Sicily that the Germans had already decided to abandon. As they advanced Kesselring commented that 'the enemy has not yet embarked on an offensive of decisive importance'. The west coast port of Trapani became a visual symbol. British journalists were shocked to find the Americans living *la dolce vita* at the height of the fighting on the east of the island; '[Patton's] Seventh Army', they implied, 'was lucky to be in the unoccupied western portion of Sicily eating grapes.'[49] The American military procession entered Palermo on 22 July 1943, but the wider effects of the Sicilian expedition had begun to reverberate around the Mediterranean even before he set out.

It was a measure of how poorly each side had been able to prepare in an information vacuum that the first genuine signs of disaffection were detected by the Allies in the eastern rather than the central Mediterranean. The British had worked hard to turn attention to the east. Officially these efforts had all been part of the great deception operation to distract from Sicily. Eddie Myers in Greece had received definitive orders that although there would not be any Allied military operations in the Balkans, he had to get the Greeks to fight. In the circumstances he did not see any alternative to an alliance with the Communists on their terms, unified resistance, no British command, no King. Reluctantly, Myers accepted the terms and signed a National Bands agreement. He pointed out to his superiors the cruelty of the deception he was being called on to implement. 'A widespread demolition plan', he signalled Cairo, 'is not executed without causing a great amount of suffering to the civilian population in the form of ruinous reprisals.' Churchill would subsequently rule that the Germans must be encouraged in this approach on the grounds that the blood of martyrs was the seed of the church.[50] The Communists, too, had turned their mind to reprisals. When Myers requested that the 'unified' resistance should resist, he was told that his demands for military action were merely a plot against 'the development of a mass patriotic movement'. The Greek forces in the Middle East were once again in ferment, whipped up on this occasion by left-wing agitators. All the expense and sacrifice of guerrilla warfare, Emanuel Tsouderos lamented, was in vain.

The centrepiece of Myers's plan was an attack on the other great eastern viaduct, the Asopus. He found, however, that the Communists were already withdrawing their bands to the west, in part to attack their rivals, in part to make sure that it was the civilians, not they, who were hit by universally expected reprisals. Instead of the expected thousand heavily armed guerrillas, Myers could spare only six British personnel armed with rubber coshes for the mission. In a 'tale of endurance, sheer "guts" and determination', this small band managed to blow the bridge. The forty or so other British officers in Greece, who had 'learned by then not to rely too much on the *Andartes*', managed a respectable range of complementary sabotage operations. By the time Operation *Animals* ended, British teams had cut the Salonika–Piraeus railway in twenty different places.[51]

It was the very moment at which arguments about 'loyalty' and 'sacrifice' amongst the Greeks were reaching a crescendo in Cairo, that reports began to filter in about Italian generals willing to explore terms with the Allies. Italy's army of occupation in the Balkans was a sizeable force comprising thirty-two divisions. By way of contrast, nine divisions were in the process of disintegration on Sicily. Italian commanders in the Balkans were kept in the dark about what was going on in Rome but they could read the runes of Sicily as well as their superiors. At least three divisional commanders in Greece made contact with the intermediaries whom they correctly believed had the means to get in touch with the British. The question each asked was the same: if they declared for the Allies, would the British save them from the Germans and Greeks? In return for their turning coats, what guarantees would the British be willing to offer about the survival of the Italian empire in the Mediterranean?[52]

Despite the various speculations about Italian reactions prior to the invasion, there were no good answers to these questions. Cairo was soon signalling London and Algiers looking for guidance. Were they supposed to encourage the Italians 'to remain Fascists' whilst spreading a 'surrender mentality'? Alternatively, should they encourage treachery on the periphery to undermine the centre? Most ambitiously of all, should they enter into negotiations, and then drag them out, until real operations in the Balkans and the Aegean could be undertaken? Although all Allied discussions had taken place on the understanding that there was to be no eastern Mediterranean front, merely a deception operation to distract the Axis, it was this last suggestion that set British pulses racing.[53]

On 18 July 1943, Eisenhower and his three chief subordinates, all

British, met in Tedder's office at La Marsa, looking east over the Bay of Tunis. They agreed that caution needed to be thrown aside. The Italian collapse on Sicily made an ambitious assault on the Italian mainland, not just a hop across the Straits of Messina into Calabria, the Toe of Italy, a viable prospect. 'I recommend carrying the war to the mainland of Italy immediately Sicily has been captured,' Eisenhower wrote to his reluctant bosses in Washington. Ike's conversion to the operation long advocated by his British colleagues was something of a coup. Within days, however, Alexander and Churchill were in correspondence, agreeing that although Sicily was indeed the jumping-off place for an invasion of Italy, the key to the control of the Mediterranean was the Balkans.[54]

The eastern Mediterranean stole a march on the central Mediterranean. The first low-level envoys from Italy did not set off towards the west – specifically Lisbon – until the head of steam in the east had started to build.[55] The majority of the Fascist bosses were convinced that in order to save their own power they had to get rid of Mussolini. He unwittingly forced their hand by summoning a grand council of the Fascist leadership to apportion blame for the Sicilian disaster. If Mussolini was not to blame then others would surely be sacrificed. Not only was the Sicilian front visible proof that the *Duce*'s rhetoric no longer had any sway except in his own mind, but the Allies gave them a brutal reminder of their own vulnerability when they staged a major air raid on Rome. As chance would have it Mussolini was absent from the city, in conclave with Hitler. Even the *Duce* was shocked by the view from his returning aeroplane. Rome appeared to be 'wreathed in black smoke'.

The plot against Mussolini evolved in four parts: a Fascist plea to the King to take over the direction of the war; the dismissal and arrest of Mussolini; the creation of a military dyarchy with Badoglio and Ambrosio sharing power between them; and a public commitment by that military regime to the Axis. Such a difficult and high-risk manoeuvre allowed little room for long-range plans. The first priority was to survive. Accordingly, the Fascists were willing to surrender some of their power in return for military protection. There was general agreement that some kind of deal with the Allies must also be explored.

Mussolini fell headlong into the plot in a way that is difficult to explain satisfactorily. His own verdict was that 'his frame of mind might be called in retrospect positively naive'. On 25 July 1943, the *Duce* was whisked away, a prisoner of the plotters, in an unmarked ambulance. The next day Badoglio was at the radio station promising that 'the war continues'. 'Italy, cruelly hurt in its invaded provinces, in its destroyed cities,' the Marshal declared, 'keeps faith to its pledged word.' Roatta issued orders that anyone who protested against the continuation of the war should be shot, 'a little bloodshed at the beginning will save rivers of blood later'. His orders were carried out in Bari, where the army opened fire on an anti-war demonstration.[56]

Mussolini's fall found committed Mediterraneanists and outsiders at odds. The Darlan experience had bitten deep, particularly for Roosevelt. He had taken great pains to distance himself from that flirtation with Mediterranean morality. The Mediterranean, he observed, had a life of its own. Even his most trusted lieutenants ignored his direct orders. The President had told Eisenhower, in terms much plainer than he was accustomed to use, to preserve Giraud. The General was the sole means, however poor, by which American policy could be defended against charges of incompetence, dishonour or both. Roosevelt had given Giraud his personal imprimatur, entertaining him at the White House. Eisenhower had chosen to pursue an entirely different course. He had relied more on the advice of Churchill's political appointee, Harold Macmillan, than Roosevelt's, Robert Murphy.[57] 'The Americans here', Macmillan rejoiced, 'are absolutely sound now.'[58] Eisenhower bought into Macmillan's fantasy that there was a party of French moderates in Algiers who might supplant both Giraud and de Gaulle. As a result de Gaulle's power waxed whilst that of Giraud faded away. His key subordinates were picked off by the Gaullists, his control of the army was undermined. It was against this background that Roosevelt told Churchill that he had a particular aversion to Eisenhower cutting more deals. Unconditional surrender was about the management of US domestic politics, and he took domestic politics very seriously. In order to make sure that his own subordinates had little room for manoeuvre, the President himself took to the airwaves with an uncompromising clarification of his remarks at Casablanca: 'our terms of surrender to Italy', he told both his domestic and international audiences, 'are the same as our terms to Germany and Japan – unconditional surrender'. Eisenhower himself was given permission to broadcast to the Italian people only if he eschewed any mention of an 'honourable peace'.[59]

The President's attempts at remote control from across the Atlantic proved fruitless. So too did tugs at the rein from London, equally disturbed by Mediterranean autonomy, if not by the prospect of a deal with Badoglio. Whatever the politicians might say, Eisenhower and his chief of staff, Walter Bedell Smith, who did the political heavy lifting for his boss, regarded the Darlan deal as a success. Eisenhower said that his biggest failure in North Africa had been the result of kow-towing to Washington's demands. He should have opposed the pointless invasion of Morocco and concentrated solely on the Mediterranean, as the British had advo-cated.[60] In playing his superiors, Eisenhower had on his side the plea of military necessity, the undoubted successes of the Sicilian operation, and the continual lure of the 'quick fix'.[61] 'There might occur', Eisenhower advised Marshall, 'a vast but possibly fleeting opportunity to accomplish all we are seeking in the Italian peninsula.'[62]

When Eisenhower broadcast to the Italian people on 29 July 1943, calling upon them to surrender, he was still speaking into a vacuum. 'We have not been able to gather much information on the internal situation in Italy,' Eisenhower confirmed a week after his broadcast.[63] The actual evidence of Italian willingness to deal was still centred on the eastern Mediterranean.

In the absence of any firm information, Eisenhower and his coterie, Bedell Smith, Macmillan and AFHQ's British intelligence chief, Kenneth Strong, were subject to fierce criticism.[64] Churchill accused them of being 'too fond of "propaganda" and [making] too many "statements" and "proclamations to the Italians"'. Macmillan was dispatched back to London to defend their conduct.[65] As it happened, however, events were unfolding much as they had predicted. The first instinct of Badoglio and his fellow plotters was to 'stall'.[66] Nothing could be done, they told each other, until a new foreign minister was appointed to replace Mussolini. Their chosen candidate, Raffaele Guariglia, 'a shrewd functionary who ties his ass where his master tells him', only arrived back from his post as ambassador to Turkey on the last day of July 1943.[67] The next day German 'reinforcements' started to enter northern Italy. Four days of discussion ensued until messengers were dispatched to Lisbon and Tangier to make contact with British diplomats. The plotters received a nasty shock when Guariglia held his first meeting with Ribbentrop. The Nazi foreign minister assured him that the Germans knew full well that he was negotiating with the Allies. This unpleasant encounter at Tarvisio focused the mind of the plotters. The exploration of possibilities, the purpose of the original envoys, had already put them in great danger.

General Ambrosio decided instead to send his 'suave Sicilian' deputy, Giuseppe Castellano, to Lisbon, so that military commander could speak to military commander. This was exactly the kind of contact Eisenhower and his team had hoped for, not least because they, rather than the professional diplomats, would become the arbiters of what was right and possible.[68]

The team in Algiers was right about the composition of the Castellano mission but wrong about its meaning. Tarvisio did more than quicken the pace, it determined the priorities of the plotters. They had no real interest in a deal that stabbed the Germans in the back in return for a Mediterranean empire. Tarvisio confirmed that their most important priority should be survival, preferably political, most certainly physical. The plotters had no intention of fighting the Germans; rather, they wished to ensure that the Allies would fight the Germans on their behalf. The Eisenhower team hoped that a military representative such as Castellano would open the door to the 'quick fix' they so passionately desired. Castellano's sponsors hoped that Eisenhower could conjure up a protective cordon reaching as far as Rome. Both were deluding themselves. Such was the excitement, however, that even those who claimed to be ideologically inoculated against deals with 'fascists' were taken in. The socialist politician Richard Crossman, one of the Mediterranean 'psychological warfare boys', weaned the Americans away from their chosen terminology for Victor Emmanuel, 'the moronic little King', whilst championing Badoglio's 'good faith'.[69] Those who warned that the likely outcome of dealing with the Italian military would be another 'Darlan deal', a blow against democracy and liberalism without any countervailing military palliation, were far away, specifically in Quebec where Roosevelt and Churchill were holding a summit. In any case the nay-sayers rendered themselves ridiculous with alternative proposals for braid-bedecked acts of surrender.[70]

The Germans began to withdraw from Sicily on 11 August 1943. On 26 July, the German operational commander, General Hube, had reluctantly concluded that the days of the 'swinging door' and the defence of Catania were numbered. Kesselring ordered plans for evacuation to be put in motion. In the meantime, the Germans established a shorter 'swinging door', this time 'hinged' on the inland town of Centuripe and 'swinging' away from Catania and up the slopes of Etna.

In a brilliant attack on 'Cherry Ripe' the British 78th Division 'unhinged' that door on 1 August. 'As it grew light so we could see the bulk of Etna away to our right front, still smoking, and very soon the sun was up and the warm night was changing into hot morning,' an artillery officer acting as forward observer began his account of the battle. He offered a detailed account of the landscape: 'the town of Centuripe lay 5000 yards ahead of me connected by a narrow strip of ground possibly a 100 yards wide on either side of which were deep ravines. This strip of ground appeared to be the only possible approach to the town – to attack up the ravines would not only be difficult it would be sheer madness. The top slopes of the ravines had been cultivated into terraces, but below these the ground sloped away at angles steeper than 45 degrees. It was a very strong defensive position.' The key to British victory was the proper application of superior firepower:

> I suppose I directed several thousand shells into enemy positions that day [the forward observer recalled]. The first was on considerable enemy troop movement away to my right just the other side of the ravine . . . I considered this important enough to engage with the entire regiment, so I gave the order 'Monkey target' and a map reference. A couple of ranging rounds and I was near enough to order '10 rounds gun fire'. 240 shells landed in an area not much bigger than a football pitch and in the space of 60 seconds. . . . I was kept busy all day but fortunately there was very little counter-artillery or mortar fire from the Germans – it was very much one way but the leading companies were pinned down by small arms fire and it wasn't until late afternoon that the [infantry] were able to make a real advance into the town.[71]

The British still had to fight their way around Etna, however. There were other 'cherry ripes': hilltop towns defended by determined German rearguards.

On the same day as 'Cherry Ripe', American troops advancing east from Palermo, along both the coast road and an inland route, towards Messina, hit their first determined German opposition. They soon saw what the British had been up against. 'Like other Sicilian towns,' wrote the operations officer of the US 1st Division, 'Troina sat atop a conical hill, the highest in the vicinity, approached by a hairpin road. The entrenched German defenders, protected by stone buildings, had an open field of fire and an excellent observation point. The valleys below were devoid of natural cover.' Troina was defended by the German 15th Panzer Grenadier Division. Like the *Hermann Göring* and the parachutists to the south-east, they made good use of the terrain. The battle of Troina lasted for five blood-soaked days. The US 3rd Division had a similar experience as they tried to fight their way along the coast road past the roadblocks and ambushes of the 29th Panzer Grenadier Division. Some British observers argued that once in combat the Americans did rather better than their British opposite numbers. They attempted, for instance, to use landing craft to get along the coast behind the German defences. 'On the whole I think the Americans have done rather better than our [British] Eighth Army,' ABC Cunningham wrote. 'They have fought with more imagination and used their seapower to greater effect. Our people have gone in for slogging matches.'[72] But neither British nor American methods made fast enough progress.

For their own reasons the Italians were determined to get their men out of Sicily. Indeed the Italian troops started to fight much more effectively to escape Sicily than they had ever done to defend it. There thus developed two separate operations in the same waterway, as both Germans and Italians ferried men and equipment across the Strait of Messina. The short sea crossing between Messina on the north-east tip of Sicily and Reggio on the underside of the toe was an enormous boon to the escapees. The small but sophisticated craft which plied the passage at night needed no harbours, merely a jetty to embark and disembark. This Axis Dunkirk was aided immeasurably by an Allied intelligence failure. The extent and purpose of the operation was only rumbled when it was close to success. The American and British armies finally stumbled into Messina on 17 August 1943. Something of the order of 60,000 Germans and 75,000 Italian troops had escaped. 'Messina was not very healthy,' a British commando officer who arrived at 10.00 observed, 'the bombing of the town and port had been severe. Now the coastal guns on the other side of the Strait, at Reggio, were beginning to open up, to add to the Chaos.'[73]

General Castellano burst onto the Allied scene at the dramatic moment of Axis escape. On 15 August he presented himself to Sir Samuel Hoare in Madrid. Four days later he was closeted in the British Embassy in Lisbon with Bedell Smith and Kenneth Strong. They initiated a contentious series of negotiations that soon moved fully within the Mediterranean sphere when transferred to Algiers and Sicily. Castellano's was, however, not the highly charged trans-Mediterranean mission of August 1943. The plotters in Rome were desperate not to acknowledge the wider Mediterranean implications of their actions. Badoglio insisted that on no account should the military commanders of the Empire be told what was going on. A pan-Mediterranean conspiracy was bound to leak, endangering its main purpose, 'protection and support' for the Rome clique. Nevertheless, as the Italians in Greece independently sought some kind of understanding with the Allies, so too did the Greek parties themselves.

Just as speculation about an Italian mission had been transformed into action by the success of military operations in Sicily, the same was true of Greece. Everybody wanted to talk to the likely victors. Despite the disappointment of the lack of resistance cooperation with *Animals*, Myers was determined to try again. He based this optimism on a particular reading of the Greek 'mentality and psychology', as it had revealed itself over the previous months. 'The Greeks', he reasoned, 'are Asiatic. They are not European. One cannot judge them by our moral standards.' This being so, 'one has got to deal with them like sentimental children, to lead them, not to order them'. On 9 August 1943, Myers led his 'children' onto an aeroplane for the six-hour flight to Cairo. Given his views on the Greek character he proved remarkably susceptible to sharp practice. Myers had originally planned to bring out a sympathetic Communist and two representatives of non-Communist bands. At the moment of departure, however, the Communist leadership arrived at the airstrip insisting that the aircraft would only be taking off if Myers took a further three Communists. The plane that arrived in Cairo thus carried an over-whelmingly Communist delegation.[74]

The initial pleasure that many in Cairo felt at seeing Myers – the by now fabled destroyer of Gorgopotamos and Asopus – and at the prospect of a unified government of resisters soon turned to gall when the nature of the mission became apparent. The practical problem was that, for all their political disagreements and personal jealousies, the delegation and the Cairo Greek politicians agreed that the King's position was untenable. A carefully crafted promise of institutional reform after his return was useless. There could be no royal return until after the politicians had 'reformed' the political system. Given their ugly mood, any agreement to the formation of a national government would mean King George 'practically signing his abdication'.[75] A violent series of arguments flowed from this realization, between the King and his own government, between the British and the Tsouderos government, between the British and the delegation, and most spectacularly of all between the British themselves. Myers and Rex Leeper, the British ambassador to the Greek government in exile, developed a poisonous relationship. Leeper viewed Myers as a dangerous fool. Myers's friends responded by portraying Leeper as a cowardly, effete, insecure, power-hungry, egomaniac. A low point was reached with a botched Leeper-inspired attempt to bundle the delegation back onto their plane and drop them back into the middle of Greece as if they had never existed. Leeper accused SOE of trying to instigate a Communist revolution; SOE responded that he was trying to get their officers in Greece killed. They were still arguing when the negotiations with the Italians became public.[76]

The coeval attempts of Algiers to negotiate with Italy, and of Cairo to negotiate with Greece, had one consistent feature: the determination of London and Washington to undermine any claims made for the autonomy of the Mediterranean. In the case of the Italian negotiations, a surprising move by the Italians themselves prompted such an intervention. Castellano had made the point of telling Smith and Strong that Mario Roatta had been deliberately excluded from the plot as an untrustworthy 'lone wolf'. Upon Castellano's departure, however, another Italian general, Giacomo Zanussi, arrived in Lisbon, announcing himself as Roatta's envoy, denouncing Badoglio and the King as 'used men'. On orders from London, and to the anger of Algiers, the British ambassador not only briefed Zanussi about Castellano but presented him with a set of 'unconditional' surrender terms, agreed by Churchill and Roosevelt, but different from those Smith had expounded to Castellano. Zanussi was swiftly transferred to Algiers in an attempt to undo the damage. 'The plot is thickening,' Macmillan moaned, 'and the sub-plots and counter-plots and the cross-plots are increasing. London has gone quite mad!'[77]

The strands were finally reunited when Zanussi, and the returning Castellano, were put in the same tent at Cassibile, Alexander's Sicilian HQ. The Cassibile meeting revealed the complete hollowness of all the big talk about a 'quick fix' at the very moment that it was too late to do anything about it. Smith and his team realized that the plotters were 'pathetic' and 'scared'. They were 'merely frightened individuals that are trying to get out of a bad mess too badly demoralised to face up to consequences'. Although Smith had no access to the plotters' actual discussions in Rome, their fearful paralysis would have confirmed his suspicions.[78]

The die had been cast a month previously. The invasion plans had taken their final form the day after news of Mussolini's fall reached Tunis. Eisenhower and his commanders had agreed on a two-pronged approach. One invasion force would cross the Messina strait directly into the Toe of Italy, 'a yachting trip across the Narrows [that] looked more like the Henley Regatta than anything else'.[79] The second force would set out from Oran, Bizerta and Tripoli for Salerno, at the head of the bay immediately to the south of the Bay of Naples. The Toe force was due to land on 3 September 1943, the Salerno force on the 9th. The Salerno convoys had started loading in North Africa just as Smith flew to Lisbon for his first meeting with Castellano. The ships sailed as the Cassibile meeting convened.

Despite later special pleading about Allied deceit – nearly all the Italian participants wrote memoirs blaming the Allies, and each other, for the failure of the plot – Smith was perfectly straight with Castellano about what was going on. He wanted a surrender document to be broadcast as the British and American troops were on their final run-in to the Salerno beaches. Smith's only act of 'bad faith' was his realization that the 'quick fix' was ebbing away. He came to believe that the best that could be hoped for was the disruption of the Axis at the moment of the invasion. Nevertheless, he still strove for a 'strategic' coup. The Allied negotiators continued to believe that the Italian fleet might sail itself into Allied hands, 'an advantage that will be felt throughout the world'. At least one direct radio link was established with Rome so that the plotters could signify their assent to the terms offered and to warn them when the invasion was imminent.[80] A radio message from Badoglio enabled Castellano to sign the Armistice late on 3 September, as the first British troops landed in the Toe.

Smith's one concession to the fears of the plotters was an offer to drop a parachute division into Rome, to help the Italian army protect their own leaders against the Germans. A British motor torpedo boat was detailed to take the American airborne commander, Max Taylor, from Palermo to Gaeta, so he could make a personal inspection of the situation in Rome. It did not take Taylor long to confirm the Allies' worst suspicions. The plotters had never had any intention of fighting for Rome. The only force that had made any serious preparations was the *Regia*

ABOVE: Churchill in Cairo: the Middle East War Council in the garden of the Embassy in Cairo (back row, left to right: Tedder, Brooke, Harwood, Auchinleck, Wavell, Sir Charles Wilson, Cadogan. Front row, left to right: Smuts, Churchill, Lampson and Casey), August 1942.

BELOW: Cuthbert: A nervous Panyiotis Kanellopoulos waits to meet Churchill in Cairo, kept company by an unimpressed Alan Brooke and the Lampsons, August 1942.

The Unacceptable Face of the Mediterranean: Admiral Darlan and his wife in their Moorish villa, Algiers, the day before his assassination, 24 December 1942.

The Odd Couple: Giraud (in gold-braided képi) stares unhappily at de Gaulle's back upon the latter's arrival in North Africa, May 1943.

Eating the French: Sir Edward Spears greets Richard Casey (in dark suit) at Beirut airport; fittingly the spook Brigadier Clayton keeps his back to the camera, November 1943.

The AFHQ team in Tunisia: Eisenhower, Tedder, Alexander and Cunningham stand on the bottom step, Macmillan stands behind Eisenhower, Bedell Smith behind Tedder, July 1943.

Churchill in Turkey: Churchill peers out of the cockpit of his Liberator on the ground at Adana, January 1943.

Churchill in Algiers: AFHQ conference, June 1943 – perched around the table are (left to right) Eden, Brooke, Churchill, Marshall and Eisenhower; Tedder, Cunningham, Alexander and Montgomery stand.

RIGHT: The Return of the King: King George VI sails into Malta in triumph, 20 June 1943.

LEFT: Victory: The White Ensign flies over Reggio, September 1943.

RIGHT: The New Masters: Italian POWs wash themselves under British guard in the harbour of Pantelleria, June 1943.

ABOVE: Ungenerous and Dishonourable: An unhappy Badoglio (centre) is shepherded around a warship anchored at Malta by (left to right) Gort, Tedder, Mason-Mac, Ike and Alex, September 1943.

RIGHT: The New Order: Rommel bids his final farewell to Mussolini; Rudolf Rahn, Germany's Mediterranean 'fixer' looks on, November 1943.

ABOVE: The Favoured Son: Churchill and Alexander, August 1944.

LEFT: SACMED: Jumbo Wilson arrives at Athens airfield, October 1944.

LEFT: Difficult Allies: General Leclerc (with walking stick) of the Fighting French and Colonel Gigantes of the Greek Sacred Squadron confer at a Tunisian roadside, March 1943.

ABOVE: Mediterranean Refuge: Tito inspects his British protectors on the Island of Vis, August 1944.

LEFT: The Fruits of Resistance: Napoleon Zervas and his well-fed guerrillas with British special forces, Epirus, October 1944.

The Newer Masters: James Forrestal (with tie) and Mark Clark inspect Japanese-American troops in the ruins of Leghorn, August 1944.

Behind the Scenes: Bob Murphy and Ben Cohen in Moscow, March 1947.

Mick Carney's Mediterranean: Admiral Robert B. Carney sitting in front of a map of the Mediterranean, 1953.

Marina, which had prepared two escape plans, one for the King, Badoglio and the leaders of the armed forces, the second for the fleet. On the morning of 8 September Badoglio sent a radio message disowning the Armistice. In return he received a sharp reply from Bizerta that the Allies' psywar radio stations would announce that the Italians had deserted the Germans, whatever the reality. When the plotters met in their final conclave their initial decision was to stand shoulder-to-shoulder with their German brothers. It was left to a junior officer to point out that since the Allies had a signed copy of the Armistice, they would not be choosing the Germans over the Allies but rather becoming the enemies of both. Finally, a compromise was reached. Badoglio was dispatched to Radio Rome to announce that the Italians had accepted an Armistice from the Allies. Orders were issued to all units not to fight the Germans. Badoglio was to gather up the Royal Family; they, and the military leaders, would head for a ship standing by on the Adriatic coast and flee for their lives.[81] 'In this cockleshell,' Badoglio remembered, 'we steamed south without the slightest idea where we would drop anchor.'[82]

The sudden self-decapitation of the Italian regime certainly succeeded in throwing the Italians themselves into a state of confusion. The flight and whereabouts of the monarch were known only to the plotters themselves – civilian members of the government were abandoned in Rome. Yet anyone who cared to listen to Allied radio could hear the constant loop of the Armistice declaration. Some Italian units had orders not to fight the Germans, others had no orders. At the very points where the Italians might have aided the Allies, they were of no help at all. The Italian command for southern Italy was based at Potenza, the central communications hub between Toe and Heel. A British army had been in the Toe for six days. Immediately upon hearing the Armistice announcement the Potenza commander left his headquarters seeking to get as far away from both Allies and Germans as possible. His choice of refuge indeed, as far into the Heel as possible, mirrored that of the eventual royal refugee. His deputy commander did do the 'honourable' thing, committing suicide. Their leaderless troops proved easy meat for the Germans. The Italian commanders in Naples, the target for the Salerno invasion force, took a similar view of their situation, put on civilian clothes and fled.

The most effective collaboration was offered by the *Regia Marina*. The admirals' minds were made up by the loss of their flagship *Roma*, a new battleship that had joined the fleet in 1942. Their original plan had been to play for time, sending the fleet to Sardinia. When reports arrived that the naval base of La Maddalena, on the northern tip of the island, was being occupied by the Germans, *Roma* turned south. Unfortunately for the battleship, it was shadowed by a specialist *Luftwaffe* anti-shipping unit operating from Istres in the south of France. The attack aircraft were equipped with a new class of weapon, guided bombs. Two of these weapons hit the ship, causing it to explode with enormous loss of life. The German air attack left its survivors desperately looking for a safe berth. The capital ships headed for Malta at high speed to surrender to the British. The naval base at Taranto was also handed over, intact, to a hastily arranged landing by British paratroopers.

The picture was equally confused wherever Italians were found around the Mediterranean. On Sardinia, the target of Allied special forces, some units mutinied so that they could join the Germans. La Maddalena's defection to the Axis came about when the Italian garrison commander did a deal with his German counterpart allowing the Germans to transfer both their own, and 'loyalist' Italian, units across the narrow seaway to Corsica. On Corsica itself, by contrast, the commander of Bastia, the north-eastern port of egress for the mainland, emboldened by the promise of both Allied special forces and a sizeable Resistance, did turn against the Germans. Unfortunately most of the Resistance wanted to fight the Italians rather than the Germans. The Germans seized Bastia and evacuated both the Sardinian and Corsican garrisons, unmolested by the Italians, the Resistance or by the Giraudist French who landed on the west of the island.[83]

A similar pattern repeated itself in the eastern Mediterranean. Faced with resolute American refusal to become involved with an operation in the Dodecanese, Cairo developed a 'shoestring' operation, not dissimilar to that proposed by the Giraudists for Corsica. They scraped together troops from the Malta garrison, some destroyers and an array of special forces, most notably Lord Jellicoe's SBS. The great potential prize was the island of Rhodes, on which the Italians had developed sophisticated air and submarine bases since the 1930s. It housed the headquarters of the Italian commander for the entire Aegean. The Italian garrison commander on Rhodes was one of those who had made independent contact with Cairo. Everyone who looked seriously at the plan was sceptical about its chances, not least because Ultra had charted the steady stream of German reinforcements who had arrived to 'aid' the Italians in the defence of Rhodes. The same source had also shown that the *Luftwaffe* in the eastern Mediterranean, removed from Kesselring's control, had been reinforced. This was a particular problem. For the first time Mediterranean Air Command did possess long-range fighter aircraft that could have operated successfully over the Dodecanese. The remarkable twin-boom Lockheed P-38 could not only reach Rhodes from Derna but also outfight opposing German aircraft. Just as the Liberator had transformed and shrunk the Mediterranean for bombing, travel and supply, the P-38 did the same for air fighting. Although Mediterranean Air Command was the formation that most symbolized the unity of the Mediterranean, the P-38 issue revealed its limitations. All the aircraft belonged to American squadrons and their American commanders had no intention of using them in an operation of which they disapproved. A 'balbo' of P-38s cruised to Derna, but were recalled to Tunisia before they could do anything useful.[84]

Military logic suggested that an operation launched against an enemy with a powerful air force, operating from well-appointed bases close to the action, without air support, would fail. The Italian wild card was the factor that overrode this logic. The excitement about the Italian surrender had, after all, begun in the eastern Mediterranean. As in the western Mediterranean, however, the prospect was overrated. When a joint SBS-SOE team parachuted onto Rhodes, they discovered that they were already too late. The German commander on the island had arrested his treacherous opposite number and had turned the *Luftwaffe* on potential opposition. The senior Italian commander in the Aegean rapidly surrendered his forces. British special forces did succeed in occupying seventeen islands where there were no German troops. There was no Italian opposition, but neither was there much enthusiasm for their arrival. When a senior British officer arrived on Samos, the Italian commander 'refused to order his troops to open fire should a Fascist coup d'etat or German landing be attempted'. Just as in Italy itself, albeit on a much smaller scale, the 'quick fix' proved nothing of the sort.[85]

There were exceptional Italian units who were willing to fight the Germans, but their adherence was not necessarily an unalloyed benefit. The commander of the *Pinerolo* Division at Larissa signed a deal with Christopher Woodhouse, now the ranking SOE leader in Greece. He agreed to Woodhouse's proposal that members of the division should cooperate with British officers in attacking the airfields from which the Germans were operating into the Aegean. Most of these attacks, however, were thwarted by the Greeks. They bore no love for a formation notorious for its massacres. *Pinerolo* eventually fell prey, not to the Germans, but to Communist guerrillas.

The most intense opposition to the Germans actually occurred in the area where the Allies had neither operators nor plans for operations, the Italian-occupied islands to the west of Greece. Cephalonia controlled the entrance to the Gulf of Corinth, Corfu was the main fortified base on the eastern side of the Straits of Otranto. Their loss not only potentially disabled German supply routes across the Adriatic but, if the Allies had ever intended such an operation, they would have been the perfect stepping stone for an invasion of the Balkans from the Toe of Italy. When the *Acqui* Division opposed the German troops landing on Cephalonia, over a thousand were killed. The Germans executed a further 5,000 men after they had surrendered. The division was finally wiped out when the ships carrying the survivors into captivity were sunk by an Allied air strike. The Germans killed another 700 Italians when they moved on to Corfu a few days later.[86]

The Germans had been so little discommoded by the disappearance of the Italian King and his generals that many speculated that they had connived in its execution. Their most spectacular public response, played for the maximum propaganda advantage, was the liberation of Mussolini by a force of paratroopers and SS from his mountaintop prison at Gran Sasso. In a daring mission, paratroopers landed by glider on 12 September 1943 and defeated the Italian guards. To their commander's undying chagrin the SS leader Otto Skorzeny claimed most of the credit for the raid. A light aeroplane, called a 'stork', was brought in to fly Mussolini to safety. 'Great, fat Skorzeny, who weighs two hundredweight, climbed into the Storch' with Mussolini, observed the paratroop commander, nearly causing it to crash on take-off. Mussolini did, however, reach a German aerodrome from whence he was flown out to Austria. A joke went the rounds in Italy that Hitler had awarded Skorzeny the Knight's Cross for freeing Mussolini but he should get the Oak Leaves for taking him back.[87]

Of more practical importance was Rudolf Rahn's appointment as 'plenipotentiary of the Greater German Reich in Italy'. Rahn viewed Mussolini as a broken reed. When he met him in Germany, 'it was evident he would have preferred to go and bury himself quietly in a library'. As ever Rahn masked with 'well-studied courtesy the obvious hardness of his character'. Nevertheless, Mussolini was often visibly agitated in the presence of his keeper. As Kesselring observed, 'Dr Rahn brought order out of chaos by speedily forming a strong administration, the Italian bureaucracy under German control.' Rahn told Kesselring that 'I consider my role to squeeze the neo-Fascist and therefore Italian lemon beyond the possible, and what matters is only the means of succeeding in that'. The steady cooperation of officials was well under way long before Mussolini declared the overthrow of the monarchy and the creation of a republic. By the time the *Duce* flew himself back to Italy a fortnight after his rescue, he no longer had any part to play in the Mediterranean. The Germans confiscated Adriatic Italy and merged it with Austria. Mussolini was allocated Gargnano, a small town on Lake Garda, as his new capital. The location of the ministry of foreign affairs and the ministry of popular culture in Salò, another small town on the lake, gave the new republic its name.[88] The *Duce* was reduced to a new model of governance through 'companies of death'. Many of them were formed from the remnants of *Decima Mas*, the naval special forces whose *mezzi insidiosi* had, barely two years previously, almost brought British naval power in the Mediterranean to its knees. Now they achieved nothing apart from the creation of vicious death squads settling old scores. The judicial execution of Galeazzo Ciano was but one example of a state run by and for terrorists.[89] German officials reported that ordinary citizens were much more helpful in specifically Nazi projects, such as the rounding up of Rome's Jewry, than Mussolini's men, who resented their 'vassalage'.[90]

The most immediate proof of German poise was the swift and effective attack they were able to mount on the Salerno bridgehead. A few weeks before the Allied landing Kesselring had created the German 10th Army to defend southern Italy. Although the Germans did not know where the Anglo-Americans might come ashore, they had a shrewd appreciation of possible landing sites. The Allied goal was 'to seize the port of Naples and secure the airfields in the Naples area with a view to preparing a firm base for future offensive operations'.[91] Their plan was to land an army on the alluvial plain to the south of Naples. The plain had enough space for the deployment of a large number of troops. Around the town of Salerno there were twenty miles of inviting beaches over which a force might land. That force then had to penetrate twelve miles eastwards inland in order to secure the plain. Thereafter the invading troops could turn north and head for Naples.

The Allied landing force comprised three divisions. The Northern Attack Force, which would seize Salerno itself, comprised two assault divisions, the British 46th and 56th. These divisions were joined by British commandos and US Rangers, whose job was to land north of Salerno and seize the passes across the mountain ridges of the Sorrentine peninsula that separated Salerno from Naples. The Southern Attack Force, which would secure the town of Paestum further down the coast, was led in by the US 36th Division. The US 45th Division would join the 36th in due course. Watching that stretch of coast was the German 16th Panzer Division. The old 16th Panzer had been destroyed at Stalingrad. The new formation had a core of about 4,000 Eastern Front veterans, including Russian volunteers. The division was filled out with new drafts, thus presenting an odd combination of experience and naivety in combat.

The view of many Allied soldiers was that the landing would be a cakewalk, especially once news of the Italian surrender was announced on the ships at 18.30 on 8 September 1943. 'We really believed the Krauts didn't know when and where the invasion would hit,' wrote a sergeant in an American infantry battalion. 'Man! Were we off base! It was Fritz who threw the curve, not us.'[92] The troops who took part concluded that the war had entered a new, more difficult, phase. An experienced American landing-craft commander disembarking the British 46th Division concluded that 'nothing during the invasions of French Morocco and Sicily approached the experience of the hour's time spent on this beachhead. It was only by the grace of God that we were not badly shot up for they certainly had the range of the beach and several shells exploded directly overhead.'[93] His landing craft 'ramped up' and got off the beach at 05.40 on 9 September. It was not until late morning that fire support from Allied warships really began to find its range, forcing the German guns inland and making conditions on the beaches much easier. As a crewman on a US destroyer described the experience, 'it was at this time that we started to fire on to the beach with our 5-inch guns guided by a fire control party . . . the firing was so rapid that we had to use fire hoses to cool down the barrels . . . the battle with the tanks was very interesting because . . . the German tanks with the 88s were a match for our 5-inch guns. The only way we won the fight was to head to the shore at full speed and then turn so we could give a broadside of our six 5-inch guns, and then go full in reverse.'[94] In truth, the German coastal defences were thinly spread, and in the end could do little to prevent the landing. It had always been their intention to keep forces further inland until it became clear what the main landing site was, then counter-attack. By the end of 9 September the three Allied divisions had made their way five miles inland, suffering casualties in the hundreds rather than the thousands. The resistance to the landing nevertheless had given them a taste of what was to come.

The battle-space had elements that favoured the German defenders. According to Allied intelligence, after the fall of Sicily, 'the expected recovery of the GAF in the Mediterranean completely failed to materialise. This failure was to some extent due to increased demands on fighter forces on both the Western and Russian Fronts, but primarily to heavy losses on the ground both in Sicily and Italy, owing to the success of Allied attacks on airfields and the abandoning of repairable aircraft in Sicily.' Nevertheless, the bomber effort against Salerno was the most intense mounted by the Germans since their attack on Malta in March 1942.[95] A lynchpin of the Allied plan had been the capture of the main airfield on the alluvial plain at Montecorvino. It was indeed secured on 11 September but proved unusable during the battle, being within artillery and mortar range of German troops. Only a limited number of high-performance fighters could operate over the assault area at any one time because of the distance to and from their bases on Sicily. The same *Luftwaffe* unit that had sunk the *Roma* did serious damage to Allied warships engaged in shore bombardment. On the morning of 11 September one of its guided bombs tore the bottom out of the American cruiser USS *Savannah*. There was no naval fire support on that day, as other ships struggled to save the *Savannah* whilst looking to their own safety.

The German commanders had decided that Salerno was the only landing area by the early morning of 10 September. They ordered the 16th Panzer to attack, reinforced by another recent post-Stalingrad recreation, the 29th Panzer Grenadier Division. Elements of a further four divisions were heading towards the battlefield. According to Kesselring:

On 10 September I had already drawn on a map our successive defence positions in the event of retirement from southern Italy; they were more or less kept to when we later withdrew. The impression I had of the first two days was that we must be prepared for considerable sacrifice of ground, but that it might still be possible to go over to the defensive south of Rome, perhaps on a line running through Monte Mignano (the later Reinhard line) or on the Garigliano–Cassino line (later the Gustav line). If there were to be any hope of halting the enemy these positions must be consolidated and fresh construction and fighting units brought up. It was up to von Vietinghoff and his 10th Army to gain us the time we needed. I did not depart from this basic idea.

Von Vietinghoff, however, did not believe that he was fighting a mere delaying action: his intention was to drive the enemy into the sea. When he and Kesselring conferred in person he told his superior that he was going to defeat the Allies.

On 'Black Monday', 13 September 1943, the task forces assembled by von Vietinghoff from his various divisions struck the Allied forces with ferocity. Their main target was the Americans in the south. Their aim was to drive along the River Sele from Ponte Sele, at the apex of the alluvial plain, all the way to the sea. Some American units disintegrated under the assault. These tactical victories convinced von Vietinghoff that he had indeed won. 'After a defensive battle lasting four days,' he reported, 'enemy resistance is collapsing. 10th Army pursuing enemy on a wide front . . . the Battle of Salerno appears to be over.'[96] Some Allied commanders reached a similar conclusion. The Americans started making plans to evacuate the beachhead. The British were more sanguine. General Alexander slapped his breeches with a swagger stick, saying, 'Oh, no! We can't have anything like that. Never do. Never do.'[97] They thought that the best outcome was 'hold on at all costs' until they were rescued by Montgomery. The Germans had an equally good day in anti-shipping operations. The fire support from the ships for which the beleaguered troops called out was rarely forthcoming because those ships were too busy dodging guided missiles and bombs. The British cruiser HMS *Uganda* was hit and crippled. It was not until after 21.00 that the naval guns opened up to any effect.

Early on the morning of 14 September, a German staff conference concluded that they were making little headway against the British defending Salerno itself. The commander of the *Hermann Göring* Panzer Division in the north reported that he was losing tanks to the 'exceptionally tough' and well-dug-in British. The main thrust would continue against the 'retreating' Americans. The surprise of the initial assault had been lost, however. Near one of the most recognizable features of the battlefield, the so-called 'Tobacco Factory', a large agricultural depot internally divided by fences into tennis-court-sized areas, a 26th Panzer Division advance turned, for the British defenders, into 'a Gunner's dream; plenty of targets, all in the open, lots of ammunition, and nothing coming back at us'.[98] Allied commanders had had enough of a fright to commit large-scale air and naval forces to the defence, whatever the risk of casualties. British battleships sailed inshore to add their 15-inch guns to the defensive bombardment. That the dangers of such a manoeuvre had not been overestimated was demonstrated when HMS *Warspite* was crippled by an air-launched guided missile. The German troops, however, could no longer advance. The 29th Panzer Grenadier Division reported that 'even though we already knew from Sicily what Allied air superiority meant the strafing that we underwent at this time, and particularly on the 14th September, put all our previous experiences in the shade. It was an achievement if one small vehicle made one short journey, darting from cover to cover, and completed it unscathed.' The 9th Panzer Grenadier Division noted that the town of Eboli had been reduced to ruins by naval gunfire and that its men 'were much affected by the non-stop strafing'.

By the time Kesselring visited von Vietinghoff again, the mood had changed. The operational commander admitted that although he could continue to 'strike' at the bridgehead he no longer expected to throw the invaders back into the sea. His army had turned into the delaying force that Kesselring had always envisaged. On the evening of 15 September 1943 Kesselring formally reported to Hitler that naval bombardment and overwhelming Allied air superiority had forced him on to the defensive. German troops began withdrawing from the alluvial plain, ready to fight a rearguard action when the Allies decided to force the northward passage to Naples. During the battle the Germans had suffered about 3,500 casualties, the Allies nearly 9,000. As Eisenhower, visiting the beachhead on 16 September, concluded, 'there was every indication that the Germans had expended their energy and were battle-weary: signs of withdrawal were evident all along the front; but it was a certainty that this withdrawal would be planned to impede our advance and to inflict the greatest number of battle casualties on us'.[99] The Germans had made it clear that 'the Tommies will have to chew their way through us, inch by inch, and we will surely make hard chewing for them'.[100]

It was hardly surprising then that the Allied delegation that motored from Taranto to Brindisi to meet the King and his commanders face to face were unimpressed. The plotters were shop-soiled goods. The whole venture in Italy appeared cursed – the Salerno landing was a 'doomed' exercise. 'The Brindisi Party' could 'hardly be dignified by the name of Government, all their divisions, in Italy and the Balkans, are "surrounded" by a smaller number of German troops. There is an atmosphere of well-bred defeatism.'[101]

It was, however, their very powerlessness that saved the motley royal party that unconvincingly claimed to rule Italy from Brindisi. Those in the Mediterranean found that 'to dabble in politics and king-making' was much more 'amusing' than 'to slog along with dull administration'.[102] Those outside the Mediterranean were delighted to find that these royalist playthings could provide their long-desired ceremonial act of abnegation.[103] Despite bitter complaints, the royal government was presented with surrender terms as complete and 'unconditional' as the Allied governments desired. Their treatment was, Badoglio complained, 'ungenerous and dishonourable': but he had no choice but to acquiesce. He dutifully trooped aboard a cruiser whose very name, *Scipio l'Africano*, had once symbolized Italy's Mediterranean ambitions. He sailed from Brindisi to Malta, where the battleships of the *Regia Marina*, signed away a few days previously, awaited disposal by the Allies.

On 29 September 1943 Badoglio signed the terms presented to him.[104] Aided not one whit by the final Italian act of surrender, but rather by the massive application of firepower, the Anglo-Americans finally cracked the German line at Salerno and made for Naples. They entered the city on 1 October. One could read the counter-point between the bloody capture of Naples and the ceremonies on Malta differently according to perspective. For military Europeanists, this was, at best, the avoidance of catastrophe. For navalist Mediterraneanists, the possession of Italy's Mediterranean naval bases, its entire fleet and the ritual humiliation of its leader on a British battleship was a 'fine show'.[105]

TWELVE

The Last Supper

Jumbo Wilson was an unlikely overlord of the Mediterranean. His superiors worried about his ever-increasing girth. The unavoidable lot of any Mediterranean commander was constant air travel. His staff winced each time General Jumbo was faced with egress from the small portal of a military transport. One day, they feared, he would get stuck.

In any case no vacancy appeared to be open. Dwight Eisenhower was firmly ensconced as the Mediterranean's premier commander, and was defending his position with gusto. His superiors had told him they intended to give command of a European invasion to the Chief of Staff of the US Army, George C. Marshall. Although Marshall's man, the news had provoked a strong response from Ike. He had no wish to give up his Mediterranean command in order to return to Washington as Marshall's replacement. Neither did he relish the transformation of the Mediterranean into 'Europe, South', run from London. 'Direct operational command of forces in this theater', he warned Marshall, 'could not be efficiently done from London.' It would be a 'tragedy to introduce any project' that would undermine the 'Allied unity of command'. Bedell Smith was dispatched Stateside to lobby against any plans to break up the Mediterranean.[1] Indeed Eisenhower went on to argue for the 'pure' Mediterranean. There should not be any question of the eastern Mediterranean being regarded as part of the Middle East, the Middle East was in 'Africa and Asia'. Instead one command, his own, should control the entire littoral.[2]

When the commanders of West and East met on 9 October 1943 at La Marsa in Tunisia, Jumbo came to Ike as a supplicant. A few days previously the Germans had begun rounding up the garrisons he had scattered around the eastern Aegean. Their first target, Cos, was caught by surprise. Cairo had, Wilson signalled Churchill in self-exculpation, 'no intelligence at our disposal which would have led us to foresee that the enemy would be able to collect and launch at such short notice an expedition of the magnitude which made the assault on Cos'.

Attempts to use the Aegean crisis to revivify the hope of American assistance in the east were rebuffed. 'I believe', Churchill wrote in impassioned terms to Roosevelt, 'it will be found that the Italian and the Balkan peninsulas are militarily and politically united and that really it is one theatre which we have to deal with. It may not be possible to conduct a successful Italian campaign ignoring what happens in the Aegean. The Germans evidently attach the utmost importance to this Eastern sphere. What I ask for is the capture of Rhodes and of the other islands of the Dodecanese.'[3] At La Marsa, Eisenhower refused Wilson's request for aid, telling him 'that our resources in the Mediterranean are *not* large enough to allow us to undertake the capture of Rhodes and at the same time secure our immediate objectives in Italy'.[4]

At first sight Eisenhower's refusal to help appeared to be an exercise in American muscle-flexing. Italy was important, he implied, because it was part of Europe; the Aegean was not because it was part of the Mediterranean. In fact Eisenhower was supported by most British Mediterraneanist opinion, which blamed Wilson's problems on Churchill for forcing him into such a cockeyed 'quick fix' in the Aegean. At La Marsa, Ike was backed up by his phalanx of British senior commanders, Cunningham, Tedder and Alexander, none of whom wished to go east. Harold Macmillan, on a flying visit to London, lamented that he simply could not get Churchill to focus on the Mediterranean as whole, 'he was only interested in Cos, Leros, Rhodes'.[5] 'Another day of Rhodes madness', snarled Alan Brooke, 'he is in a very dangerous condition, most unbalanced, and God knows how we shall finish this war if this goes on.'[6]

Britons as well as Americans believed that Churchill's claims for the Mediterranean were incredible. 'We can all see', he rumbled, 'how adverse to the enemy are conditions in Greece and Yugoslavia. When we remember what brilliant results have followed from political reactions in Italy induced by our military efforts should we not be shortsighted to ignore the possibility of a similar and even greater landslide in some or all of the countries I have mentioned?'[7] In fact very few others could see any of these things. The claimed brilliant results in Italy were hard to detect. Despite initial hopes to the contrary, the six political parties of the southern Italian Committee of National Liberation, much less the best known anti-Fascists, Benedetto Croce and Carlo Sforza, refused to have anything to do with their tainted monarch. 'I suppose', Macmillan wrote after another fruitless Neapolitan encounter with Sforza and Croce, one 'vain and dishonest', the other a 'dwarf professor', 'it is just as confusing for the Italians as for us to remember which side they are on.' All he could foresee was endless talk and no action.[8] 'It is becoming more and more evident', Brooke admitted at the same moment, 'that our operations in Italy are coming to a standstill.'[9]

The main feature of the situation in both Greece and Yugoslavia was not an anti-German landslide, but the slide into civil war. As Churchill wrote, Communist forces launched a pan-Greek offensive against their rivals. The joint headquarters so painfully stitched together by Myers ceased to exist. When Wilson got back to Cairo from Tunis, the immediate crisis he had to deal with was the news that a young New Zealand liaison officer in Greece, Lieutenant Hubbard, had been murdered by Communist insurgents, 'who were like half-crazed beasts'.[10] The eighty or so liaison officers with Communist forces were 'in effect hostages'. The British had no control over the Communists. A denunciation of the insurgents would merely 'lead us into the humiliating position of uttering threats which we, ELAS and the Germans know cannot be backed by force, and of standing helplessly by while our BLOs were murdered'. The final compromise worked out in Cairo was that the 'pro-Communist' Eddie Myers should be banned from ever returning to Greece, whilst the death of Hubbard would be hushed up altogether.[11] Even before the death of Hubbard, Wilson had taken steps to 'militarize' the effort in Greece. The champion of subversion, Christopher Glenconner, was sacked in the yearly purge of special forces. 'The military claim', sneered Eden's private secretary, 'that without the Communists we could not blow up bridges behind the German lines, we much doubt this.' The incoming commander of special forces, who had been on a tour of inspection in Greece at the time of the Hubbard murder, reported that there were already too many 'commando' types in Greece.[12]

As far as Yugoslavia was concerned, the situation was clear only to the BBC, who, with official connivance in London, eulogized the Partisans. Two brigadiers, Fitzroy Maclean for Tito and Charles Armstrong for Mihailovic, parachuted into Yugoslavia to take a definitive, high-ranking, look at what was really happening, had barely started work in early October 1943.[13] The brigadiers had been inserted by the now well-flown Mediterranean route from North Africa by air. There was, of course, now a much shorter route into coastal Yugoslavia from the Heel of Italy. Every imaginable intelligence and special operations outfit hustled for facilities on the coastal strip from Bari to Brindisi. Many came as representatives of their Cairo headquarters, thus blurring the boundary between the central and eastern Mediterranean.[14] A senior OSS officer from Cairo established himself in Bari, crossed over to the Adriatic island of Vis, did a deal to see Tito, and was soon in Bosnia being paraded under British noses as the Communist leader's new best friend.[15] Whether the watchers reported to Cairo or Algiers, however, only those ideologically committed to the Communists agreed with Churchill's assessment of the situation on the Adriatic coast.[16]

When an authoritative voice did emerge from Yugoslavia to endorse Churchill's ideas, it was one that he himself had carefully planted. Brigadier Fitzroy Maclean was supposed to give Wilson military advice on the situation in the country. He was, however, Churchill's personal emissary to Tito, a Conservative MP, whose military experience amounted to a temporary captaincy in the SAS before his sudden elevation. Charles Armstrong, a real brigadier, sent to Mihailovic, was equally carefully selected for his lack of political skill or contacts.[17] Maclean carefully chose the moment of a stop-over in Cairo by Anthony Eden, on his way home from Moscow, to fly out with the message that 'we should put our money on Tito, who represents the future of Yugoslavia whether we like it or not'.[18] Mihailovic's retreat into Serbia, combined with the collapse of the Italian divisions, had made it easy for the Partisans to predate the coastal Chetniks. The most spectacular Partisan success was the annihilation of the leadership of the Montenegrin Chetniks, surrounded and massacred in their monastic refuge. The war near the Mediterranean coast was a civil conflict of which the Partisans were undoubted beneficiaries.

The other beneficiaries were the Germans. The new Nazi plenipotentiary, Hermann Neubacher, reversed previous policy and sought collaboration. The leader of Dalmatia's Chetniks, near the top of the German hit list in September 1943, was being courted as a potential ally by November 1943. The new policy was particularly successful in Montenegro, where leaderless Chetniks helped a few German troops keep firm control. A full *Abwehr* account of the Montenegrin negotiations, intercepted by the usual methods, caused a stir when Bletchley Park forwarded a copy to Cairo for the attention of Churchill and Roosevelt. Further down the coast in Albania, a recently arrived British mission was reporting that their main contact in the north, a feudal chief, was showing 'a marked distaste for engaging German troops at close quarters or provoking them'. A supposedly anti-German national front broke down in November 1943. Yet another brigadier was sent in to find out what was going on. He had found direct evidence that the Germans were allied to the Albanian resistance when he was ambushed, shot and captured by a joint German-Albanian war band.[19]

Although the Germans chased the Partisans away from all the major cities on the Dalmatian coast, Dubrovnik, Split and Zara, German commanders were far from sanguine about their position. Von Weichs pointed out that he had deployed troops to the coast to defend against an English invasion that was now most unlikely to materialize. Meanwhile, in the interior, the Partisans had become a real military menace. With the Italians gone, the grand sweeps like *Weiss* and *Schwarz* were a thing of the past: manpower was too tight. The mere occupation of territory was not sufficient; more imaginative counter-insurgency techniques were necessary. Whatever their private concerns, however, the Germans were still formidable. Vis became the meeting point between the Partisans and the Italian-based Allied special forces because, as the major Dalmatian island furthest from the mainland, it was the one Mediterranean asset that the Partisans had managed to hold.

The autumn scorecard of military stalemate, lack of a political settlement in Italy, German victory in the Aegean and along the Balkan coast, and civil war between the Allies' putative collaborators in Greece, Albania and Yugoslavia was always likely to create tension, and it did. Brooke blamed the Americans for his problems: 'we are now beginning to see', he wrote sarcastically, 'the full beauty of the[ir] Mediterranean strategy!! It is quite heartbreaking when we see what we might have done if our strategy had not been distorted by the Americans.'[20] Eisenhower also criticized his countrymen's contention that the only part of the Mediterranean that was of interest was southern France. Such thinking was 'strategically unsound' he cautioned, 'the south of France cannot logically be considered by itself; southern France, Italy and the Balkans form a belt'.[21] Often tension was just as high between the Mediterranean team and their masters in London and Washington, as it was between British and Americans. 'This was', as Macmillan put it, 'partly due to the incompetence of some of the people at AFHQ (Algiers) but much more to the incredible stupidity, lack of imagination, and really insane legalistic confusion' of London and Washington.[22] The AFHQ empire had many British enemies. They compared it to 'Cairo at its worst'.[23] Just as Cairo's crime had been to become a semi-independent satrapy, so too now was Algiers's.

The crime of 'Britishness' was added to the Mediterranean by the vagaries of presidential whim. The closest that Roosevelt had hitherto come to the Mediterranean was his stay on the Atlantic coast of Morocco in January 1943. He actually entered the sea in December 1943, albeit on his way to somewhere else. Churchill's response to the débâcle in the Aegean was to call for a new Mediterranean conference, on the model of Casablanca. Roosevelt had replied that although he did not mind coming to the Mediterranean, the sea itself was beneath them. They should be discussing the future of the world, not a minor region. Roosevelt envisaged a great 'world conference' that would include both Stalin and the Chinese leader, Chiang Kai-shek. The grandiose 'world conference' foundered on Stalin's reluctance to travel very far beyond the borders of the Soviet Union. In its place emerged a kind of rolling meeting. The battleship-borne Roosevelt and Churchill would progress through the Mediterranean to Cairo. Roosevelt had USS *Iowa* deposit him at Oran, flying on first to Tunis and then Egypt; Churchill sailed to Malta before emplaning. There they would meet each other and the Chinese. From Cairo they would fly to Teheran to meet Stalin, and then return together to Cairo for a post-mortem. Roosevelt conceived this unwieldy structure in part for the avoidance of any serious discussion of the Mediterranean with Churchill. He wanted to move on. The Mediterranean was only to be the subject of conversation as part of the campaign against north-west Europe.

Roosevelt had no desire to be cajoled by Churchill; the Washington Americans were as one in resisting another dunning by British dialecticians. Roosevelt's real business was with Stalin in Teheran.[24] The Cairo meetings had an element of farce, not least because of the reactions of the middle-aged male herd to the sheer silken outfits encasing the tight body of Madame Chiang Kai-shek, the first woman negotiator to sit at a wartime conference table. 'We were dumbfounded,' wrote an incandescent Alan Brooke of the Americans, 'they have completely upset the whole meeting by wasting our time with Chiang Kai-shek and Stalin, now they propose to disappear into the blue and leave all the main points connected with the Mediterranean unsettled! It all looks like some of the worst sharp practice that I have seen for some time.'[25]

One consequence of Roosevelt's burgeoning world ambitions was his decision, reputedly one that troubled his conscience, to veto Marshall's planned departure for Europe. Surrounded by sycophants, the President would not sacrifice the one figure upon whose independence of judgement he could rely. Instead, Roosevelt told Churchill in Cairo, he would nominate Eisenhower for the supreme command in Europe. There was little Churchill could say to the *fait accompli*, beyond enthusiastic acquiescence. He had always accepted that the European command was in the President's gift. His immediate concern was to ensure that the 'new centralised Mediterranean command', designed for Eisenhower, should be assigned to a British officer.[26] Such an arrangement suited Roosevelt perfectly.

The main argument was between the British themselves as to who was best suited to the role. Churchill, encouraged by Brooke, had initially said it should be Jumbo Wilson because, 'he knew ½ Mediterranean intimately'. Doubts were raised by Harold Macmillan. He immediately saw that if there was to be 'one commander, there must also be one Resident Minister'.[27] He intended that Minister to be him and that Algiers should take over the eastern Mediterranean, not that AFHQ should be taken over by Cairo. Macmillan had just concluded a power struggle with his opposite numbers, Spears in Beirut and Casey in Cairo.[28] He had shown that the Levant could be run from Algiers. On 11 November 1943, Jean Helleu, the French Commissioner-General in the Levant, had launched a surprise coup in Beirut. He arrested the independence-claiming Lebanese government. The actual coup caught the British by surprise, but trouble had been brewing for months. Solh and Spears were at one in their desire to oust the French. Spears and Casey's proposed solution to Helleu's seizure of power was the imposition of martial law by the British. They characterized the French, Gaullist zealots and neo-Vichyites alike, as enemies who, in the end, would have to be dealt with violently. Macmillan on the other hand had constructed a vision of a moderate France emerging in Algiers.[29] When Churchill's battleship had stopped at Algiers, Macmillan was able to lobby him in person.[30] As the British travelled on to Cairo, Catroux was allowed to carry out shuttle diplomacy between Algiers and Beirut. The final solution was Casey and Spears's in substance, the French were forced to sack Helleu and release the Lebanese government, but Macmillan's in spin, the French in Algiers were allowed to pretend that Helleu was a rogue whom they had disowned of their own volition. The consensus in Cairo was that Casey had to go, that 'the Lebanese would now have to put a little water in their wine' and that 'being a popular hero in the Levant' had gone to Spears's head.[31]

Fresh from this east–west conflict, Macmillan whispered that 'General Wilson was too old and too set in his ways to undertake the Cromwellian reforms which are necessary if Algiers and Cairo are to be made to work; after all, Wilson has had command in Cairo for nearly a year, and the Augean stables are still uncleaned'.[32] When Churchill appeared to have 'pushed old Jumbo Wilson aside' in favour of 'wanting Alexander as Supreme Commander for the Mediterranean', Brooke retorted that 'Macmillan knew he could handle Alex, and that he would be a piece of putty in his hands'.[33] The argument raged all the way from Cairo back to Tunis. Brooke finally got his way, not least because Churchill suffered a serious collapse. Even Churchill's elephantine constitution could no longer stand the constant travelling. With fears for his life growing, he was shipped off for a rest cure at Marrakesh.

The creation of the 'Jumbocracy' was announced at the end of December 1943. It did not have a happy beginning. Eisenhower immediately began to cherry pick the most effective commanders and staff officers for transfer back to England.[34] Wilson himself arrived in the central Mediterranean with the best of intentions towards furthering Anglo-American relations, but was surrounded by a tight coterie of trusted intimates from Cairo.[35] When John Slessor, the new head of the RAF in the Mediterranean, arrived in mid-January 1944 he reported a difficult situation. The large AFHQ organization that was supposed to run the Mediterranean was in Algiers. Other headquarters were scattered higgledy-piggledy around the Mediterranean. An efficient Mediterranean radio net had proved elusive. Quite often commanders flying around the theatre found that they arrived before their host knew they were coming. Wilson himself spent the bulk of his time with his small personal staff at Caserta, the huge palace of the Neapolitan Bourbons that 'squatted in squalid disorder at the base of the sharp hills that separated the Neapolitan Plain from the Volturno Valley'. Caserta was certainly big enough for any headquarters that chose to pitch camp there, with over 1,200 rooms, albeit coated with 'two centuries accumulation of flies and filth'. But Wilson was the johnny-come-lately: Caserta was already the domain of his rival General Alexander, commander of the Allied Central Mediterranean Force.[36] Resident Minister Macmillan remained an outspoken partisan of Alexander. Neither did Churchill ever warm overly to his appointee, for 'old Jumbo Wilson was not as pliable in Churchill's hands as Alex would have been. Wilson was a tough old specimen and let Winston's abuse run over him like water rolls off a duck's back.'

The brief handover period between Eisenhower and Wilson was a 'tangle' caused by 'the PM convalescing in Morocco and trying to run the War'.[37] Indeed Churchill, balked by Roosevelt in the matter of Mediterranean strategy, turned instead to Mediterranean operations. His pet plan was for ambitious, although small-scale, amphibious landings around the small coastal town of Anzio. This plan was based on three assumptions. First, landings on the Italian coast would outflank the German troops who had stopped the advance of the Allied armies up the western littoral. Second, that since Anzio was the coastal terminus of the road to Rome, its capture would lead to the rapid seizure of the capital. Third, that the capture of Rome would liberate many political leaders to do a deal with the King and Badoglio.

None of these assumptions was correct; none was probed in sufficient detail. The Prime Minister enrolled Alexander as a champion and used his enthusiasm to overcome the sceptics. When Churchill expounded the plan to Eisenhower and Wilson in Tunis, Ike was already packing to leave, Wilson had not yet received formal confirmation of his appointment. The Anzio operation was given the green light on the same day as Wilson actually took up office. Whereas Eisenhower had had a major say in strategy, Wilson was given little chance to leave his imprint. As the American commander of the initial assault confided to his diary, 'the whole affair has the strong odour of Gallipoli and apparently the same amateur is still on the coach's bench'.[38]

Another product of Churchill's Marrakesh period was the order that Tito must receive maximum support. In particular the island of Vis was not to be allowed to fall into German hands, even if this meant mounting a British operation to defend it. Von Weichs's solution to the problem of dealing with a complex insurgency with an insufficiency of men, was an attempt to decapitate the Partisans. Instead of trying to roll up local Partisan units and garrison the coast, he argued that the key was the Partisan leadership itself. The day after the Anzio operation was agreed, German troops captured the Bosnian capital of the Partisans, Jajce. Fitzroy Maclean was sent back into Bosnia to find Tito at his new base. As a token of Churchill's personal commitment to the Partisan cause, he was accompanied by the Prime Minister's son, Randolph.

Although many of the technical limitations of Wilson's command were solved over the next few months, it never really recovered from its difficult birth. It was saddled with the Anzio operation, which turned into a fiasco.

The troops got ashore smoothly enough on 22 January 1944. This in itself was a great achievement for Allied combined operations. On the eve of the operation, many had predicted disaster. Lucian Truscott, commanding one of the two assault divisions, the 3rd US, feared that his troops would not even be able to get onto the beaches. Their final practice run had been chaotic. The transport ships had anchored so far out from shore that no armour had been able to land with the infantry battalions. The landing ships had opened their bows and bundled out the amphibious vehicles into the dark but the Mediterranean was so rough that most of them had foundered. 'Against opposition the landing would have been a disaster,' Truscott warned. Pleas for more time to get things right were ignored. Luckily the landing was not opposed.

The armada sailed on schedule out of Naples harbour on midday on 21 January. The landing ships arrived off the Bay of Anzio twelve hours later. The German naval commander in Italy admitted to his superiors that 'the enemy surprised us'. In any case, 'the landing has come at a very bad time for us' because all his ships were already committed to escorting coastal convoys. He had no means of attacking the enemy fleet. 'Landing craft lowered into the water, and proceed towards beach,' a diarist on the British infantry-landing ship *Princess Beatrix* recorded, 'everything OK and quiet until 1:30 when our ships shell the enemy positions, port and starboard of us, where other landings are taking place by other troops and Commandos. Terrific explosions going on within the town as we beach our landing craft, all troops got ashore OK, but for getting wet up to the waist.'[39] Truscott's 3rd Division landed to the south of Anzio, without his feared snafu, and advanced three miles inland before setting up a defensive perimeter. To the north of Anzio the British 1st Division advanced a similar distance inland. By the end of the day 36,000 troops had been landed at the cost of a dozen lives.

The harbour of Anzio itself was secured by lightly armed special forces. This undramatic victory proved to be the key to the whole battle. The initial landings had proved as unwieldy as Truscott had feared. The armoured vehicles were delayed on their ships. In daylight a landing craft was lashed under the bows of a tank-landing ship and the ship's ramp was dropped onto the craft's deck. Another landing craft came alongside the first: the tanks drove down the ship ramp, across the first landing craft and onto the second. That landing craft then went ashore. Each landing ship carried nineteen tanks, sixteen half-tracks, five armoured cars and nineteen other vehicles, so it was slow, cumbersome work. By the time the landing ships had made their way back to Naples, picked up another load, and returned on 24 January, they were able to sail directly into the harbour. That manoeuvre itself was tense and difficult. 'By this time it was very dark', wrote a British landing-ship commander in his diary, 'and there was no light to show where the harbour entrance was . . . it was not until 2245 that we were secured to the quay and were able to unload. It had taken four hours of painstaking manoeuvring from the time we left the anchorage only 300 yards away. I left the bridge and retired to my cabin, sat down quite exhausted and shed a few tears.'[40] Yet despite the challenges of Anzio harbour it was irreplaceable. The gear needed to land at sites other than the harbour was seriously damaged by a storm that came in on 25 January and 'blew undiminished for two days'. The storm wrecked a large number of landing craft and washed the pontoon causeways under construction as landing ramps so far inland 'that the salvage of pontoons was not accomplished until after two months of heartbreaking work'. 'Had not the port of Anzio been able to operate at three or four times its expected capacity for LSTs,' concluded the naval commander of the operation, 'the loss of these pontoons would have doomed the beachhead.'[41] 'The one factor that has allowed us to get established ashore has been the port of Anzio,' confirmed his army opposite number, 'without it our situation by this time would have been desperate with little chance of a build-up of adequate strength.'[42]

Whilst the port of Anzio proved a vital, if low-key, success, there was no stunning victory to be had. As soon as the troops got ashore Allied propaganda cranked into action. It claimed that German troops to the south would soon be cut off by a 'classic battle of encirclement'.[43] But there were plenty of German forces to the north of Anzio, near Rome, as well as to the south. They were the encirclers rather than the encircled. The leading elements of the panzer division *Hermann Göring* reached the outskirts of the bridgehead by the day after the landings. On 23 January too, the *Luftwaffe* began to launch serious air strikes against ships offshore. The first casualty was a British destroyer sunk by a torpedo-bomber. The German airmen were hampered by the strength of the Allied fighter forces. Daytime attacks were risky. At night it was hard to hit anything. So they settled on dusk for the deadliest hours. Their effectiveness was soon demonstrated by the order that went around to Allied ships: that they must clear the invasion area by four o'clock each afternoon. Although the Germans had failed to identify the time or place of the landing they had made contingency plans to contain such an eventuality. Kesselring was able to appeal successfully to OKW for reinforcements from around *Festung Europa*. On 25 January the next wave of two Allied divisions began to land, but the Germans established the headquarters of the 14th Army near Anzio in order to conduct a major battle aimed at obliterating the invasion force. 'I myself was convinced,' Kesselring recalled, 'even taking their powerful naval guns and overwhelming air superiority into consideration, that with the means available we must succeed in throwing the Allies back into the sea. I constantly kept in mind the psychological effect of their situation on the staff and troops of US 6th Corps. Penned in as they were on the low-lying, notoriously unhealthy coast, it must have been damned unpleasant . . . It seemed to me of paramount importance that we should attack as quickly as possible.'[44] By the end of January 1944, over 70,000 German troops were fighting just over 60,000 Allied soldiers.

As the Allied front line pushed tentatively forward, it met heavier and heavier resistance. When British troops entered Aprilia, soon to be infamous as 'the Factory', they were immediately counter-attacked and thrown out of the small town. When the British themselves counter-attacked they pushed through 'the Factory' even further north to create a salient known as 'the Thumb', due to its shape on the map. The fighting was intense. One battalion lost its CO, all its company commanders and nearly seventy per cent of its men, killed, captured or wounded. Surveying the battlefield the commander of the US 1st Armored Division reported: 'I have never seen so many dead men in one place.' The Americans tried a similar advance to the south of Anzio. Their Rangers had scored a strategic coup with their near-bloodless capture of Anzio; but never got to enjoy the fruits of the victory. A battalion of nearly 800 men entered the town of Cisterna. There they were ambushed by German armour. 'For half an hour the Rangers fought the tanks with bazookas and sticky grenades and then everything was over.' Only half a dozen men made it back to Allied lines.

The battle was playing out much as John Lucas, the sceptical Allied invasion commander, had thought it would. 'I think', he confided to his diary on 28 January, 'more has been accomplished than anyone had a right to expect. This venture was always a desperate one and I could never see much chance for it to succeed, if success meant driving the Germans north of Rome.' If he had got off the beaches and pushed inland at high speed,

> nothing would have been accomplished except to weaken my force by that amount because the troops sent, being completely beyond supporting distance, would have been completely destroyed. The only thing to do was what I did. Get a proper beachhead and prepare to hold it. Keep the enemy off balance by a constant advance against him with small units, not committing anything as large as a division until the Corps was ashore and everything was set. Then make a coordinated attack to defeat the enemy and seize the objective. Follow this by exploitation. This is what I have been doing, but I had to have troops in to do it with.[45]

That Lucas could justify his conduct did not make it any more palatable to his superiors or his more gung-ho juniors. A British artillery officer who joined Lucas's staff a few days later was far from impressed. 'General Lucas', he believed, 'was far too old a man, who seemed dazed by what was happening.' 'There were', the British officer observed, 'far too many senile officers, of the rank of full colonel and above, they were too old, no idea of the technique of modern war and lived in an atmosphere of 1917 warfare. No one seemed to like to make a decision, and the baby used to be passed on and on, with no one ready or willing to hold it, decide something and give orders . . . indecision, slowness and inexperience was all there.'[46] References to Anzio being like a First World War battle were to flow thick and fast in the coming month. Cisterna became Ypres. 'So back to World War I,' wrote a Scottish infantry officer, 'oozing thick mud. Tank hulls. The cold, God, the cold. Graves marked by a helmet, gashed with shrapnel. Shreds of barbed wire. Trees like broken fishbones.'[47]

On 3 February 1944 the Germans attacked 'the Thumb' and forced the British to retreat with heavy casualties. Four nights later they repeated the operation against 'the Factory' with similar success. The British 1st Division had been reduced to less than half its initial strength. Like wildfire the word went out to sea that the battle was a German victory. On 9 February, a British officer bobbing off the coast in his armed trawler noted in his diary that 'they are blaming the gales for failure at Anzio . . . for there is no longer any question it is a failure. Instead of cutting off the Germans in the South all that has been achieved is a second Tobruk, which will only be maintained with great difficulty against heavy attack now starting. Tiger tanks and SS troops are attacking the British . . . the salient has gone.'[48] Ashore, the troops were united in misery. 'To make it worse,' a member of the battalion headquarters of the Grenadier Guards wrote in his diary, 'it started to rain and before long everyone was soaked . . . we were open to fire from every side and what was worse to every wind and in our sodden state it was freezing.'[49] A company commander in a German panzer grenadier battalion agreed. 'It was', he wrote, 'a struggle to keep anything dry. Weapons rusted unless constantly attended to, there was filthy mud everywhere – it got into your hair, your eyes, your food – our feet were constantly wet and our clothes clung to our bodies. We turned into human icicles at night.'[50]

Some of Lucas's critics, such as the Mediterranean air-force commander, John Slessor, sneered that 'I have not the slightest doubt that if it had been Germans or Russians landing at Anzio, we would have had . . . Rome by now'.[51] But the Germans found offensive operations just as deadly as had the Allies before them. Some panzer grenadiers even claimed that fighting was worse than at Stalingrad where they had also served. Kesselring had been much too sanguine about Allied firepower, naval and land. German units suffered horrific casualties when they went forward in the face of Allied barrages. They attributed over three-quarters of their casualties to artillery fire. The war correspondent Ernie Pyle reported the ubiquity of slang that referred to attempts to avoid German artillery fire: the Anzio Amble, Anzio Anxiety, Anzio Foot, Anzio Walk. Yet Allied gunners fired ten times the number of rounds as their German opposite numbers. One German infantry division reported that it had been reduced to one thousand combat effectives, less than one-tenth of its establishment.

Reviewing the situation, the commander of the US 1st Armored Division concluded that 'not only our line troops but many of our offi-cers were despondent and, as I could readily see, at the point of crack-up. . . . Fortunately, there were among my brother commanders some sturdy characters who realised that if we were near exhaustion, the Germans must be tuckered too.'[52] He was right. The German counter-offensive ground to a halt on 20 February. The commander of the 14th Army reproached Kesselring for his reckless search for total victory. As a result young untrained men, 'not prepared to meet Allied troops in battle', had diluted the battle-hardened veterans. Numerical superiority had been an illusion. 'Due to this the Army was unable to wipe out the beachhead with the troops on hand.' They could not go on. 'The tactics that have been employed, namely to reduce the bridgehead gradually by concentrated attacks,' warned the army commander, 'cannot be continued much longer.' He had lost 29,000 men in these large-scale attacks. Now was the time to accept that the Germans had to change both their goal and their tactics. Instead of trying to destroy the bridgehead they would dig in, 'to enable us to meet the large-scale enemy attack from the beachhead with adequate numbers of troops and supplies'.[53] Kesselring knew that such blunt speaking could be fatal, unless carefully handled. After some thought he sent his chief of staff, along with a gaggle of other officers, to convince Hitler of the 'unvarnished truth': victory at Anzio was impossible.

For the Germans, the strategic battle of Anzio ended with Kesselring's declaration on 6 March 1944. But a stalemate, stretching for months ahead, was hardly what Anzio's original boosters had had in mind either. 'I thought we should', Churchill said of his own brainchild, 'fling a wildcat ashore and all we got was an old stranded whale on the beach.'[54] To the south Allied forces remained pinned down in the similarly dreadful battles around Monte Cassino. There was little that Wilson could do about these operations: they were planned and carried out by Alexander, with the advantage not only of operational command but high-level political protection.

Just as it had been under Eisenhower, the main role of AFHQ was as much political as military. Wilson had to apportion resources and responsibilities around the Sea, whilst preventing authority, men and equipment from fleeing the theatre altogether. In doing so, he frequently offended old friends. His decisions on Greece, for instance, evinced howls of protest from Cairo. There was anger that his knowledge of '½ the Mediterranean' did not mean rulings in favour of the East.[55] 'A Supreme Commander is necessary in the Mediterranean theatre, but at the same time geographical and political factors make some decentralisation essential,' Casey's successor, Walter Moyne, argued on behalf of the Cairo panjandrums. 'On predominantly political issues, or where it is a question of appreciating political or military intelligence, he would not normally have sufficient grounds to call into question the Cairo view.' The Cairo view was that 'there could be no case for subordinating political considerations to military'.[56] Wilson, on the other hand, took the view that 'sabotage' was more useful than politicking, even if this meant supporting Communists.[57] He tried to impose some degree of consistency. Support for the Communists in Yugoslavia was a Churchillian pet project. It seemed bizarre not to apply the same logic to Greece, and possibly to Italy itself.[58] His special forces had forged links with the recently formed Action Party.[59] But not only was Action opposed to the Badoglio government, its 'Justice and Liberty' bands were reluctant to attack the Germans.[60] The Communists on the other hand proved passable, if unpredictable, allies. The Soviets recognized the legitimacy of the royal government at the beginning of March 1944.[61] In the same month, a Communist cell carried out the most famous single act of anti-German resistance in Italy when a bomb killed thirty SS police troops marching along the *Via Rasella* in Rome.[62] Wilson demanded that special operations across the whole Mediterranean should be centralized in the Caserta–Bari–Brindisi triangle under a single commander, although, 'it is realised that this means moving a great deal from Cairo'.[63]

With the wholehearted support, in this instance, of Macmillan, Wilson had some success in imposing his will on Cairo.[64] Nevertheless, Churchill seriously considered dismissing him only two months into his term of office.[65] His offence was to take too seriously the 'allied' portion of his mandate. 'This arose', Macmillan observed, 'from the poor general trying to be too honest and sending all kinds of messages to the Combined Chiefs of Staff (whose servant he is) on Italian politics and military plans without first ascertaining that they coincided with the wishes of HMG!'[66] In the end Wilson came out of the contretemps with a promotion of sorts. He was raised to the dignity of 'Supreme Allied Commander' of the Mediterranean. The new title was invented to give him parity of esteem with Eisenhower, who was appointed Supreme Allied Commander in Europe. It certainly cheered Wilson personally. 'Jumbo Wilson in the greatest of good form,' Miles Lampson reported of SACMED's first appearance in Cairo. 'He is very pleased with the three flags which he now flies on his motor car as Supreme Commander in the Mediterranean – these he showed us with great glee.'[67]

The extensive but flaccid grip of the 'Jumbocracy' created a paradox. His appointment as Supreme Commander was the high point of the concept of a united Mediterranean.[68] He had unrivalled mobility around the sea, not only for himself but for his representatives. With over 12,000 aircraft under his titular command, he was even able to insist on transports with comfortable seats. But the result of travel was not more

authority, but yet more movement. A whole class of political entrepreneurs roved around the Mediterranean.

Even as Wilson left Cairo, another complex Greek crisis was coming to
the boil. Through the good offices of the Metropolitan of Athens,
Archbishop Damaskinos, Tsouderos sent repeated pleas to political leaders
to leave Greece and join a government of national unity. In March 1944
a message arrived in Cairo from Damaskinos, with the terms dictated by
the party politicians. They refused to form a liberation committee, refused
to leave Greece, and demanded a secret convention preventing the return
of King George to Greece. The Communists dissented even from this
offer. They declared that the true government of Greece existed in the
mountains in the form of a newly created Committee of National
Liberation – the PEEA. Within days of news of the PEEA reaching Egypt,
troops near Alexandria mutinied, as did ships in the harbour itself.
Tsouderos had little choice but to resign.[69]

The Greek troops who mutinied at Alexandria were awaiting embarkation for Italy. Yet whilst the Communists tried to overthrow one king,
their Italian leader was coming to the aid of another monarch. A few
days beforehand, Palmiro Togliatti, the leader of Italian Communism,
had arrived in Naples from Moscow to announce the *svolta di Salerno*,
the Salerno U-turn. 'Under orders from Moscow,' Macmillan noted, 'they
have let it be known that they will enter a Government *without* first
raising the question of the King and the monarchy.' At the same moment
in Alexandria and Naples, fear of the Communists gave the British a stick
with which to beat careerist politicians. They proposed, in both cases,
broad-bottomed governments under cowed monarchs. In Greece the
King should offer a plebiscite on the future of the monarchy and accept
Communists into the government. In Italy the King should also offer a
plebiscite on the future of the monarchy and accept Communists into
the government. Each monarch should pay a severe forfeit, according
to his circumstances. Victor Emmanuel should announce his intention
to retire in favour of his son, Umberto. King George should issue a
self-denying ordinance preventing him from actually having any power
over the conduct of the plebiscite.[70]

In Italy, Victor Emmanuel offered to hand over power to Prince
Umberto, but only when the Allies had recaptured his capital. This

compromise proved good enough for the politicians of the south, fearful
of being squeezed between monarch and comrade. There followed days
of horse trading but Badoglio was able to unveil a new, 'all party' government in which he remained both prime and foreign minister. The
situation in Egypt was dealt with more forcibly. Royalist officers seized
mutinous ships in Alexandria. British troops surrounded and starved out
the army mutineers. The 'wretched' Greek politicians in Cairo, with 'no
aim but political intrigue and self-advancement', 'reaped a whirlwind
beyond their puny control'.[71]

The Germans helped resolve the problem.[72] The SS was rapidly
expanding the ambitions and reach of its organization. Its leader in Greece
was determined to purge all those not committed to the Nazi cause,
including even those officers who had been most active in recruiting
'security battalions', an anti-Communist militia willing to fight alongside the Germans.[73] The one Greek politician who had dared to utter
even veiled criticisms of the regime, finally agreed to flee. The British
smuggled George Papandreou to Egypt. For the first time since
Kanellopoulos's escape there was a charismatic figure outside Greece
around whom a new government might be constructed. Following in
Papandreou's wake was a somewhat disoriented delegation from the
PEEA. Lacking instructions on how to deal with the new situation, the
delegation was sucked into negotiations for an 'all party' Cairo government. To subsequent howls of dismay from their comrades left behind
in Greece, the Communist representatives signed a deal to support the
Papandreou government at Beirut in May 1944.[74] The British believed
that 'it will certainly have a great effect in other parts of the Balkans and
do a great deal towards stabilising things'.[75]

The Beirut agreement on Greece was still being mulled over when
another entrepreneur, quite unexpectedly, crossed the Mediterranean. In
Algiers, Harold Macmillan wrote that 'with modern communications as
rapid as they are, and the universal listening to radio', it was barely defensible to support Badoglio, a neo-Fascist reactionary, in Italy, Papandreou,
a social democrat, in Greece, and Tito, a 'romantic and dramatic'
Communist brewing a 'cauldron of hate', in Yugoslavia.[76] Yet there did
not seem any point in those who dissented from the Tito myth even
reporting their experiences in Yugoslavia. Captain Hudson, the officer
who had led the first mission onto the Montenegrin coast in 1941, and
remained in Yugoslavia for three years, said in disgust of his treatment
in Bari: 'at least refrain from treachery to your officers in the field. Such

conduct is unworthy of prostitutes.'[77] Tito's personal representative had been sent out of Bosnia along with his backers, Fitzroy Maclean and Bill Deakin, to be lionized, first in the Mediterranean and then in London. Going the other way were Soviet missions. Soviet helpfulness over Italian politics was paid for in Russian facilities in the special forces 'golden triangle' of Bari, Brindisi and Naples. The facilities supported an NKVD mission that had finally opened up direct contact with Tito in February 1944. By May 1944 the Partisan leader had a conveyor belt of supplies, personnel and plenipotentiaries flowing to and fro across the Mediterranean. Indeed the route seemed so secure that complacency set in. The physical traffic, as well as the insecure signals traffic, that bounced in and out of his base at Drvar was of interest to the Germans. On 25 May an SS airborne battalion landed by glider and parachute in Drvar with the intention of killing or capturing Tito. Although he succeeded in escaping, the operation turned him into a fugitive. His salvation was the Mediterranean connection.

An American-supplied Soviet aeroplane, operating from a British air base, and escorted by American fighters, landed in Bosnia, picked up the fugitive and flew him safely to Bari. Commanders around the Mediterranean were woken with the news and set about protecting not only Tito but his legend. There was an argument that Tito's status as a helpless refugee could be exploited to turn him into a political client. The counter-argument was that Tito the refugee would become a pathetic figure, no better than the helpless exiled monarchs with whom the Allies already had to deal. Tito was deposited on Vis by a British warship two days later. Allied naval and air protection meant that there was no possibility that the Germans would be able to pursue their prey out into the Adriatic.[78]

Tito's plight was not big news anywhere apart from in AFHQ. The 'Knight's Move' saga coincided with rather more immediately eye-catching events. On the same day as the Drvar operation, involving some hundreds of troops, the Allies finally broke the siege of Anzio. Three hundred thousand men had fought for five months, along a front only sixteen miles long. The inability of the Germans to contain the Anzio pocket any longer, opened up the road to Rome, the original prize of the operation. The opportunity plunged the Allied command into a bitter argument. Mark Clark, the commander of the operation, demonstrated why so few of his fellow generals trusted him. He was determined to take Rome for the greater glory, firstly, of Mark Clark, and secondly, of America. He was not keen on pursuing the retreating German forces. 'We not only wanted the honour of capturing Rome,' he wrote, 'but felt we deserved it.' He threatened that if British troops moved towards the city they would have 'another all-out battle on their hands, namely with me'. He reacted with scorn when his British superiors 'kept pulling on me the ideas that we were to annihilate the entire German army'. He was 'disgusted' with their attitude. Tito was being rescued at the same time as American units – with military police deployed to keep the British out – marched into the Italian capital.[79] As it happened, Clark's thunder was cruelly stolen by events elsewhere. If Clark was gazumped in the news by D-Day, 6 June 1944, the landing of Allied troops on the beaches of Normandy, then the unlading of Tito on Vis was barely noticed.

In the short term, the effect of great events was surprisingly slight for those trying to run the Mediterranean. The fate of kings continued to dominate the political landscape. Indeed with the attention of London, Washington and Moscow diverted elsewhere, the Mediterranean political entrepreneurs operated for the moment on an even looser rein.[80] As Wilson and Macmillan told one another on D-Day, 'London cannot hurt us'.[81] Bob Murphy, recently returned from Washington, reported that it was increasingly difficult to get anyone outside the Mediterranean to focus on its affairs.[82] Churchill famously read about the settlement of the Italian question in the press. The capture of Rome triggered Victor Emmanuel's promise to hand over power to Prince Umberto. It also brought to a head the long-running argument between Macmillan and General Noel Mason-MacFarlane, acting head of the Allied Control Commission for Italy. 'Mason-Mac' believed that he did all the work and Macmillan took all the credit. Mason-Mac saw his opportunity. He insisted that he should take Umberto and the royal government to Rome as soon as possible. He dismissed Macmillan's warning that the politicians in Rome, as much as those in Greece, might be reluctant to bow the knee to their acting monarch. The matter turned out as Macmillan predicted. The Roman politicians, led by Ivanoe Bonomi, told Umberto that his so-called 'all party' government was not one that they recognized. Mason-Mac was forced to dismiss Badoglio and appoint Bonomi in his place. 'It seems to be working out as I foretold,' wrote Macmillan, who had retreated to Algiers in order to be as far away from the political fall-out as possible.[83] Whilst this Italian crisis was in full swing, Wilson received a telegram telling him that the 'boy king', Peter of Yugoslavia, accompanied by his new ally, the former Ban of Croatia, Subasic, was on his way to 'land at Vis and take possession of kingdom'. Frantic telegraphing had Peter's aircraft diverted to Algiers. Once he had the King in his hands, Wilson was able safely to divert him into purdah on Malta. Ban Subasic alone was allowed to travel on to Vis to meet Tito.[84]

The outcome of the parallel royal crises was much the same. Mason-MacFarlane was summoned by Wilson, told that 'he was intrinsically right – the Bonomi government is probably an improvement on Badoglio', scolded for his incompetent handling of the affair, and ordered to have a mental breakdown so that he might be relieved of his position. Wilson approved the formation of the Bonomi government, despite the refusal of the Roman politicians to give any assurances about the long-term survival of the monarchy. King Peter never did get to travel on to Yugoslavia. Instead Subasic signed away many of his rights on Vis. Tito, rather than the now reviled 'traitor' Mihailovic, became the approved leader of the Yugoslav military resistance. He, too, gave no promises about the long-term survival of the monarchy.[85]

The palpable sense of confidence – perhaps overconfidence – amongst the Mediterranean policy entrepreneurs was expressed most fully during a grand dinner held at Caserta on 19 June 1944. That dinner was hosted by Ira Eaker, the American commander of the Mediterranean Allied Air Forces. The guests of honour were George C. Marshall and Hap Arnold, chief of the US Army Air Force. Two figures less sympathetic to the Mediterranean venture it would have been hard to find. Arnold was a champion of crushing Germany by bombing. He had recently transferred Eaker to the Mediterranean 'back-water' because he was not pursuing the main bombing campaign from England with sufficient ruthlessness. Marshall saw little value in further Mediterranean campaigns other than those that diverted German forces away from the main front in Normandy. The best he was willing to offer the Mediterranean commanders was the chance to participate in the diversionary invasion of southern France – codenamed *Anvil*. In this endeavour the Mediterranean would act as little more than an access route and a supply base. The Franco-American landing force would operate as part of the European theatre. Control of resistance groups from Algiers had already been handed over to Eisenhower's headquarters, SHAEF. The Supreme Commander in the Mediterranean acted as little more than the franchisee of the Supreme Commander in Europe. Giraud, for months little more than an embarrassing reminder of Allied failure to corral de Gaulle, had been retired without a ripple. Thereafter it was hard to get the FCNL in Algiers to focus on the Mediterranean, 'about which they talk so much'. The truth was that the Metropolitan French were 'thinking about nothing but France'.[86]

Nevertheless, the staffs of Alexander, Wilson and Macmillan had been beavering away for some weeks on an entirely different approach. The plans that Alexander had wired to London the day before were unveiled to the visiting Americans at the dinner. Alexander disavowed the invasion of southern France in favour of a major offensive launched from within the Mediterranean. His forces would move up the eastern coast of Italy and around the head of the Adriatic. From there they would invade Yugoslavia, striking across Slovenia for the Ljubljana Gap. Their eventual target would be Vienna and a direct attack on the 'soft underbelly' of the Reich.[87]

The most remarkable thing about the Ljubljana Gap plan was that its authors thought that it had any chance of serious consideration. On the night of the dinner, Marshall and Arnold were, in the interests of Allied amity, polite enough. Immediately after the meal Harold Macmillan and Wilson's chief of staff, James Gammell, took off from Naples, picking up express aeroplane relays in Algiers and Casablanca, so they might rush to London, striking whilst the iron seemed hot. Their journey was so quick that they arrived, as planned, 'unheralded'.[88] Wilson could manipulate Allied communications to achieve such an effect. He had no control, of course, over direct communications within the US Army. Marshall and Eisenhower signalled to one another. Whilst the delegation was still in the air, they had agreed that 'to contemplate wandering off overland via Trieste and Ljubljana' was little more than a fool's errand.[89]

Thus when Macmillan called upon Churchill he was 'able to get the PM to see the picture as we saw it in the Mediterranean' but when Gammell had a similar exploratory interview with Eisenhower, the latter 'said he wanted *Anvil* and he wanted it quick'.[90] This disconnection between Caserta and the outside world was not, at least in its origins, purely an Anglo-American affair. The reaction of many in London to the Mediterranean entrepreneurs was equally lukewarm. Alan Brooke described 'Alexander's wild hopes of an advance on Vienna' as 'not based on any real study of the problem, but rather the result of elated spirits after a rapid advance'. The Mediterranean was producing little more than 'strategic ravings'.[91]

Nevertheless, the joint enthusiasm of Churchill and the entrepreneurs carried all before them. Macmillan was invited down to Chequers to finalize the plan for transmission to Washington.[92] They were able to buttress their case with 'the most marvellous intercept' evidence of Hitler's orders to Kesselring.[93] The Mediterranean balloon was, however, pricked by the 'rude', 'brusque' and 'offensive' retort from Washington. For nine days the Mediterranean enthusiasts had deluded themselves. They provoked the Americans into a series of straightforward statements about the Mediterranean. The invasion of southern France would go ahead as part of the European campaign; American ships and troops would move towards their embarkation ports, whatever the orders British commanders in the Mediterranean might choose to issue. The Caserta dinner turned out to be not a new beginning but the last supper. The great days of Mediterranean semi-independence came to an abrupt end.

THIRTEEN

Mission Impossible

In purely technical terms the unified Mediterranean reached its organizational peak in the summer of 1944. SACMED had bedded in. His signalling system now worked. His Mediterranean-spanning photographic reconnaissance organization had been centralized, so that he might call up aerial views of his theatre at a moment's notice. The great palace of Caserta was now fully operational. In July 1944 AFHQ finally pulled out of Algiers completely and settled permanently in Italy.[1] Memories of the winter, when officers strove to conduct the far-flung Mediterranean war 'without benefit of files, typewriters, lights or even passable communications', were fading. One still had to dodge 'around the bedraggled Italian scrubwomen interminably stirring up the dust in the interminable halls' but at least it was warm. The military and political arbiters of the Mediterranean lived a sybaritic lifestyle. At Caserta itself, they took over not only the palace but surrounding lodges and villas. A few miles away around Naples they provided themselves with palaces and the grandest apartments.

But amongst the gay atmosphere, there remained a sense of decay. The move to Caserta had a profound psychological impact. Until that moment the Mediterranean had been a living experience, with constant commuting from shore to shore. Increasingly, air travel became a matter of short hops, up and down the Italian peninsula. Horizons narrowed. The excitement that had surrounded the great Caserta dinner, when the hall had fizzed with rumours of great plans for a rapid breakthrough to Yugoslavia, soon faded. With the reluctant British acceptance of *Anvil*, that dinner really did feel like the last supper. In place of the hopes of only a few weeks before, the talk was of 'scraping' together forces from around the Mediterranean so at least some attempt could be made to keep the Italian campaign going.[2]

Taking their cue from Washington, the Americans in the Mediterranean became openly dismissive of its importance. Their most experienced Mediterranean political operative, Bob Murphy, an important player since 1940, announced that he was leaving. His next posting was indicative of American sentiment. He was transferred to north-western Europe, as Eisenhower's political adviser. The main job of Alexander Kirk, Murphy's replacement, was as Ambassador to Italy. His other functions were residual.

The only pan-Mediterranean figure the Americans deployed in the summer of 1944 was an obscure Republican politician, W. S. Culbertson. Culbertson was dispatched to make a study of the Mediterranean as an economic area, with a view to developing post-war American trading relations.[3] He was instructed to visit three areas – French North Africa, the Middle East and Italy. Culbertson and his team arrived in Algiers at the beginning of August 1944 and spent the rest of the year travelling around the sea.[4] He heard many tales of British iniquity. In Cairo, in particular, many American officials, both professional diplomats and wartime appointments, had grown tired of the supercilious British, whom, they believed, thwarted them at every turn. On the surface the British gave the Americans a fair crack of the whip. In reality they were so deeply embedded in the political life of the Middle East that it was almost second nature for them to thwart American interests. This was particularly galling since the money and the goods that kept local economies in reasonable health was largely American, much of it supplied 'free' through the Lend-Lease scheme. James Landis, the senior American official attached to the Middle East Supply Council, was particularly vocal on this score. Landis told Culbertson that the MESC was so effective that it was imperative that Americans should destroy it. The Anglo-American organization should then be reinvented as a purely American body working for purely American interests.[5]

Sadly for Culbertson and Landis, officials in Washington chose to hear only half of their message, about dismantling the organization. Even before Culbertson had left America, the most ambitious scheme to further American interests in the Middle East had foundered in the quagmire of Washington interest-group politics. At the beginning of 1944 a committee led by an obscure Mid-western senator called Harry Truman had issued a report on the importance of oil for American power. Truman warned that, at current rates of consumption, the oil stocks of the western hemisphere would be exhausted within fifteen years. The oil fields of the

Middle East would become the pivot of future world power. Truman's warning was manna for Roosevelt's Secretary of the Interior, and wartime petroleum coordinator, Harold Ickes. He had developed a plan to build a huge pipeline from Saudi Arabia and Kuwait, in whose, as yet undeveloped, oilfields American companies had a major share, to the Mediterranean coast. From a Mediterranean terminal – probably Alexandria – oil supplies could be shipped west. Ickes insisted that oil supply was not merely a matter of private profit, it was a central strategic requirement of the state. Thus his pipeline would be financed, built and owned by the American government. Although the oil that flowed along it would be owned by private oil companies, the government would take, at its own discretion, what it needed in times of crisis. Ickes's plan was savaged in Congress as an unconscionable interference with private enterprise, kleptomaniac New Dealerdom running wild on the world stage. It was dropped in July 1944. Both the pipeline and the wider idea of American politico-economic intervention in the east would soon return, but there was little appetite for them in 1944.[6] By the end of Culbertson's mission the British had decided not to waste 'powder and shot' on refuting his conclusions. Harold Macmillan, always an acute observer of American power, dismissed him as 'rather a dreary old man, on some vague mission here'.[7]

The British were more than aware that there were some Americans with grand Mediterranean aspirations inimical to their own interests. They were happy to see them confuted. Such visionaries were, however, not the main problem. There were plenty of Americans without such a Mediterranean vision, but with the same political ambitions as Culbertson or Landis. As often as not British policy was opposed by American officials hoping to appeal to a specific ethnic group back home: Italian, Greek and Jewish. Such a perception could have been dismissed as sour grapes if it were not for the repeated and frank admission by Roosevelt that this was indeed so. 'For purely political considerations over here,' he told Churchill, 'I would never survive even a slight set back.'[8] As the fate of Ickes's pipeline demonstrated, American domestic politics, Presidential, Congressional and gubernatorial, were running at full bore in 1944. Roosevelt had every reason to fear that he might not be re-elected for his desired fourth term in November 1944.

If the Americans had little idea of what to do with the Mediterranean, neither did the British. To outsiders it appeared that as the war wound down normal service might be restored: that, as a popular American news magazine put it, 'the Mediterranean is likely to be after the war, more than ever before, a *mare nostrum* of Britain'. Such an outcome seemed much less clear to insiders. The high-water mark of an integrated Mediterranean had been reached. Many believed that it should now begin to recede.[9]

As so often, a forthcoming visit of Churchill to the Mediterranean in August 1944 brought the question to the fore. His presence was dictated by a desire to witness an operation he had done much to sabotage, the invasion of southern France by Franco-American forces, scheduled for the middle of August. He also wanted to see British troops in Italy in action. In between the battles Churchill would hold court in Naples and Rome. He would rule on who should rule in the Mediterranean. The great man was becoming increasingly irascible, unpredictable and quixotic, 'perspiring in white ducks'.[10] The SACMED question became as much a matter of personalities as strategy. Was Britain fighting a campaign in Italy, or was it fighting a war in the Mediterranean? Was her premier commander Alexander or Wilson? Churchill himself made little secret of his preference. He constantly talked of Alexander's armies, Alexander's plans, Alexander's needs. Quite often Roosevelt had to reintroduce SACMED back into any discussion from which Wilson's name was wilfully excluded by Churchill.[11]

Alexander's partisans could, and did, take contradictory views about the role of SACMED. On one day, they might argue that Wilson was a monkey on Alexander's back. AFHQ at Caserta merely added an unnecessary layer of bureaucracy over Alexander's Allied Armies Italy (AAI) HQ, which had moved by July 1944 to Lake Bolsena. Wilson, it was claimed, second-guessed and interfered with Alexander. Wilson and the whole SACMED superstructure should go.[12] On the next day, they could argue that Wilson's power should be augmented in order to assist Alexander. Following the reallocation of American forces to the invasion of southern France, the British would have to increase their own efficiency. There was no point tying down forces on local security and garrison duty in the eastern Mediterranean. Rather, the remaining assets of Middle East Command in Cairo should be transferred to SACMED. He would then be able to 'scrape' the area for men and supplies, thus feeding Alexander with sufficient resources to attempt to break, rather than merely contain, Kesselring's armies. If enough forces could be raised in this way, Alexander's grand ambitions for a breakout into Yugoslavia – just rejected – could be resurrected.

There was also a countervailing view, unfriendly to both Wilson and Alexander, held by many in Cairo, still smarting that their own authority had been transferred to SACMED and the Minister Resident at Caserta. If they could not run the Mediterranean they would prefer that no one did. Italy, in their view, had become a cuckoo in the nest. What happened there had little relevance for the rest of the Mediterranean. There was little point sending resources to Italy; they would be wasted. Instead, Britain had to recognize that the grand titles and baroque organizations thrown up by the war had little relevance to the future. What remained were a series of knotty local problems which had little to do with one another. If any coordination was needed, it should come from London not via extra-territorial Mediterranean intermediaries.[13] 'It is odd', Harold Macmillan observed, 'how people seem to want impossible assignments and quarrel to get insoluble problems entrusted to them.'[14]

The two 'impossible assignments' that defined the extent of the Mediterranean in the summer of 1944 were Palestine and Greece. There was a good argument that Palestine was the pivot of the Mediterranean, 'the link between the three continents' of Europe, Asia and Africa. The Mediterranean ports of Palestine were natural lading and unlading points for travel between the Middle East and Europe. Palestine already housed the Mediterranean terminal of the existing pipeline from the interior to the coast. As the Ickes plan indicated, the demand for such facilities was bound to grow in the future. Not only did Palestine control the point where land met sea, it guarded the pure sea route itself: possession of Palestine was essential for the security of the Suez Canal. Nevertheless, Palestine became abstracted from the Mediterranean. Those who wanted to regard Palestine in strategic terms were fighting a losing battle.[15] In 1939 the Palestine White Paper had assumed that Jewish immigration into Palestine would be terminated in 1944. As a result, the politics of Zionism reached an apogee in 1944. In summer 1944 both Democrats and Republicans adopted Zionist platforms for the forthcoming American elections. Roosevelt had already denounced the end of immigration. However reluctantly, he was moving to the conclusion that the open endorsement of a Jewish state in Palestine was necessary for his re-election.[16]

As Churchill prepared for his visit to the Mediterranean, he was also considering Auschwitz. Faced with incontrovertible proof that the Nazis'

technology of murder was now capable of meeting their ideological aspirations, he noted that 'there is no doubt that this is probably the greatest
and most horrible crime ever committed in the whole history of the
world'. Yet whatever Churchill might scribble for the benefit of posterity,
Britain's real 'Jewish problem' was not the Holocaust.[17] The reality was
that the primary enemy of the Jews *in Palestine* was not the Nazis,
but the British themselves. In the early years of the war many Britons
sympathetic to Zionism – most especially Churchill himself – had seen
the Jews as natural allies. The army had raised Jewish units with the
assistance of the Jewish Agency. SOE had adopted Revisionist Zionist
radicals as 'friends'. In doing so the British had armed the very Jews who
preferred to fight Britain rather than the Axis.[18] The official position of
mainstream Zionism was that Jewish troops should be brigaded together
under the Star of David and sent to Italy to fight the Germans. Whilst
in Italy, Churchill ordered the army to adopt this idea.[19] Established Jewish
leaders such as Chaim Weizmann were amongst those who wished to see
the Middle East 'scraped' to further the wider Mediterranean war. Many
of those in British uniform, however, owed their main loyalty to the
Jewish Agency's own secret army, the Haganah. The High Commissioner
in Palestine, Harold MacMichael, described Jewish troops in British
uniform as 'a highly organised racket'.[20]

If the Haganah was the ultimate threat, it was the Revisionists, however,
who presented the most immediate problem. In the spring of 1944 their
military wing, the Irgun, denounced the 'treacherous British oppressors'
as the main enemy and launched a terrorist campaign. They framed their
campaign in an explicitly Mediterranean context. The Revisionists
compared the British to the Nazis in Yugoslavia and Greece, and their
own resistance to that of partisans in those countries. The most violent
terrorists were a splinter faction of the Irgun, known as the Stern Gang.
On the eve of Churchill's departure for the Mediterranean the Stern
Gang ambushed Harold MacMichael as he drove from Jerusalem to Jaffa;
it was only by luck that he escaped with minor injuries to his arm and
thigh. Zionist politics in America and Zionist terrorism in the Middle
East made it almost impossible to regard Palestine as anything other than
a special problem.[21]

Just as they tried to keep Palestine out of the general run of
Mediterranean affairs, the Cairene authorities attempted the same gambit
with regard to Greece, albeit with less success. The habitual axis of Greek
affairs ran between Athens and Cairo. The Greek government and exiles

existed easily within the milieu of the Greek diaspora in Egypt. This was no longer necessarily seen as an advantage. Although factional fighting amongst the Greeks had abated to an extent since the rise of Papandreou, its recrudescence was daily expected in 'the poisonous atmosphere of intrigue which reigns in Cairo. All previous Greek governments in exile have been broken in the bar of Shepheard's Hotel.'[22] Cairo and Jerusalem had once been seen as the main centres for Yugoslav exiles as well. Now virtually all business had been shifted to Italy. Tito was established at Vis, and, as Churchill approached the Mediterranean, finally consented to come over to visit Italy, creating a 'favourable impression' at Caserta. Representatives of the Albanian Communist leader Enver Hoxha were also in Italy negotiating for recognition and support.[23] The same special forces 'golden triangle' was also handling the attempt to create a unified Italian partisan movement. The fall of Rome had seen the burgeoning of the resistance from a few bands into many hundreds, amounting to tens of thousands of men. As Tito introduced himself around Caserta, General Raffaele Cadorna was departing to be parachuted near Bergamo to establish a supreme command of the Volunteers of Liberty. The supplies earmarked for Tito or Cadorna could with the greatest of ease be given to the Greeks: they were the same supplies, at the same bases, flown in by the same Allied aircrews.[24]

Even before Churchill left the UK, British intelligence intercepts indicated that German commanders in Greece felt that it was no longer worth trying to hold the country. Whilst Churchill was in Italy, the Red Army launched its long-awaited thrust into the Balkans via Rumania. On 23 August 1944 von Weichs attended a meeting with Hitler. Although the Führer was characteristically unwilling to hear of retreats, he was persuaded to allow the redeployment of Army Group F 'further north'. Permission was even granted for German commanders in Greece, who had already opened lines of communications to British officers in their areas, to collaborate with the British if this would smooth the 'redeployment'.[25]

Churchill was already a firm supporter of British intervention in Greece. He was easily persuaded that intervention could best be launched from Italy, organized by SACMED. The corollary of this decision was that Papandreou's government should also be transferred from Cairo to Italy, and that all further political direction of Greek affairs should come from across the Adriatic rather than across the Mediterranean.[26] At the same time Churchill and his party were exposed to a rehearsal of

SACMED's virtues.[27] His champions pointed out the danger of dividing the Mediterranean into two zones: the central Mediterranean – Italy, Yugoslavia, Albania and North Africa – where the British and the Americans cooperated, and the eastern Mediterranean, where the British chose to go it alone.[28] The political dangers of such an attempt to twit the Americans were plain for all to see. In June 1944 Roosevelt had agreed to give Churchill a relatively free hand in the Balkans, as long as nothing politically embarrassing was done behind his back. The Mediterraneanists had, in any case, a clinching practical argument beyond high politics. They had already succeeded in integrating Mediterranean transport. Both shipping and air travel were subject to American agreement, and quite often took place in planes and ships controlled by the Americans. To pursue an independent policy was to risk embarrassing paralysis. In Slessor's words, 'the necessity for the continuance of AFHQ was so obvious that it was hardly worth stating'.[29] With the threat of extinction lifted, 'the whole circus [was] back in great form'.[30]

On one level Churchill's visit was a triumph for the idea of the Mediterranean. By the time he left Naples, the British were indulging in bold talk about extending the life of SACMED beyond the end of any war with Germany. AFHQ was touted as the best organization to deal with questions of post-war relief and political instability. The string of airfields and ports all coordinated from around Caserta bound the Mediterranean countries together like never before. But although the political side of AFHQ had had its authority enhanced by Churchill, any thoughts of developing grand Mediterranean plans quickly degenerated into a series of trouble-shooting exercises. The Mediterranean horizon narrowed to a concentration on Greece more rapidly than was expected.

Churchill delivered on his promise to give Macmillan more authority in Italy by making him head of the Allied Commission. The next stage of the plan, that Macmillan should travel to America in order to persuade the Americans that the future of Italy meant something more than the projection of domestic politics, never came to fruition. Macmillan ignored pleas from the staff at AFHQ that they should be allowed to leave Caserta for Rome, before another beastly winter set in, on the grounds that 'our territory covers far more than Italy. If we are at Naples, the Mediterranean command is a reality. If we are at Rome, we seem to emphasise the *Italian* aspect, and General Wilson will be continually harassed by members of the Italian government and representatives of the Vatican.'[31] In the event he found it hard to spend enough time in his Rome office to properly

conduct Italian affairs. If Italian politics were neglected, then neither did
military operations prosper. Alexander's hopes of breaking through the
German Gothic line rapidly, foundered. Macmillan found him near Siena,
three weeks into the battle, 'rather tired, even strained' and railing bitterly
against his neglect 'by the powers-that-be'.[32]

In the Adriatic, supplying the Partisans in Yugoslavia had become a matter
of routine business. The routine lulled its participants into a false sense
of security. Reports from both uniformed British liaison officers and SIS
agents about the inefficiency and corruption with which these supplies
were handled were steadfastly ignored. So, too, were indications that
Partisans were beginning to treat the British with something akin to
contempt. In the first week of September 1944 Tito received an unprece-
dented level of Allied air support, direct attacks as well as supply drops.
Operation *Ratweek* managed to halt through traffic on the railway lines
between Zagreb and Belgrade, Belgrade and Salonika. As the Allied airmen
began to celebrate a success, however, it became clear that the Partisans
were less and less interested in cutting German communications. German
troops were still formidable opponents. Partisans and Germans avoided
each other as much as possible, as the Partisans took over the areas of
Serbia not directly protected by German units.[33] At the end of *Ratweek*,
the 'well behaved' Tito suddenly disappeared. He boarded a Soviet plane
and flew away from Vis, never to return. In August the British had boasted
to the Americans that 'Tito is conscious that his present value is not as
great or necessary as it was'. He had been properly impressed by British
power in the Mediterranean.[34] The truth was rather the other way around.
The Partisan leader no longer needed his status as a British client in the
Mediterranean. He was able to return to his natural allegiance. The next
the British heard of him, he had arrived in Moscow. As Fitzroy Maclean
cheerfully proclaimed when he got out to Caserta, there was absolutely
nothing further the Mediterraneanists could do. The die was cast. There
would not be much of a civil war. Mihailovic had no chance against Tito's
forces, equipped with 'the splendid equipment we have given him',
supported by the Russian army that had just crossed the Yugoslav border.[35]

The only practical option open to AFHQ was to concentrate on Greece.
As Maclean delivered his verdict on Yugoslavia, planning for the descent
on Greece moved into top gear.[36] Wilson's career had almost been

terminated by the Dodecanese débâcle which he presided over from Cairo. He had little intention of inviting a similar disaster in Greece or the Aegean. He proceeded with justifiable caution. He was particularly allergic to demands for quick action.[37] By late September 1944 the talk was mainly of 'anti-scorch' operations, preventing the destruction of critical infrastructure and the potential collapse of civil society. The point at issue was whether it was the Nazis or the Communists who were more likely to do the scorching.[38] SACMED would send forces to both the northern coast of the Peloponnese and to Athens. It was unclear whether they would cooperate with the Communists against the Nazis, or with the rightists against the Communists.[39]

Individuals long involved in Greece undoubtedly had strong personal opinions, upon which confusion allowed them to act. Many others were simply tired. 'One gets the impression', SOE concluded about their long-serving chief representative in the country, 'that Woodhouse was very disillusioned towards the end and is anxious to have nothing more to do with the Greeks for the time being.'[40] At root most agreed that Papandreou offered the best solution not least because he was willing, albeit speaking in 'idiomatic and fluent French', to espouse a vision of the Mediterranean that accorded very much with British expectations. He portrayed Greece as a 'fortress guarding the Imperial route' through the Mediterranean. In return Greece would be fortified by 'British protection against Slav aggression'. He admired British policy in Italy. They had shown great wisdom in depriving her for ever of 'her African colonies so that the southern shores of the Mediterranean could never again be a source of danger to our Imperial communications'. In both Greece and Italy, 'the question of the monarch' was relatively unimportant.[41]

Papandreou espoused his vision of Britain in the Mediterranean in the aftermath of a brief but bracing encounter with Churchill, who had made a four-hour stop-over in Naples on his way to Moscow. To the embarrassment of the British, as well as the Greek participants, Churchill had delivered a paean of praise for the Greek monarchy, declaring that nothing but its full restitution would do. The next person whom Churchill spoke to about Greece was treated to a more controlled display. On 9 October 1944, as Papandreou made his pitch on Britain's Mediterranean role to Macmillan in Italy, Churchill was having a similar discussion with Stalin in Moscow. With the original 'free hand' Roosevelt had offered Churchill in the Balkans now expired, but the American presidential election still a month away, Churchill seized his opportunity. 'Britain',

Churchill said to Stalin almost as soon as they met, 'must be the leading Mediterranean Power.' Stalin immediately agreed. He 'understood that Britain had suffered very much owing to her communications in the Mediterranean having been cut by the Germans. It was a serious matter for Britain when the Mediterranean route was not in her hands.' 'In that respect,' he concluded, 'Greece was very important.' Encouraged, Churchill also threw Italy into the mix. He was, he confided, having many problems with Roosevelt. American actions were dictated solely by ethnic politics at home. As for the Italians themselves, 'he did not think much of them as people, but they had a good many votes in New York'. Would Stalin 'soft-pedal the Communists in Italy and not stir them up'? Once more Stalin was happy to oblige. Togliatti, he reassured Churchill, was 'a wise man, not an extremist, and would not start an adventure in Italy'. There was no need to fear *il vento del Nord*. Within a few minutes Churchill had received all the Soviet help in the Mediterranean for which he had asked.[42]

Churchill and Eden spent the next eight days of their visit paying for Stalin's largesse. One *quid pro quo* they had always intended to offer – the withdrawal of support from the Polish government in London – had nothing to do with the Mediterranean. Whenever the conversation was switched to the Mediterranean itself, they realized that the Soviets took a very literal view of the deal that had been struck. Soviet negotiators were happy to reiterate Stalin's promise that no succour would be offered to the revolutionary aspirations of the Greeks or the Italians. When it came to Yugoslavia, British complaints about Tito leaving Vis for Moscow and his continued presence in the city were met with less sympathy. Stalin was willing to concede that both Russia and Britain would have influence over Yugoslavia, but it was clear from the tone of the conversations that the Soviets were confident of their own prime position. By the Mediterranean, they meant strictly the Mediterranean. Belgrade was not on the Mediterranean. It was far inland in Serbia. They would take care of such inland centres but have 'nothing to do with regard to affairs on the coast'. Eden even found himself arguing against the proposition that the Mediterranean should be a 'British lake', and indeed the offer that 'the Soviet Union was prepared to help Britain be strong in the Mediterranean'.[43]

Whilst Churchill talked, the main British armada made its way towards Athens. One hundred and twenty ships sailed from Taranto on 14 October 1944, carrying the designated commander of British forces, Ronald Scobie,

Resident Minister Macmillan and the Greek government. They rendezvoused with a similar convoy sailing from Alexandria, and by evening the impressive fleet was anchored off the eastern coast of Greece.[44] Landing parties were sent ashore to assess their likely reception. On the day Churchill left Moscow for Cairo, the representatives of British power, military and civil, Scobie and Macmillan, disembarked in the Piraeus. They drove from Piraeus to Athens 'through crowded streets, filled with cheering crowds'. The observation that 'whenever a British uniform appeared, great enthusiasm and applause' was, however, double-edged.[45] Many Communist fighters also wore British battledress. The ubiquity of Communist propaganda was clear for all to see. When Papandreou made the same drive the next day, he was greeted in Constitution Square by a huge demonstration. The Communist banners were everywhere. His speech was interrupted by choruses of 'We-want-no King'. The whole affair, the relieved British noted, seemed fairly good-natured because, they presumed, 'the order from Moscow had been given'.[46] Assuming mission accomplished, the Resident Minister left Athens to receive Churchill on his return to Caserta.

An odd mixture of peevishness and euphoria greeted Churchill's return to Italy. The Moscow visit was garlanded with the success of Athens. Stalin's promises of help in Italy showed signs of paying off too. One of SIS's agents in Milan acted as *cicerone* for a delegation of Italian guerrilla leaders, including a Communist representative, that set off on a journey south to acknowledge the authority of both AFHQ and the legitimacy of the Italian government. They were received with satisfaction. 'On the one side,' recalled their leader, Ferruccio Parri, 'imposing and majestic as a pro-consul, Sir H. Maitland Wilson, on the other the four of us. A glass of something, a word or two, a hand-shake, and then the signing. I ask myself if whenever the British pro-consuls sign agreements with some sultan of Baluchistan or the Padramut it is not a little the same.'[47] On the other hand Alexander's military failures created a poor atmosphere within the British high command.[48] Roosevelt added fuel to the fire by claiming that Wilson's reports on the Mediterranean contradicted those of Churchill. The 'treacherous' Jumbo thus became fair game. Whilst Churchill was at Caserta, a plot was hatched to finally get rid of Wilson. 'There must be drastic changes,' Alexander and Macmillan agreed.[49]

The chance for the blow rapidly presented itself. Once Churchill had departed, Wilson and Macmillan flew back to Athens to meet Eden and Lord Moyne, flying in from Cairo. It was to be the last occasion on which the Mediterranean proconsuls met. Macmillan had done his best to liquidate Moyne as a force in Mediterranean politics. 'I really do not know what these people in Cairo have been doing for two years,' he had complained. Moyne had been a 'disgraceful failure'.[50] Macmillan insisted on the 'placing of Greece quite clearly in my sphere, and no longer balanced uncertainly between me and Lord Moyne'.[51] In the event Moyne's termination was much more dramatic than anyone could have imagined. The Athens meeting was his last Mediterranean venture. When he returned to Cairo he was assassinated by the Zionist terrorists of the Stern Gang.[52] Although provoking much rhetorical outrage, Moyne's death changed remarkably little on the Mediterranean scene.[53]

Macmillan had wasted no opportunity to belittle Moyne, but his main purpose was to belittle Wilson. When he said that he wanted to wield power on behalf of SACMED, he was talking of Alexander. When Alexander himself met Eden in Italy he, too, had 'whined about being crushed by Wilson's HQ'.[54] If needed, further proof of Wilson's unfitness for office was provided by his usual habit of reporting to his titular superiors in Washington. In Athens, the British had discussed shifting resources from Italy to Greece. These plans were in direct contradiction to Wilson's orders and Roosevelt's preferences. The President had insisted that the Italians must be better fed than Greeks or Yugoslavs 'because of the great number of Italians in this country'.[55] Wilson's accurate report of the meeting put the Americans 'up in arms'. If Wilson liked the Americans so much, Eden and Churchill agreed, he could have them. He would be transferred to Washington. Alexander would become SACMED. He would retain also his office as Commander-in-Chief of the armies in Italy. The lustre of the whole Mediterranean enterprise would be restored by a single, charismatic figure. 'How wonderful Alex was,' Churchill claimed. 'What a grasp! What a quick appreciation of the situation! What a master mind!'[56]

The news was not received well by Alexander's military superiors.[57] 'I cannot imagine', Alan Brooke wrote, 'that Alex will ever make a Supreme Commander, he has just not got the brains for it.'[58] Alexander, Brooke predicted, would become little more than Macmillan's tool. Macmillan had a strong sense of Mediterranean autonomy. As he described his own technique, the trick was to make 'a joint politico-military plan'. Faced with a united front, London found it hard to unpick decisions made in the Mediterranean. Alexander, without 'a single idea in his head of his own', would become 'completely lost in this damned Greek business'.[59]

The fear that the command in the Mediterranean would be swallowed by a crisis in Greece proved eminently well founded. Summing up the experience in March 1945, Alan Brooke wrote that 'Alexander . . . has forgotten the main object of the War, and no longer remembers that there are such people as Germans! To him the situation in Greece is of paramount importance.'[60] At the end of November 1944 Wilson, Alexander and Macmillan were summoned back to London to effect the handover of command. Whilst they were away from Italy, war broke out in Greece. The Greek Mountain Brigade, which had distinguished itself in fighting around Rimini, was sent to Greece to provide the Papandreou government with a strong military arm. Despite being warned off by Moscow, the Greek Communists concluded that they would have to fight for their own survival.[61] The KKE in Athens faced a difficult dilemma. They were at their military peak, decked out with all the equipment that they had stockpiled from British supply drops. Witnessing insurgents 'in British battledress, with British weapons', Harold Macmillan ululated, 'Oh, Dr Dalton. Oh, Lord Selborne, what things were done in your name.'[62] On the same day, special forces in Cairo reported that they had sent Odysseus, their tobacco-smuggling paladin, who had set the whole Greek affair in motion, to a lunatic asylum in the Sudan, suffering from 'temporary fits of insanity'.[63] Papandreou had no real control anywhere. The structures of local government had been replaced by the shadow government of soviets the Communists had so carefully built over the previous years. Anti-Communist forces in rural Greece were a broken reed. Chris Woodhouse, the long-time leader of British special forces in Greece, left Athens for Epirus on the first day of December 1944. He arrived in time to witness the annihilation of the leading non-Communist military leader, Napoleon Zervas. Attacked by the Communists, Zervas's forces showed little stomach for the fight. It was all over within a fortnight. All that Woodhouse could do for his former ally was to arrange his evacuation to Corfu.[64]

But in Athens, Papandreou was getting money and supplies from the British. With those resources he could, in time, rebuild the government. The KKE's attempts to prevent the people being fed and workers from being paid might be overridden by a White Terror. The Communists had to act.[65] A Communist demonstration in Constitution Square turned into a bloody massacre. Communist forces converged on Athens. 'It could hardly be worse,' Macmillan commented upon his return. 'We have really been taken by surprise, the British forces (and the Embassy) are besieged and beleaguered in the small central area of Athens.'[66] The most humiliating loss was the headquarters of the RAF in Greece. Whilst the Mediterranean air forces lorded it over the Germans there, ground crew proved all too vulnerable to lightly armed insurgents. The captured men were sent on a bitter long march to northern Greece: many never returned. 'All my worst forebodings coming true!' declared Alan Brooke. It was impossible to stand by and watch British forces being killed or captured. Eighty thousand British troops would be dispatched to Greece to fight the Communists.[67]

The Americans were unsympathetic. In the first hours of the crisis American commanders refused to help the British ship forces to Greece from elsewhere in the Mediterranean. The British, they said, were merely reaping what they had sown. The Brits 'always acted in the Mediterranean' without consulting them. The British, Ambassador MacVeagh wrote, 'have not been either deft enough or understanding enough'. They had presented the Communists with a 'marvellous opportunity'. The 'Greek problem' would 'plague Britain, and us too' for years to come.[68] In the meantime American policy would continue to be governed, as it was on all Mediterranean issues, by the ethnic politics of the Democratic Party.[69] 'No one will understand better than yourself', Roosevelt told Churchill, 'that I . . . am necessarily responsive to the state of public feeling. It is for these reasons that it has not been and I am afraid will not be possible for this Government to take a stand with you in the present course of events in Greece.'[70]

Within their beleaguered Athens garrison the British desperately searched for a plan. Their best hope of survival, they decided, was to declare Archbishop Damaskinos, the Metropolitan of Athens, Regent. Damaskinos 'shares our view that there must be no reprisals and no counter-revolution'.[71] Apart from the risk of being 'either murdered or captured' by Communist insurgents, their main problem was that they could trust very few non-Communists. The British sent out peace feelers to the Communists suggesting a ceasefire.[72] The Royalists on the other hand wanted a White Terror. Calculating that once British troops started pouring into the country the military situation would be reversed,

Papandreou was willing to give it to them. He had to be told in no un-certain terms by the British military commander, General Scobie: 'we were not prepared to become a tool of a right-wing reaction throughout Greece . . . we would not allow ourselves to be dragged into a long war from one end of Greece to exterminate the Communist Party'.[73] Unfortunately, the one Briton who did wish British forces to become the tool of right-wing reaction was Churchill. In a 'sozzled' outburst he denounced the Metropolitan of Athens as a 'Quisling' and his own men on the spot as 'fussy-wuzzies'.[74] He then announced that he personally would take command of the Greek situation.[75] Not only would the British Minister Resident in the Mediterranean be dealing almost exclusively with Greek problems, but so too would the British Prime Minister. Athens for Christmas was to be yet another of Churchill's direct interventions in Mediterranean affairs. If Churchill insisted on going to Athens then the foreign secretary, Eden, insisted on coming too. They were, one aide commented, 'like two house-maids answering every bell'.[76]

On Christmas Eve, 1944 the two men took off in the Prime Minister's new aeroplane, a Douglas C-54 Skymaster, 'a huge and luxurious thing . . . but alas American'. The advanced long-range transport made the journey to the Mediterranean with ease. Stopping only to pick up Alexander in Italy, the party arrived in Athens on Christmas Day.[77] An armoured convoy was assembled at the airport to ensure that Churchill could get from the airfield to the British cruiser HMS *Ajax*, anchored off Phaleron, without being shot. Churchill immediately demonstrated his capacity for unpredictability. When Macmillan brought Damaskinos to see him, 'the Archbishop impressed the PM as much as he had the rest of us, and we are now in the curiously topsy-turvy position of the PM feeling strongly pro-Damaskinos (he even thinks he would make a good Regent)'.[78] The British party, nearly all of whom had travelled to Athens in the 1930s as lovers of classical culture, could not be other than struck by the contrast between their once Mediterranean dream and the current Mediterranean reality. Pierson Dixon wrote, in an unconscious echo of Huxley, that 'rocket-firing Beaufighters were circling over the Piraeus and swooping down on a target and then sweeping up again steeply over the brown background of hills – the trail and sound of their rockets breaking a scene which, above all other in the world, has up to now meant the acme of peace and content to me'. 'The sentimental approach', he added, 'with which I have lived for twenty years and which has, I see, clouded my political vision, has been warped forever.'[79]

On Boxing Day 1944, Churchill, Eden and Alexander, the leaders of a technically advanced, global war effort, crouched under the light of a few hurricane lamps waiting for a Communist delegation to wait on them. Finally, 'three men in English battledress' came in. Alexander read an appeal for a ceasefire. 'Instead of me pouring men into Greece,' he said, 'you ought to be pouring men into Italy to join my victorious armies against the enemy.' For British ears only, he added the thought that 'of course we could go quicker [attacking the Communists] if we stormed our way through streets and Rotterdamed whole quarters by air bombard-ment, but apart from other disadvantages of such a policy, the troops would refuse to do it'.[80] Many in the British party disagreed. When Eden visited the Rifle Brigade, he found that 'the troops seemed keen to kill as many [Communists] as possible – showing none of the distaste for the Greek campaign attributed to them in England'.[81] Luckily, it did not appear that the opinion of the troops would ever be put to the test. Damaskinos told the British team that the negotiations were genuine, for 'the Communists wanted a way out in spite of their brave words but they would prefer to see the war ended . . . they would struggle hard to get themselves into a favourable political position, so as to be able to achieve their ends by other means'. The British then took their leave of the negotiations, although they bugged the conference room so that they might listen in on the discussions between the Greeks themselves. The conclusion they reached was that although the Greeks would continue to abuse each other, there was a deal to be done. Churchill ordered British officials in the Mediterranean to throw their full weight behind the Damaskinos as Regent solution. He admitted that Macmillan had been right all along. He told Alexander and Macmillan that they had to close a deal by 16 January 1945, when he would have to defend his own volte-face in front of Parliament.[82] Churchill, Eden, Alexander and Macmillan then left Greece to return to Italy.[83]

Despite physical absence Alexander and Macmillan believed that their priority remained Greece rather than the wider Mediterranean. Macmillan commented that his neglected responsibilities were piling up in his Rome office, but that he had to get back to Athens: 'the Greek position is a running sore – it drains away both our military strength and political prestige at home and abroad'.[84] Not everyone was impressed by their efforts. 'Winston', Alan Brooke recorded, 'has done a spectacular rush to Greece . . . he does not appear to have achieved much. The rest of the 46th Division is off to Greece, this completes the 80,000 men I had originally predicted! And what shall we get out of it all? As far as I can see, absolutely nothing.'[85] Pierson Dixon agreed that making Greece the centre of the world had had its cost. 'I think', he wrote in a post-visit assessment, 'the PM hoped that the effect of his descent into the Greek situation like a V2 would be to alarm and disintegrate [the Communists]. On them it had the precisely opposite effect. That the British PM and Foreign Secretary, abandoning their world pre-occupations and their Christmas Dinner, should fly across Europe, all because of [the Communist insurgents] sent their sense of importance soaring.'[86]

In the end, however, the British made their self-imposed deadline with four days to spare. The reinforcements, that Alan Brooke so resented, made all the difference. At New Year 1945, British troops began cleansing Athens of Communist insurgents. They started to move out into Attica. It became clear that the British had the strength to secure central Greece.[87] Negotiations turned to the question of the whereabouts of a ceasefire line, with 'Red Greece' to the north.[88] 'It looks as if our policy in Greece is going to triumph,' gloated Churchill's private secretary in London, 'to the discomfiture of our critics.'[89] As he had planned, Churchill was able to make a barnstorming speech when Parliament reconvened. With victory and a ceasefire in his hand he was able to trounce the critics of his Greek policy. The view from Moscow was not dissimilar. 'I advised not starting this fighting in Greece,' Stalin said. The Communist insurgents were dangerous idiots. They had failed to understand Greece's wider context. 'They've taken on more than they can handle,' Stalin went on. 'They were fools if they thought he would waste the Red Army on them. They were even greater fools if they believed that Britain would tolerate a "red" Greece threatening their vital communications to the Middle East.'[90]

British victory in Greece, however, merely highlighted uncertainties elsewhere in the Mediterranean. 'Make no mistake,' Churchill said, 'all the Balkans, except Greece, are going to be Bolshevised; and there is nothing I can do to prevent it.'[91] In his triumphant House of Commons oration, Churchill slipped in a rebuttal of 'power politics in the Mediterranean'. His comment that 'we need Italy no more than we need Spain, because we have no designs that require the support of such powers' was soon transmogrified into the bald statement that 'we do not *need* Italy' and broadcast widely across the Mediterranean.[92] Fears were aroused of an Italian insurgency on the Greek model with '100,000 so-called patriots' dressed in British battledress, declaring a Communist Republic. On 7 February 1945 Communist guerrillas murdered nineteen non-Communist partisans at Porzus. The Italian violence did not, in the end, escalate. But there were tens of thousands of armed partisans washing around northern Italy, more interested in settling scores than fighting the Germans.[93]

Churchill and Eden arrived back in Greece in mid-February 1945 to add their imprimatur to the final all-party agreement negotiated in the month since the ceasefire.[94] Whilst they were in the country the KKE issued its instruction to all party organizations to conceal large quantities of arms for use in an 'hour of emergency that could present itself to us'. As Macmillan commented, the problems of the Mediterranean had a depressing samey-ness. There were Communist insurgents, although they were not necessarily the worst problem. There was always a Darlan/Giraud/Badoglio figure to deal with: currently in Greece it was the former Republican dictator General Plastiras, 'authoritarian and anti-British', 'a sort of Quisling in 1940 and 1941'.[95] North Africa, Italy and Greece were 'very similar': 'after the military phase comes the frightful tangle of economic difficulties'. And always there was the 'same puzzle'. 'Either there is no power, or no machinery, or no raw material, or no labour, or no money. If by any chance all the necessary ingredients to production can be put together, at one time and in one place, it is a miracle. And if this miracle (which is not uncommonly performed) is not immediate and automatic, then the British military authorities are subject to violent criticism and attacks – locally, but much more cruelly at home, by the pundits of the *Times*, the *Manchester Guardian* and the *New Statesman*.'[96]

FOURTEEN

Goodbye Mediterranean

The world war ebbed away from the Mediterranean. Although Charles de Gaulle had passed out of the Mediterranean long since in his rush for Paris, it was he who marked the war's passing in most spectacular fashion. VE-Day, 8 May 1945, dawned with a violent massacre of Algerians. The French feared that the Anglo-American victory over Germany, plus the American-led festivities for the formation of the UN in San Francisco, might lead the natives to believe that liberation was a Mediterranean, as well as a European, phenomenon. A combination of troops, aeroplanes and warships made short work of potential Algerian rebels. The '45,000 martyrs' of Arab propaganda was grossly exaggerated; but thousands were most certainly killed.[1]

De Gaulle was far from finished twitting the Anglo-American Mediterranean order. Two days before the Sétif massacre, a French flotilla had docked at Beirut. Not only did it restore the French Levantine station, destroyed by the British in the war of 1941, but it carried African re-inforcements. Edward Spears had laboured hard to build a strong bulwark against the day that he knew would come; the French welching on the promises of independence he had forcefully extracted from them in 1943. He can hardly be said to have succeeded. The response of the native governments to French provocation was a general strike. The response of the French to sullen resistance was military action. On 29 May 1945, French artillery opened fire on Damascus. Terence Shone, who had replaced Edward Spears in the Levant, reported that, 'the French have instituted nothing short of a reign of terror in Damascus. Apart from indiscriminate shelling, their troops, black and white, are behaving like madmen, spraying the streets with machine-gun fire . . . they do not spare vehicles flying the British flag.' 'It is useless', he concluded, 'to appeal to the French authorities who are clearly out to win a merciless war against the Syrians.'[2]

In the end the French achieved what Spears had always wanted Churchill to do; give the order for direct military intervention. Faced with a British army ordered to face them down, the French reluctantly returned to their barracks. De Gaulle was furious in his denunciations from Paris. He had authorized a ceasefire, not a flight to barracks; the crisis was solely the responsibility of British plotters and *provocateurs*.[3] The American representative in the Levant described French actions and their justifications as being characterized throughout by 'unblushing hypocrisy'.[4]

The Levantine rebuff did little to diminish de Gaulle's capacity for military adventurism. Churchill had been careful to bring the new American president, Harry Truman, on board before he confronted the French in Syria.[5] Truman's attention was forced more directly onto such problems when the Americans themselves were faced with the possibility of fighting the French. De Gaulle took the view that the day the war in Europe ended, so too did the authority of so-called Supreme Commanders. The French army disregarded orders and crossed the border into Italy so they might occupy those areas desired by France in a future peace settlement.[6] Their commander came with orders from de Gaulle to 'use all necessary means without exception' to prevent the establishment of Allied military government in north-western Italy. Washington's immediate response was to prepare a statement that spoke of an incipient state of war between America and France. In the meantime frantic diplomacy took place in Italy itself.[7]

The Gaullist moment in the Mediterranean was brief. It enjoyed little success. The architect of the Sétif massacre boasted that it had secured France in Algeria for a decade. Few outside France took him seriously, although remarkably the estimate proved accurate to within a year. In Europe the moment soon faded from memory. For a few months French action was at the heart of Arab nationalist politics, dominating the affairs of the Arab League formed at the 'Dumbarton Palms' conference in March 1945.[8] French villainy in the Maghreb and the Levant was, however, soon displaced by British, American and Zionist perfidy in Palestine. De Gaulle himself was removed from the picture by the vagaries of French domestic politics. In the summer of 1945, nevertheless, the Americans were caught by surprise. De Gaulle, at least, had had a plan. The Americans did not. They had many resources in the Mediterranean. Military forces and civil government officials were particularly strong in Italy. Secret warfare, too, had reached almost baroque proportions on the peninsula. When the OSS's senior operational officer had attempted to estimate how many partisans the Americans were paying, he was surprised to find that thirty organizations, most of them 'secret', had an interest in the question.[9] Some of these organizations were ready to 'close up shop', others were settling in for the long haul.[10] There was, however, no controlling theme. The Americans in the Mediterranean reported up the chain of command and awaited instruction; they had no independent vision of what their presence meant.

It would take a threat rather more serious than that posed by Charles de Gaulle to get the Americans to take the Mediterranean seriously. Few ever did. In mid-1945 those in Washington concerned with the conduct of the war had eyes only for the Pacific, and the challenge of Japan. For Pacific-firsters the Mediterranean was merely a subsidiary supply route to the Indian Ocean. Optimists were gathered in San Francisco, talking about the wonder of the United Nations. Those of a gloomier cast of mind pondered the fate of central Europe. A few *cognoscenti* talked of the coming importance of the 'Near East'. Businessmen and officials noticed that Roosevelt, on his final visit to the Mediterranean, had taken the trouble to meet Ibn Saud, creator and ruler of the titular kingdom. After Roosevelt's death it proved hard to define what either side had promised. That Saudi Arabia and its oil would become an area of special interest for the United States was, however, clear.[11]

For most politicians, however, the Near East was understood through only one prism: Palestine. Outside the circle of true-believing Zionists, Palestine was part of a European problem. The survivors of the Nazi attempt at genocide were still in camps, no longer victims, it was true, but DPs, displaced persons. Most had nowhere to go, for home no longer existed. The first official report of the Truman Presidency, completed in August 1945, commented that the treatment of Jewish DPs was little different under the Allies than it had been under the Germans, 'except we do not exterminate them'. The authors of the report argued for the 'quick evacuation of all non-repatriable Jews to Palestine'. Truman's response to that report was indicative of a wider set of assumptions: he sent it to the British Prime Minister. Clement Attlee had been in post for but a few weeks after his Labour Party had routed Churchill's Conservatives in the first general election since the 'Abyssinian crisis' poll of 1935. He was less than delighted with Truman's assumption that the

...terranean was Britain's problem, except on specific occasions when the Americans wanted something to happen.[12]

Truman's attitude was typical. The Americans were developing a global turn of mind to run alongside old-fashioned parochialism.[13] It took them much longer to develop what would later be called 'regional policy'. There was, however, one major American politician with a growing interest in Mediterranean affairs who began to hope that diverse US interests could be shaped into a coherent whole. The job of Secretary of the Navy wished the Mediterranean upon Jimmy Forrestal.[14] His fervent belief in a Soviet threat imprinted it on him. The belief would later turn to obsession and the obsession to tragedy. In the summer of 1945, however, Forrestal was very much a coming man in Washington, appointed by Roosevelt, continued by Truman. In his early fifties, self-made, with ambitions for the very top, Forrestal had built up a formidable reputation for dynamism at the Navy Department. In the summer of 1944 his duties had taken him on a major tour of the Mediterranean. He had been a fascinated spectator of the fleet's involvement in the landings in southern France. Before and after the landings he had taken the opportunity to travel widely around the western Mediterranean. His itinerary had taken in Morocco, Italy, the Riviera, Corfu, Sicily, Algeria and Gibraltar.

Forrestal would later conclude that the world view he brought to the Mediterranean had been seriously at fault. No one could have been a more orthodox advocate of official American policy. Forrestal's large warship was buzzed by Churchill's speedboat off Capri. The act seemed symbolic: Forrestal viewed contemporary British approaches to the Mediterranean as little more than annoying importunities. He believed that the enemy was Germany, the battle was in Europe, the invasion of southern France furthered hopes of quick victory, and that British arguments to the contrary were fatuous.[15]

On his return from the landings, Forrestal gave the Mediterranean little further thought: he was consumed by the much greater challenge of preparing the final naval campaigns against Japan. When Roosevelt went to Yalta to meet Stalin and Churchill in February 1945, Forrestal clipped some of the briefing papers prepared for the conference into his diary without comment or demur. The briefings assumed that the Mediterranean was of interest as an area of Anglo-Soviet rivalry, but that the deal Churchill had struck in Moscow in October 1944 would hold. In Italy, Moscow would continue to recognize that the British had a greater stake in that country than the USSR. Russian strategic interests in Greece were 'greater potentially than in any other Mediterranean country and her capabilities for exerting influence are, potentially at least, also great'. But Moscow had recognized the primacy of British interest in Greece. The pivot of Soviet interest, if it was to emerge, would be in Salonika, as the Aegean port for a South Slav Balkan federation. In the Adriatic, Moscow's 'capabilities for exerting influence in Yugoslavia' were much greater than those of Britain. A Slav Federation, which carved Aegean Macedonia out of Greece and handed it over to Yugoslavia, might be of interest to Moscow but, the Americans noted, Stalin had expressed no clear view on the subject. In the Near East, 'the classic area of Russo-British power politics', Russia would probably recognize that 'British interests and capabilities for exerting influence are overwhelmingly greater'. Only in Turkey did Britain and Russia have near equal traction. The major issue would be the control of the Straits. It was 'not expected', however, that Russia would demand control of the Straits for fear of antagonizing Britain. There seemed little probability of Moscow taking any such risks. In all likelihood she would be satisfied with a modification of the Montreux convention.[16]

Such a framework of understanding was quite capable of encompassing the first proof of Anglo-Soviet rivalry in the Mediterranean. The Trieste crisis of May 1945 was coeval with the various 'de Gaulle' crises. Indeed SACMED was dealing with de Gaulle in the north-west and Tito in the north-east at the same moment. When Forrestal was in the Mediterranean in September 1944, Alexander had been pleading to be allowed to race to the Ljubljana Gap in Slovenia. In reality his forces only managed to get across the River Po, in north-eastern Italy, at the end of April 1945. He immediately received instructions that he should push on for Venezia Giulia. A force of New Zealanders was sent forward into the 'witch's cauldron of conflicting politics and nationalisms' that was Trieste. At the head of the Adriatic, the New Zealanders met the Yugoslavs coming the other way. 'On the great cornice road which cuts into the rock above the sea between Monfalcone and Trieste,' recalled the divisional intelligence officer, 'our supply trucks wound in and out of the columns of marching Tito troops with faces as dark as Moors.'

On his most recent visit to Moscow, Tito had successfully lobbied Stalin to be allowed to take not only the long-disputed cities of *Italia irredenta*, but Trieste itself. To those who met him in the Soviet capital, Tito seemed supremely sure of himself. 'General impression,' noted Georgi Dimitrov, the leader of the Bulgarian Communists, '*too arrogant*, heavy dose of conceit and sure signs of "dizziness with success".'[17] His partisans gave the same impression. As soon as their leader returned they started arresting British special forces in Yugoslavia. When the New Zealanders had first entered Trieste, Alexander's main worry had been that any conflict with their 'gallant allies', the Partisans, could lead to a mutiny. Two weeks of watching the brutalities of the Yugoslavs quite changed minds. Alexander felt free to denounce Tito's behaviour as 'all too reminiscent of Hitler, Mussolini and Japan'. Despite such rhetoric the British all along preferred a deal with Tito: the city for them, the countryside of Venezia Giulia for the Yugoslavs. The Soviets reacted in much the way that the documents in Forrestal's diary predicted. Once it became clear that the British would fight for Trieste, Stalin ordered Tito to get his men out of the city. Grumbling, Tito complied.[18]

Trieste itself barely rated Forrestal's attention. Over the next month, however, the Soviet threat in the Mediterranean began to prey on his mind. He started keeping reports from American diplomats in Turkey about Soviet claims on Turkish territory.[19] Other reports from Italy urged him to rethink his, and America's, approach to Mediterranean affairs.[20] The difficulties of Ferruccio Parri, the organizer of the partisans, and Allied secret services' most favoured Italian, as prime minister, might leave Forrestal 'cold' but, one correspondent suggested, 'it shouldn't'. The Italians were hungry and facing the potential disaster of 'disoccupation'. This was not a case of 'thinking of the sentimental question of saving hungry babies, but merely of the fact that hunger and poverty and lack of work provide fertile soil for Communist activity and then it will be too late'. 'Don't forget', Forrestal was told, that 'what happens in Italy affects every other country out of proportion, and Greece and Spain and all the Mediterranean countries will inevitably follow'. 'Most Americans think this is a purely British baby,' but they were wrong. The Mediterranean was 'everybody's baby'.[21]

The opinions of Forrestal's friends were not, however, the opinion of Forrestal's department. The US Navy was well advanced in its plans to leave the Mediterranean. As they had been since 1942, American ships were still assigned to what they called 'North-west African waters'. The squadron actually assigned to the Mediterranean comprised little more than a cruiser and her escorts. It was slated to return to the Atlantic within months. There was little Forrestal could do to halt this process without some more general change of heart amongst his colleagues. Their general line was that the Communists were not causing trouble in Italy. Indeed Togliatti, the Italian Communist leader, viewed Tito as little more than an opportunistic land-grabber. The Turks had been subject to a 'friendly exchange of views and no concrete threats had been made'.[22]

Luckily for Forrestal, the Soviets chose the summer of 1945 to try their luck in the Mediterranean.[23] The 'Black Sea for Russia, Mediterranean for England' line had worked well. With Bulgaria and Rumania safely in Russian hands it was time for something more ambitious.[24] Soviet thinking on the 'Mediterranean prison' was not dissimilar to that of Mussolini in the 1930s. The British held the 'keys' to the prison, but they could be pried out. If the Soviet Union could gain control of the Straits they would have free access to the Mediterranean. Once they could freely penetrate into the Sea, then they could establish strongholds in the Mediterranean. As British power was undermined, the Atlantic and the Indian Ocean beckoned. There were good prospects for such a course. The revolt of the Jews in Palestine presented many opportunities for *mezzi insidiosi*. It was a fertile breeding ground for Anglo-American conflict, fanned by 'Jewish capital'. The Soviets had ways of making life more difficult for Britain, assisting on one hand the movement of Jewish DPs towards Palestine, liberally impregnated with Soviet agents, whilst on the other helping the Arab radicals, who had once thrown in their lot with the Nazis, to return to the Middle East. Regretfully, the Soviets concluded that they had little chance themselves of taking over in Palestine; it was merely a means of sowing discord.[25] With regard to Italy, however, they had greater hopes. The former Italian colonies were under British occupation. Their fate would be formally decided in the negotiations for a final peace treaty with Italy. Stalin's specialists saw no reason why they could not prise an Italian colony or two out of British hands. Tripoli, they decided, would make an excellent naval base.[26]

The unveiling of these plans to the world, by the Soviet foreign minister, Vyascheslav Molotov, at the London Conference in September 1945 was a gamble that went badly wrong. In private the British Prime Minister, Clement Attlee, thought that nearly everything that had been written about and done in the Mediterranean since 1935 was wrong-headed. The so-called life-line of the Empire was nothing of the sort. In any case the war had shown that Britain, at the height of its power, had been incapable of keeping the Mediterranean open. For good measure Attlee added that he didn't even think that Soviet claims in the Mediterranean were unreasonable. They had a good argument for influence over the Straits, access to the Mediterranean, a say in North Africa and the Levant. In public, however, it was the Mediterraneanist consensus, articulated by the British foreign secretary, Ernest Bevin, which held sway. Bevin angrily rejected Molotov's arguments that 'Great Britain cannot have a monopoly in the Mediterranean'. Once it became clear that the American Secretary of State, James Byrnes, intended to support Bevin, Stalin ordered Molotov to back off.[27]

There were two ways to read Soviet behaviour at the London Conference. It might be no more than a storm in a teacup. According to this school of thought, the Soviets did not really care about the Mediterranean. Their vital security interests lay in Europe. They had bid high on Tripoli so that they might subsequently retreat, in return for compensation in more important areas. The alternative view was rather more sinister. 'Soviets, like Hitler,' the American ambassador in Turkey signalled, 'have become drunk on victory and are embarking on world domination.'[28] Those already predisposed to fear Soviet expansionism were seriously spooked by the drive to the south. Forrestal was in the 'world domination' camp. So were others, but it was Forrestal, and a few allies, who focused particularly on the Mediterranean. In December 1945, Loy Henderson, the head of Near Eastern affairs at the State Department, whose reputation stood, and later fell, with that of Forrestal, penned a paper entitled 'The Present Situation in the Near East – a Danger to World Peace' in which he concluded that 'the Soviet Union seems to be determined to break down the structure which Great Britain has maintained so that Russian power and influence can sweep unimpeded across Turkey and through the Dardanelles into the Mediterranean'.[29] Forrestal himself engaged in frequent self-criticism for not having seen the truth sooner. 'Churchill's eyes were always on the Mediterranean,' Forrestal wrote, and he had been quite right.[30] America had to make amends for being so slow on the uptake.[31]

Long before most of his colleagues, Forrestal had come to the conclusion that America must act in the Mediterranean. He accepted the Soviet view that Palestine was an important part of the Mediterranean jigsaw. At the beginning of 1946 the Soviet Union's fixer in the Levant had written that Palestine was 'the most vulnerable point, the centre of Anglo-American differences'.[32] But, Forrestal found, most of the other important players in Washington saw Palestine as a hot potato, to be avoided, or even exploited, for domestic political gain. In particular he began to distrust the judgement of Secretary of State James Byrnes – another Democrat of high ambition. Byrnes appeared to his colleague both an avoider and a manipulator. An Anglo-American Committee of Inquiry began hearings on Palestine at the beginning of 1946.[33] When it became clear that Truman was interested only in endorsing the Zionist position on the immigration of DPs, Byrnes ostentatiously washed his hands of the Palestine problem, implying that if the White House wanted it, they were welcome. Forrestal could not help noticing that Byrnes's chief henchman, Ben Cohen, had excellent Zionist credentials. Forrestal had had his eye on Cohen for some time as someone who might be willing to cut a backstairs deal with the Soviets. The threat of the double stab in the back, from Soviets and Zionists, began to coalesce in Forrestal's mind.

Whilst America was weak in the Mediterranean, Forrestal believed, it was all too likely that vital interests would be sold out before public opinion had been properly alerted to the danger. He needed to move the Mediterranean issue out of the smoke-filled chamber and into the real world of guns and steel. In February 1946 he started changing America's naval posture to achieve that result. The Navy Department quietly dropped the euphemism of 'North African Waters' and stated that it now had an admiral commanding naval forces in the Mediterranean.[34] The name-plate change meant little unless that admiral had some ships. Forrestal took up a plan to send the embalmed body of the former Turkish ambassador to the US back home by warship. He failed, however, to convince his colleagues. They agreed to the dispatch of the battleship *Missouri* – one of the most powerful in the American fleet and famous for having had Japan's surrender signed on its foredeck. But they cavilled at Forrestal's idea of having the *Missouri* lead a large task force into the Mediterranean, thus flaunting American naval power under Soviet noses.[35] Forrestal had to endure a ticking-off from his adopted hero Churchill. Out of government, Churchill visited America to deliver his call to Cold War arms, a dire – if geographically inaccurate – warning of an 'Iron Curtain' splitting Europe from 'Stettin in the Baltic to Trieste in the Adriatic'.[36] In a private interview he told Forrestal that 'he was very glad of our sending the *Missouri* to the Mediterranean but was very much disappointed when I told him the plans to have this ship accompanied by a Task Force of substantial proportions had been abandoned. He said a gesture of power not fully implemented was almost less effective than no gesture at all.'[37]

Almost immediately, the legend of Churchill's preternatural insight seemed to be confirmed. His old bugbear, Greece flared back into life. The Greek Communists had acquired a new leader. As an unwilling guest of the Germans, Nikos Zahariadis had taken no part in the wartime events. He returned at the end of 1945 determined to prove his mettle as a revolutionary. He found the KKE in worse straits than when they had launched their revolt in October 1944. The wartime system of soviets gave them power in the countryside, particularly to the north of the ceasefire line defined by the British at the end of the war. The armed forces were thoroughly riddled with Communist sympathizers, but the British were doing such a good job of re-equipping and retraining those forces that sooner or later the government would be able to launch a purge. Elections had been organized for the end of March 1946 but if the Communists continued to play a role in national politics they might legitimize their enemies, without being able to seize power for themselves. In the worst case a White victory might herald the return of George II to the throne. The line from Moscow was 'wait and see'. In particular, the Soviets said, the KKE should contest the forthcoming elections. Fearing the Whites in Athens more than the Reds in Moscow, Zahariadis disobeyed the instruction. The KKE boycotted the elections. On the eve of the poll, the 'Democratic Army' started a series of attacks on isolated police and government posts in the north-east.[38]

The different timetables of the US Navy and the Greek politics meshed rather well. Just as the KKE revolted in Greece, the *Missouri* reached the Mediterranean. At the beginning of April 1946 she sailed into the Dardanelles. Having delivered her melancholy cargo, she remained anchored off Istanbul for nearly a week. The Americans monitored press coverage of her progress, which was most satisfactory, whether in the praises of sympathizers or the bile of opponents. Naval power played a large role in Stalin and Tito's 27 May 'snack meeting' – so-called because after a brief, if pregnant, late-night exchange, Stalin suggested a light bite. The *vodzh* told his cocky client that naval power in the Mediterranean was vital, and that he should be cautious. Stalin laughed menacingly when he told Tito that the Anglo-Americans were not going to allow him to get his hands on Trieste. To complete a less than successful supper party, Tito also received a 'gentle' warning about his plans to take over Albania.[39] Stalin was willing to try pressure on all points around the Mediterranean over the summer of 1946: Tripoli, Trieste, Salonika, the Straits. The Russians also tried a number of indirect pressure points from

Palestine to Spain.[40] Official party propaganda took the line that the generous offer of a 'small' Mediterranean sphere of influence made to Churchill in 1944 was no longer on the table.[41] Stalin retained, however, a healthy respect for America's potential to exert power through its navy: if necessary he was willing to modify each aspect of his policy.

Forrestal was happy to oblige with further naval displays. On the eve of the Paris Peace Conference he was able to persuade Byrnes that 'the visit of the *Missouri* had been most effective and had produced most satisfactory results'; therefore a regular rota of American warships should sail into the Mediterranean 'so that we may establish the custom of the American Flag being flown in those waters'.[42] Whilst the proceedings in Paris were ongoing Forrestal himself set off for a world tour. His two main Mediterranean stop-overs, Cairo and Rome, merely served to convince him that he was on the right track. The final meeting of minds within the higher councils of the American government occurred upon Forrestal's return to Washington.

Whilst showing some give-and-take on other Mediterranean issues, Stalin decided to ratchet up the pressure on Turkey for a new Straits settlement. In the first week in August 1946, the Soviet government delivered a formal note to the Turks calling for a revision of the treaty governing the passage of the Straits. As American intelligence analysts pointed out, many of the proposed revisions were in line with those that both British and Americans had indicated they could accept. The real problem was the demand that it should be the Black Sea powers – such as the Soviet Union, Rumania and Bulgaria – who were responsible for the Straits, rather than Mediterranean powers such as Britain, France and, now, the United States.[43]

The demands finally succeeded in bringing everyone who mattered in Washington to sign up to the line that Forrestal had been peddling for months. Indeed, Forrestal no longer even had to take the lead in articulating American policy, he was able to defer to the superior persuasive skills of Dean Acheson who was in temporary charge at State.[44] Acheson had the inestimable advantage of being, in contrast to Forrestal, liked and admired by Harry Truman.[45] When the principals of the main departments filed in to see the President, Acheson was able to tell him that they had reached a unanimous conclusion. The Soviet demands on Turkey 'reflected a desire to control and dominate the country; that acceding to these demands would be followed next by infiltration and domination of Greece by Russia with obvious consequences in the Middle East and the obvious threat to the line of communications of the British'. Truman responded: 'we might as well find out whether the Russians were bent on world conquest now as in five or ten years'. Looking back Acheson concluded that this had been the tipping point. A meeting about a technical diplomatic note had given the green light to those who believed in – an as yet unnamed – Cold War.[46]

In the short term, Forrestal's navy did the heavy lifting. All available destroyers were immediately ordered from the Atlantic approaches into the Mediterranean. At last, his colleagues endorsed Forrestal's wish for a proper task force to be sent into the Mediterranean. The giant modern carrier *Franklin D. Roosevelt* and its escorts were diverted from a visit to Lisbon. 'For the first time,' the press commented, 'the active assertion of seapower in the Mediterranean rests with a country other than Britain.'[47] Despite the talk about toughness, it was ordered to follow a cautious itinerary. A visit to Istanbul itself was ruled out as too provocative. Even Forrestal was perturbed when the commander of the task force gave a news conference in which he openly discussed the possibility of war in the Mediterranean. Instead the *FDR* was routed into the Piraeus. The battlegroup arrived only two days after a plebiscite on the future of the Greek monarchy. The right-wing landslide of March 1946 had made possible the carefully stage-managed return of George II. A suspiciously large proportion of the Greek population voted for the return of the King.[48]

It was not, however, in Forrestal's nature to be satisfied. He observed that they still had a lot to do. It would be a hard task convincing the American people that they should be interested in the Mediterranean. Unlike Greece, Italy or Palestine, Turkey had little cultural resonance in the United States. The principals agreed on a determined, trickle-down approach. They would work the proprietors and the well-known syndicated columnists of the big newspapers. In addition Forrestal insisted that the government must publicly declare that it had a Mediterranean strategy; that 'the American fleet have been in the Mediterranean and will continue to be there in the future'. The statement released over his name was bland enough, talking of the support of American forces in Europe, backing the words of diplomats and 'educating the Fleet'. The carefully briefed press hailed it both as a definitive statement of long-term intent and an immediate counter-move to Soviet attempts to win power around the sea, as much to do with Tripoli and Trieste as Turkey.[49] Stalin for one was convinced: 'one could see the manifestations of the new USA reactionary trend,' he remarked to Molotov.[50]

The President had been convinced that there was a Russian threat but he was reluctant to spend much more money on meeting it. Here was an issue on which commander-in-chief and Secretary of the Navy might fall out.[51] Both the growing band of 'Cold Warriors' and the much smaller, but seemingly empowered, group of Mediterraneanists suspected that Truman took neither cause seriously enough. What was the point, they asked, of supporting the 'arch' of the Mediterranean – Turkey – if the United States was willing to kick away one of its 'pillars' – Palestine? By October 1946 it was quite clear that World War Three was not going to break out in the Mediterranean. The Paris Peace Conference ended with signs of compromise on most Mediterranean issues. At one moment it appeared that the Soviets, the Americans and the French might even agree to hand the Italian empire back to Italy. It was Britain that insisted on the need to create a new, independent, state of Libya. The American negotiators, surprised at how easily they had nearly bought a Soviet line, fell in with their fellow Anglo-Saxons: but the fluidity of the negotiation suggested that all these issues could be solved by the normal processes of diplomacy. Trieste was temporarily declared a 'free territory' belonging to neither Italy nor Yugoslavia. American intelligence concluded that the Russians, Turks and Americans would probably come to an amicable agreement about the Straits.[52] Truman's attention shifted to more important issues, specifically how the mid-term elections of November 1946 would affect his own chances of re-election in November 1948. His political advisers were particularly exercised as to how the Palestine issue might play in these elections. They were worried about Jewish votes in key electoral battlegrounds; they were worried about Gentile votes in areas threatened by large-scale immigration; they were worried about funding the election campaign. Most immediately, they were worried that Truman's presumed electoral rival, Thomas Dewey of New York, seemed likely to announce his support for a Jewish state. On the Day of Atonement, Truman addressed all of these problems by making a speech endorsing what he called a 'viable Jewish state' in Palestine. The speech spurred on Zionists who saw the Mediterranean as merely the sea off the coast of *eretz Israel*, rather than Palestine as a 'pillar' of the Mediterranean.[53]

Probably the most interested observer of how Mediterranean affairs were playing out in the US was Britain's Foreign Secretary, Ernest Bevin.

Bevin had had a tough year. Negotiations over Palestine had failed. Negotiations with Egypt about the Canal Zone had reached an impasse. Bevin came to America in November 1946 to attend the New York Conference of Foreign Ministers. Nothing he saw or heard improved his humour, which in any case was ill-advised: to the question, 'Why do you put the Jews in Cyprus: why not the Waldorf Astoria?' he replied: 'Because there isn't room, my dear.' 'It was', his private secretary recorded, 'a horribly uncomfortable party, really, and I was never so glad to leave a place as New York . . . the poor S. of S. was almost unmanageable'.[54] In private American diplomats sympathized with the difficulties of their British counterparts. The gap between fair words behind closed doors and public rhetoric only led to the conclusion that the Americans spoke out of both sides of the mouth on Palestine. He left convinced that Britain could expect little help or even good faith from the Americans over Palestine. On his return he got into another argument with Attlee about the importance of the Mediterranean.

Formally, 'the defence of the Middle East' was enshrined as the third 'pillar' of British defence policy. In reality Attlee's argument that the Mediterranean was a route to nowhere survived in a dawning realization that Britain could not go on as it was. There had been much talk about Palestine becoming the main British base in the eastern Mediterranean. But what was the point of planning to 'hold Palestine' six years hence when no one was sure whether control would last for six months?[55] On 22 July 1946 the headquarters of the British army in Palestine, the King David Hotel in Jerusalem, was wrecked by a massive bomb blast. The bomb had been set by Britain's one-time 'friends', the Irgun. The war in Palestine was unwinnable not because of the effectiveness of Jewish terrorism, although it was indeed effective, but because other powers were only too happy to use the Jews to damage Britain. Above all, as Bevin had seen for himself, the only thing one could rely on America for in Palestine was a stab in the back.[56]

The British said that they were still committed to keeping a grip on the Suez Canal. But the value of the Canal was no longer clear, with the Indian empire disappearing in smoke. Since the Canal's so-called 'inner bastion', Palestine, was about to be handed over to the mercy of the UN, maybe it was not worth that much. Greece was the 'outer bastion' of the Canal. Even the capture of Greece and Crete had not enabled the Germans to cripple Suez. But aircraft had become more powerful since 1941. The Red air force operating from Greece would, in all probability, be able to close the Canal from the air. Perhaps that didn't matter. Britain was going to build nuclear weapons. America had nuclear weapons. The Soviets would have A-bombs as well. There was not much point worrying about the Canal in a world war, when in all likelihood Egypt was going to be incinerated. What then was the point of an 'outer bastion'? There was already a shooting war in Greece. In a perfect world Britain would continue to fight there. But since Britain was going to abandon the 'inner bastion', it would be illogical to fight too hard for the 'outer bastion'.[57] The Greek war had never been popular, especially in the Labour Party. Even British diplomats admitted that the Greeks with whom they were allied – such as Napoleon Zervas – were 'extremists'.[58] The decision to let Greece go required remarkably little soul-searching.

Forrestal learnt of the British decision when George Marshall, recently appointed Secretary of State, caught up with him just before they went in to meet the President. The British ambassador had called at the State Department with the news that 'Britain could no longer be the reservoir of financial-military support of Turkey and Greece . . . Britain simply could not afford it.' Forrestal and Marshall's first response was irritation: 'this dumped into our lap another most serious problem'. Their second response was to greet the dawning of an opportunity: 'it was tantamount to British abdication from the Middle East with obvious implications as to their successor'.[59] Many came to believe that Bevin had laid down bait for the Americans, luring them towards confrontation with the Soviets. If there was ever such an intention, the Americans were only too ready to bite.[60]

Many of the same players who had come together to make an issue of the Soviet threat to Turkey, did the same over Greece. The KKE had launched a full-scale insurrection, supported by Yugoslavia, Albania and Bulgaria. The Communists were cutting northern Greece away from government control along a line that stretched from Mount Grammos on the Adriatic coast to Mount Olympus on the Aegean coast. The politicians in Athens squabbled with each other to little effect.[61] They had frittered away the gains from British aid and military reform. Just days before the British announced they were getting out, the American team in Greece had sent a 'situation critical' report to Washington. It was, they wired, 'impossible to say how soon collapse might be anticipated, but we believe that to regard it as anything other than imminent would be highly unsafe'.[62]

As Acheson said in briefing the President, 'the Greek government was not a satisfactory one to us; that it contained many elements that were reactionary; that much of the success of Russian propaganda was due to the knowledge the people had of corruption and inefficiency'.[63] Indeed the prospects of success seemed so good that Stalin had finally decided to go full-out in support of the KKE. When Zahariadis went to Moscow to 'meet the Old Man' in May 1947 he finally received a cordial welcome and all the promises he could wish for.[64]

In August 1946, Truman had said that the decision to confront the Soviet Union over Turkey was his most important decision since Hiroshima. He said that now, in March 1947, 'he was faced with a decision more serious than had ever confronted any President'.[65] Possibly Lincoln, Wilson and Roosevelt would have been surprised by that claim: it was, however, music to the ears of men like Forrestal. As had been the practice established over Turkey, the decision to announce American intervention was being prepared by their meetings with the great and good of the press. The *New York Times*, for instance, explained intervention in Greece in exactly the terms British imperialists might once have used. 'Interest in Greece', it suggested, 'is not mere sentiment. Greece controls Eastern Mediterranean strategy. Should Greece turn Communist, Turkey would be politically outflanked and could no longer resist pressure that is already onerous. Without Turkey, Iran would go under . . . behind the pie-crust of these countries linking Europe to Asia across the Hellespont, are fledgling Arab states without stability. The US has a powerful concern . . . [where] there is probably more oil than in the United States proved reserves.'[66]

Just as America was reaching the point of no return in the Mediterranean, the Mediterranean itself was in danger of being written out of the script. As reflected in the government inspired op-ed pieces of early March 1947, many ardent Cold Warriors were more exercised by 'the pie-crust', more formally known as the Northern Tier, than the Mediterranean *per se*. Greece was important because of Turkey; Turkey was important because of Iran; Iran, Iraq and Saudi Arabia were important because of oil. There were certainly plans afoot to create a physical link between Middle Eastern oil and the Mediterranean. The great wartime pipeline plan that the oil lobby had scuppered in 1945, reappeared. Both America's ARAMCO and Britain's AIOC were engaged in feverish negotiations to build wide-gauge pipelines from Middle Eastern oilfields to the Mediterranean coast. Both were clearly in cahoots with their own governments. Both had come to the conclusion that the ports of Palestine, Lebanon or Syria offered the best outlet. The oil issue was, however, of limited overall importance in March 1947. It was a minor issue in Palestine and would later have a very localized and specialist importance, particularly for the development of American political warfare.[67] When faced with the hypothetical question of how America might defend Middle Eastern oil against a Soviet incursion into Iran and Iraq, the simple response of the military was: we won't, we'll blow it up. Forrestal commented that since 'ample petroleum stocks can be obtained from the Middle East, but it is possible that our supply from this area might be shut off in the event of hostilities', the wisest solution would be to develop alternatives.[68]

In the event, the Mediterranean barely featured in the eighteen-minute speech that Truman gave to Congress on 12 March 1947. His speechwriters had come to the conclusion that 'the Truman doctrine' could not be about any specific geographical area.[69] Greece and Turkey had to be aided, not because of their geographical location, but because they were bastions of freedom. As Acheson said, 'the concept of individual liberty is basic . . . [as is] the protection of democracy everywhere in the world'. Truman did speak of 'confusion and disorder' in the Middle East. His main theme, however, was that at that moment 'nearly every nation must choose between alternative ways of life'. One way would be 'based on the will of the majority, and is distinguished by free institutions, representative government, free elections, guarantees of individual liberty, freedom of speech and religion, and freedom from oppression'. The other way was 'the will of a minority forcibly imposed on the majority'. Greece and Turkey were merely starting points. From now on, 'it must be the policy of the United States to support free peoples who are resisting attempted subjugation by armed minorities or by outside pressures'.[70] When Truman's subordinates appeared on the Hill to reinforce this message, they were well drilled on the party line. Forrestal, who could usually be relied upon to introduce the importance of the Mediterranean into discussions, was delighted by Truman's universalist rhetoric. He aligned himself more with the Europeanists than the Middle Easterners in believing that if the Greek domino fell, the next victims would be Italy and France rather than Turkey and Iran. But that was not really the point. As he said during the drafting of the speech, the important argument was 'the very real danger' that America itself 'as we know it, may cease to exist'. In face of such peril the 'country cannot afford the deceptive luxury of waging defensive warfare . . . our victory, and our survival, depend on how and where we attack'.[71] Forrestal contented himself before the Senate Foreign Relations Committee by speaking 'in general terms of the importance to the United States of the Mediterranean'. The Navy also took the opportunity to formalize their new mission. What had been the US Navy in Europe was rechristened the US Navy in the Eastern Atlantic and the Mediterranean.

Forrestal was a true believer in the global course announced by the President in March 1947. Both he and the US Navy, however, had had good parochial reasons for trying to keep the Mediterranean pot on the boil. The idea of building a powerful Mediterranean fleet, and placing the Mediterranean at the epicentre of the Cold War, gave the Navy a new and important mission. It was a mission that they needed. Since the end of the war a great deal of Forrestal's time and effort had been given over to the problem of 'unification'. The creation of a new structure for the armed services did not necessarily appeal to naval officers. They feared that if and when a separate United States Air Force was spun out of the Army, it would become a cuckoo in the nest. Bernard Brodie of the air-force-funded RAND corporation most famously articulated the view that the 'absolute weapon' had changed the function of the armed forces. They no longer existed to fight wars, but to deter them. The air-force programme for a massive force of nuclear-armed bombers, indeed for an air-force monopoly of nuclear weapons, mobilized a formidable following in Congress. The President himself seemed to favour the air force because nuclear deterrence offered both a 'strong defence' and a 'balanced budget'. The Navy feared that when a civilian Secretary of Defense was appointed to oversee the armed services, he would be a politician dancing to the air force's tune.

Forrestal did all he could to limit the powers of such an appointee.[72] It was thus a nice irony when Truman appointed him to become the United States' inaugural Secretary of Defense in the summer of 1947. Forrestal was faced by a defence establishment united in their determination to meet the Soviet threat but divided on how, when and where that should be done. He had few powers, beyond his persuasive ability, to get the now constitutionally established Joint Chiefs of Staff to go along with him. Both Forrestal and the Navy believed that the Mediterranean should be at the centre of American efforts to fight the Cold War – he used a flare-up of tension in Trieste to push through his final confirmation by the Senate – but they were no longer automatic allies.[73] Indeed Forrestal found himself with a decreasing circle of allies, whether military or civil.

Without a powerful guiding intelligence, the meaning of the Mediterranean to America remained fuzzy. Despite the high-flown rhetoric, aid to Greece and Turkey was governed by strict legislation. The officials and officers swept up in the Truman Doctrine were soon dealing with the mechanics of aid.[74] The best minds in the national security establishment moved on to other matters, in particular the wider problem of European instability. The centrepiece of their approach was a package of aid offered to all European countries willing to organize themselves to receive it. The idea was adumbrated in a speech that Secretary of State Marshall made in June 1947, and the aid was thereafter known colloquially as the Marshall Plan. The narrower aid package to Greece and Turkey thus came to be viewed increasingly as part of a wider *European* endeavour. Indeed both countries were enrolled in the Marshall Plan. For a while both the Mediterranean and the Middle East 'pie-crust' faded into the background.

In the 1930s there had been a slew of books dealing with the 'Mediterranean problem'. Only one such book was written in America at this time, and its theme was the fuzziness of American thinking itself. There was 'general feeling' but no policy. William Reitzel's Yale study was issued in the same series that had shaped important ideas in the post-war consciousness, most notably Brodie's 'absolute weapon' and William Fox's notion of 'the superpowers'. Reitzel argued that the Americans were making two mistakes. On one hand, they thought only of what they might do elsewhere from positions in the Mediterranean, without giving any thought to the 'ardent and diverse' Mediterranean societies they encountered. On the other hand they became too caught up in local problems. The trick was to intervene to maintain stability, without becoming too obsessed by the details of local or ethnic issues. The very organization of American government, Reitzel said, exacerbated such tendencies. The State Department alone had divisions of Middle Eastern Near Eastern, Western European and Southern European affairs. No one dealt with the Mediterranean itself. Yet 'while there are daily Greek, Spanish and Palestinian questions,' Reitzel argued, 'these questions do not necessarily build up into a Greek, Spanish or a Palestinian problem . . . there are instead Greek, Spanish, or Palestinian aspects of Mediterranean problems.'[75]

Forrestal could not have agreed more. Within his crushingly busy schedule getting the National Military Establishment off the ground, the time he gave to Mediterranean affairs was limited. Nevertheless, he arranged with Robert Lovett, temporarily in charge of the State Department, that the inaugural meeting of the National Security Council should be devoted to the Mediterranean. Their 'typical example' of a model discussion focused on one of Forrestal's favourite hobby horses. Was there, they asked, the possibility of a coup in Italy?[76] The Christian Democrat politician Alcide De Gasperi had eased the Communists out of his Cabinet. Yet the combination of Communists and leftist Socialists were, by all accounts, the most popular force in the country. If they were sensible, they would await the upcoming elections with every prospect of success. But something seemed to be going on. The Soviets ratified the peace treaty with Italy. The ratification would trigger the withdrawal of the American and British troops who had remained in the country after the war, the last remnant of the old AFHQ and SACMED. The Communists had maintained their old guerrilla cadres. Palmiro Togliatti boasted that he had 30,000 men under arms and was ready to unleash them on the government. Were the Communists preparing for a violent insurrection? [77]

Events in Italy, the NSC agreed, were linked to Soviet strategy both in the Mediterranean and in the Northern Tier. Failure to act against the Communists there would undo any good the Truman Doctrine might do in Greece and Turkey for the 'obvious reason that Italy lies athwart the line of communications to those regions'. Furthermore, 'the whole position in the Middle East would be threatened to the extent that, with the line of communications through the Mediterranean dominated by a Russian satellite, both [sic] Iran and Iraq and Saudi Arabia would have to reassess their position vis-à-vis Russia'.[78] It would be necessary to use wartime contacts with the Italian intelligence services to reconstitute a 'secret army' capable of resisting Communism. Handily, for instance, the Italian ambassador in Washington had been a member of the first special forces team to land in wartime Italy. As the US Army withdrew from its post-war garrison duties it would be replaced by the US Marine Corps, technically in CINCNELM's ships, paying visits to Italian ports. Not only did the Mediterranean naval force, of which Forrestal was the architect, become the visible guarantee against Communism, Forrestal pushed himself forward as the right man to coordinate the invisible effort.[79]

Truman was reluctant to take Forrestal's advice on Italy, not least because he did not relish another special session in which he would have to repeat his Truman Doctrine aid sales-pitch. Forrestal was relieved to find allies in the White House willing to badger the President on the Italian issue. Nevertheless, he was becoming increasingly obsessed with the manner in which, after bursts of activity in the Mediterranean, Turkey in 1946, Greece in spring 1947, Italy in winter 1947, everyone returned to business as usual. What America said and did was self-contradictory. There was a failure to live up to rhetoric. There was a failure to apply the test of greater necessity to minor problems. Such hypocrisy was eating away at American power. To Forrestal, the source of this weakness was clear: grubby, behind-the-scenes political deals. Who was making those deals, and why? That too was clear: Jews. The White House was inundated by organized write-ins on Palestine. Over half of all Senators and Governors had signed pro-Zionist petitions. The President's aides were drawing up projections that showed that Jewish votes were essential for his re-election.[80] Forrestal was repulsed by the casual way in which Jewish money and foreign policy were hitched together in meetings. Bob Hannegan, Truman's fixer in the Democratic Party, told the Cabinet that the Day of Atonement speech had been a fantastic success in 1946 and that they needed a repeat in 1947. Hannegan said that 'very large sums were obtained a year ago from Jewish contributors and that they would be influenced in either giving or withholding by what the President did on Palestine'.[81]

America could not have a Mediterranean strategy, Forrestal believed, because of the Jews. The Jews undermined attempts to build bridges with potential allies. They 'spiked' any sensible plan.[82] The general consensus amongst officials was that there was no point in trampling over British sensibilities.[83] 'The significance of the British system of authority in supporting the American interest can scarcely be exaggerated,' Reitzel wrote; 'the unvarnished fact of the moment is that the British system and American resources are a Siamese-twin power in the Mediterranean.'[84] The British wanted to make a deal. They sent delegations, secretly, to Washington to thrash out differences all around the littoral. Both military and diplomatic parties found a warm welcome. The British and the Americans discovered that they agreed about nearly everything.[85] The Army, Navy and USAF all received British promises of aid setting up bases in the Mediterranean.[86] Probably the most spectacular of these plans was for American facilities on British-administered territory at Wheelus Field outside Tripoli. Despite its singular name the intention was to build up to seven air bases in the complex.[87]

Everyone involved in the negotiations knew, however, that Palestine was the elephant in the room.[88] Dwight Eisenhower, now the head of the US Army, said bluntly to the British that American politics would trump a military alliance and they should get out of Palestine as quickly as possible.[89] Loy Henderson, Forrestal's long-term ally, led the diplomatic team in the 'Pentagon talks'. Before those talks even began, he was summoned to the White House to explain why he had dared to write that the Truman Doctrine would be a waste of time if Mediterranean allies were alienated by America's support of Zionism. That month the Arab League established an Arab Liberation Army to seize Palestine by force. The convinced Zionists on Truman's staff, Clark Clifford and David Niles, had tried, Henderson said, 'to break me down and humiliate me in the presence of the President'. They had impugned Henderson's knowledge, judgement and motives. The President announced his support for the UN's plan to partition Palestine, denounced by Henderson as a disaster, during the Anglo-American military talks, and four days before the diplomatic teams were due to convene. Whilst the British and Americans talked in Washington, American diplomats and politicians were lobbying in New York to ensure that the General Assembly approved the plan. Henderson told his friends that the Zionists had won America.[90]

Just as the Pentagon talks were coming to an end, Forrestal bearded Howard McGrath, the chairman of the Democratic National Committee, as he would many other notables in the coming months, with the demand that 'the Palestine question be taken out of politics and by that I meant that no group in this country should be permitted to influence our policy to the point where it would endanger our national security'. McGrath dismissed him with the comment that 'there were two or three pivotal states which could not be carried without the support of people who were deeply interested in the Palestine question'. When Forrestal plied him with the latest CIA intelligence assessments in an attempt to make him see the dangers, McGrath rebuffed him again, this time with the argument that 'Jewish sources are responsible for more than fifty per cent of the contributions to the Democratic National Committee'. 'These contributions', the Senator stressed, 'are made with the distinct idea on the part of the givers that they will have an opportunity to express their views and have them seriously considered.'[91] Lovett complained to Forestal that, 'never in his life had he been subject to such pressure as he had been from the Jews'. The President's own attempts to explain his approach – whatever bloodbath developed in Palestine, he would never allow

American troops to take part in peacekeeping – merely struck Forrestal as the abrogation of strategic and moral logic.[92]

Insider Washington knew how Jimmy Forrestal thought. Many had been buttonholed by him personally. His acquaintances told him it was time to back off. He should be satisfied with the way things were going. He had the Mediterranean in his grip. There were some serious warships inbound, under commanders who believed that the Mediterranean was a vital theatre of operations. His precious Marines were bobbing around off the Italian coast. Covert operations were under way, and Defense had a slice of the action. American military aid was re-equipping and encouraging the Italian armed forces to take on the Communist underground. The air force was surveying North Africa, preparatory to cutting sod on impressive bases. American military advisers had started arriving in Greece.[93] The war there had clearly reached its critical stage.[94] In February 1948 the Communists had failed in their long-awaited attack on Salonika. According to Stalin, the failure in Salonika represented the triumph of the West. 'What do you think,' he said regarding backers of the KKE with barely concealed menace, 'that Great Britain and the United States – the US, the most powerful state in the world – will permit you to break their line of communication in the Mediterranean Sea! Nonsense. And we have no Navy. The uprising in Greece must be stopped, and as quickly as possible.'[95]

All Forrestal had to do was to accept that the glass was more than half full. All he had to do was let go of this obsession with Palestine. Zionism and the Cold War could rub along. It was ridiculous, as Clark Clifford put it, that the US should be 'trembling before threats of a few nomadic desert tribes . . . why should Russia or Yugoslavia . . . treat us with anything but contempt in the light of our shilly-shallying appeasement of a few Arabs?'[96] The Arabs were terrorists pure and simple. They were led by the Grand Mufti. In revenge for British actions in Syria, the French intelligence services had sent the Mufti, in need of new protectors after the demise of the SS, back to Egypt. He reached the high point of his power in February 1948 when, in a repeat of his 1936 attempt to cut Palestine off from the Mediterranean, his insurgents cut the route between Tel Aviv and Jerusalem.[97] It was a particularly sensitive moment.

The leading Jewish power-broker in the Democratic Party, Bernard Baruch, warned Forrestal off with the threatening advice, 'not to be active in this particular matter . . . in my own interests'.[98] That advice came too late. Forrestal had already committed the cardinal sin of going public.

Testifying before the House Armed Services Committee, he stated his view that the policy of the President on Palestine was inimical not only to American interests in the Middle East but to the very national security of the United States. Soon it was open season on Forrestal. The story was kept on the boil by popular syndicated columnists. Forrestal was disloyal to the President and the Democratic Party; he was a closet Republican and his talks with Republican leaders over Palestine proved it. He was Wall Street's leading Jew-baiter in a street of Jew-baiters. Thrown in for good measure were innuendoes about Forrestal's unhappy private life; why did he see his wife so seldom? The architect of America's Mediterranean began to crack. He scratched the same spot on his scalp continually. It bled. It scabbed. He scratched off the scab. A bowl of water was a permanent feature on the Secretary of Defense's desk. He constantly dipped his fingers into the bowl and ran them across his lips, complaining that he could never moisten his mouth. He said he was being followed, watched. He was convinced that his shadows were Zionists. When the head of the Secret Service investigated, he became convinced that Forrestal was heading for a 'total psychotic breakdown . . . characterised by suicidal features'.[99]

Forrestal's melancholy situation was a stern warning to anyone else who might wish to say anything about the essential unity of the Mediterranean.[100] When William Reitzel published his study of the Sea, he was careful to mention Palestine as little as possible – it made its first appearance in a footnote on page 151. It was not that important things were not happening in the Mediterranean – the Italian elections passed off without insurrection; Stalin accused Tito of planning the annexation of Albania and turned on Yugoslavia; the State of Israel was declared – rather that few wished to talk openly about the Mediterranean.

The Mediterranean was an embarrassing subject. Franco's lobbyists, for instance, spread around a lot of money in the summer of 1948.[101] He established excellent relations with the Arab League.[102] The League put into 'cold storage' any demands in Spanish Morocco; he pledged support for their struggle against imperialism and Zionism. It was, the British reported, 'tiresome' but 'in other ways inevitable . . . the Arabs tend to understand and like autocracies'.[103] Konstantine Tsaldaris of Greece, whom the Americans had forced to resign as prime minister because of his enthusiasm for the White Terror, threw out ideas for Mediterranean match-ups with fierce energy, 'frantically grabbing at any straw to give a fillip to Greek morale and his own position'.[104] He championed the 'Byzantine ideal': Britain and America should 'assist the Greeks in imposing Hellenism and Greek Orthodoxy in the Eastern Mediterranean at the expense: of the Slav influence; of the Latin influence; and of the Moslem and Turkish influence'.[105]

Tsaldaris asked a realistic and embarrassing question in the summer of 1948: was Italy a Mediterranean country?[106] The embarrassment lay in the fact that whilst grand Mediterranean strategies were definitely out of fashion, a grand European strategy had started to brew in Washington. American and British representatives were secretly in negotiation over the idea of forming a North Atlantic Pact.[107] Many said that it was ridiculous to include Italy; she was self-evidently a Mediterranean country – if Italy was included in a Euro-American deal then, by definition, it would no longer be North Atlantic. When some European governments were let in on the secret negotiations, the position of Italy became the most contentious issue. The French ended up championing Italy, the British trying to keep her out.[108] In private both were ambivalent. As the British said, Italy was on the cusp, 'Italy is a Western European country, and an Eastern European or Middle Eastern country.' But she had to go somewhere. In the end, the British concluded, Tsaldaris' ideas were not so bad after all. She, along with 'Greece, Turkey, Great Britain and France and conceivably with certain Middle Eastern countries such as Syria, Lebanon, Egypt, and ... eventually Israel' could form a Mediterranean alliance.[109]

The best argument for Italy's inclusion in Europe emanated from Forrestal's Pentagon.[110] To leave out Italy was 'like a man going out to dinner in evening clothes minus his trousers, thereby exposing a part of the body which should never be exposed'.[111] Forrestal himself addressed the issue on his last trip abroad. In London, the British said that they had always liked his idea of naval task forces in the Mediterranean. Anglo-American discord was temporarily defused by a joke, Bill Slim, the head of the British army, quoting Napoleon to the effect that 'if the Italians were against you, it would require four divisions to defeat them; if they were neutral it would require six divisions to watch them; if they were on your side, it would take twelve divisions to rescue them'.[112] But by this point Forrestal had little capacity for laughter. Politically, he was a dead man, walking. He had expended his political and emotional capital to no avail over Palestine. He couldn't contain himself in National Security

Council meetings, where everyone talked in serious tones about 'national interest' and 'strategy'. 'Actually,' Forrestal said in one outburst, 'our Palestine policy had been for "squalid political purposes" and had largely been the work of David Niles and Clark Clifford . . . he hoped that some day he would be able to make his position on this issue clear.'[113] His ally in the fight against Israel, Loy Henderson, was removed from any dealings in Mediterranean affairs. The election was coming, and Truman Democrats regarded him as a turncoat. Others were already agitating for his job. He was caught in a vice between Truman, who told him he wanted the Cold War for $15 billion, and the military chiefs who said he would be lucky to have it for double that. Whilst the Navy wanted extra funding for Mediterranean commitments, the Army and Air Force retorted they had more important priorities. Their proposal was to put a line through all the Navy's Mediterranean budget items.[114] The only way out for Forrestal would have been Truman's defeat. The President was, however, a much better politician than the Secretary of Defense. The money and the votes he had amassed over Palestine proved vital in the closest election in living memory. He waited until the post-election euphoria had died down and then, as a final insult, nominated his chief fundraiser to take Forrestal's job. Of course, Truman had to get rid of Forrestal. He was a man on the edge. Two months after leaving office Jimmy Forrestal committed suicide. Out of the window of the Bethesda Naval Hospital went the idea of a grand strategy for the Mediterranean.

There was a notably low-key postscript to the great Mediterranean controversy. Forrestal's old collaborators in the Navy and State found a new pigeonhole for the Mediterranean idea. A few weeks after Forrestal's suicide, George McGhee was elevated to a newly created Assistant Secretaryship of State for the 'Near East, South Asia and Africa'. In other words McGhee was to oversee those parts of the world not important enough to warrant Secretary of State, Dean Acheson's, constant attention. Acheson was too wily a bird to be caught out, Forrestal-like, in trying to make sense of the Mediterranean. As one of his officials put it, 'we work as soundly and constructively as the latest lunacy permits', assuming at all times that 'our Arab policy is a captive of Israeli policy working through the Zionist pressure group in this country'.[115]

McGhee was enthusiastic about his task; he was determined to shift military minds away from an unhealthy fixation with Europe. For the first time since Robert Murphy had left the Mediterranean five years previously, America installed an official with a wide brief and extra-territorial authority. But although McGhee spent a great deal of time roving the Mediterranean, he was no Mediterraneanist. He defined his mission as being to 'The Middle World', the 'lands stretching on a west-east axis from Morocco and the Pillars of Hercules, at the western end of the Mediterranean, to the Indian subcontinent and the Bay of Bengal on the east'.[116] A legacy of his two years as aid coordinator for Greece and Turkey was an intense enthusiasm for the Turks. One of his first acts was to bring all America's senior diplomats from around the Near East to Istanbul in the 'drab, overcast days of November 1949'. The press speculated that McGhee and his men had arrived in Istanbul to throw their weight behind the idea of a Mediterranean pact of the kind that Tsaldaris had been hawking. In fact they had no interest in what the Soviets called 'the Mediterranean plans of American imperialism'.[117] All their talk was of the threat of Soviet subversion in the Middle East. McGhee championed the old idea that the true aim of the US was to create the Northern Tier: a line of anti-Communist, Muslim states from Istanbul to Lahore. Behind this 'pie-crust', the states of the Middle East would remain safe from the Communists. American 'psywar' specialists believed that the 'basic values and aspirations of the Mohammedan religion are akin to those of the Christian religion, and the peoples of the area are spiritually anti-Communist'.[118] As McGhee explained to his men in Istanbul, they were creating a new concept of the Middle East in which psychology was all important. In 1946 Acheson had helped put American capital ships in the eastern Mediterranean. In 1949 McGhee was not allowed even to bring the commander of Forrestal's legacy, the US Navy's Sixth Task Force, soon to be renamed the Sixth Fleet, to Istanbul.[119] Above all, the Americans gathered in Istanbul had to pretend that the creation of Israel was not the greatest obstacle to the creation of their desired Middle East. Instead the villains must be those 'imperial stereotypes', Britain and France.[120]

The final attempt to define the Mediterranean revolved round an old cause, the need to appoint a Supreme Allied Commander. The old SACMED had petered out in 1947. The SACMED idea was resurrected during the Korean War panic. In the shock of the first few hours of North Korea's invasion of the South, Harry Truman's mind leapt to

McGhee's bailiwick. 'Korea is the Greece of the Far East,' he told an aide the day after the invasion, 'if we are tough enough now, if we stand up to them like we did in Greece three years ago, they won't take any steps.' As to the future, he predicted that 'if we just stand by, they'll move into Iran and they'll take over the whole Middle East'.[121] Dwight Eisenhower was called out of retirement and appointed once more as Supreme Allied Commander in Europe, SACEUR. With one element of the Second World War system restored, one could argue for the rest. The new SACMED was supposed to be an admiral who would command the length of the Cold War Mediterranean. He should be, the British argued, British.

Times had changed, the British conceded. The unity of the Mediterranean was no longer anything to do with the old west–east route. The Suez Canal was of little importance. Rather the Mediterranean was the means by which a global war against the Soviet Union could be prosecuted. The Mediterranean was Eisenhower's 'Southern Flank'; the Balkans were the 'soft underbelly' of the Soviet Empire; a string of air bases from Morocco to Suez would be the launching point for bomber attacks on Russia; Egypt was a base from which the battle for oil could be won or lost. Eisenhower was willing to sign up to many of these ideas. As he put it, Europe was like a bottle in a bathtub. Russia was the wide part of the bottle, western Europe was the neck of the bottle. The North Sea and the Mediterranean were the water in the bathtub, England and North Africa were the sides. He would squeeze the bottle from the bath water.[122]

It was the British who put the idea on the table, but it was their critics who made the best use of it. Initial negotiations were put in the hands of Mick Carney, current holder of the post of CINCNELM created by Forrestal. Carney was one of those Americans who didn't even bother to hide their disdain for the 'no ships' British. The time had come, he said, to properly examine 'Freedom's resources'. Such an audit revealed that it would be America doing all of the work. It was the US Navy that would go to the aid of Italy, Greece and Turkey if they were ever attacked. 'It is over these predominantly American forces', he complained, 'that the British advocate British command.' 'The sensitivities of British pride is understandable', he continued, 'but the immutable fact is that the British Navy is not only much smaller than the US Navy, but it lacks the comprehensive armoury of weapons and techniques possessed by the US Navy . . . it would appear to be our responsibility to our own country and to the world to retain leadership where the facts of leadership are established by existing and future relative strength and capabilities.' The Italians, the Greeks and the Turks, 'all of whom prefer American command, and all of whom regard British overlordship as distasteful', were well aware of these disparities. The British were living in a dangerous fantasy land; 'the term Supreme as applied to the Mediterranean would lead to the common British belief in the actuality of such supremacy'. To concede the title would be disastrous, 'the designation of SACMED would inevitably lead to dissatisfaction, confusion and hard feeling'. Americans would be disgusted when they found out that they did all the work whilst the British took all the glory. In fact, the whole idea was plain dangerous.[123]

Carney drew on a fine old tradition of Anglophobic rhetoric, long perfected by the US Navy. He enjoyed, however, articulate support from McGhee. Unlike the Irish-American Carney, the Oxford-educated McGhee fitted in with his English peers. But behind all the mutual friendships, shared interests and bonhomie, he knew they had to go. 'McGhee seemed very sure of himself,' a perceptive British diplomat who met him in Cairo wrote, 'and has the idea at the back of his mind that we British are making rather a mess of Middle East. . . . I think he may have a vision of dwindling British and increasing American power and influence which within eighteen months will completely change the picture here.'[124] McGhee dismissed any idea of relying on the British. Ignore the rhetoric, he warned, look at British war plans. The British had no intention of using the Mediterranean to join the Middle East to Europe in some kind of grand anti-Soviet manoeuvre. They were still locked into old thinking about the Suez Canal. If there was a war scare, British troops would roll across the border into central Israel. There they would dig in and do nothing. They had no intention of going to the aid of Turkey. Protection of American interests in Saudi was explicitly excluded. In return for massive American aid, the British would change their plans in one particular: they might go as far as northern Israel before stopping. This they called the Inner Ring strategy. The British were still in the world of 1940, with a semi-autonomous Middle East Command holding out on the eastern shores of the Mediterranean, hoping that something might turn up. McGhee bearded the Army and Air Force on Carney's behalf. Thanks to Korean rearmament, they now had more money than they could ever have dreamed of in Forrestal's day. Forrestal had been driven insane trying to extract an extra $3 billion for defence; in one year the US defence budget leapt by over $30 billion.[125] It was time to commit to the defence of the Northern Tier. He received a dusty response. 'We are kidding ourselves and kidding them', said 'Lightning Joe' Collins, the head of the Army, if McGhee started bruiting it about that America would soon arrive in the eastern Mediterranean in force. The 'Big Job', 'first, last and always' was to 'win the battle in Europe'. McGhee was unabashed. It was time for the Americans to provide a realistic 'insurance policy'. The Army insisted that they had no interest in defending the Middle East, only in fighting a war in Europe. The solution was simple: Turkey and Greece were no longer part of the eastern Mediterranean but of southern Europe. They, as much as France or Italy, comprised Eisenhower's 'Southern Flank'.[126]

Immediately after his rumbustious encounter with Collins, McGhee set off for Istanbul for a repeat of his November 1949 conclave. Waiting for him in Turkey was Mick Carney. They did not bother to pretend that they had come to persuade the Turks that they were an eastern Mediterranean country which must look to Britain for guidance and support. Instead they put together an end-run around any such policy. McGhee went off to see the President of Turkey, Celal Bayar. He reported directly to Truman that all the work done since 1946 was now in jeopardy. The Turks had done everything that America had ever asked of them. American money had been well spent. Bayar was President because the Kemalists had peacefully given up power after free elections. The new Democratic Party government had sent troops to fight in Korea, and they had fought well. But the Turks were tired of being treated like second-class citizens. Their ally was America, not Britain. If they were fobbed off with some kind of British-led organization, they might well think better of it and 'veer towards a policy of neutralism instead'. McGhee and Carney put their names to a demand that Turkey should be recognized as a European nation and allowed to join NATO.[127]

The admiral and the diplomat convinced the Turks that Washington would soon agree to such a plan. A few days after McGhee and Carney left Istanbul, General Brian Robertson arrived to outline British plans for Turkey's role in the Middle East. He was met with smug indifference. This could best be discussed, his hosts assured him, when Turkey and Britain were co-equal members of NATO. It was a message that Carney himself rubbed in a few days later when he and Robertson met on Malta, to discuss 'co-operation'.[128] Although officially the Americans hewed to the line that they supported the British idea of a MEC, the body language of their Mediterranean representatives told an entirely different story. As Eisenhower pointed out, any kind of British commander – by this time there was talk of a SACMEDME – would have little real worth. It was time to face reality, and admit that the commander of all significant armed forces in the Mediterranean would be under the command of an American admiral.[129] In April 1951 he appointed Carney as his CINCSOUTH, 'responsible in the Mediterranean for the sea communications for the Southern Flank'.[130] When Eisenhower came to Naples to inspect the work of his new commander, he liked what he saw. The Marines were planning amphibious landings on Malta, American bombers flying from French Morocco were trialling minelaying off Sicily. Although the Mediterranean was 'frothing into a bad storm', a helicopter 'windmilled through the grey, moist skies' and gingerly deposited a grinning Eisenhower on the deck of the *Roosevelt*. Carney treated him to a demonstration of the 'Navy's Corsairs, Skyraiders and twin-jet Banshees bombing and strafing a ten-foot-square wooden target floating abeam of the carrier'. Around them bobbed a thirty-strong fleet of warships. When Eisenhower became president of the United States less than two years later, he immediately declared Carney a 'heavyweight thinker' and appointed him head of the US Navy.[131]

The last British attempt to undo these American manoeuvres ended in predictable failure. Carney's appointment as CINCSOUTH, they conceded, made the western and central Mediterranean American territory. Britain could still have the eastern Mediterranean if they kept Turkey out of NATO. Then an Anglo-Turkish-Egyptian combination would be possible. The Americans played along with this scheme. Acheson feared that the British were receiving such a pummelling that general relations might be in danger. McGhee, on the other hand, described the whole affair as 'hopeless'. Neither the Turks nor the Egyptians were willing to sign up to anything. American diplomats and agents were frankly incredulous when the British decided that the answer to their problem in Egypt was the increasingly dissolute and hopeless figure of Farouk. When Herbert Morrison, the new British foreign minister, visited Washington, a deal was struck over McGhee's head. If Britain would agree to Turkey, and less contentiously, Greece, joining NATO, America would support MEC. America would send its senior military figure, the chairman of the JCS, Omar Bradley, to Turkey to persuade the Turks to join MEC as well as NATO. McGhee would be marginalized. His immoderate love of the Turks would be requited by sending him to Ankara.

The ink was barely dry before everything unravelled. The Egyptian government unilaterally denounced the 1936 treaty with Britain. Wafd radicals, in uneasy alliance with jihadists, unleashed 'liberation squads' in the Canal Zone. In such rancorous circumstances, American and British diplomats in Cairo agreed with one another, it was pointless pursuing the MEC.[132] At the same time Bradley, however, accompanied by his British opposite number, Bill Slim, arrived in Ankara to sell the MEC to the Turks. The outcome in Ankara was as predictable as that in Cairo. Stop treating us like Asiatics when we are Europeans, the Turks said. Give us Carney, they demanded. The idea of SACMED, SACME, SACMEDME, whatever it was called, was dead.[133] The 'geographical division of the Mediterranean Sea . . . is not desirable', the Americans declared. The southern flank of Europe would comprise 'western Turkey, the Straits, the Balkans, the Mediterranean Sea, and North Africa, west of Egypt'. Carney had the Sixth Fleet. Relieved of Atlantic responsibilities, he, and his successors, would command the Mediterranean from Naples.[134]

CONCLUSION

Post-war Europeans needed little encouragement to think about the Mediterranean. In France, Braudel composed his great paean to the Mediterranean's historical unity. In England, Elizabeth David introduced jaded British palates to the joys of Mediterranean cuisine.[1] David's wartime odyssey – in flight from the Germans, in pursuit of lovers – had taken her from Corsica to Greece to Cairo. When she published *A Book of Mediterranean Food* in 1950, austerity-raddled Britons headed for their chemists so that they might extract olive oil from remedies formerly kept for softening ear wax. Book-reading publics embraced the Mediterranean. Inhabitants of the wartime Mediterranean demi-mondaine, such as David, had followed their instincts towards 'the light'. Now they were looking back, trying to make sense of an intense but irreproducible encounter. As a pre-war theorist of 'Mediterranean culture', George Sarton, said, the Mediterranean was a fleeting sensual experience, for him olfactory: 'a kind of subtle resemblance in all the towns, a smell *sui generis*, which is unmistakable'. Through the nose, 'Galata, Beirut, Alexandria, Tunis, Tangiers, Malaga, Naples, or Piraeus, in spite of their infinite differences, have enough in common to proclaim their Mediterranean kinship'.[2] Lawrence Durrell, like David a wartime refugee fleeing from Greece to Egypt, later asked, 'What was the Mediterranean tapestry all about anyway?' His answer: the Mediterranean lands 'all had the same light and the same garden produce. They were all garlic countries.' Like Proust's madeleines, the smell of the Mediterranean evoked rather than explained. The smell of garlic hung in the air but the world in which David and Durrell had found themselves flotsam had disappeared.[3]

The struggle for mastery in the Mediterranean had been a mighty endeavour. It neither began with the outbreak of the Second World War nor ended with Victory in Europe. Its end point was not a great victory or a great defeat. Rather the Mediterranean was dismantled, in a blurred, indistinct fashion, in the smoke-filled rooms of Ankara, Cairo, Paris, Lisbon, and all the cities where negotiations for the new Cold War world took place. In its place rose Southern Europe, North Africa and, above all, the Middle East.

In 1952 the British geopolitical writer Gordon East, a long-time champion of the 'pivotal' importance of the Mediterranean, returned to a subject that he had first tackled in 1937. Then he had been sure that the Mediterranean 'should be regarded in its entirety . . . as part of the continent of Europe, with which its relationships, physical and human, have been closest'.[4] The Mediterranean 'problem' was the clash of empires for 'command of the sea'. A disciple of the father of geopolitics, Sir Halford Mackinder, East believed that the war had vindicated those who believed in the superiority of the 'shipmen' over the 'heartlanders'. 'The "Mediterranean" school of strategists had justified its views,' he wrote in his post-war retrospect, 'and the grandiose strategy of the enemy, which would have outflanked the Allied position in the Mediterranean by a gigantic pincer movement directed toward the Middle East from the Caucasus and from Libya, came to nothing.' But, East admitted, the triumph of the British 'shipmen' had had entirely unpredicted consequences: 'the revolutionary advent of the state of Israel and the creation of an independent Libya in place of Italian North Africa'.[5]

Independence for Libya at the end of 1951 was seen as the last fruit of the epoch that had begun in 1935. To some observers, however, it seemed as if the final rolling up of Mussolini's 'imperialist map' was a paltry return for a decade and a half of death, destruction and the expenditures of treasure. The Italians had failed to make Libya a going concern. Neither they, nor their British successors, ever realized that Libya was floating on a huge oil field. 'Recognition in December 1951 of full Libyan independence', wrote the leader of a British geographical survey of Cyrenaica, 'brought into being a new state . . . only slenderly endowed with natural resources, and hence supporting a population of less than one-and-a-half million. As a geographically isolated area lying well to the south of the main currents of activity in the Mediterranean, Libya is overshadowed in many ways by the more powerful units of Egypt and French North Africa. Unlike some of the Levant states, intrinsic poverty

in resources and inhabitants is not compensated for by a favourable location, which might act as the facade of a larger and more productive
hinterland. Libya is unlikely to become a route-centre of the first importance; no oil pipelines cross its territories, and its strategic potentialities,
though not unimportant, are less prominent than those of Egypt, Cyprus,
Malta and Turkey.'[6]

The 'not unimportant' strategic potential of Libya lay in the developing Wheelus Field base complex around Tripoli. Now it was the
Americans who were dominant in the Mediterranean. The 'Mediterranean
problem' had been solved. In brief, the story of the Mediterranean in the
mid-twentieth century had been that the Italian Empire challenged the
British Empire for hegemony, to the ultimate benefit of the American
Empire. Mick Carney's 'fleets of NATO' ruled its waters, having at their
disposal 'the many mainland and insular bases and harbours of Britain,
France, Italy, Greece and Turkey'. It was nevertheless 'not surprising' that
the United States had been 'at pains' also to seek a military agreement
with Franco's Spain. In January 1952 the US Sixth Fleet steamed into
Barcelona and seven other Spanish ports. In Majorca, the Balearic base
that Franco had never granted Mussolini, the visiting American admiral
made clear the wider political and geographical scope of his mission.
Spain and Turkey, he said, were the 'two most anti-Communist nations
in Europe today'. The Americans were tired of being beholden to the
British for the use of Gibraltar and Malta. Spain's 'long, indented
Mediterranean shoreline' would be an ideal base of operations. The
American admirals held out the offer of 'many pesetas' to modernize the
east-coast harbours to accommodate US capital ships.[7] The United States
was 'thus quietly writing a new page in history by replacing Britain as
the principal guardian of the western gateway to the Mediterranean'.

The Mediterranean question may have been resolved, yet in its place
was arising the question of 'that large region which we oddly call the
"Middle East"'. This was not necessarily a comfortable development. 'If
Western defence in the Mediterranean area appears firmly grounded,'
East warned, 'it is weak and growing weaker in the Middle East.' His
enumeration of the problems of the Middle East, fresh in 1952, would
soon become a familiar litany: 'Recollection of American support for the
new Israel . . . desire for revenge against Israel and fear of her expansion,
distrust of alliances with Great Powers, the aspiration for full independence in countries whose faith and culture are alien to those of the West.'[8]

The 'geopolitical value of the Mediterranean Sea', East suggested in

1952, had hitherto rested on 'British control of Egypt, junction of sea routes from the outer oceans and passageway between them'. But Egypt would no longer play ball with Britain. Britain was on its way out militarily once any hope of a British admiral becoming SACMEDME had been scuppered by the Americans the year before. Strategic bankruptcy was only heightened by further political change during 1952. King Farouk's decadent and fumbling rule was finally terminated by a military coup. The first prime minister of the new regime was an 'old friend' of the British: Ali Maher. This seemed the final, ironic, pay-off for Fascism's challenge to British hegemony. Ali Maher had been a genuine enthusiast for Islamo-Fascism, albeit one who had tried to cover his tracks. He was soon shunted aside by the most charismatic member of the military junta, Gamal Abdel Nasser. In a further bitter irony, however, Nasser did a thing strange to post-war European eyes, although perfectly logical by his own lights: he exaggerated his role as a Nazi and Fascist fellow-traveller in order to boost his Anglophobe credentials.[9] Only the most misty-eyed imperialists could believe that Egypt was ever coming back.[10]

The British were not at all sure that they were happier with the Middle East than the Mediterranean. The Mediterranean, at least, had been 'near-white'.[11] Now they had an ugly premonition that there would be something even worse than radicals expounding their debt to Fascism. Coming up behind the nationalists was 'a Moslem Caliban', 'screaming hate for the rich and the foreign; he fires palaces, hotels, night clubs and cinemas, while the radio endlessly repeats the *suras* of the Koran exhorting the faithful to a Holy War'. British writers had the uncomfortable suspicion that this 'Caliban' was the unnatural offspring of their own Mediterranean crisis. Something had changed; very specifically, since 1935.[12]

Albert Hourani, during the war a controversial source of many political intelligence briefings circulated in the Middle East, after it the rising star of British 'oriental studies', recalled a conversation he had had in 1935 with the leading pre-war Arabist, Philip Hitti. There was, Hitti remarked, no Arabic history worthy of the name, if one was interested in the exercise and transmission of political power, after the Christian fourteenth century. The past 150 years merited nothing other than a 'short epilogue'.[13] However, the leading French commentator on the Arab world, Robert Montagne, much read in the Anglophone sphere, argued that 1935 marked the end of that 'epilogue'. Islamo-Fascism might seem irrelevant after the defeat of Italy and Germany, but the rising generation had drunk deeply at the well: 'the student youth rapidly abandoned liberal principles and began modelling itself on the Fascist organizations ... there sprang up paramilitary youth organizations, with different coloured shirts and gaudy emblems ... at the same time the universities (especially in Egypt) became hotbeds of agitation,' observed Montagne, who had been living and working in Syria in 1935. 'Learning was at a discount, replaced by patriotic zeal ... to this enthusiastic but badly-educated youth,' he concluded.[14]

But Arab youth had also learnt from the West. What had begun in 1935 came to a 'climax' in 1943, noted Hamilton Gibb, Montagne's direct contemporary in England, and the West's most influential Arabist, 'with ... the removal of all fears of direct involvement in the War in consequence of the Allies' successes in the Mediterranean theatre'. 'It seemed clear ... to the Arabs that all their troubles were due to Europe; to the war between the European nations, to the closing of export outlets, to the restriction of imports, to their dependence on European shipping,' Gibb wrote. 'The conclusion seemed as plain,' he continued. 'Why should not the Arab countries assert their independence, keep clear of European entanglements, organize their own life and exploit their own resources in their own interests?' 'The sense of grievance focused on the Middle East Supply Centre,' Gibb observed. 'That the MESC had narrowly averted actual famine in more than one country on more than one occasion was an argument that carried little weight in face of the daily struggle to get the necessities of life and to make ends meet.' The MESC had been wound up in the summer of 1945, but its legacy was a reinforced sense of the 'the Middle East' as a discrete area.[15]

Both Gibb and Montagne knew that there were British organizations more secret and less benign than the publicly reviled MESC. Cairo had been also the hub of the pan-Mediterranean 'hidden hand'. From Cairo the British had sponsored 'terrorists' ranging from the Irgun to Balkan Communists. 'The Second World War re-awoke the inclinations toward violence everywhere in the region,' observed Montagne, 'the examples of the Irgun and the Stern Gang, or the European resistance and of Communist group activities, incited the organization of terrorist movements divided into cells and operated by secret and remote control.'[16] Assassination was becoming the common currency of politics of the Middle East: Cairo was murder central. The chief procurers of murder were Islamic extremists, most notably the Grand Mufti. Prime ministers and princes were amongst the victims. The most famous casualty was King Abdullah of Jordan, who fell to one of the Mufti's assassins in 1951.

One possible future Gibb predicted as early as July 1944 was 'a Moslem Revolution, an anti-Western movement appealing to the old Moslem sense of solidarity, aiming at the reunion of the Arab lands under the banner of Islam by means of a violent upthrust of the Moslem masses, the driving out or extirpation of all the superficial Western institutions that seem to have brought only division and corruption, the reassertion of the supremacy of the Moslem, of Moslem Law and of Moslem institutions in their own homelands'.[17]

The Mediterranean had been more modern than any of the empires of the old world, with their clearly defined colonies, protectorates and mandates. It was more modern than the feared Middle Eastern future. It lacked the iron curtains and the inviolable frontiers of the emerging new Europe. Yet its delicate complexity made it difficult to maintain. The cost of Mediterranean unity was almost impossibly high. Such unity required a hegemon. The hegemon required a Mediterranean ideology *and* enormous material resources.

The Americans certainly possessed the material resources to rule: but they lacked any grand idea of Mediterranean unity. They had come by the Mediterranean in a fit of absence of mind: 'the sudden invasion of the Mediterranean by the American forces during World War II, the perennial desire of Russia for an outlet on the Mediterranean and the insistence for a share in the control of the Straits,' commented Gordon East's opposite number in the USA, the Czech-American geopolitical writer Joseph Roucek, 'have resulted in making the Mediterranean the United States' *Mare Nostrum*.'[18] The Americans had demonstrated, 'the "unwilling willingness" to take over the position in the Mediterranean from the weak hands of Great Britain'. 'But today,' East himself warned, 'when so much has changed politically both inside and outside the Mediterranean basin, it does not follow automatically that the part which this sea played for Britain in the past is the one it should now play for the American-led Western World.' The future was 'obscure'.[19]

Forrestal, the prophet, had gone to his grave over his failure to create a coherent vision of the Mediterranean. His one-time instrument, the US Navy, took the narrow view. When American commentators addressed the Mediterranean they wrote extensively about the past, whether classical or British, little about the present. Although the Sixth Fleet was 'the

Mediterranean Fleet', it remained essentially a task force, using the Mediterranean to strike away from the Mediterranean. 'The supreme importance of the Mediterranean' was purely operational. The old British 'artery' mattered little more than the defunct Italian 'fourth shore'. 'This vast body of water with its flanking land masses offers a potential strategic gateway into the great Eurasian land mass,' Roucek concluded. 'It provides, in other words, a field of deployment along the coastal "fringelands" for the arm in which the United States is still strong vis-à-vis Russia – sea-air power. The eastern part of the Mediterranean region and the North African littoral offer potential bomber bases for US strategic air power from which many important Russian industrial centres could be reached . . . domination of the Mediterranean region gives the United States a strategic "ace in the hole".[20] This unsubtle doctrine reached its full fruition in 1954: the first operational nuclear weapons deployed outside American territory went to Morocco.[21]

NOTES AND REFERENCES

INTRODUCTION

1 Bruno Waterfield (Tripoli), 'Gaddafi attacks Sarkozy Plan for Union of the Med', http://www.telegraph.co.uk/news/world news/europe/2277517/Gaddafi-attacks-Sarkozy-plan-for-Union-of-the-Med.html

2 Heather Nicholson, 'At Home and Abroad with Cine Enthusiasts: Regional Amateur Filmmaking and Visualizing the Mediterranean, 1928–1962', GeoJournal, 59 (2004), 323–33.

3 Denis Cosgrove, 'John Ruskin and the Geographical Imagination', Geographical Review, 69 (1979), 43–62, 58.

4 Garret Mattingly, review of La Méditerranée et le monde Méditerranéen à l'époque de Philippe II in American Historical Review, 55 (1950), 349–51.

5 Fernand Braudel, 'Personal Testimony', Journal of Modern History, 44 (1972), 448–67; Howard Caygill, 'Braudel's Prison Notebooks', History Workshop Journal, 57 (2004), 151–60.

6 Ian Morris, 'Mediterraneanization', Mediterranean Historical Review, 18 (2003), 30–55; J. de Pina-Cabral, 'The Mediterranean as a Category of Regional Comparison: A Critical View', Current Anthropology, 30 (1989), 399–406.

7 Lawrence Martin, 'The Miscalled Middle East', Geographical Review, 34 (1944), 335–6; C. G. Smith, 'The Emergence of the Middle East', Journal of Contemporary History, 3 (1968), 3–17; Alford Carleton, '"Near East" versus "Middle East"', International Journal of Middle East

Studies, 6 (1975), 237–8; Matthew Jacobs, 'The Perils and Promise of Islam: The United States and the Muslim Middle East in the Early Cold War', Diplomatic History, 30 (2006), 705–39.

8 I. S. O. Playfair et al. (eds), The Mediterranean and the Middle East (London, HMSO, 6 vols [physically 8], 1954–1987). The British official military history, when read in conjunction with its companion volumes on intelligence – which reveal information about Ultra unavailable to the original team – remains the fullest and best extended treatment of the 1939–1945 conflict.

9 Trumbull Higgins, 'The Anglo-American Historians' War in the Mediterranean, 1942–1945', Military Affairs, 34 (1970), 84–8.

10 David Reynolds, In Command of History: Churchill Fighting and Writing the Second World War (London, Penguin, 2005), 52–3.

11 Douglas Porch, Hitler's Mediterranean Gamble: The North African and the Mediterranean Campaigns in World War II (London, Weidenfeld & Nicolson, 2004).

CHAPTER ONE

1 Aldous Huxley, Eyeless in Gaza (London, Chatto & Windus, 1936). The novel sets the dropping of the dog at noon on 30 August 1933. Huxley's essays on Mediterranean travel, Along the Road, were published in 1925. Huxley took heed of his own warning, abandoned the

Mediterranean and decamped for California.

2 Claudio Segrè, *Italo Balbo: A Fascist Life* (Berkeley, University of California Press, 1987), 194–7.

3 Tim Benton, 'Dreams of Machines: Futurism and *l'Esprit Nouveau*', *Journal of Design History*, 3 (1990), 19–34, 34.

4 R. J. B. Bosworth, *Mussolini* (London, Arnold, 2002), 143–4, 307–11.

5 Ray Moseley, *Mussolini's Shadow: The Double Life of Count Galeazzo Ciano* (New Haven, 1999), 17–20.

6 Galeazzo Ciano, *Diary, 1937–1943* (London, Phoenix Press, 2002), 28 August 1937. The specific projects were Spain and Albania.

7 Andrew Ryan, *The Last of the Dragomans* (London, Geoffrey Bles, 1951), 334.

8 Elizabeth Monroe, *The Mediterranean in Politics* (Oxford, OUP, July 1938), 11.

9 Denis Mack Smith, *Mussolini's Roman Empire* (London, 1976), 89–90.

10 Record by Sir Alexander Cadogan of a conversation with Signor Fracassi, 5 September 1936, *British Documents on Foreign Policy*, Series II, XVII.

11 Robert Mallett, *The Italian Navy and Fascist Expansionism, 1935–1940* (London, 1998), 54–8.

12 Lawrence Pratt, *East of Malta, West of Suez: Britain's Mediterranean Crisis, 1936–1939* (Cambridge, 1975), 46, 121.

13 D. H. Cole, *Imperial Military Geography: General Characteristics of the Empire in Relation to Defence* (London, Sifton Praed, 8th edition, April 1935), 89–112, 291–2.

14 Lieutenant-Colonel A. C. Arnold, 'The Italo-Abyssinian Campaign, 1935–36', *Journal of the Royal United Service Institution*, 82 (1937), 71–85.

15 Churchill to Hoare, 29 August 1935, *Churchill Papers* (Printed Papers, London, Heinemann, 1966 onwards).

16 Major-General Robert Haining in discussion with Lieutenant-Colonel A. C. Arnold, 'The Italo-Abyssinian Campaign, 1935–36', *Journal of the Royal United Service Institution*, 82 (1937), 85–8.

17 R. A. C. Parker, 'Great Britain, France and the Ethiopian Crisis, 1935–1936', *English Historical Review*, 89 (1974), 293–332, 296.

18 Steven Morewood, *The British Defence of Egypt, 1935–1940: Conflict and Crisis in the Eastern Mediterranean* (London, 2005), 84–5.

19 Quoted in Nicholas Rankin, *Telegram from Guernica* (London, Faber & Faber, 2003), 33.

20 Angelo Del Boca, *The Ethiopian War, 1935–1941* (Chicago, Chicago University Press, 1969), 80–1. Although the Italian use of gas was notorious, Fascist propaganda retained its grip for decades. The Italian Ministry of Defence only officially admitted to the gas campaign in November 1995.

21 Sir Warren Fisher to Sir Robert Vansittart, 21 April 1936, quoted in Pratt, *East of Malta, West of Suez*, 35.

22 Robert Mallett, 'Fascist Foreign Policy and Official Italian Views of Anthony Eden in the 1930s', *The Historical Journal*, 43 (2000), 157–87.

23 Mack Smith, *Mussolini's Roman Empire*, 119–20.

24 Nicholas Doumanis, *Myth and Memory in the Mediterranean: Remembering Fascism's Empire* (Basingstoke, Macmillan, 1997), 45.

25 Dilek Barlas, 'Turkish Diplomacy in the Balkans and Mediterranean: Opportunities and Limits for Middle-power Activism in the 1930s', *Journal of Contemporary History*, 40 (2005), 441–64.

26 Anthony Eden to Winston Churchill, 16 April 1937 and Winston Churchill's speech to the House of Commons, 14 April 1937 in *Churchill Papers, 1936–1939*; Chargé d'Affaires, Paris to Foreign Ministry, Berlin, 25 September 1937 in *Documents on German Foreign Policy*, Series D, III; Paul Preston, 'Italy and Spain in Civil War and World War, 1936–1943' in Sebastian Balfour and Paul Preston (eds), *Spain and the Great Powers in the Twentieth Century* (London, Routledge, 1999), 151–84.

27 Moseley, *Mussolini's Shadow*, 27.

28 Raymond Proctor, 'They Flew from Pollensa Bay', *Aerospace Historian*, 24 (1977), 196–202 and *Hitler's Luftwaffe in the Spanish Civil War* (Westport, Greenwood, 1983); Robert Whealey, *Hitler and Spain: The Nazi Role in the Spanish Civil War, 1936–1939* (Lexington, University of Kentucky Press, 1989), 57.

29 Morten Heiberg, 'Mussolini, Franco and the Spanish Civil War: An Afterthought', *Totalitarian Movements & Political Religions*, 2 (2001), 55–66.

30 John Coverdale, *Italian Intervention in the Spanish Civil War* (Princeton, Princeton University Press, 1975), 248–60. The CTV was lured to disaster only when it transferred to central Spain and attempted to seize Madrid. John Coverdale, 'The Battle of Guadalajara, 8–22 March 1937', *Journal of Contemporary History*, 9 (1974).

31 Ciano, *Diary*, 19 September 1937; James Sadkovich, 'The Development of the Italian Air Force Prior to World War II', *Military Affairs*, 51 (1987), 128–36.

Italian air operations 1935–9			
	Abyssinia	Spain	Total
Aircraft used	500	710	1,210
Aircraft lost	8	226	265

32 'Barcelona Bombed; Daylight Raid', *The Times*, 15 March 1937, 14.

33 Brian Sullivan, 'Fascist Italy's Military Involvement in the Spanish Civil War', *Journal of Military History*, 59 (1995), 697–727, 722.

34 Sullivan, 'Fascist Italy's Military Involvement', 724.

35 Sullivan, 'Fascist Italy's Military Involvement', 722; James Corum, 'The *Luftwaffe* and the Coalition Air War in Spain, 1936–1939', *Journal of Strategic Studies*, 18 (1995), 68–90.

36 Memorandum by the Foreign Minister, 30 June 1938, *Documents on German Foreign Policy*, Series D, III; Sadkovich, 'Development of the Italian Air Force', 128–36; James Corum, 'The Spanish Civil War: Lessons Learned and Not Learned by the Great Powers', *Journal of Military History*, 62 (1998), 313–34.

37 Luigi Federzoni, 'Hegemony in the Mediterranean', *Foreign Affairs*, 14/1 (1935/36), 395. Federzoni was Fascist Minister of the Interior. One side-effect of the Abyssinian war was a veritable 'battle of the books' commenting on the Mediterranean situation. Examples include Elizabeth Monroe's 1938 work, cited above, Margaret Boveri, *Mediterranean Crosscurrents* (1938), George Martelli, *Whose Sea? A Mediterranean Journey* (1937), Sir Charles Petrie, *Lords of the Inland Sea: A Study of the Mediterranean Powers* (1937), George Slocombe, *The Dangerous Sea: The Mediterranean and its Future* (1937).

38 Morewood, *The British Defence of Egypt*, 24.

39 Roderick Watt, '"*Wanderer, kommst du nach Sparta*": History through Propaganda into Literary Commonplace', *Modern Language Review*, 80 (1985), 871–83.

40 William Hoisington, 'The Mediterranean Committee and French North Africa, 1935–1940', *The Historian*, 53 (1991), 255–66.

41 Martin Thomas, 'At the Heart of Things? French Imperial Defence Planning in the Late 1930s', *French Historical Studies*, 21 (1998), 325–61.

42 Coverdale, *Italian Intervention in the Spanish Civil War*, 127–8.

43 Record of a conversation with Vice-Admiral Darlan and Rear Admiral Decoux, 5 August 1936, *Documents on British Foreign Policy, 1919–1939*, Second Series, XVII; Reynolds Salerno, 'The French Navy and the Appeasement of Italy, 1937–39', *English Historical Review*, 112 (1997), 66–104; Peter Jackson, 'French Strategy and the Spanish Civil War' in Christian Leitz and David Dunthorn (eds), *Spain in an International Context* (Oxford, 1999), 55–79.

44 Churchill to Clementine Churchill, 30 December 1935 in *Churchill Papers*; William Hoisington, 'The Selling of Agadir: French Business Promotion in Morocco in the 1930s', *International Journal of African Historical Studies*, 18 (1985), 315–24.

45 Brock Millman, 'Turkish Foreign and Strategic Policy, 1934–1942', *Middle Eastern Studies*, 31 (1995), 483–508; Gary Leiser, 'The Turkish Air Force, 1939–45: The Rise of a Minor Power', *Middle Eastern Studies*, 26 (1990), 383–95.

46 Claudio Segrè, 'Liberal and Fascist Italy in the Middle East, 1919–1939' in Uriel Dann, *The Great Powers and the Middle East, 1919–1939* (New York, Holmes & Meier, 1983), 199–212. Smyrna, on the west coast of Turkey, had been renamed Izmir by the Kemalists; the province of

Adalia on the south coast equated to Antalya.

47 Peter Jackson, 'French Intelligence and Hitler's Rise to Power', *The Historical Journal*, 41 (1998), 795–824.

48 Dilek Barlas and Serhat Güvenç, 'To Build a Navy with the Help of an Adversary: Italian-Turkish Arms Trade, 1929–32', *Middle Eastern Studies*, 38 (2002), 143–68.

49 Brock Millman, *The Ill-Made Alliance: Anglo-Turkish Relations, 1934–1940* (Montreal, McGill-Queen's University Press, 1998), 57.

50 Millman, *The Ill-Made Alliance*, 64.

51 Borden Painter, 'Renzo De Felice and the Historiography of Italian Fascism', *The American Historical Review*, 95 (1990), 391–405; Stephen Azzi, 'The Historiography of Fascist Foreign Policy', *The Historical Journal*, 36 (1993), 187–203; MacGregor Knox, 'The Fascist Regime: Its Foreign Policy and its Wars: An Anti-Fascist Orthodoxy', *Contemporary European History*, 3 (1995), 347–65.

52 'Italian Role in Europe; Mediterranean Interests; Duce and British Policy', *The Times*, 2 November 1936, 14.

53 Heather Hyde Minor, 'Mapping Mussolini: Ritual and Cartography in Public Art during the Second Roman Empire', *Imago Mundi*, 54 (1999), 147–62.

54 Martin Moore, *Fourth Shore: Italy's Mass Colonization of Libya* (London, Routledge, 1940). Moore covered the huge convoy that crossed the Mediterranean in October 1938 taking thousands of colonists to Libya as a correspondent for the *Daily Telegraph*.

55 Sir John Russell (Director, Rothamsted Experimental Station), 'Agricultural Colonization in the Pontine Marshes and Libya', *The Geographical Journal*, 94 (1939), 273–89, 289. Sir John gave his lecture in May 1939 but it was published after the outbreak of war.

56 Meir Michaelis, 'Italy's Mediterranean Strategy, 1935–1939' in Michael Cohen and Martin Kolinsky (eds), *Britain and the Middle East in the 1930s: Security Problems, 1935–39* (Basingstoke, Macmillan, 1992), 41–60, 55–6.

57 Reynolds Salerno, *Vital Crossroads: Mediterranean Origins of the Second World War, 1935–1940* (Ithaca, Cornell UP, 2002), 106.

58 Jack Greene and Alessandro Massagnani, *The Black Prince and the Sea Devils: The Story of Valerio Borghese and the Elite Units of the Decima Mas* (Cambridge, Da Capo, 2004), 9–58. The Special Weapons Section became the 'Tenth Light Flotilla', or *Decima MAS*, in March 1941.

59 Esmonde Robertson, *Mussolini as Empire-Builder: Europe and Africa, 1932–1936* (London, 1977), 123.

60 Roberta Suzzi Valli, 'The Myth of *Squadrismo* in the Fascist Regime', *Journal of Contemporary History*, 35 (2000), 131–50.

61 MacGregor Knox, 'Conquest, Foreign and Domestic, in Fascist Italy and Nazi Germany', *Journal of Modern History*, 56 (1984), 1–57.

62 Robert Mallett, *The Italian Navy and Fascist Expansionism*, 50–1; Gerhard Schreiber, 'Italy and the Mediterranean in the Power-Political Calculations of German Naval Leaders, 1919–1945' in John Hattendorf, *Naval Policy and Strategy in the Mediterranean: Past, Present and Future* (London, 2000), 108–43.

63 'Conversation between the Duce and Herr Frank, Palazzo Venezia, Rome, 23 September 1936' and 'Conversation with the Fuehrer, Berchtesgaden, 24 October 1936' in Malcolm Muggeridge (ed.), *Ciano's Diplomatic Papers* (London, Odhams Press, 1948).

64 'Italian Liner on Fire: British Seamen to the Rescue', *The Times*, 19 October 1935, 12.

65 Lawrence Fernsworth, 'Mediterranean Tug-of-War', *Current History*, 47 (December 1937), 46–52. Fernsworth was the *New York Times* correspondent in Spain.

66 Arthur Marder, 'The Royal Navy and the Ethiopian Crisis of 1935–36', *The American Historical Review*, 75 (1970), 1327–56.

67 Rosaria Quartararo, 'Imperial Defence in the Mediterranean on the Eve of the Ethiopian Crisis (July to October 1935)', *The Historical Journal*, 20 (1977), 185–220.

68 Ciano, *Diary*, 28 August 1937.

69 Willard Frank, 'Naval Operations in the

Spanish Civil War, 1936–1939', *US Naval War College Review*, 37 (1984), 24–55.

70 'Seafox', 'Some Destroyer Experiences in the Mediterranean', *Royal United Services Institute Journal*, 83 (1938), 782–90.

71 Ciano, *Diary*, 2 September 1937.

72 William Mills, 'The Nyon Conference: Neville Chamberlain, Anthony Eden and the Appeasement of Italy in 1937', *International History Review*, 15 (1993), 1–22.

73 Peter Gretton, 'The Nyon Conference – the Naval Aspect', *English Historical Review*, 90 (1975), 103–12.

74 Ciano, *Diary*, 14 and 21 September.

75 Michael Alpert, 'Contrasting Ways of War in Spain, 1936–1939', *War in History*, 6 (1999), 331–51; Dominic Tierney, 'Franklin D. Roosevelt and Covert Aid to the Loyalists in the Spanish Civil War, 1936–1939', *Journal of Contemporary History*, 39 (2004), 299–313.

76 M. E. Yapp (ed.), *Politics and Diplomacy in Egypt: The Diaries of Sir Miles Lampson, 1935–1937* (Oxford, British Academy, 1997), 10 November 1936.

77 Morewood, *The British Defence of Egypt*, 5–6.

78 Lampson, *Diary*, 18 November 1936; Robert Mallett, 'The Anschluss Question in Italian Defence Policy, 1933–37', *Intelligence & National Security*, 19 (2004), 680–94.

79 *Ciano's Diplomatic Papers*, 57.

80 David Alvarez, 'Left in the Dust: Italian Signals Intelligence, 1915–1943', *International Journal of Intelligence and Counter-intelligence*, 14 (2001), 388–408.

81 Sir Robert Vansittart's minute on a Note by Leslie Hore-Belisha (Secretary of State for War) on his meeting with Dino Grandi (Italian ambassador in London), 22 June 1937, *British Documents on Foreign Policy*, Second Series, XIX.

CHAPTER TWO

1 *The Times*, 9 November 1937.

2 Dick White, 'Report on a visit to the Middle East, January 26th to February 28th, 1943', 29 March 1943: Part II, Appendix 1 – 'The Evolution of SIME and its Present Constitutional Foundation', KV4/240. All archival references are to papers held in The National Archives: Public Record Office, Kew unless otherwise specified.

3 Francis Nicosia, 'Arab Nationalism and National Socialist Germany, 1933–1939: Ideological and Strategic Incompatibility', *International Journal of Middle East Studies*, 12 (1980), 351–72; Ami Ayalon, 'Egyptian Intellectuals versus Fascism and Nazism in the 1930s' in Dann, *The Great Powers and the Middle East, 1919–1939*, 391–404; Stefan Wild, 'National Socialism in the Arab Near East between 1933 and 1939', *Die Welt des Islams*, New Series 25 (1985), 126–73; Israel Gershoni, 'Egyptian Liberalism in the Age of "Crisis of Orientation": *Al-Risala*'s Reaction to Fascism and Nazism, 1933–39', *International Journal of Middle East Studies*, 31 (1999), 551–76; *idem, Beyond Anti-Semitism: Egyptian Responses to German Nazism and Italian Fascism in the 1930s* (Florence, EUI Working Paper 2001/32).

4 Lampson to Eden, 24 February 1936, *British Documents on Foreign Affairs*, Part II, Series B, Vol. 11.

5 Lampson, *Diary*, 1 April 1935.

6 Manuela Williams, *Mussolini's Propaganda Abroad: Subversion in the Mediterranean and the Middle East, 1935–1940* (London, Routledge, 2006), 65.

7 Callum MacDonald, 'Radio Bari: Italian Wireless Propaganda in the Middle East and British Countermeasures, 1934–1938', *Middle Eastern Studies*, 23 (1977), 195–207.

8 Segrè, *Italo Balbo*, 294–301.

9 Krystyna von Henneberg, 'Imperial Uncertainties: Architectural Syncretism and Improvisation in Fascist Colonial Libya', *Journal of Contemporary History*, 31 (1996), 373–95.

10 Mack Smith, *Mussolini's Roman Empire*, 117; Alexander De Grand, 'Mussolini's Follies: Fascism in its Imperial and Racist Phase, 1935–1940', *Contemporary European History*, 13 (2004), 127–47.

11 E. D. O'Brien, 'With the Duce in Libya', *English Review*, 64 (May 1937), and McClelland (Tripoli) to Drummond (Rome), 1 April 1937, *British Documents on Foreign Affairs*, Series F: Europe, XIII.

12 Robert Gale Woolbert, 'Pan Arabism and the Palestine Problem', *Foreign Affairs*, 16 (1937/8), 309–22, 314.

13 Yehoshua Porath, *The Palestinian Arab National Movement*, II: *From Riots to Rebellion* (London, Frank Cass, 1977), 116–17; Yehuda Taggar, *The Mufti of Jerusalem and Palestine Arab Politics, 1930–1937* (New York, Garland, 1986), 285; Philip Mattar, *The Mufti of Jerusalem: Al-Hajj Amin al-Husayni and the Palestinian National Movement* (New York, Columbia UP, rev. edn, 1988), 50–64; Zvi Elpeleg, *The Grand Mufti: Haj Amin al-Hussaini, Founder of the Palestinian National Movement* (London, Frank Cass, 1993); Joseph Nevo, 'Palestinian Arab Violent Activity during the 1930s' in Cohen and Kolinsky, *Britain and the Middle East in the 1930s: Security Problems*, 169–89; Martin Kolinsky, *Britain's War in the Middle East: Strategy and Diplomacy, 1936–1942* (Basingstoke, 1999), 49–50.

14 Nicosia, 'Arab Nationalism and National Socialist Germany, 1933–1939', 351–72.

15 Charles Tripp, 'Ali Mahir Pasha and the Palace in Egyptian Politics, 1936–1942' (Ph.D, University of London, 1984).

16 James Jankowski, 'The Egyptian Blue Shirts and the Egyptian *Wafd*, 1935–1938', *Middle Eastern Studies*, 6 (1970), 77–95.

17 Lampson to Hoare, 12 July 1935, *Documents on British Foreign Policy, 1919–1939*, Second Series, XIV.

18 Lampson, *Diary*, 12 May 1936.

19 Laila Morsy, 'The Military Clauses of the Anglo-Egyptian Treaty of Friendship and Alliance, 1936', *International Journal of Middle East Studies*, 16 (1984), 67–97; Morewood, *The British Defence of Egypt*, 91–7.

20 Lampson, *Diary*, 5 July 1935 and 31 December 1936.

21 Ahmed Gomaa, 'The Syrian Throne: Hashemite Ambition and Anglo-French Rivalry, 1930–35' in Dann, *The Great Powers and the Middle East, 1919–1939*, 183–95; Peter Shambrook, *French Imperialism in Syria, 1927–1936* (Reading, Ithaca Press, 1998).

22 Philip Khoury, *Syria and the French Mandate: The Politics of Arab Nationalism, 1920–1945* (London, I. B. Tauris, 1987), 471–6.

23 'Liberal and Fascist Italy in the Middle East, 1919–1939' in Dann, *The Great Powers and the Middle East, 1919–1939*, 199–212; Wild, 'National Socialism in the Arab Near East between 1933 and 1939', 126–73; Manuela Williams, *Mussolini's Propaganda Abroad*, 79; Porath, *The Palestinian Arab National Movement*, II: *From Riots to Rebellion*, 118–39; Mustafa Kabha, 'The Palestinian Press and the General Strike, April to October 1936: *Filastin* as a Case Study', *Middle Eastern Studies*, 39 (2003), 169–89.

24 Porath, *The Palestinian Arab National Movement*, II, 118–39.

25 Kabha, 'The Palestinian Press and the General Strike, April to October 1936', 169–89.

26 Morton Stratton, 'British Railways and Motor Roads in the Middle East, 1930–1940', *Economic Geography*, 20 (1944), 189–203; Zachary Lockman, 'Railway Workers and Relational History: Arabs and Jews in British-Ruled Palestine', *Comparative Studies in Society and History*, 35 (1993), 601–27.

27 James Jankowski, 'Egyptian Responses to the Palestine Problem in the Interwar Period', *International Journal of Middle East Studies*, 12 (1980), 1–38; *idem*, 'The Government of Egypt and the Palestine Question, 1936–1939', *Middle Eastern Studies*, 17 (1981), 427–53; Israel Gershoni, 'Rejecting the West: The Image of the West in the Teachings of the Muslim Brotherhood, 1928–1939' in Dann, *The Great Powers and the Middle East, 1919–1939*, 370–90; *idem*, 'The Muslim Brothers and the Arab Revolt in Palestine, 1936–39', *Middle Eastern Studies*, 22 (1986), 367–97; Philip Khoury, 'Divided Loyalties: Syria and the Question of Palestine, 1919–39', *Middle Eastern Studies*, 21 (1985), 324–48.

28 Kolinsky, *Britain's War in the Middle East*, 49–50.

29 H. J. Simson, *British Rule, and Rebellion* (Edinburgh, Blackwood, 1937), 226.

30 Michael Cohen, 'Sir Arthur Wauchope, the Army and the Rebellion in Palestine,

1936', *Middle Eastern Studies*, 9 (1973), 20–34; Porath, *The Palestinian Arab National Movement*, II; Taggar, *The Mufti of Jerusalem and Palestine Arab Politics*.

31 MacKereth's Despatch from Damascus, 14 September 1937, reprinted in Elie Kedourie, 'The Bludan Conference on Palestine, September 1937', *Middle Eastern Studies*, 17 (1981), 107–25.

32 Tom Bowden, 'The Politics of the Arab Rebellion in Palestine', *Middle Eastern Studies*, 11 (1975), 147–74; Charles Townshend, 'The Defence of Palestine: Insurrection and Public Security, 1936–1939', *The English Historical Review*, 103 (1988), 917–49; Martin Kolinsky, 'The Collapse and Restoration of Public Security' in Cohen and Kolinsky, *Britain and the Middle East in the 1930s*, 147–68.

33 Lampson, *Diary*, 12 November 1937; Michael Cohen, 'British Strategy and the Palestine Question, 1936–39', *Journal of Contemporary History*, 7 (1972), 157–83; Townshend, 'The Defence of Palestine', 917–49.

34 Francis Nicosia, *The Third Reich and the Palestine Question* (London, I. B. Tauris, 1985); H. D. Schmidt, 'The Nazi Party in Palestine and the Levant, 1932–1939', *International Affairs*, 28 (1952), 460–9; Michael Wolffsohn, 'The German-Saudi Arabian Arms Deal, 1936–1939 Reconsidered' in Dann, *The Great Powers and the Middle East, 1919–1939*, 283–300, 292; Renate Dieterich, 'Germany's Relations with Iraq and Transjordan from the Weimar Republic to the End of the Second World War', *Middle Eastern Studies*, 41 (2005), 463–79.

35 German Ambassador in Rome to Foreign Office, Berlin 10 September 1940, *DGFP*, Series D, Vol. XI.

36 Kolinsky, 'The Collapse and Restoration of Public Security' in Cohen and Kolinsky, *Britain and the Middle East in the 1930s*, 147–68.

37 Notes on the Near East by the Intelligence Officer, Khartoum (Edward Atiyah), July–August 1937, forwarded to London from Cairo, 9 September 1937, *British Documents on Foreign Affairs*, Part II, Series B, Vol. 12.

38 Luksasz Hirszowicz, *The Third Reich and the Arab East* (London, Routledge, 1966), 20-61.

CHAPTER THREE

1 'Itiy' was Cunningham's spelling of the term of abuse. Cunningham to Rear Admiral Hugh England, 23 November 1940, reproduced in Michael Simpson (ed.), *The Cunningham Papers*, Volume I: *The Mediterranean Fleet, 1939–1942* (Aldershot, Ashgate, 1999).

2 H. N. Brailsford, 'Impressions of Tunis and Libya', *International Affairs*, 18 (1939), 361–79; Brailsford was speaking in May 1939. George Deasy, 'The Harbors of Africa', *Economic Geography*, 18 (1942), 325–42.

3 Jackson, 'French Strategy and the Spanish Civil War' in Leitz and Dunthorn, *Spain in an International Context*, 55–79; Thomas, 'At the Heart of Things? French Imperial Defence Planning in the Late 1930s', 325–61.

4 Maxime Weygand, 'How France is Defended', *International Affairs*, 18 (1939), 459–77, 475. Weygand was speaking in July 1939.

5 Pratt, *East of Malta, West of Suez*, 187.

6 Reynolds Salerno, 'The French Navy and the Appeasement of Italy, 1937–39', *English Historical Review*, 112 (1997), 66–104.

7 Lucio Ceva, 'The Strategy of Fascist Italy: A Premise', *Totalitarian Movements & Political Religions*, 2 (2001), 41–54.

8 Ciano, *Diary*, 30 November 1938.

9 Perth to Halifax, 30 November 1938, *BDFP*, Series III, Volume 3.

10 Perth to Halifax, 2 December 1938, *BDFP*, Series III, Volume 3.

11 Ciano, *Diary*, 30 November 1938.

12 Ciano, *Diary*, 3 December 1938.

13 Ciano, *Diary*, 9 December 1938.

14 Salerno, *Vital Crossroads*, 106.

15 Described in Robert Young, 'French Military Intelligence and the Franco-Italian Military Alliance, 1933–1939', *The Historical Journal*, 28 (1985), 143–68, 147.

16 Mallett, *The Italian Navy and Fascist Expansionism*, 65 and 115–16.

17 John Gooch, *Mussolini and his Generals: The Armed Forces and Fascist Foreign Policy, 1922–1940* (Cambridge, CUP, 2007), 384–449.

18 Salerno, *Vital Crossroads*, 89–90.

19 Bernd Juergen Fischer, 'King Zog and the Struggle for Stability in Albania' (Ph.D thesis, University of California, 1982), 487.

20 Moseley, *Mussolini's Shadow*, 55.

21 Ciano, *Diary*, 7 April 1939.

22 Ciano, *Diary*, 1 December 1938.

23 Ciano, *Diary*, 29 March 1939.

24 Morewood, *The British Defence of Egypt*, 131.

25 Dawn Miller, 'Dark Waters: Britain and Italy's Invasion of Albania, 7 April 1939', *International Journal of Intelligence and Counter-intelligence*, 16 (2003), 290–323.

26 Ryan, *The Last of the Dragomans*, 334, 340.

27 Ciano, *Diary*, 7 April 1939.

28 Bernd Fischer, *Albania at War, 1939–1945* (West Lafayette, Purdue University Press, 1999), 23.

29 Military Co-ordination Committee Minutes, 8 February 1940 printed in *Churchill War Papers* (New York, Norton, 1993 onwards), I, 731–2.

30 Playfair, *The Mediterranean & Middle East*, I, 31–5.

31 DCOS, 33rd Meeting, 30 January 1939, CAB104/72.

32 Victoria Schofield, *Wavell: Soldier and Statesman* (London, John Murray, 2006), 127.

33 RAF Narrative (First Draft): The RAF in Maritime War, Vol. 6: The Mediterranean and Red Sea, AIR41/19.

34 DCOS, 33rd Meeting, 30 January 1939, CAB104/72.

35 RAF Narrative (First Draft): The RAF in Maritime War, Vol. 6: The Mediterranean and Red Sea.

36 Cunningham to Pound (from Malta), 31 October 1939, *Cunningham Papers*.

37 Cunningham to Pound, 18 December 1939, *Cunningham Papers*.

38 Beaumont-Nesbitt (DDMI) to Ismay (CID), 26 October 1938, CAB104/72.

39 Vivian (SIS) to Hollis (JIC), 'Note on Proposed Combined Intelligence Bureau for Middle East', 16 December 1938, CAB104/72.

40 JIC 79, 'A Combined Intelligence Bureau for the Middle East', Note by the Deputy Director of Air Intelligence, 14 November 1938, CAB104/72.

41 Beaumont-Nesbitt (DDMI) to Ismay (CID), 26 October 1938, CAB104/72.

42 Miller, 'Dark Waters: Britain and Italy's Invasion of Albania, 7 April 1939', 290–323.

43 CID, Minutes of the 365th meeting, 11 May 1939, CAB104/72.

44 JIC (39) 21, 22 October 1939, CAB104/73.

45 F. H. Hinsley, *British Intelligence in the Second World War: Its Influence on Strategy and Operations* (5 vols, London, HMSO, 1979–1990), I; Michael Howard, *British Intelligence in the Second World War*, Volume V: *Strategic Deception* (London, HMSO, 1990); History of the Italian Military Section of the Combined Bureau Middle East, HW51/14; Synopsis for a History of Naval Sigint in the Mediterranean, 11 December 1945, HW50/39; Cunningham to Pound, 19 August 1940, *Cunningham Papers*.

46 Admiralty Views on Anglo-Turkish Relations, 30 August 1939, and Godfrey to Pound, 5 September 1939, quoted in Mustafa Sitki Bilqin and Steven Morewood, 'Turkey's Reliance on Britain: British Political and Diplomatic Support for Turkey against Soviet Demands, 1943–1947', *Middle Eastern Studies*, 40 (2004), 24–58.

47 Yucel Guclu, 'Turco-British Relations on the Eve of the Second World War', *Middle Eastern Studies*, 39 (2003), 159–96.

48 Majid Khadduri, 'The Alexandretta Dispute', *American Journal of International Law*, 39 (1945), 406–25; Robert Satloff, 'Prelude to Conflict: Communal Interdependence in the Sanjak of Alexandretta, 1920–1936', *Middle Eastern Studies*, 22 (1986), 147–80; Keith Watenpaugh, '"Creating Phantoms": Zaki al-Arsuzi, the Alexandretta Crisis, and the Formation of Modern Arab Nationalism in Syria', *International Journal of Middle East Studies*, 28 (1996), 363–89.

49 Brock Millman, 'Turkish Foreign and Strategic Policy, 1934–1942', *Middle Eastern Studies*, 31 (1995), 483–509.

50 Halifax to Knatchbull-Hugessen, 19 April 1939, *DBFP*, Series 3, Volume V.

51 Millman, *The Ill-Made Alliance*, 369–71.

52 Paul Preston, *Franco* (London, HarperCollins, 1993), 319.

53 Antonio Cazorla Sánchez, 'Surviving Franco's Peace: Spanish Popular Opinion during the Second World War', *European History Quarterly*, 32 (2002), 391–411.

54 Stanley Payne, *Franco and Hitler: Spain, Germany and World War II* (New Haven, Yale University Press, 2008), 46.

55 Mogens Pelt, 'The Establishment and Development of the Metaxas Dictatorship in the Context of Fascism and Nazism, 1936–1941', *Totalitarian Movements and Political Religions*, 2 (2001), 143–72; Harry Cliadakis, 'The Political and Diplomatic Background of the Metaxas Dictatorship, 1935–36', *Journal of Contemporary History*, 14 (1979), 117–38; T. D. Sfikas, 'A Tale of Parallel Lives: The Second Greek Republic and the Second Spanish Republic, 1924–1936', *European History Quarterly*, 29 (1999), 217–50.

56 'British Guarantee to Greece: Deep Gratitude Felt', *The Times*, 17 April 1939.

57 Pelt, 'Metaxas Dictatorship', 165.

58 Salerno, *Vital Crossroads*, 131.

59 Talbot Imlay, *Facing the Second World War: Strategy, Politics and Economics in Britain and France, 1938–1940* (Oxford, OUP, 2003), 49.

60 Ciano, *Diary*, 21–23 May 1939.

61 Gerhard Schreiber, 'Italy and the Mediterranean in the Power-Political Calculations of German Naval Leaders, 1919–1945' in Hattendorf, *Naval Policy and Strategy in the Mediterranean*, 108–43.

62 Mallett, *The Italian Navy and Fascist Expansionism*, 150–1.

63 Salerno, *Vital Crossroads*, 134–6.

64 Brian Sullivan, 'A Fleet in Being: The Rise and Fall of Italian Sea Power, 1861–1943', *International History Review*, 10 (1988), 106–24, 120.

65 George Fielding Eliot, 'Italy's Over-Estimated Power', *Harper's Monthly Magazine*, 176 (1938/9), 511–19.

66 Angela Raspin, *The Italian War Economy, 1940–1943: With Particular Reference to Italian Relations with Germany* (New York, 1986), 118–19.

67 Raspin, *Italian War Economy*, 110–12.

68 Moseley, *Mussolini's Shadow*, 82 and 106.

69 MacGregor Knox, *Mussolini Unleashed, 1939–1941: Politics and Strategy in Fascist Italy's Last War* (Cambridge, CUP, 1982), 44–133; Segrè, *Italo Balbo*, 377–83.

70 Harry Cliadakis, 'Neutrality and War in Italian Policy, 1939–1940', *Journal of Contemporary History*, 9 (1974), 171–90.

71 Mack Smith, *Mussolini's Roman Empire*, 207.

72 Salerno, *Vital Crossroads*, 191.

73 Morewood, *The British Defence of Egypt*, 142–3.

74 Salerno, *Vital Crossroads*, 191.

75 Mack Smith, *Mussolini's Roman Empire*, 213.

76 Ciano, *Diary*, 13 May 1940.

77 Knox, *Mussolini Unleashed*, 87.

78 Segrè, *Italo Balbo*, 377–83; Ciano, *Diary*, 9 June 1940.

CHAPTER FOUR

1 Hector Bywater, 'The Changing Balance of Forces in the Mediterranean', *International Affairs*, 16 (1937), 361–87.

2 Playfair, *Mediterranean and Middle East*, I, 90–7; Richard Overy, *The Air War 1939–1940*, Table 12; MGFA, *Germany and the Second World War*, III: *The Mediterranean, South-east Europe and North Africa, 1939–1941* (Oxford, OUP, 1995), 89.

The Balance of Power in the Mediterranean: Naval and Land-based Air Strength, Summer 1940

	Britain	Italy
Battleships	5	4
Aircraft-carriers	1	0
Heavy cruisers	0	7
Light cruisers	9	12
Submarines	12	113
Fighters	125	594
Bombers	150	783
Ground reconnaissance	24	268
Sea reconnaissance	10	151
Aircraft production in 1940	15,049	1,800

3 See table on the next page.

4 Marc' Antonio Bragadin, *The Italian Navy in World War II* (Annapolis, US Naval Institute, 1957), 15.

West–East passages of the Sicilian Narrows by multiple surface ships, 1940–41

Gibraltar sailing date	Purpose	Codename
30 August 1940	Warship reinforcements for eastern Mediterranean	HATS
7 November 1940	Warship reinforcements for eastern Mediterranean	Coat
25 November 1940	Tank transporters and troop transports to Alexandria	Collar
7 January 1941	Tank transporters to Alexandria, reinforcements to Piraeus, warship reinforcements to eastern Mediterranean	Excess
5 May 1941	Tank transporters and troopships to Alexandria	Tiger
21 July 1941	Naval reinforcements and convoy to Malta	Substance
30 July 1941	Naval reinforcements and troopships to Malta	Style
24 September 1941	Convoy to Malta	Halberd
16 October 1941	Naval reinforcements for eastern Mediterranean	Callboy
11 December 1941	Naval reinforcements for eastern Mediterranean	–
22 December 1941	Naval reinforcements for Malta	–

5 Cunningham to Pound, 27 June 1940 and 3 August 1940, *Cunningham Papers*.

6 Cunningham, *War Diary*, 6 August 1940, *Cunningham Papers*.

7 Cunningham to Pound, 22 September 1940, *Cunningham Papers*.

8 Bragadin, *Italian Navy*, 15–77; James Sadkovich, *The Italian Navy in World War II* (Westport, Praeger, 1994), 53–4, 100–5.

9 Cunningham to Pound, 17 June 1940, *Cunningham Papers*.

10 Somerville to Cunningham, 5 August 1940, reproduced in Michael Simpson (ed.), *The Somerville Papers: Selections from the Private and Official Correspondence of Admiral of the Fleet Sir James Somerville* (Aldershot, Scolar Press, 1995).

11 Raymond Dannreuther, *Somerville's Force H: The Royal Navy's Gibraltar-based Fleet, June 1940 to June 1942* (London, Aurum, 2005).

12 Jack Greene and Alessandro Massignani, *The Naval War in the Mediterranean, 1940–43* (Rochester, Chatham Publishing, 1998).

13 G. A. Titterton, *The Royal Navy and the Mediterranean*, I, *September 1939–October 1940* (London, Whitehall Publishing, 2001 reprint of 1952 Naval Staff History), Section 28; Hinsley, *British Intelligence in the Second World War*, I, 208–9.

14 MacGregor Knox, 'Fascist Italy Assesses its Enemies, 1935–1940' in Ernest May (ed.), *Knowing One's Enemies: Intelligence Assessment Before the Two World Wars* (Princeton, Princeton University Press, 1986), 347–72.

15 Alvarez, 'Left in the Dust: Italian Signals Intelligence, 1915–1943', 388–409, 399.

16 Moseley, *Mussolini's Shadow*, 105–6.

17 Somerville, Report on Proceedings, 30 August to 3 September, 14 September 1940, *Somerville Papers*. The formal designation of the Gull was CANT Z.501.

18 Ciano, *Diary*, 24 September 1940.

19 RAF Narrative (First Draft): The RAF in Maritime War, Vol. 6: The Mediterranean and Red Sea.

20 Darlan to Fernet, 'Can the British Reproach Us?', July 1940, in Hervé Coutau-Bégarie and Claude Huan (eds), *Lettres et Notes de l'Amiral Darlan* (Paris, Economica, 1992), Document 115.

21 Darlan's Notes on Events, 16 June to 31 December 1940, in Coutau-Bégarie and Huan, *Darlan*, Document 97.

22 David Brown, *The Road to Oran: Anglo-French Naval Relations, September 1939 to July 1940* (London, Frank Cass, 2003), 79.

23 War Cabinet Minutes, 22 June 1940, printed in *The Churchill War Papers* (New York, 1993 onwards), II, 395–7.

24 Brown, *Road to Oran*, 93–5.

25 'Considerations on the Continuation of the War from North Africa', 24 June 1940, in Coutau-Bégarie and Huan, *Darlan*, Document 106.

26 Ciano, *Diary*, 18 June 1940.

27 Somerville to Lady Somerville, 6 July 1940, *Somerville Papers*.

28 Philippe Lasterle, 'Could Admiral Gensoul Have Averted the Tragedy of Mers el-Kébir?', *Journal of Military History*, 67 (2003), 835–44.

29 Somerville to Lady Somerville, 24 July 1940, *Somerville Papers*.

30 Cunningham to Admiralty, 25 June 1940, *Cunningham Papers*.

31 Cunningham to Pound, 27 June 1940, *Cunningham Papers*.

32 Account of an interview between the British Naval C-in-C, Mediterranean Station, and Admiral Godfroy, Commanding French Force X, held on board *Warspite*, 3 July 1940, *Cunningham Papers*.

33 Cunningham to Admiralty, 4 July 1940, 13:17, *Cunningham Papers*.

34 Cunningham to Admiralty, 4 July 1940, 15:29, *Cunningham Papers*; Cunningham to Admiralty, 5 July 1940, *Cunningham Papers*.

35 Ronald Chalmers Hood, *Royal Republicans: French Naval Dynasties between the World Wars* (Baton Rouge, LSUP, 1985), 179–80.

36 Somerville to Lady Somerville, 4 July 1940, *Somerville Papers*.

37 Ciano, *Diary*, 4 July 1940.

38 Report on Proceedings, 11–14 September 1940, *Somerville Papers*.

39 Darlan's Explanation of the Armistice to Navy Officers at Vichy, 9 July 1940 in Coutau-Bégarie and Huan, *Darlan*; Martin Thomas, 'After Mers-el-Kébir: The Armed Neutrality of the Vichy French Navy, 1940–43', *English Historical Review*, 112 (1997), 643–70.

40 Somerville to Lady Somerville, 24 September 1940, *Somerville Papers*.

41 Somerville to Lady Somerville, 25 September 1940, *Somerville Papers*.

42 Mack Smith, *Mussolini's Roman Empire*, 222–8.

43 Moseley, *Mussolini's Shadow*, 109.

44 Ciano, *Diary*, 13 July 1940.

45 Cunningham, Report on an Action with the Italian Fleet, 9 July 1940, *Cunningham Papers*; Somerville, Report on Proceedings, 6–11 July 1940, *Somerville Papers*.

46 *The Royal Navy and the Mediterranean*, I, Section 22.

47 Cunningham, Report, 9 July 1940, *Cunningham Papers*.

48 Ciano, *Diary*, 13 July 1940.

49 Cunningham to Pound, 13 July 1940, *Cunningham Papers*.

50 Somerville, Report, 8 July 1940, and Somerville to Pound, 13 July 1940, *Somerville Papers*.

51 Churchill to Alexander and Pound, 15 July 1940, printed in *CWP*, II, 524–5.

52 Cunningham to Admiralty, 21 September 1940, enclosing Captain Collins's account of 20 July 1940, *Cunningham Papers*.

53 Ciano, *Diary*, 22 July 1940.

54 Cunningham, Rescue of Survivors from Enemy Ships, 22 July 1940, *Cunningham Papers*.

55 Somerville to Pound, 11 August 1940, *Somerville Papers*.

56 Bernard Freyberg, *Diary*, 8 July 1940, printed in *CWP*, II, 494–5.

57 Defence Committee Minutes, 12 August 1940, printed in *CWP*, II, 656.

58 Pound to Cunningham, 14 August 1940, *Cunningham Papers*.

59 Churchill to A. V. Alexander, 7 September 1940, printed in *CWP*, II, 785–6; Cunningham, Operation HATS, 29 August to 5 September 1940, 14 January 1941, *Cunningham Papers*; Somerville, Report on Proceedings, 30 August to 3 September 1940, 14 September 1940, *Somerville Papers*.

60 Churchill to Ismay, 19 September 1940, printed in *CWP*, II, 838.

61 Ciano, *Diary*, 3 August 1940.

62 *CWP*, 25 August 1940.

63 Ciano, *Diary*, 7 September 1940.

64 Graziani's diary, 7 September 1940, quoted in Knox, *Mussolini Unleashed*, 163.

65 Mussolini to Graziani, 18 August 1940, quoted in Knox, *Mussolini Unleashed*, 161.

66 Mediterranean Fleet War Diary, 10 to 14 June 1940, *Cunningham Papers*.

67 De Vecchi to Ciano, 12 July 1940, quoted in Knox, *Mussolini Unleashed*, 167.

68 Ciano, *Diary*, 12 August 1940.

69 Knox, *Mussolini Unleashed*, 170–3.

70 Ciano, *Diary*, 30 September 1940.

71 Norman Goda, 'The Riddle of the Rock: A Reassessment of German Motives for the Capture of Gibraltar in the Second World War', *Journal of Contemporary History* 28 (1993), 297–314, 299.

72 Martin van Creveld, 'October 25 1940: A Historical Puzzle', *Journal of Contemporary History*, 6 (1971), 87–96.

73 Ciano, *Diary*, 25 October 1940.

74 Ian Kershaw, *Hitler: Nemesis, 1936–1945* (London, Penguin, 2000), 327–32.

75 Ciano, *Diary*, 12 October 1940.

76 Preston, *Franco*, 393–8; Payne, *Franco and Hitler*, 87–113.

77 Darlan to Pétain, 8 November 1940, in Coutau-Bégarie and Huan, *Darlan*, Document 142.

78 Ciano, *Diary*, 28 October 1940.

79 Konstantinos Polyzois *et al.*, *An Abridged History of the Greek-Italian and Greek-German War (Land Operations)* (Athens, Army History Directorate Editions, 1997), 36–111.

80 James Sadkovich, 'Italian Morale during the Italo-Greek War of 1940–41', *War and Society*, 12 (1994), 97–123, 107–8.

81 Ciano, *Diary*, 12 November 1940.

82 Ciano, *Diary*, 1 November 1940.

83 Somerville to Blake, 7 July 1940, *Somerville Papers*.

84 Report on Fleet Air Operations against Taranto on 11 November 1940, 16 January 1941, *Cunningham Papers*.

85 Report on Operation MB8, 6–14 November 1940, 3 March 1941, *Cunningham Papers*; Somerville, Report on Proceedings, 7–11 November 1940, 12 November 1940, *Somerville Papers*.

86 Ciano, *Diary*, 12 November 1940.

87 Somerville to Lady Somerville, 15 November 1940, *Somerville Papers*; Somerville to Lady Somerville, 17 November 1940, *Somerville Papers*.

88 Cunningham to Pound, 21 November 1940, *Cunningham Papers*.

89 Report on Operation COLLAR, 23–30 November 1940, 20 July 1941, *Cunningham Papers*.

90 Somerville to Lady Somerville, 11 December 1940, *Somerville Papers*.

91 Report on Proceedings, 19–29 November 1940, 5 December 1940, *Somerville Papers*.

92 Report on Proceedings, 19–29 November 1940, 5 December 1940, *Somerville Papers*.

93 Somerville, Observations on the Action off Cape Spartivento, 18 December 1940, *Somerville Papers*.

94 Somerville to Lady Somerville, 28 November 1940, *Somerville Papers*.

95 Report on Proceedings, 19–29 November 1940, 5 December 1940, *Somerville Papers*.

96 Somerville to Admiralty, 6 December 1940, *Somerville Papers*; Cunningham to Somerville, 30 December 1940, *Somerville Papers*; Somerville to Cunningham, 8 January 1941, *Somerville Papers*.

97 Ciano, *Diary*, 5 December 1940.

98 Playfair, *The Mediterranean and Middle East*, I, 257–75; Schofield, *Wavell: Soldier and Statesman*, 145–64.

99 War Cabinet Confidential Annex, 16 December 1940, printed in *CWP*, II, 1243.

100 Directive No. 21, 'Case Barbarossa', 18 December 1940, in Hugh Trevor-Roper (ed.), *Hitler's War Directives, 1939–1945* (Edinburgh, Birlinn, 2004).

101 Ciano, *Diary*, 20 December 1940.

CHAPTER FIVE

1 Schofield, *Wavell*, 170.

2 Ciano, *Diary*, 11 January 1941.

3 'Mr. Churchill Speaks to the Italian People: Mussolini's Deed of Shame and Folly', *The Times*, 24 December 1940.

4 Ciano, *Diary*, 22 January 1941.

5 Fred Taylor (ed.), *The Goebbels Diaries, 1939–1941* (New York, Putnam's, 1983), 20 and 22 December 1940.

6 Charles Burdick and Hans-Adolf Jacobsen (eds), *The Halder War Diary, 1939–1942* (London, Greenhill, 1988), 5 December 1940.

7 James Corum, 'The *Luftwaffe* and its Allied Air Forces in World War II: Parallel War and the Failure of Strategic and Economic Co-operation', *Air Power History*, 51 (2004), 4–20.

8 Report on Operation *Excess*, 19 March 1941, *Cunningham Papers*.

9 Cunningham to Pound, 18 January 1941, *Cunningham Papers*.

10 Ciano, *Diary*, 10 January 1941.

11 Goebbels, *Diary*, 22 December 1940.

12 Halder, *Diary*, [9] January 1941.

13 Ciano, *Diary*, 17–21 January 1941.

14 Minutes of Defence Committee (Operations), 13 January 1941, printed in *CWP*, III, 84–6 and Minutes of

Defence Committee (Operations), 20 January 1941, printed in *CWP*, III, 101–4.

15 Robert Rhodes James (ed.), *Chips: The Diaries of Sir Henry Channon* (London, Phoenix, 1996), 2 January 1941.

16 Ciano, *Diary*, 18–19 November 1940; Halder, *Diary*, 18–19 November and 28 November 1940; Hitler Directive No. 20, 20 December 1940.

17 Channon, *Diary*, 8–9 January 1941.

18 Channon, *Diary*, 10 January 1941.

19 Channon, *Diary*, 12 January 1941.

20 Somerville, 6 and 10 February 1941, *Somerville Papers*.

21 Halder, *Diary*, 3 February 1941.

22 Goebbels, *Diary*, 13 February 1941.

23 Minutes of Defence Committee (Operations), 10 February 1941, printed in *CWP*, III, 200–1; Cadogan, *Diary*, 10 February 1941 in David Dilks (ed.), *The Diaries of Sir Alexander Cadogan 1938–45* (London, Cassell, 1971); Churchill to Wavell, 12 February 1941, printed in *CWP*, III, 212–14; Pierson Dixon, *Diary*, 15 February 1941, in Piers Dixon, *Double Diploma: The Life of Sir Pierson Dixon* (London, Hutchinson, 1968).

24 Dixon, *Diary*, 19 February 1941.

25 Lampson, *Diary*, 19 February 1941, in Trefor Evans (ed.), *The Killearn Diaries, 1934–1946: The Diplomatic and Personal Record of Lord Killearn (Sir Miles Lampson), High Commissioner and Ambassador, Egypt* (London, Sidgwick and Jackson, 1972).

26 Channon, *Diary*, 3 January 1941.

27 Dixon, *Diary*, 20–21 February 1941; Martin van Creveld, 'Prelude to Disaster: The British Decision to Aid Greece', *Journal of Contemporary History*, 9 (1974), 65–92; Sheila Lawlor, 'Greece, March 1941: The Politics of British Military Intervention', *Historical Journal*, 25 (1982), 933–46.

28 Eden to Churchill, 20 February 1941, *Cunningham Papers*; Cadogan, *Diary*, 23 and 24 February 1941.

29 Dixon, *Diary*, 26 February 1941.

30 Cadogan, *Diary*, 28 February and 1 March 1941; Churchill to Eden, 1 March 1941, printed in *CWP*, III, 299.

31 Cadogan, *Diary*, 5 March 1941; Churchill to Eden, 5 March 1941, printed in *CWP*, III, 311–12 and War Cabinet Minutes, 6 March 1941, printed in *CWP*, III, 324–5.

32 Cunningham, *War Diary*, January and February 1941, *Cunningham Papers*.

33 Goebbels, *Diary*, 14 January 1941.

34 Cunningham, *War Diary*, February 1941 and Cunningham to Pound, 11 March 1941, *Cunningham Papers*.

35 Cadogan, *Diary*, 19 March 1941.

36 Charles Burdick, '"Moro": The Resupply of German Submarines in Spain, 1939–1942', *Central European History*, 3 (1970), 256–84.

37 Somerville to Lady Somerville, 5 January 1941, *Somerville Papers*.

38 Robert Melka, 'Darlan between Britain and Germany, 1940–41', *Journal of Contemporary History*, 8 (1973), 57–80; Darlan, 'Reflections on the Situation of the Belligerents', 7 April 1941, Coutau-Bégarie and Huan, *Darlan*.

39 Churchill to Eden, 2 May 1941, printed in *CWP*, III, 593.

40 Churchill to Halifax, 18 March 1941, printed in *CWP*, III, 366; War Cabinet Minutes, 27 March 1941, printed in *CWP*, III, 411–12.

41 Goebbels, *Diary*, 20 April 1941.

42 Churchill to Eden, 5 March 1941, printed in *CWP*, III, 311–12.

43 War Cabinet Minutes, 6 March 1941, printed in *CWP*, III, 324–5.

44 Cadogan, *Diary*, 6 March 1941.

45 Lawlor, 'Greece, March 1941', 933–46.

46 Channon, *Diary*, 14 March 1941.

47 Pound to Cunningham, 16 March 1941, *Cunningham Papers*.

48 Cunningham to Pound, 11 March 1941, *Cunningham Papers*.

49 Cadogan, *Diary*, 19 March 1941.

50 Dixon, *Diary*, 25 March 1941.

51 Lampson, *Diary*, 15 March 1941; Dixon, *Diary*, 18–19 March 1941.

52 Goebbels, *Diary*, 21 March 1941 and Halder, *Diary*, 20–21 March 1941.

53 Cunningham's Dispatch on the Battle of Matapan, 27–30 March 1941, 11 November 1941, *Cunningham Papers*; Colville, *Diary*, 30 March 1941, quoted in *CWP*, III, 423–4.

54 Goebbels, *Diary*, 27, 30 and 31 March 1941.

55 David Stafford, 'SOE and British Involvement in the Belgrade Coup d'Etat of March 1941', *Slavic Review*, 36 (1977), 399–419; Simon Trew, *Britain, Mihailović and the Chetniks, 1941–42* (Basingstoke, 1998), 37.

56 Andrzej Krzak, 'Operation *Marita*: The Attack Against Yugoslavia in 1941', *Journal of Slavic Military Studies*, 19 (2006), 543–600.

57 Hitler Directives, 25, 26 and 27; Goebbels, *Diary*, 27 and 28 March 1941, 6 April 1941.

58 Goebbels, *Diary*, 7 April 1941.

59 James Sadkovich, *Italian Support for Croatian Separatism, 1927–1937* (New York, Garland, 1987).

60 Jozo Tomasevich, *War and Revolution in Yugoslavia, 1941–45: Occupation and Collaboration* (Stanford, 2001), 58–9.

61 Dixon, *Diary*, 27–28 March 1941.

62 Lampson, *Diary*, 27 March 1941.

63 Goebbels, *Diary*, 1 April 1941.

64 Goebbels, *Diary*, 2 April 1941.

65 Dixon, *Diary*, 31 March 1941.

66 Larry Addington, 'Operation Sunflower: Rommel versus the General Staff', *Military Affairs*, 31 (1967), 120–30.

67 Churchill to Eden, 3 April 1941, quoted in *CWP*, III, 445.

68 Goebbels, *Diary*, 6 April 1941.

69 Lampson, *Diary*, 5, 6 and 20 April 1941.

70 Dixon, *Diary*, 6 April 1941; Channon, *Diary*, 7 and 10 April 1941; Cadogan, *Diary*, 7 and 10 April 1941.

71 Goebbels, *Diary*, 9 April 1941.

72 Cunningham to Pound, 10 April 1941.

73 Lampson, *Diary*, 14 April 1941.

74 Lampson, *Diary*, 20 April 1941; Dill to Churchill, 6 May 1941, quoted in Alex Danchev, '"Dilly-Dally", or Having the Last Word: FM Sir John Dill and PM Winston Churchill', *Journal of Contemporary History*, 22 (1987), 21–44.

75 Churchill to Alexander and Pound, 12 April 1941, quoted in *CWP*, III, 483; Churchill to Wavell, 14 April 1941, quoted in *CWP*, III, 492.

76 Minutes of ME Cs-in-C Meeting, Cairo, 9 April 1941, *Cunningham Papers*.

77 Cunningham to Pound, 10 April 1941, *Cunningham Papers*.

78 Pound to Cunningham, 11 April 1941, *Cunningham Papers*.

79 Churchill to Alexander and Pound, 12 April 1941, quoted in *CWP*, III, 483.

80 Admiralty to Cunningham, 15 April 1941 and Cunningham to Admiralty, 15 April 1941, *Cunningham Papers*.

81 Report of an Action against an Italian Convoy, 15–16 April 1941, 8 June 1941', *Cunningham Papers*.

82 Churchill to Longmore, 18 April 1941, quoted in *CWP*, III, 512–13.

83 Churchill to Cunningham, 16 April 1941, *Cunningham Papers*.

84 Halder, *Diary*, 15 April 1941; Goebbels, *Diary*, 16 April 1941.

85 Goebbels, *Diary*, 23 and 29 April 1941; Ciano, *Diary*, 27 and 28 April 1941.

86 SOE Activities in Greece, 1940–1942, by Major Ian Pirie, October 1945, HS7/150.

87 Cunningham to Pound, 22 April 1941; Pound to Cunningham, 23 April 1941, *Cunningham Papers*.

88 Cunningham to Pound, 25 April 1941; Churchill to Cunningham, 26 April 1941, printed in *CWP*, III, 545–6.

89 Cunningham to Churchill, 29 April 1941, *Cunningham Papers*.

90 Cunningham to Pound, 26 April 1941, *Cunningham Papers*.

91 Ismay to Churchill, 11 November 1946, recalling the meetings with the COS on 20 April 1941, quoted in *CWP*, III, 521.

92 Admiralty to C-in-C, Mediterranean, 1 May 1941; Churchill to Cunningham, 1 May 1941; Cunningham to Admiralty, 2 May 1941, *Cunningham Papers*.

93 Channon, *Diary*, 6 May 1941 and Cuthbert Headlam, Diary, 6 May 1941 in Stuart Ball (ed.), *Parliament and Politics in the Age of Churchill and Attlee: The Headlam Diaries, 1935–1941* (Cambridge, CUP, 1999).

94 Cadogan, *Diary*, 30 May 1941.

95 Ciano, *Diary*, 3 May 1941; Goebbels, *Diary*, 3 and 11 May 1941, Halder, *Diary*, 11 May 1941.

96 Somerville, Report on Proceedings, 28 April to 12 May 1941, and Somerville to Dudley North, 14 May 1941, *Cunningham Papers*; Colville, *Diary*, 9 May 1941, printed in *CWP*, III, 641; Cunningham to Pound, 18 May 1941.

97 Hitler Directive No. 28, 25 April 1941.

98 Cunningham to Pound, 23 May 1941; Cunningham to Admiralty, 26 May 1941, *Cunningham Papers*.

CHAPTER SIX

1 Olivia Manning, *The Balkan Trilogy*, III: *Friends and Heroes* (London, Arrow, 2004. The Balkan Trilogy was written between 1956 and 1964).

2 Walter Ansel, *Hitler and the Middle Sea* (Durham, Duke UP, 1972).

3 Halford Mackinder, 'The Geographical Pivot of History', *Geographical Journal*, 23 (1904), 421–37; *idem*, 'Progress of Geography in the Field and in the Study during the Reign of His Majesty King George the Fifth', *Geographical Journal*, 86 (1935), 1–12.

4 Hitler Directive No. 32, 11 June 1941.

5 Klaus Schmider, 'The Mediterranean in 1940–1941: Crossroads of Lost Opportunities?', *War & Society*, 15 (1997), 19–41.

6 Cunningham to Pound, 28 and 30 May 1941, *Cunningham Papers*.

7 Cunningham to the Admiralty, 2 June 1941, *Cunningham Papers*.

8 RAF Narrative (First Draft): The RAF in Maritime War, Vol. 6: The Mediterranean and Red Sea.

9 Darlan's Message to the Council of Ministers, 14 May 1941 in Coutau-Bégarie and Huan, *Darlan*.

10 Geoffrey Warner, *Iraq and Syria, 1941* (London, Davis-Poynter, 1974).

11 Winston Churchill, Draft Note on Syrian Policy, 19 May 1941, printed in *CWP*, III, 686–7.

12 Khoury, *Syria and the French Mandate*, 584–618.

13 H. O. Dovey, 'Security in Syria, 1941–1945', *Intelligence and National Security*, 6 (1991), 422; Maxime Rodinson, 'Aux Origines du "Pacte Nationale": Contribution à l'Histoire de la Crise Franco-Libanaise de Novembre 1943', *Die Welt des Islams*, 28 (1988), 445–74.

14 D/HP to CD, 19 May 1941, HS3/154.

15 N. E. Bou Nacklie, 'The 1941 Invasion of Syria and Lebanon: the Role of the Local Paramilitary', *Middle Eastern Studies*, 30 (1994), 512–29, and 'Les Troupes Speciales: Religious and Ethnic Recruitment, 1916–1946', *International Journal of Middle East Studies*, 25 (1993), 645–60.

16 Lenni Brenner, 'Zionism-Revisionism: The Years of Fascism and Terror', *Journal of Palestine Studies*, 13 (1983), 66–92, and *Zionism in the Age of the Dictators* (London, 1983); Hava Eshkoli-Wagman, 'Yishuv Zionism: Its Attitude to Nazism and the Third Reich Reconsidered', *Modern Judaism*, 19 (1999), 21–40; Ronald Davies, 'Jewish Military Recruitment in Palestine, 1940–43', *Journal of Palestine Studies*, 8 (1979), 55–76.

17 Report by D/HO on SO Activities in Palestine and Transjordan, 2 May 1941, HS3/154.

18 'History of SOE in the Arab World', September 1945, HS7/86.

19 Dalton to Wavell, 11 June 1941, HS3/189.

20 Saul Kelly, 'A Succession of Crises: SOE in the Middle East, 1940–45', *Intelligence and National Security*, 20 (2005), 121–46; Simon Anglim, 'MI(R), G(R) and British Covert Operations, 1939–1942', *Intelligence and National Security*, 20 (2005), 631–53.

21 Simon Trew, *Britain, Mihailović and the Chetniks*, 42–3.

22 'History of SOE in the Arab World', September 1945.

23 Nicholas Tamkin, 'Britain, the Middle East, and the "Northern Front", 1941–42', *War in History*, 15 (2008), 314–36.

24 Somerville to North, 15 June 1941 and Somerville, Report on Proceedings, 7–15 June 1941, 18 June 1941, *Somerville Papers*.

25 Minute by W. H. B. Mack (reviewing the history of Force X), 17 July 1942, FO371/31894.

26 Cunningham, *War Diary*, June 1941 and Report on Syrian Campaign, 2 September 1941, *Cunningham Papers*.

27 Schofield, *Wavell*, 194–211.

28 Darlan's notes on foreign affairs, 6 June 1941; Darlan to Weygand, 17 June 1941; Darlan's notes on the Syrian Campaign, 24 July 1941; in Coutau-Bégarie and Huan, *Darlan*.

29 Churchill to Auchinleck, 6 July 1941, printed in *CWP*, III, 901–3.

30 'The German-Arab *Lehrabteilung* and other recent Abwehr Activity in North Africa', 22 February 1943, HW13/52.

31 Hirszowicz, *The Third Reich and the Arab East*, 173–92.

32 Lampson to Eden, 12 July 1941, FO954/5.

33 G. E. Maguire, *Anglo-American Policy towards the Free French* (Basingstoke, Macmillan, 1995); A. B. Gaunson, *The Anglo-French Clash in Lebanon and Syria, 1940–45* (Basingstoke, Macmillan, 1987); Martin Thomas, *The French Empire at War* (Manchester, MUP, 1998); Meir Zamir, 'De Gaulle and the Question of Syria and Lebanon during the Second World War', *Middle Eastern Studies*, 43 (2007), 675–708.

34 Cunningham to Pound, 25 July 1941, *Cunningham Papers*.

35 Lyttelton to Churchill, 15 August 1941 and Lyttelton to Foreign Office, 17 August 1941, quoted in Gaunson, *Lebanon and Syria*, 57–9.

36 Dovey, 'Security in Syria, 1941–1945', 418–46.

37 Lyttelton to Dalton, 10 July 1941, FO954/24.

38 Jean-Louis Crémieux-Brilhac, *La France Libre: De l'appel du 18 Juin à la Libération* (Paris, Gallimard, 1996), 143–70.

39 Mrs Warner, Preliminary Brief on the Early History of the Middle East Supply Centre, CAB102/432.

40 Violetta Hionidou, 'Black Market, Hyperinflation, and Hunger: Greece, 1941–1944', *Food & Foodways*, 12 (2004), 81–106.

41 Ciano, *Diary*, 9 October 1941.

42 SOE Activities in Greece, 1940–1942 by Major Ian Pirie, October 1945.

43 Milovan Djilas, *Wartime* (New York, Harcourt Brace Jovanovich, 1977), 68–9; William Mackenzie, *The Secret History of SOE: Special Operations Executive, 1940–1945* (London, St Ermin's Press, 2000, a published version of the official history of SOE finished in 1947), 117–18; Mark Wheeler, 'Pariahs to Partisans to Power: The Communist Party of Yugoslavia' in Tony Judt (ed.), *Resistance and Revolution in Mediterranean Europe, 1939–1948* (London, Routledge, 1989), 110–56.

44 Alan Moorehead, *African Trilogy: The Desert War, 1940–1943*, II: *A Year of Battle: The Year of Auchinleck, 1941–42* (London, 1944), 194.

45 Crookshank to Eden, 22 August 1941, FO954/31.

46 Churchill to Ismay, 20 June 1941, printed in *CWP*, III, 828–9.

47 Cunningham to Pound, 25 July 1941, *Cunningham Papers*.

48 Hinsley, *British Intelligence in the Second World War*, I, 375–402 and II, 277–340.

49 Corum, 'The *Luftwaffe* and its Allied Air Forces in World War II', 4–20.

50 Somerville, Report on Operation SUBSTANCE, 4 August 1941 and Somerville to North, 30 July 1941, *Somerville Papers*.

51 Somerville, Report on Operation *Halberd*, 24–30 September 1941, 9 October 1941, and Somerville to Cunningham, 6 October 1941, *Somerville Papers*.

52 Sönke Neitzel, '*Kriegsmarine* and *Luftwaffe* Co-operation in the War against Britain, 1939–1945', *War in History*, 10 (2003), 448–63.

53 CX/M33/202/T11, 1941, HW1/42.

54 Churchill to Pound, 3 September 1941, printed in *CWP*, III, 1150.

55 Cunningham to Pound, 25 July 1941, and 18 September 1941, *Cunningham Papers*.

56 Cunningham, *War Diary*, September 1941, *Cunningham Papers*.

57 Ciano, *Diary*, 1 October 1941 and 1 November 1941.

58 Report of the Commander-in-Chief, Navy to the Fuehrer, 20 April 1941; Conference of the Commander-in-Chief, Navy with the Fuehrer at HQ Wolfsschanze in the afternoon of 25 July 1941; Report by the Commander-in-Chief, Navy to the Fuehrer in Berlin, 12 December 1941, *Fuehrer Conferences on Naval Affairs, III, 1941* (London, Admiralty, October 1947); The RAF in Maritime War, Volume VII, Part I: Mediterranean Reconquest and the Submarine War, May 1943–May 1944, Appendix 5: German U-Boats Detailed for the Mediterranean and the Account

of their Fate, September 1941 to September 1944, AIR41/54.

Strength of U-boat force in the Mediterranean

Date	Total in Med.
10 October 1941	6
30 November 1941	13
18 January 1942	21
4 August 1942	15
30 October 1942	18
11 November 1942	25
31 December 1942	23
28 March 1943	17
24 April 1943	18
7 May 1943	20
30 May 1943	18
12 September 1943	12
30 October 1943	14
30 November 1943	15
16 December 1943	13
30 January 1944	18
6 April 1944	14
21 May 1944	11
24 September 1944	0

59 Conference of the Commander-in-Chief, Navy with the Fuehrer at HQ Wolfsschanze in the afternoon of 25 July 1941, *Fuehrer Conferences on Naval Affairs, III, 1941* (London, Admiralty, October 1947).

60 Cunningham to Pound, 11 September 1941, *Cunningham Papers*.

61 Pound to Cunningham, 11 October 1941, *Cunningham Papers*.

62 Ciano, *Diary*, 9 and 10 November 1941.

63 Lawrence Paterson, *U-Boats in the Mediterranean* (London, Chatham Publishing, 2007).

64 Somerville to Lady Somerville, 14 November 1941 and Somerville to Cunningham, 18 November 1941, *Somerville Papers*.

CHAPTER SEVEN

1 Selborne to Eden, 9 June 1942, HS3/155.

2 Eden to Dalton, 12 February 1942, HS3/189.

3 David Garnett, *The Secret History of PWE: The Political Warfare Executive, 1939–1945* (London, St Ermin's Press, 2002, published version of classified official history completed c. 1945), 143–7.

4 Minister of State, Cairo to Foreign Office, Tel. 3806, 3 December 1941, HS3/189.

5 Moorehead, *A Year of Battle*, 248.

6 Churchill to Ismay, 24 November 1941, printed in *CWP*, III, 1502–4.

7 John Ferris, 'The "Usual Source": Signals Intelligence and Planning for the Eighth Army *Crusader* Offensive, 1941', *Intelligence and National Security*, 14 (1999), 84–118.

8 Hermione Ranfurly, *To War with Whitaker: The Wartime Diaries of the Countess of Ranfurly, 1939–1945* (London, Mandarin, 1997), 10 February 1941.

9 Moorehead, *A Year of Battle*, 234. Italian intelligence intercepted and decoded his reports. Fellers's detailed commentary on the unfolding battle, won with such initiative, was favoured reading in Rome.

10 Bill Close, *A View from the Turret: A History of the 3rd RTR in the Second World War* (Tewkesbury, Dell & Bredon, 1998), 62–3.

11 Close, *View from the Turret*, 63–4.

12 Playfair, *Mediterranean and Middle East*, III, 46.

13 Basil Liddell Hart (ed.), *The Rommel Papers* (London, Collins, 1953), 23 November 1941.

14 Rommel, *Papers*, 27 November 1941.

15 Walker, *Iron Hulls, Iron Hearts: Mussolini's Elite Armoured Divisions in North Africa* (Marlborough, Crowood, 2006), 92–3.

16 Ciano, *Diary*, 29 November 1941.

17 ACAS (I), *The Rise and Fall of the German Air Force, 1933–1945* (Air Ministry, Restricted Report, 1948, published by the National Archives, 2008), 129–59; 'GAF Supply Organization in the Libyan Campaign', 12 February 1942, HW13/52.

18 Albert Kesselring, *Memoirs* (London, William Kimber, 1953), 103–36.

19 Anthony De Luca, '*Der Grossmufti* in Berlin: The Politics of Collaboration', *International Journal of Middle East Studies*, 10 (1979), 125–38; Hirszowicz, *Third Reich and Arab Near East*, 218–21.

20 Ciano, *Diary*, 1 December 1941.

21 Lucio Ceva, 'The North African Campaign, 1940–1943: A Reconsideration', *Journal of Strategic Studies*, 13 (1990), 84–104; James

Sadkovich, 'Of Myths and Men: Rommel and the Italians in North Africa, 1940–1942', *International History Review*, 13 (1991), 284–313.

22 Moorehead, *A Year of Battle*, 252.

23 Rommel, *Papers*, 12 December 1941.

24 Rommel, *Papers*, 20 December 1941.

25 Hans Ahlmann, 'La Libye Septentrionale: Études de Géographie Physique et Humaine', *Geografiska Annaler*, 10 (1928), 1–118.

26 Moorehead, *A Year of Battle*, 254–7.

27 Sadkovich, *The Italian Navy in World War II*, 203.

28 Pound to Cunningham, 23 November 1941; Churchill to Cunningham, 23 November 1941; Cunningham to Pound, 24 November 1941; Cunningham to Churchill, 1941, *Cunningham Papers*.

29 Cunningham to Pound, 4 December 1941, *Cunningham Papers*.

30 Somerville to Cunningham, 5 December 1941, *Somerville Papers*.

31 Somerville to Cunningham, 16 December 1941, *Somerville Papers*.

32 Ciano, *Diary*, 13 December 1941.

33 Ciano, *Diary*, 17 December 1941.

34 Cunningham, *War Diary*, December 1941 and Cunningham to Pound, 28 December 1941, *Cunningham Papers*.

35 Luigi Durand de la Penne and Virgilio Spigal, 'The Italian Attack on the Alexandria Naval Base', *United States Naval Institute Proceedings*, 82 (1956), 125–35.

36 Cunningham, *War Diary*, December 1941, *Cunningham Papers*.

37 Ciano, *Diary*, 10 December 1941.

38 Verbal Note of Juin's Report to Darlan and Pétain upon his return from talks with Göring and Warlimont, 22 December 1941, Coutau-Bégarie and Huan, *Darlan*.

39 Darlan's Thoughts on the Situation, December 1941/January 1942, *Darlan*.

40 Ciano, *Diary*, 5 February 1942.

41 'Vichy Supplies to Rommel', *The Times*, 11 February 1942.

42 Note by Darlan, 9 February 1942; Darlan to Head of Italian Armistice Commission, 10 February 1942, Coutau-Bégarie and Huan, *Darlan*.

43 Ford to Cunningham, 3 January 1942, *Cunningham Papers*.

44 Cunningham to Pound, 28 December 1941, *Cunningham Papers*; Willis to Cunningham, 2 February 1942, *Cunningham Papers*.

45 Douglas Austin, *Malta and British Strategic Policy, 1925–1943* (London, Frank Cass, 2004), 125.

46 Cunningham to Moore, 9 January 1942, *Cunningham Papers*.

47 Cunningham to Admiralty, 10 January 1942, *Cunningham Papers*.

48 Playfair, *Mediterranean and Middle East*, III, 126–7.

49 Rommel, *Papers*, 17 January 1942.

50 Rommel, *Papers*, 21 January 1942.

51 Rommel, *Papers*, 23 January 1942.

52 Rommel, *Papers*, 25 January 1942.

53 Rommel, *Papers*, 4 February 1942.

54 Martin Kitchen, *Rommel's Desert War: Waging World War II in North Africa, 1941–1943* (Cambridge, CUP, forthcoming).

55 Charles Smith, '4 February 1942: Its Causes and its Influence on Egyptian Politics and the Future of Anglo-Egyptian Relations, 1937–1945', *International Journal of Middle East Studies*, 10 (1979), 453–79.

56 Maunsell to Petrie, 24 January 1942, KV4/306.

57 Lampson, *Diary*, 22 January 1942.

58 Lampson, *Diary*, 2 February 1942.

59 Lampson, *Diary*, 4 February 1942.

60 Lampson, *Diary*, 5 February 1942.

61 Report by DSO, The Borsa Incident, 1 May 1942, FO371/31563.

62 T. H. Preston (Middle East Relief and Refugee Agency, British Embassy Repatriation Office, Cairo) to Secretary, External Affairs Department, Government of India, 11 February 1942, FO371/31563.

63 RAF Section, CSDIC ME Report No. A.11/1944, 2 March 1944, AIR 40/3111.

64 V.w. Report 28, 30 June 1942, KV3/74.

65 Middle East Joint Planning Staff Paper No. 73: Subversive Activities Middle East, 5 December 1941, HS3/155.

66 Stevan Pavlowitch, 'Out of Context – The Yugoslav Government in London, 1941–1945', *Journal of Contemporary History*, 16 (1981), 89–118.

67 SOE Activities in Greece, 1940–1942, by Major Ian Pirie, October 1945.

68 SOE Cairo to SOE London, Tel. 540, 18 September 1942, HS5/472; Christina Goulter-Zervoudakis, 'The Politicization of Intelligence: The British Experience in Greece, 1941–1944', *Intelligence and National Security*, 13 (1998), 165–94; Spyridon Ploumidis, 'British Propaganda towards Greece, 1940–1944', *Southeast European and Black Sea Studies*, 6 (2006), 407–26.

69 SOE Activities in Greece, 1940–1942, by Major Ian Pirie, October 1945.

70 Mark Mazower, *Inside Hitler's Greece: The Experience of Occupation, 1941–1944* (New Haven, YUP, 1993), 107.

71 Brooke, *Diary*, 17 April 1942 in Alex Danchev and Dan Todman (eds), *Field Marshal Lord Alanbrooke: War Diaries, 1939–1945* (London, Weidenfeld & Nicolson, 2001).

72 Cunningham to Pound, 15 March 1942, *Cunningham Papers*.

73 Cunningham, Memorandum on Command in the Middle East, 10 June 1942, *Cunningham Papers*.

74 Cunningham, *War Diary*, February 1942, Cunningham to Pound, 14 February 1942 and Cunningham to Pound, 15 March 1942, *Cunningham Papers*.

75 Report by the Commander-in-Chief, Navy to the Fuehrer, 13 February 1942, *Fuehrer Conferences on Naval Affairs, IV, 1942* (London, Admiralty, June 1947).

76 Brooke, *War Diary*, 24 February 1942.

77 Winston Churchill, *The Second World War, IV: The Hinge of Fate* (London, Cassell, 1951), 268–9.

78 W. J. Hudson, *Casey* (Melbourne, OUP, 1986), 137–55.

79 Kesselring, *Memoirs*, 122.

80 The Hon. Mabel Strickland, 'Malta, G. C., Yesterday, To-day and To-morrow', *Journal of the Royal Society of Arts*, 92 (1943), 18–28.

81 Michael Simpson, 'Superhighway to the World Wide Web: The Mediterranean in British Imperial Strategy' in Hattendorf, *Naval Policy and Strategy in the Mediterranean*, 51–76.

CHAPTER EIGHT

1 Alan Levine, *The War Against Rommel's Supply Lines, 1942–1943* (Westport, 1999).

2 Ciano, *Diary*, 21 June 1942.

3 Hinsley, *British Intelligence*, II, 341–98.

4 Channon, *Diary*, 1 July 1942.

5 Ciano, *Diary*, 20 May 1942.

6 Ciano, *Diary*, 11 June 1942.

7 MGFA, *Germany and the Second World War, VI: The Global War, 1941–1943* (Oxford, OUP, 2001), 661–92; Playfair, *Mediterranean and Middle East*, III, 223–52; Crémieux-Brilhac, *La France Libre*, 352–68.

8 Ralph Erskine, 'Eavesdropping on Bodden: ISOS v. the *Abwehr* in the Straits of Gibraltar', *Intelligence & National Security*, 12 (1997), 110–29.

9 Stephen Roskill, *The War at Sea, 1939–1945*, II: *The Period of Balance* (London, HMSO, 1956), 63–72.

10 Ian Walker, *Iron Hulls, Iron Hearts*, MacGregor Knox, *Hitler's Italian Allies: Royal Armed Forces, Fascist Regime, and the War, 1940–1943* (Cambridge, CUP, 2000).

11 Davide Rodogno, 'Italian Soldiers in the Balkans: The Experience of the Occupation, 1941–43', *Journal of Southern Europe and the Balkans*, 6 (2004), 125–44 and *idem*, *Fascism's European Empire: Italian Occupation during the Second World War* (Cambridge, CUP, 2006).

12 Mackenzie, *Secret History*, 126–8.

13 Pavlowitch, 'Out of Context', 89–118.

14 Frank Verna, 'Notes on Italian Rule in Dalmatia under Bastianini, 1941–1943', *International History Review*, 13 (1990), 528–47.

15 Ciano, *Diary*, 22 January 1942.

16 James Burgwyn, 'General Roatta's War Against the Partisans in Yugoslavia, 1942', *Journal of Modern Italian Studies*, 9 (2004), 314–29; Srdjan Trifkovic, 'Rivalry between Germany and Italy in Croatia, 1942–43', *Historical Journal*, 36 (1993), 879–904; Milos Kovic, 'From Persecutors to Saviours: The Italian Occupation Forces of the Second World War in post-1989 Serbian Historiography', *Journal of Southern Europe and the Balkans*, 6 (2004), 109–23.

17 Rommel, *Papers*, 16 June 1942.

18 'Axis Gloats Over Libya; British Mistakes in Publicity; Chance Seized by Berlin', *The Times*, 23 June 1942, 4.

19 Rommel, *Papers*, 26 June 1942.

20 Ciano, *Diary*, 22 June 1942.

21 Kesselring, *Memoirs*, 124–5.

22 Rommel, *Papers*, 29 June 1942.

23 Hirszowicz, *Third Reich and Arab East*, 229–49.

24 Brooke, *Diary*, 30 June 1942.

25 Minutes on French Fleet at Alexandria, 29 June 1942 and C-in-C Mediterranean to Admiralty, Tel. 918, 2 July 1942, FO371/31893.

26 Moorehead, *A Year of Battle*, 383.

27 Maunsell's comments on the Middle East Situation as of 4 July 1942, KV4/307.

28 'History of SOE in the Arab World', September 1945.

29 Lampson, *Diary*, 2 July 1942.

30 Lampson, *Diary*, 12 July 1942.

31 Ciano, *Diary*, 6 July 1942.

32 Cadogan, *Diary*, 3 August 1942.

33 Brooke, *War Diary*, 4 August 1942.

34 Raspin, *The Italian War Economy, 1940–1943*, 233–45.

35 Joel Hayward, 'Too Little, Too Late: An Analysis of Hitler's Failure in August 1942 to Damage Soviet Oil Production', *Journal of Military History*, 64 (2000), 769–94.

36 'When Rommel Failed', *The Times*, 1 August 1942, 4.

37 Brooke, *War Diary*, 6 August 1942.

38 Ciano, *Diary*, 13 August 1942.

39 Greene and Massignani, *Naval War in the Mediterranean*, 242–63.

40 Field-Marshal Lord Wilson of Libya, *Eight Years Overseas, 1939–1947* (London, Hutchinson, 1948), 134–5.

41 Austin, *Malta*, 160–1.

42 Hirszowicz, *Third Reich and Arab East*, 250–68; De Luca, 'Der Grossmufti'.

43 Dick White, Report on a visit to the Middle East, January 26th to February 28th, 1943, 29 March 1943, KV4/240; 'The German-Arab *Lehrabteilung* and other recent Abwehr Activity in North Africa', 22 February 1943.

44 BJSM, Washington to COS, London, Tel. 375, 3 September 1942, HS3/166.

45 Sir William Croft to Lord Moyne, 26 February 1944, FO921/176.

46 Aviel Roshwald, 'The Spears Mission in the Levant, 1941–1944', *Historical Journal*, 29 (1986), 897–919, 904.

47 General H. M. Wilson to Brigadier Clayton, 26 July 1942; MEIC/SYR/35,

July 1942; Clayton (MEIC) to Hopkinson (Minister of State's Office), 29 July 1942; Bennett to Hopkinson, 26 August 1942, FO921/31.

48 Georges Catroux, *Dans La Bataille de Méditerranée: Égypte, Levant, Afrique du Nord, 1940–1944 Témoignages et Commentaires* (Paris, René Julliard, 1949), 285.

49 Harvey, *Diary*, 14 and 17 September 1942 in John Harvey (ed.), *The War Diaries of Oliver Harvey, 1941–1945* (London, 1978).

50 Philip S. Khoury, 'Continuity and Change in Syrian Political Life: The Nineteenth and Twentieth Centuries', *The American Historical Review*, 96 (1991), 1374–95.

51 Meir Zamir, 'An Intimate Alliance: The Joint Struggle of General Edward Spears and Riad al-Sulh to Oust France from Lebanon, 1942–1944', *Middle Eastern Studies*, 41 (2005), 811–32.

52 Khoury, *Syria and the French Mandate*, 587–618.

53 DPA to Controller, 9 February 1942, HS3/213.

54 Memorandum by DH226 [B. T. Wilson] on Events in Palestine and Syria from 5 December 1941 to 6 June 1942, 24 August 1942, HS3/154.

55 Aide-Memoire by M. Tsouderos, 5 August 1942, HS5/296.

56 Sir Orme Sargent to CD, 4 September 1942, HS5/296.

57 Lord Glenconner to Minister of State, August 1942, HS5/154.

58 Cadogan, *Diary*, 21 August 1942.

59 Brooke, *Diary*, 21 August 1942.

60 Warner, Preliminary Brief on the Early History of the Middle East Supply Centre.

61 Ciano, *Diary*, 30 August 1942.

62 Ciano, *Diary*, 30 August 1942.

63 D/HV to V/CD, 22 October 1943, HS5/422.

64 SOE Activities in Greece, 1940–1942 by Major Ian Pirie, October 1945.

65 Niall Barr, *The Pendulum of War: The Three Battles of El Alamein* (London, Jonathan Cape, 2004), 226–40.

66 Ciano, *Diary*, 9 September, 12 September and 9 October 1942.

67 Ciano, *Diary*, 4 and 9 September 1942.

68 Jozo Tomasevich, *The Chetniks* (Stanford, Stanford UP, 1975), 166–75.

69 Trifkovic, 'Rivalry between Germany and Italy in Croatia, 1942–43', 879–904.

70 SRM 140 – Recording of the Conversation of Crüwell (captured 29 May 1942) and *General der Panzertruppe* von Thoma (captured 4 November 1942), WO208/4136.

CHAPTER NINE

1 Hadley Cantril, 'Evaluating the Probable Reactions to the Landing in North Africa in 1942: A Case Study', *Public Opinion Quarterly*, 29 (1965), 400–10.

2 Leon Borden Blair, 'Amateurs in Diplomacy: The American Vice Consuls in North Africa, 1941–1943', *The Historian*, 35 (1973), 607–20.

3 Alan Moorehead, *African Trilogy: The Desert War, 1940–1943*, III: *The End in Africa: The Year of Eisenhower, Alexander and Montgomery, 1942–43* (London, 1944), 484–96.

4 Borden, 'Vice Consuls', 618.

5 John Herman, 'Agency Africa: Rygor's Franco-Polish Network and Operation Torch', *Journal of Contemporary History*, 22 (1987), 681–706.

6 Brooke, *War Diary*, 17 and 26 October 1942.

7 Eisenhower to Hazlett, 7 April 1943 in Robert Griffith (ed.), *Ike's Letters to a Friend, 1941–1958* (Lawrence, University Press of Kansas, 1984).

8 Brooke, *War Diary*, 22 October 1942.

9 Hinsley, *British Intelligence*, II, 463–509.

10 Aide-Memoire from the US Embassy, London, 31 August 1942, HS3/166.

11 David Walker, 'OSS and Operation Torch', *Journal of Contemporary History*, 22 (1987), 667–79.

12 Andrew Buchanan, 'A Friend Indeed? From Tobruk to El Alamein: The American Contribution to Victory in the Desert', *Diplomacy & Statecraft*, 15 (2004), 279–301.

13 Minister of State to FO, Tel. 2028, 26 November 1942, HS3/166.

14 GM.175 to AD/U, Text of Hoskins Report, 28 January 1943, HS3/166.

15 Howard, *Strategic Deception*, 55–70.

16 Conference of the Commander-in-Chief, Navy with the Fuehrer at Wehrwolf, 26 August 1942, *Fuehrer Conferences on Naval Affairs, IV, 1942* (London,

Admiralty, June 1947); Conference of the Commander-in-Chief, Navy with the Fuehrer at the Berghof, 19 November 1942, *Fuehrer Conferences on Naval Affairs, IV, 1942* (London, Admiralty, June 1947).

17 The visit of the Commander-in-Chief, Navy to Rome, 12 May 1943 to 15 May 1943, *Fuehrer Conferences on Naval Affairs, V, 1943* (London, Admiralty, May 1947).

18 Barr, *The Pendulum of War*, 369.

19 Kesselring, *Memoirs*, 135–6; Rommel, *Papers*, 323–4.

20 Ciano, *Diary*, 12 November 1942.

21 Ciano, *Diary*, 11 and 12 November 1942.

22 Eisenhower to Bedell Smith, 9 November 1942 in Alfred Chandler (ed.), *The Papers of Dwight David Eisenhower: The War Years* (Baltimore, Johns Hopkins UP, 1970).

23 Arthur Funk, 'Eisenhower, Giraud, and the Command of Torch', *Military Affairs*, 35 (1971), 103–8.

24 Barbara Brooks Tomblin, *With Utmost Spirit: Allied Naval Operations in the Mediterranean, 1942–1945* (Lexington, University Press of Kentucky, 2004), 77.

25 Ken Ford, *Battleaxe Division: From Africa to Italy with the 78th Division, 1942–1945* (Stroud, Sutton Publishing, 1999), 6–7.

26 Admiral A. B. Cunningham, Report of Proceedings of Operation *Torch*, March 1943, in Michael Simpson (ed.), *The Cunningham Papers*, II: *The Triumph of Allied Sea Power, 1942–1946* (Aldershot, Ashgate, 2006).

27 Cunningham to Ramsay, 12 November 1942, *Cunningham Papers*.

28 Murphy to State Department, 5 November 1942, *FRUS* 1942, II.

29 Rick Atkinson, *An Army at Dawn: The War in North Africa, 1942–43* (London, Little Brown, 2003), 94–6.

30 Ciano, *Diary*, 9 November 1942.

31 Atkinson, *Army at Dawn*, 163–6; William Hitchcock, 'Pierre Boisson, French West Africa, and the Postwar Epuration: A Case from the Aix Files', *French Historical Studies*, 24 (2001), 306–41.

32 Ramsay to Cunningham, 11 November 1942, *Cunningham Papers*.

33 C-in-C, Mediterranean (Harwood) to HM Ambassador, Cairo (Lampson), 29 October 1942, FO371/31895.

34 Cunningham to Ramsay, 12 November 1942, *Cunningham Papers*.

35 Atkinson, *Army at Dawn*, 157; Anthony Clayton, 'A Question of Honour? Scuttling Vichy's Fleet', *History Today*, 42 (Nov. 1992), 32–9.

36 Harwood to Cunningham, 14 November 1942, *Cunningham Papers*.

37 Cunningham to Pound and Harwood, 18 November 1942, *Cunningham Papers*.

38 Arthur Funk, 'Negotiating the "Deal with Darlan"', *Journal of Contemporary History*, 8 (1973), 81–117.

39 Steven Casey, 'Franklin D. Roosevelt, Ernst "Putzi" Hanfstaengl and the "S-Project", June 1942 to June 1944', *Journal of Contemporary History*, 35 (2000), 339–59.

40 Nigel Hamilton, *Monty*, II: *Master of the Battlefield, 1942–44* (London, Sceptre, 1987), 56–7.

41 Austin, *Malta*, 173–4.

42 Cunningham to Pound, 20 November 1942, *Cunningham Papers*.

43 Vincent Orange, *Tedder: Quietly in Command* (London, Frank Cass, 2004), 187–204.

44 Hirszowicz, *Third Reich and Arab East*, 269–74.

45 Atkinson, *Army at Dawn*, 187–93.

46 The first village soviet was established on 11 October 1942, the first district soviet on 4 December 1942. L. S. Stavrianos, 'The Greek National Liberation Front (EAM): A Study in Resistance Organization and Administration', *Journal of Modern History*, 24 (1952), 42–55; G. M. Alexander and J. C. Loulis, 'The Strategy of the Greek Communist Party, 1934–1944: An Analysis of Plenary Decisions', *East European Quarterly*, 15 (1981), 377–89; Haris Vlavianos, 'The Greek Communist Party: In Search of a Revolution' in Judt, *Resistance and Revolution*, 157–212.

47 Inside Greece: A Review by Brigadier E. C. W. Myers [25 August 1943]. Myers finally took the six-hour flight back to Cairo on 9 August 1943, HS7/152.

48 Lord Glenconner to Minister of State, 'SOE Middle East', August 1942, HS3/154.

49 FO to Minister of State, Cairo, Tel. 2342,

2 October 1942 (Personal Eden to Casey, in fact from Orme Sargent), HS5/308.

50 Xan Fielding cited in Richard Clogg, *Anglo-Greek Attitudes: Studies in History* (Basingstoke, Macmillan, 2000), 178.

51 D/HV to CD, 8 December 1942. The Vellacott–Glenconner 'agreement' had been signed on 6 December 1942, HS5/213.

52 History of OSS/SOE Relations, HS7/283; T. C. Wales, 'The "Massingham" Mission and the Secret "Special Relationship": Co-operation and Rivalry between the Anglo-American Clandestine Services in French North Africa, November 1942 to May 1943', *Intelligence & National Security*, 20 (2005), 44–71.

53 Moorehead, *End in Africa*, 483.

54 Brooke, *War Diary*, 28 December 1942.

CHAPTER TEN

1 Ranfurly, *Diary*, 23 January 1944.

2 Thaddeus Holt, *The Deceivers: Allied Military Deception in the Second World War* (London, Phoenix, 2005), 328–94.

3 Ciano, *Diary*, 6 January 1943.

4 Kenneth Macksey, *Kesselring: German Master Strategist of the Second World War* (London, Greenhill, 2000), 143–5: Geoffrey Megargee, 'Triumph of the Null: Structure and Conflict in the Command of German Land Forces, 1939–1945', *War in History*, 4 (1997), 60–80; Howard Smyth, 'The Command of the Italian Armed Forces in World War II', *Military Affairs*, 15 (1951), 38–52.

5 Hitler Directive No. 47, 28 December 1942.

6 Harold Macmillan, *War Diaries: The Mediterranean, 1943–1945* (London, Macmillan, 1984), 26 January 1943.

7 Kennedy Diary, 8 December 1942 quoted in Nicholas Tamkin, 'Britain's Relations with Turkey during the Second World War' (Ph.D thesis, Cambridge University, 2006), 142.

8 Brooke, *War Diary*, 16 January 1943.

9 Brooke, *War Diary*, 18 January 1943.

10 Brooke, *War Diary*, 28 December 1942.

11 Eisenhower, *Diary*, 19 January 1943 in Robert Ferrell (ed.), *The Eisenhower Diaries* (New York, Norton, 1981).

12 Eisenhower to Bedell Smith, 19 January 1943, *Eisenhower Papers*.

13 Ciano, *Diary*, 23 January 1943.

14 Eisenhower to Marshall, 31 December 1942, *Eisenhower Papers*.

15 Atkinson, *An Army at Dawn*, 218.

16 Brooke, *War Diary*, 27 November 1942.

17 Cunningham to Lady Cunningham, 14 February 1943, *Cunningham Papers*. The new commands were activated on 20 February 1943.

18 Egya Sangmuah, 'Sultan Mohammed ben Youssef's American Strategy and the Diplomacy of North American Liberation, 1943–1961', *Journal of Contemporary History*, 27 (1992), 129–48.

19 Michael Laskier, 'Between Vichy Antisemitism and German Harassment: The Jews of North Africa during the early 1940s', *Modern Judaism*, 11 (1991), 343–69.

20 John Boyd to Robert Murphy, 3 January 1943, FO660/64.

21 Sabin J. Dalferes to Consul-General Wiley, 'Memorandum on Concentration, Work and War Prison Camps', 16 January 1943, FO660/64.

22 Macmillan to FO, Tel. 100, 12 January 1943, FO660/64.

23 Bergeret to Macmillan and Murphy with comments from Roger Makins (Resident Minister's Office) and Kenneth Younger (MI5), 15 February 1943, FO660/64.

24 Resident Minister, Algiers to FO, Tel. 182, 21 February 1943, FO660/64.

25 Eisenhower, *Diary*, 19 January 1943, *Eisenhower Diaries*.

26 Arthur Funk, 'The "Anfa Memorandum": An Incident of the Casablanca Conference', *Journal of Modern History*, 26 (1954), 246–54.

27 Brooke, *War Diary*, 16 January 1943.

28 Tuvia Ben-Moshe, 'Explaining an Historical Puzzle: Freudian Errors and the Origin of the Declaration on the Policy of "Unconditional Surrender" in the Second World War', *Political Psychology*, 14 (1993), 697–709.

29 Cadogan, *Diary*, 7 February 1943.

30 Cunningham to Pound, 15 March 1943, *Cunningham Papers*.

31 Burgwyn, 'General Roatta's War Against the Partisans', 314–29.

32 C. M. Keble to the Secretary of the Defence Committee, GHQ, MEF, 8 April 1943, HS5/307.

33 Morton to Price (War Cabinet Office), 23 February 1943, HS3/196.

34 CD to AD/S, 1 April 1943, HS3/196.

35 Ciano, *Diary*, 31 January 1943.

36 Tamkin, 'Britain and Turkey', 148–83; Robin Denniston, *Churchill's Secret War: Diplomatic Decrypts, the Foreign Office and Turkey, 1942–1944* (Stroud, Alan Sutton, 1997).

37 Gaunson, *Lebanon and Syria*, 111.

38 Brooke, *War Diary*, 4 February 1943.

39 'The German-Arab *Lehrabteilung*'; RIS2, 'Kesselring's *Abwehr* Arm', 18 May 1943, KV3/74.

40 Eisenhower to Marshall, 18 February 1943, *Eisenhower Papers*.

41 Carleton S. Coon, *A North Africa Story: the Anthropologist as OSS Agent, 1941–1943* (Ipswich, Gambit, 1980), 64–101. Reproduction of Report by C. S. Coon, Villa Rose, 23 February 1943.

42 Hirszowicz, *Third Reich and Arab East*, 276–306.

43 Meeting at the Minister of State's Office [to discuss Greek organizations in Cairo], 17 February 1943, HS5/326.

44 Brief for Lt-Col. Sheppard [being sent into Athens], 22 August 1944, HS5/688.

45 Myers, Inside Greece.

46 Glenconner to CD, 24 January 1943, HS5/328.

47 Report No. 1 on British Intelligence Organisations by Lt-Col. E. G. Moore, 24 May 1943, KV4/234; Minutes of Meeting between Dick White (MI5), Brigadier Clayton (MEIC) and ISLD, Cairo, 17 February 1943, KV4/240.

48 Tomasevich, *Chetniks*, 240.

49 Tomasevich, *Chetniks*, 237–8.

50 Mackenzie, *Secret History*, 427–8; Heather Williams, *Parachutes, Patriots and Partisans: The Special Operations Executive and Yugoslavia, 1941–1945* (London, 2003), 110.

51 AD to CD, 'Report on Visit to Cairo Mission', 11 March 1943, HS3/155.

52 Tomasevich, *Chetniks*, 248.

53 Tomasevich, *Chetniks*, 244–6.

54 Eisenhower to CCS, 15 February 1943 and Eisenhower to Brooke, 20 February 1943, *Eisenhower Papers*.

55 Kesselring, *Memoirs*, 151–2.

56 Hinsley, *British Intelligence*, II, 592.

57 Macmillan, *War Diary*, 1 April 1943.
58 Macmillan, *War Diary*, 31 March 1943.
59 Eisenhower to Marshall, 5 April 1943, *Eisenhower Papers*.
60 Martin Thomas, 'The Discarded Leader: General Henri Giraud and the Foundation of the French Committee of National Liberation', *French History*, 10 (1996), 86–111.
61 Resident Minister, Algiers to FO, Tel. 182, 21 February 1943, FO660/64.
62 Gaunson, *Syria*, 107–22. Catroux announced the restoration of the Lebanese constitution on 18 March 1943 and the Syrian constitution on 25 March 1943. On the same day he reached a security agreement with Jumbo Wilson.
63 Macmillan, *War Diary*, 6 March 1943.
64 Macmillan, *War Diary*, 14 and 16 March 1943.
65 Hamilton, *Monty: Master of the Battlefield*, 154–5.
66 Moorehead, *End in Africa*, 547.
67 Hamilton, *Monty: Master of the Battlefield*, 161.
68 Eisenhower to Marshall, 15 April 1943; Eisenhower to Bradley, 16 April 1943, *Eisenhower Papers*.
69 Holt, *Deceivers*, 366–79.
70 Brooke, *Diary*, 10 March 1943.
71 Mackenzie, *Secret History*, 428–31.
72 F. W. D. Deakin, *The Embattled Mountain* (Oxford, OUP, 1971), 35–60; Williams, *Parachutes, Patriots and Partisans*, 149.
73 Myers, Inside Greece; Mackenzie, *Secret History*, 458–9.
74 Crémieux-Brilhac, *La France Libre*, 497.
75 Hamilton, *Monty: Master of the Battlefield*, 195.
76 Kesselring, *Memoirs*, 154.
77 Ford, *Battleaxe Division*, 54.
78 Kesselring, *Memoirs*, 155.
79 Cunningham to Edelsten, 15 June 1943, *Cunningham Papers*.
80 Kesselring, *Memoirs*, 157.
81 Crémieux-Brilhac, *La France Libre*, 472.

CHAPTER ELEVEN

1 Could one apply the concept of class to Mediterranean society? Was it worth communicating with 'the masses' in hierarchical societies? Were the opinions of merchants and intellectuals, often drawn from minorities, too 'flashy' to be trusted? How far could one rely on modern means of communication, such as newsprint and the radio, in a credulous and backward oral culture? The conversation included many agencies, both British and American: PWE and PWB, SOE, ISLD, SIME and OSS, PICME, the G-2, G-3, and G-5 branches of the major commands, and others.
2 Filippo Focardi and Lutz Klinkhammer, 'The Question of Fascist Italy's War Crimes: The Construction of a Self-Acquitting Myth (1943–1948)', *Journal of Modern Italian Studies*, 9 (2004), 330–48; Michele Battini, 'Sins of Memory: Reflections on the Lack of an Italian Nuremberg and the Administration of International Justice after 1945', *Journal of Modern Italian Studies*, 9 (2004), 349–62.
3 Giovanni Villari, 'A Failed Experiment: The Exportation of Fascism to Albania', *Modern Italy*, 12 (2007), 157–71.
4 Lidia Santarelli, 'Muted Violence: Italian War Crimes in Occupied Greece', *Journal of Modern Italian Studies*, 9 (2004), 280–99; Nicola Labanca, 'Colonial Rule, Colonial Repression and War Crimes in Italian Colonies', *Journal of Modern Italian Studies*, 9 (2004), 300–13; Effie Pedaliu, 'Britain and the "Hand-over" of Italian War Criminals to Yugoslavia, 1945–1948', *Journal of Contemporary History*, 39 (2004), 503–29.
5 James Walston, 'History and Memory of the Italian Concentration Camps', *The Historical Journal*, 40 (1997), 169–83.
6 Burgwyn, 'General Roatta's War Against the Partisans in Yugoslavia: 1942', 314–29.
7 Mark Mazower, 'Military Violence and National Socialist Values: The Wehrmacht in Greece, 1941–1944', *Past & Present*, 134 (1992), 129–58; Jonathan Gumz, 'German Counterinsurgency Policy in Independent Croatia, 1941–1944', *The Historian*, 61 (1998), 33–50.
8 Director of Intelligence (O), 'GAF Operations in the Mediterranean, 14 May 1943 to 17 August 1943: The Invasion of Sicily', 4 September 1943, AIR 20/2107.
9 Hitler Directive No. 48, 'Command and

Defence Measures in the South-East', 16 July 1943.

10 Tomasevich, *Chetniks*, 319.

11 The final result of this bewildering series of changes was that by November 1943 von Weichs was the commander of Army Group F, Löhr was commander of Army Group E and Kesselring was commander of Army Group C. There were 52 German divisions in southern Europe, 25 in the Balkans and 27 in Italy.

12 Eisenhower to Wilson, 22 August 1943, *Eisenhower Papers*; Record of a Meeting held at 64 Baker Street on Friday, 18 June 1943 on SOE Organisation in the Mediterranean Theatre, HS3/155; Draft Memorandum on OSS for Chief of Staff, AFHQ, July 1943, WO204/11600; COS to MEDC, 18 August 1943, HS3/196; AD1 to V/CD, 'Tour of the Mediterranean', 11 August 1943, HS5/150.

13 D/H131 (Noel-Baker) to D/HT, 25 January 1944, HS5/221; Office of Chief Secretary, Palestine to Brigadier Clayton, 14 September 1943, FO921/117.

14 History of OSS/SOE Relations.

15 'The Story of the North African Coastal Convoys', AIR23/7511.

16 *Mare Nostrum*, 14 September 1944, AIR23/920; Appendix 30: British, Allied and Neutral Merchant Ship Losses in the Mediterranean and the Indian Ocean due to Enemy Action, AIR41/54.

Allied merchant ship losses in the Mediterranean, 1943–4

	1943	1944
January	14	5
February	14	8
March	17	5
April	6	5
May	6	2
June	7	1
July	14	0
August	11	1
September	11	1
October	9	1
November	10	0
December	18	1

17 Cunningham to Aunt Doodles, 24 June 1943, *Cunningham Papers*.

18 Macmillan, *War Diary*, 20 June 1943.

19 Elena Agarossi, *A Nation Collapses: The Italian Surrender of September 1943* (Cambridge, CUP, 2000), 44–5.

20 Bosworth, *Mussolini*, 398–9.

21 Macmillan, *War Diary*, 20 June 1943.

22 Eisenhower to Combined Chiefs of Staff, Draft Statement to accompany the proclamation of Military Government, 7 June 1943. Revised version approved, 20 June 1943, *Eisenhower Papers*.

23 Eisenhower to Patton, 4 June 1943, *Eisenhower Papers*.

24 Questionnaire for Colonel Scott, 21 December 1942, HW14/62.

25 History of the Italian Military Section of the Combined Bureau Middle East, HW51/14.

26 Synopsis for a History of Naval Sigint in the Mediterranean, 11 December 1945, HW50/39.

27 History of SIME Special Section, KV4/197.

28 Special Report CSDIC Middle East No. ME3/4. Recording of CO of the 125th Infantry Regiment, WO208/5507.

29 'An Outline of the History of SOE Activity in Italy, 1941–1945', October 1945, HS8/436 and F. W. D. Deakin, 'Allied Forces and the Italian Resistance, 1943–1945: Collected Notes', HS7/59.

30 Eisenhower to Patton, 4 June 1943, *Eisenhower Papers*.

31 Eisenhower to Marshall, 26 June 1943, *Eisenhower Papers*.

32 Macmillan, *War Diary*, 6 August 1943.

33 Castellano to Ambrosio, 21 May 1943, quoted in Agarossi, *A Nation Collapses*, 42–3.

34 C. J. C. Molony (ed.), *The Mediterranean and the Middle East*, V: *The Campaign in Sicily and the Campaign in Italy to 31 March 1944* (London, HMSO, 1973), 18–21.

35 Solly Zuckerman, *From Apes to Warlords, 1904–1946: An Autobiography* (London, Collins, 1988), 194–6.

36 Carlo D'Este, *Bitter Victory: The Battle for Sicily, 1943* (London, Collins, 1988), 301.

37 John Follain, *Mussolini's Island: The Battle for Sicily 1943 by the People Who Were There* (London, Hodder & Stoughton, 2005), 182–3, 262–4.

38 Kesselring, *Memoirs*, 163.

39 Eisenhower to Marshall, 17 July 1943; Eisenhower to JCS, 18 July 1943, *Eisenhower Papers*.

40 Agarossi, *A Nation Collapses*, 45.

41 Benito Mussolini, *The Fall of Mussolini: His Own Story* (1948), 45. This 'book' comprised a series of newspaper articles Mussolini published in June 1944.

42 Michael Carver, *War in Italy, 1943–1945* (London, IWM, 2001), 24.

43 D'Este, *Bitter Victory*, 295–6.

44 Molony, *Mediterranean and the Middle East*, IV, 154.

45 Carver, *War in Italy*, 36–40.

46 Kesselring, *Memoirs*, 164.

47 D'Este, *Bitter Victory*, 424.

48 D'Este, *Bitter Victory*, 427.

49 Eisenhower to Churchill, 4 August 1943, *Eisenhower Papers*.

50 Tom Dyson, 'British Policies towards Axis Reprisals in Occupied Greece: Whitehall vs. SOE', *Contemporary British History*, 16 (2002), 11–28.

51 'Inside Greece: A Review' by Brigadier E. C. W. Myers, 25 August 1943, HS7/152.

52 Brigadier C. M. Keble to Joint Operational Staff, 13 July 1943, HS5/257.

53 MEDC to COS and Eisenhower, CC/260, 15 July 1943, WO214/71.

54 Eisenhower to JCS, 18 July 1943, *Eisenhower Papers*.

55 William Linsenmeyer, 'Italian Peace Feelers before the Fall of Mussolini', *Journal of Contemporary History*, 16 (1981), 649–62.

56 Agarossi, *A Nation Collapses*, 50–3.

57 Eisenhower to Marshall, 18 June 1943 and Eisenhower to Marshall, 26 June 1943; Roosevelt to Eisenhower, 8 July 1943, *Eisenhower Papers*.

58 Macmillan, *War Diary*, 5 July 1943.

59 Telephone call between Churchill and Roosevelt (transcript of German interception), 29 July 1943; Roosevelt to Churchill, 29 July 1943; Roosevelt to Churchill, 30 July 1943, 17.35 & 17.55 in Warren Kimball (ed.), *Churchill and Roosevelt: The Complete Correspondence*, II: *Alliance Forged, November 1942 to February 1944* (New Jersey, Princeton UP, 1984).

60 Butcher diary, 14 August 1943 in Harry Butcher, *My Three Years with Eisenhower: The Personal Diary of Harry C. Butcher, Naval Aide to General Eisenhower, 1942 to 1945* (New York, Simon and Schuster, 1946).

61 Macmillan, *War Diary*, 29 July 1943.

62 Eisenhower to Marshall, 29 July 1943; Eisenhower, 28 July 1943, *Eisenhower Papers*; Brooke, *War Diary*, 15 August 1943.

63 Macmillan, *War Diary*, 31 July 1943; Eisenhower to Combined Chiefs of Staff, 5 August 1943, *Eisenhower Papers*.

64 Eisenhower to Marshall, 4 August 1943, *Eisenhower Papers*.

65 Macmillan, *War Diary*, 6 August 1943.

66 Agarossi, *A Nation Collapses*, 73; Macmillan, *War Diary*, 30 July 1943.

67 Ciano, *Diary*, 8 November 1938.

68 Eisenhower to Marshall, 29 July 1943, *Eisenhower Papers*.

69 *New Statesman*, 6 October 1943, quoted in Garnett, *Secret History*, 303.

70 Eisenhower to Marshall and Cordell Hull, 30 August 1943, *Eisenhower Papers*.

71 Carver, *War in Italy*, 49–50.

72 Cunningham to Aunt Doodles, 14 August 1943, *Cunningham Papers*.

73 Carver, *War in Italy*, 57.

74 Myers, Inside Greece.

75 Sargent to Eden [in Quebec], Tel. 419, 20 August 1943, HS5/425.

76 The opposing views are recalled in E. C. W. Myers, 'The Andarte Delegation to Cairo: August 1943', C. M. Woodhouse, 'Summer 1943: the Critical Months' and Richard Clogg, '"Pearls from Swine": the Foreign Office Papers, SOE and the Greek Resistance', all in Phyllis Auty and Richard Clogg (eds), *British Policy Towards Wartime Resistance in Yugoslavia and Greece* (London, Macmillan, 1975).

77 Macmillan, *War Diary*, 28 August 1943 and Eisenhower to CCOS, 28 August 1943, *Eisenhower Papers*.

78 Butcher, *Diary*, 18, 21 August and 3 September 1943; Howard Smith, 'The Armistice at Cassibile', *Military Affairs*, 12 (1948), 12–35 and William Snyder, 'Walter Bedell Smith: Eisenhower's Chief of Staff', *Military Affairs*, 48 (1984), 6–14.

79 Cunningham to Ramsay, 20 September 1943, *Cunningham Papers*.

80 There was an 'SOE link' operated by a captured British officer parachuted into one of SIM's 'resistance' fronts. There was also a 'SIME link', as the Italians were told

that their own supposed agent network in Tripoli was an Allied front organization and that if they communicated with its wireless the messages would be passed on to AFHQ. The head of SIM, General Carboni, was also the commander of Italian troops in Rome and the leading plotter opposed to the Armistice.

81 Agarossi, *A Nation Collapses*, 82–103.

82 Pietro Badoglio, *Italy in the Second World War: Memories and Documents* (London, 1948), 85. Originally published in Italian in 1944.

83 Brooks Richards, *Secret Flotillas* (London, Whitehall, 2004).

84 Ian Gooderson, 'Shoestring Strategy: The British Campaign in the Aegean, 1943', *Journal of Strategic Studies*, 25 (2002), 1–36.

85 Philip Carrabot, 'British Military Occupation, under a British Military Governor, but without a British Military Administration: The Case of Samos, 8 September to 18 November 1943', *Journal of Modern Greek Studies*, 7 (1989), 287–320.

86 Agarossi, *A Nation Collapses*, 112–15.

87 Perry Biddiscombe, *The SS Hunter Battalions: The Hidden History of the Nazi Resistance Movement, 1944–45* (Stroud, Tempus, 2006), 27–9.

88 Ray Moseley, *Mussolini: The Last 600 Days of Il Duce* (Dallas, Taylor Trade, 2004), 36–7.

89 Luigi Ganapi, 'The Dark Side of Italian History, 1943–45', *Modern Italy*, 12 (2007), 205–23.

90 Frauke Wildvang, 'The Enemy Next Door: Italian Collaboration in Deporting Jews during the German Occupation of Rome', *Modern Italy*, 12 (2007), 189–204.

91 Molony, *The Mediterranean and the Middle East*, V, 257.

92 Tomblin, *With Utmost Spirit*, 243.

93 Tomblin, *With Utmost Spirit*, 259–60.

94 Tomblin, *With Utmost Spirit*, 251.

95 Appendix 14: Analysis of Operational Aircraft on the Strength of the Northwest African Strategic and Tactical Air Forces on 7 August 1943, AIR41/54; D. of I. (O), 24 November 1943, 'GAF Operations in the Mediterranean, 18 August to 15 October 1943', AIR20/2107.

The balance of airpower in the central Mediterranean, August 1943

Type	Allied	German
Four-engined bombers	181	0
Twin-engined bombers	557	450
Fighters	1,033	355
Total	1,771	805

96 Rick Atkinson, *The Day of Battle: The War in Sicily and Italy, 1943–44* (London, Little Brown, 2007), 227.

97 Atkinson, *The Day of Battle*, 231.

98 Molony, *The Mediterranean and the Middle East*, V, 321.

99 Molony, *The Mediterranean and the Middle East*, V, 323–4.

100 Atkinson, *The Day of Battle*, 236.

101 Macmillan, *War Diary*, 14 September 1943.

102 Macmillan, *War Diary*, 5 November 1943; Lord Rennell of Rodd, 'Allied Military Government in Occupied Territory', *International Affairs*, 20 (July 1944), 307–16.

103 Bruno Arcidiacono, 'The "Dress Rehearsal": The Foreign Office and the Control of Italy, 1943–1944', *The Historical Journal*, 28 (1985), 417–27.

104 Eisenhower to CCOS, 30 September 1943, *Eisenhower Papers*.

105 Eisenhower to Vice Admiral Willis, 30 September 1943, *Eisenhower Papers*.

CHAPTER TWELVE

1 Eisenhower to Marshall, 1 October 1943, *Eisenhower Papers*.

2 Eisenhower to Marshall, 7 November 1943, *Eisenhower Papers*.

3 Churchill to Roosevelt, 7 October 1943, 0010, *Complete Correspondence*, II.

4 Eisenhower to CCS, 9 October 1943, *Eisenhower Papers*; Churchill to Roosevelt, 10 October 1943, 1450, *Complete Correspondence*, II.

5 Macmillan, *War Diary*, 7 October 1943.

6 Brooke, *Diary*, 7 October 1943.

7 Churchill to Roosevelt, 7 October 1943, *Complete Correspondence*, II.

8 Macmillan, *War Diary*, 27 October 1943.

9 Brooke, *Diary*, 25 October 1943.

10 'Greece: Death of Lieutenant Hubbard' (Report not sent), 13 October 1943, HS5/689.

11 MEDC (43) 23rd, 18 October 1943, MEDC (43) 24th, 31 October 1943; Selborne Note for the Prime Minister, 4 November 1943, HS5/310; Oliver Harvey, *War Diary*, 7 November 1943.

12 Report of a Visit to Greece by DD/B (Barker Benfield), September-October 1943, HS5/422.

13 Fitzroy Maclean, *Eastern Approaches* (London, Jonathan Cape, 1949), 303–41.

14 Report to the Director of Special Operations, Mediterranean from Deputy Head of the Division of Security, Liaison and Personal Services, 28 March 1944, HS8/846 and 'An Outline History of SOE Activity in Italy, 1941–45', October 1945, HS8/436.

15 Note of a Meeting held at MO4, Cairo at 1500 hrs between Gubbins and Donovan, 17 November 1943, HS8/7.

16 'The History and Development of SOE Activities in Yugoslavia, Part IV' by Lt-Col. W. D. Wilson, August 1945, HS7/201. The head of the Yugoslav section of OSS/SI at Bari was subsequently relieved of his duties when he became 'more Partisan than Tito and was really a Partisan representative in Bari'. To his later intense embarrassment, Wild Bill Donovan endorsed the views of OSS's Partisan partisans, telling Roosevelt that the Partisans were not Communists.

17 Macmillan, *War Diary*, 10 June 1944.

18 Oliver Harvey, *War Diary*, 6 November 1943.

19 'Albania', n.d., HS7/69 and Section Head, B.8 to Lord Harcourt (Force 399), 'Recommendations on Policy to be adopted to Major Abas Kupi and the Movement of Legality', 14 August 1944, HS5/2; Roderick Bailey, *The Wildest Province: SOE in the Land of the Eagle* (London, Jonathan Cape, 2008), 90–127.

20 Brooke, *Diary*, 25 October 1943.

21 Eisenhower to CCOS, 29 October 1943, *Eisenhower Papers*.

22 Macmillan, *War Diary*, 7 January 1944. The specific subject of Macmillan's outburst concerned relations between AMGOT and the ACC in Italy.

23 Brooke, *Diary*, 27 October 1943.

24 Keith Sainsbury, *The Turning Point: Roosevelt, Stalin, Churchill, and Chiang Kai-Shek, 1943 – The Moscow, Cairo and Teheran Conferences* (Oxford, OUP, 1986); Robin Edmonds, *The Big Three: Churchill, Roosevelt and Stalin in Peace and War* (London, Penguin, 1991), 315–61.

25 Brooke, *Diary*, 2 December 1943.

26 Brooke, *Diary*, 4 December 1943.

27 Macmillan, *War Diary*, 5 December 1943.

28 Macmillan, *War Diary*, 17 November 1943.

29 Resmin, Algiers to FO, Tel. 2301, 11 November 1943, FO660/141.

30 Macmillan, *War Diary*, 19 November 1943.

31 Macmillan, *War Diary*, 26 November 1943; Oliver Harvey, *Diary*, 6 December 1943; Lampson, *Diary*, 11 December 1943.

32 Macmillan, *War Diary*, 7 December 1943.

33 Brooke, *Diary*, 8 December 1943.

34 Brooke, *Diary*, 31 December 1943.

35 Macmillan, *War Diary*, 19 April 1944.

36 The History of the MAAF, December 1943 to 1 September 1944, AIR41/51.

37 Brooke, *War Diary*, 4 January 1944.

38 Lucas Diary, 11 January 1944, quoted in Lloyd Clark, *Anzio: The Friction of War – Italy and the Battle for Rome, 1944* (London, Headline Review, 2006), 76.

39 Tomblin, *With Utmost Spirit*, 323–4.

40 Carver, *War in Italy*, 121.

41 Tomblin, *With Utmost Spirit*, 335.

42 Clark, *Anzio*, 132.

43 Martin Herz, 'Some Psychological Lessons from Leaflet Propaganda in World War II', *Public Opinion Quarterly*, 13 (1949), 471–86. Herz was in charge of leaflet writing and prisoner interrogation for Mark Clark's 5th Army at the time of Anzio.

44 Kesselring, *Memoirs*, 195.

45 Clark, *Anzio*, 132.

46 Carver, *War in Italy*, 132–3.

47 Atkinson, *Day of Battle*, 413.

48 Tomblin, *With Utmost Spirit*, 349.

49 Carver, *War in Italy*, 131.

50 Clark, *Anzio*, 159.

51 Atkinson, *Day of Battle*, 370.

52 Tomblin, *With Utmost Spirit*, 352.

53 Steven Zaloga, *Anzio 1944: The Beleaguered Beachhead* (Oxford, 2005), 73–4.

54 John Colville, *Diaries*, II, 3 March 1944.

55 Macmillan, *War Diary*, 4 February 1944.

56 Moyne to Macmillan, 9 March 1944, FO921/139.

57 Wilson to COS, 5 February 1944, FO921/139.

58 The counter-argument was that 'the *Andartes* of all colours are as farcical in the military sense and a danger to Greece'. Leeper to Eden, Tel. 81, 1 April 1944, HS5/224.

59 'An Outline History of SOE Activity in Italy, 1941–45', October 1945, HS8/436.

60 Mirco Dondi, 'Division and Conflict in the Partisan Resistance', *Modern Italy*, 12 (2007), 225–36.

61 Macmillan, Memorandum on Italy, 23 March 1944. Macmillan finished writing up his analysis whilst accompanying Wilson to Cairo and on the same day as the bomb exploded in *Via Rasella*. Silvio Pons, 'Stalin, Togliatti and the Origins of the Cold War in Europe', *Journal of Cold War Studies*, 3 (2001), 3–27.

62 John Foot, 'Via Rasella, 1944: Memory, Truth, and History', *The Historical Journal*, 43 (2000), 1173–81.

63 Wilson to Mideast, MEDCOS 66, 11 March 1944, FO921/139.

64 WP (44) 89, 7 February 1944, WO106/3936.

65 Brooke, *Diary*, 7 March 1944; Prime Minister to Wilson, Special Unnumbered Signal, 7 March 1944, WO214/48.

66 Macmillan, *War Diary*, 9 March 1944.

67 Macmillan, *War Diary*, 9 March 1944. Wilson formally became SACMED on that day. Killearn, *Diary*, 22 March 1944; Minister Resident, Cairo to FO, Tel. 708, 24 March 1944, FO921/139; Macmillan, *War Diary*, 21 March 1944.

68 Cunningham to Supreme Allied Commander, Mediterranean Theatre, 21 May 1944, WO214/48.

69 Report by British Embassy on Greek Affairs, 1 January 1944 to 3 April 1944, FO921/163; L. S. Stavrianos, 'The Mutiny of the Greek Armed Forces, April 1944', *American Slavic and East European Review*, 9 (1950), 302–11; Mark Jones, 'Misunderstood and Forgotten: The Greek Naval Mutiny of April 1944', *Journal of Modern Greek Studies*, 20 (2002), 367–97.

70 Macmillan, *War Diary*, 8, 9 and 10 April 1944; Macmillan, *War Diary*, 14 April 1944.

71 Leeper to Eden, Tel. 104, 24 May 1944, FO921/163.

72 Record of Yvonne, otherwise Apollo (John Peltekis), n.d. [1944], HS5/688.

73 PICME Paper, No. 55, 'Greek Security Battalions', 18 July 1944, FO921/163.

74 Lars Baerentzen, 'The Arrival of the Soviet Military Mission in July 1944 and KKE Policy: A Study of Chronology', *Journal of the Hellenic Diaspora*, 13 (1986), 77–111.

75 Macmillan, *War Diary*, 23 May 1944.

76 Macmillan, *War Diary*, 17 April 1944.

77 Williams, *Parachutes, Patriots and Partisans*, 211.

78 Ralph Bennett, 'Knight's Move at Drvar: Ultra and the Attempt on Tito's Life, 25 May 1944', *Journal of Contemporary History*, 22 (1987), 195–208; Wayne Eyre, 'Operation *Rösselsprung* and the Elimination of Tito, 25 May 1944: A Failure in Planning and Intelligence Support', *Journal of Slavic Military Studies*, 19 (2006), 343–76.

79 Clark, *Anzio*, 295–320.

80 Matthew Jones, *Britain, the United States and the Mediterranean War, 1942–1944* (Basingstoke, Macmillan, 1996), 138–80.

81 Macmillan, *War Diary*, 6 June 1944. They were discussing their decision to sack Paul Vellacott who had just arrived from London to run pan-Mediterranean political warfare.

82 Macmillan, *War Diary*, 5 June 1944.

83 Macmillan, *War Diary*, 6 June 1944.

84 Macmillan, *War Diary*, 10 June 1944.

85 Macmillan, *War Diary*, 12 and 15 June 1944.

86 Macmillan, *War Diary*, 20 May 1944.

87 Thomas Barker, 'The Ljubljana Gap Strategy: Alternative to Anvil/Dragoon or Fantasy?', *Journal of Military History*, 56 (1992), 57–86.

88 Macmillan, *War Diary*, 19 June 1944.

89 Eisenhower to Marshall, 20 June 1944, *Eisenhower Papers*.

90 Macmillan, *War Diary*, 21 June 1944.

91 Brooke, *Diary*, 22 June and 23 June 1944.

92 Macmillan, *War Diary*, 25 June 1944.

93 Brooke, *Diary*, 28 June 1944.

R THIRTEEN

d Macmillan, *War Diary*, 20 July
4.

2 Macmillan, *War Diary*, 2 July 1944.

3 John DeNovo, 'The Culbertson Economic Mission and Anglo-American Tensions in the Middle East, 1944–45', *Journal of American History*, 63 (1977), 913–36; Nathan Godfried, 'Economic Development and Regionalism: US Foreign Relations in the Middle East, 1942–45', *Journal of Contemporary History*, 22 (1987), 481–500.

4 Kingsley Rooker to Hal Mack, 15 August 1944, FO660/172.

5 Terence Shone, Cairo to FO, Tel. 1245, 24 October 1944, FO921/232.

6 Stephen Randall, 'Harold Ickes and United States Foreign Petroleum Planning Policy, 1939–1945', *Business History Review*, 57 (1983), 367–87.

7 Macmillan, *War Diary*, 19 November 1944.

8 Roosevelt to Churchill, 29 June 1944 in *The Complete Correspondence*, III and Brooke, *War Diary*, 30 June 1944.

9 Eliahu Ben-Horin, 'Arabian Oil and American Imperialism', *Harper's*, 89 (June 1944), 28–35; Laurence Babcock, 'The Explosive Middle East', *Fortune* (September 1944); Eliahu Ben-Horin, 'The Future of the Middle East', *Harper's*, 90 (December 1944), 82–90; Sidney Fay, 'Oil and the Middle East', *Current History* (April 1945), 336–40; J. M. Landis, 'Anglo-American Co-operation in the Middle East', *Annals of the American Academy of Political and Social Science*, 240 (1945), 64–72.

10 Pierson Dixon, Diary of Churchill in Italy, 10–28 August 1944 in *Double Diploma*, 96–115.

11 Roosevelt to Churchill, 30 August 1944, *Complete Correspondence*, III.

12 Brooke, *War Diary*, 21 and 22 August 1944.

13 CGS Memorandum to C-in-C on Mediterranean Strategy and System of Administration, August 1944, WO214/48.

14 Macmillan, *War Diary*, 26 July 1944.

15 Minutes of a Meeting [of British officers] held in the Supreme Allied Commander's Conference Room, 20 August 1944, WO214/48.

16 Michael Cohen, 'American Influence on British Policy in the Middle East during World War Two: First Attempts at Co-ordinating Allied Policy on Palestine', *American Jewish Historical Quarterly*, 67 (1977), 50–70; Samuel Halperin and Irvin Oder, 'The United States in Search of a Policy: Franklin D. Roosevelt and Palestine', *Review of Politics*, 24 (1962), 320–41.

17 Michael Cohen, 'Churchill and the Jews: The Holocaust', *Modern Judaism*, 6 (1986), 27–49.

18 Brenner, 'Zionism-Revisionism', 66–92; Eshkoli-Wagman, 'Yishuv Zionism', 21–40.

19 Brooke, *War Diary*, 23 August 1944.

20 Davies, 'Jewish Military Recruitment in Palestine', 55–76; PIC Paper No. 2 (Revised), 'Jewish Illegal Organisations in Palestine', 8 November 1944, FO921/154; Gil Har, 'British Intelligence and the Role of Jewish Informers in Palestine', 117–49.

21 PIC Paper No. 2 (Revised), 'Jewish Illegal Organisations in Palestine', 8 November 1944, FO921/154; J. Bowyer Bell, 'Assassination in International Politics: Lord Moyne, Count Bernadotte, and the Lehi', *International Studies Quarterly*, 16 (1972), 59–82. Based on interviews with Shamir (Stern Gang) and Begin (Irgun) and the other surviving Stern Gang leaders.

22 Macmillan, *War Diary*, 21 August 1944.

23 APC (44) 11, Hoxha's Demand for Withdrawal of BLOs from Mission to Abbas Kupi: Note by Chairman, August 1944, HS5/2.

24 Notes of a Conversation at the Foreign Office between Sargent, Leeper, Gubbins and Pirie, 17 August 1944, HS5/688.

25 Dolbey to Commander, Force 133, 8 August 1944, HS5/258.

26 COS to Wilson, Tel. 4372, 12 August 1944, WO214/48.

27 Macmillan, *War Diary*, 15 August 1944.

28 Macmillan, *War Diary*, 18 August 1944; Macmillan to Wilson, 18 August 1944 and Copy of Memorandum for Churchill on Mediterranean Command, WO214/48.

29 Memorandum for CAO by Brigadier T. J. W. Winterton, 19 August 1944, WO214/48.

30 Roosevelt to Churchill, 26 August 1944, *Complete Correspondence*, III; Macmillan, *War Diary*, 27 August 1944.

31 Macmillan, *War Diary*, 28 September 1944.

32 Macmillan, *War Diary*, 15 September 1944.

33 'The History and Development of SOE Activities in Yugoslavia, Part IV (January 1944 to June 1945)' by Lt-Col. W. D. Wilson, August 1945; HS7/201; Joyce to Donovan, 8 August 1944, quoted in Kirk Ford, *OSS and the Yugoslav Resistance, 1943–45* (College Station, Texas A&M Press, 1992).

34 Murphy to Secretary of State, 16 August 1944, *FRUS 1944*, IV.

35 Macmillan, *War Diary*, 25 September 1944.

36 Macmillan, *War Diary*, 25 September 1944.

37 Macmillan, *War Diary*, 7 and 12 September 1944.

38 Brief for Lt-Col. Sheppard on situation in Athens, 22 August 1944.

39 Greece: Narrative Account [1945], HS7/158.

40 D/HT to AD/H, 15 February 1945, HS5/227.

41 Macmillan, *War Diary*, 9 October 1944.

42 Record of a Meeting at the Kremlin, Moscow, 9th October, 1944, at 10 p.m., *Diplomatic History*, 3 (1979).

43 Minutes of Meetings Held at the Kremlin on 9, 10 and 13 October 1944, *Diplomatic History*.

44 Macmillan, *War Diary*, 14 and 15 October 1944.

45 Macmillan, *War Diary*, 17 October 1944.

46 Macmillan, *War Diary*, 18 October 1944.

47 An Outline of the History of SOE Activity in Italy, 1941–1945, October 1945, HS8/436.

48 Churchill to Roosevelt, 8 October 1944, *Complete Correspondence*, III.

49 Macmillan, *War Diary*, 22 October 1944.

50 Macmillan, *War Diary*, 4 October 1944; Notes on a Conference held at Lord Moyne's Villa, 20 October 1944, FO921/182; Oliver Harvey, *War Diary*, 20 October 1944.

51 Macmillan, *War Diary*, 28 October 1944.

52 Michael Cohen, 'The Moyne Assassination, November 1944: A Political Analysis', *Middle Eastern Studies*, 15 (1979), 358–73.

53 Cairo to FO, Tel. 2398, 18 November 1944 and Colonial Office to Jerusalem, Tel. 89, 27 November 1944, FO921/154.

54 Brooke, *War Diary*, 7 November 1944.

55 Roosevelt to Churchill, 21 November 1944, *Complete Correspondence*, III.

56 Brooke, *War Diary*, 12 December 1944.

57 Brooke, *War Diary*, 7 and 15 November 1944.

58 Brooke, *War Diary*, 17 November 1944.

59 Macmillan, *War Diary*, 12 January 1945 and Brooke, *War Diary*, 12 January 1945.

60 Brooke, *War Diary*, 15 March 1945.

61 Macmillan, *War Diary*, 9 and 15 November 1944.

62 Macmillan, *War Diary*, 11 December 1944. Dalton and Selborne were the government ministers with responsibility for SOE.

63 SOE Liq.Med, Cairo to D/H.109, London, 11 December 1944, HS5/363.

64 Col. The Hon. C. M. Woodhouse, Report on Final Phase of the Allied Military Mission in Greece, September 1944 to January 1945, HS5/227.

65 Macmillan, *War Diary*, 23 December 1944.

66 Macmillan, *War Diary*, 11 December 1944.

67 Brooke, *War Diary*, 3 December 1944, *Complete Correspondence*.

68 MacVeagh to Roosevelt, 8 December 1944 in John Iatrides (ed.), *Ambassador MacVeagh Reports: Greece, 1933–1947* (Princeton, PUP, 1980).

69 Macmillan, *War Diary*, 9 February 1945.

70 Roosevelt to Churchill, 13 December 1944, *Complete Correspondence*, III.

71 Macmillan, *War Diary*, 14 and 23 December 1944.

72 Macmillan, *War Diary*, 22 December 1944.

73 Macmillan, *War Diary*, 17 December 1944.

74 Harvey, *War Diary*, 21 December 1944.

75 Harvey, *War Diary*, 24 December 1944.

76 Dixon, *Diary*, 1 January 1945.

77 Dixon, *Diary*, 24 December 1944.

78 Colville to John Martin, 26 December 1944 in John Colville, *The Fringes of Power: Downing Street Diaries, 1939–1955* (London, 1985).

79 Dixon, *Diary*, 26 and 27 December 1944.

80 Macmillan, *War Diary*, 26 December 1944.

81 Dixon, *Diary*, 27 December 1944.

82 Macmillan, *War Diary*, 26 and 27 December 1944.

83 Dixon, *Diary*, 28 December 1944.

84 Macmillan, *War Diary*, 31 December 1944.

85 Brooke, *War Diary*, 30 December 1944.

86 Dixon, *Diary*, 1 January 1945.

87 Macmillan, *War Diary*, 4 January 1945.

88 Macmillan, *War Diary*, 10 January 1945.

89 Colville, *Diary*, 11 January 1945.

90 Georgi Dimitrov, *The Diary of Georgi Dimitrov* (New Haven, Yale UP, 2003), 10 January 1945.

91 Colville, *Diary*, 23 January 1945.

92 Macmillan, *War Diary*, 23 January 1945.

93 Dondi, 'Division and Conflict in the Partisan Resistance', 225–36; Massimo Storchi, 'Post-war Violence in Italy: A Struggle for Memory', *Modern Italy*, 12 (2007), 237–50; D. J. Travis, 'Communism in Modena: The Provincial Origins of the PCI, 1943–1945', *Historical Journal*, 29 (1986), 875–95.

94 Macmillan, *War Diary*, 15 February 1945.

95 Macmillan, *War Diary*, 15 December 1944, 29 January 1945, 4 February 1945, 3 March 1945, 7 April 1945.

96 Macmillan, *War Diary*, 26 January 1945; Alan Foster, 'The Politicians, Public Opinion and the Press: The Storm over British Military Intervention in Greece in 1944', *Journal of Contemporary History* 19 (1984), 453–94.

CHAPTER FOURTEEN

1 Manfred Halpern, 'The Algerian Uprising of 1945', *Middle East Journal*, 2 (1948), 191–202; Charles-Robert Ageron, 'Les troubles du nord-constantinois en mai 1945: Une tentative insurrectionnelle?', *Vingtième Siècle*, 4 (1984), 23–38; Martin Thomas, 'Defending a Lost Cause? France and the United States Vision of Imperial Rule in French North Africa, 1945–1956', *Diplomatic History*, 26 (2002), 215–47; *idem*, 'France's North African Crisis, 1945–1955: Cold War and Colonial Imperatives', *History*, 92 (2007), 207–34.

2 Gaunson, *Syria*, 174.

3 SOE Near East Organisation, March 1945: Report on Tour of Inspection by Lt-Col. L. J. W. Richardson, HS7/86; CD/G to RW, 11 October 1945, HS7/86.

4 James Melki, 'Syria and the State Department, 1937–1947', *Middle Eastern Studies*, 33 (1997), 92–106.

5 Churchill to Truman, 30 May 1945 and Truman to Churchill, 31 May 1945 in G. W. Sand (ed.), *Defending the West: The Truman–Churchill Correspondence, 1945–1960* (Westport, Praeger, 2004).

6 John Wildgen, 'The Liberation of the Valle d'Aosta, 1943–1945', *Journal of Modern History*, 42 (1970), 21–41.

7 PM to SACMED, June 1945 and Alexander to Churchill, 15 June 1945, WO214/53.

8 Majid Khadduri, 'Towards a League of Arab States', *American Political Science Review*, 40 (1946), 90–100; *idem*, 'The Arab League as a Regional Arrangement', *American Journal of International Law*, 40 (1946); Paul Seabury, 'The League of Arab States: Debacle of a Regional Arrangement', *International Organization*, 3 (1949), 633–42.

9 Colonel John Riepe (G-3, Spec. Ops, 15th Army Group) to Colonel George King (G-3, Spec. Ops, AFHQ), 15 March 1945, WO204/10300.

10 R. S. Mantho, Director, A Desk, SI, Caserta to Earl Brennan, Chief, Italian and Albanian SI, Washington, 29 June 1945, DDRS [Declassified Documents Reference System]; Timothy Naftali, 'ARTIFICE: James Angleton and X-2 Operations in Italy' in George Chalou (ed.), *The Secrets War: The Office of Strategic Services in World War II* (Washington, NARA, 1992), 218–45.

11 Barry Rubin, 'Anglo-American Relations in Saudi Arabia, 1941–45', *Journal of Contemporary History*, 14 (1979), 253–67.

12 Arieh Kochavi, 'Anglo-American Discord: Jewish Refugees and the United Nations Relief and Rehabilitation Administration Policy, 1945–47', *Diplomatic History*, 14 (1990), 529–52; Michael Ottolenghi, 'Harry Truman's Recognition of Israel', *The Historical Journal*, 47 (2004), 963–88.

13 Arnold Offner, '"Another Such Victory": President Truman, American Foreign Policy, and the Cold War', *Diplomatic History*, 23 (1999), 127–55.

14 Arnold Rogow, *James Forrestal: A Study in Personality, Politics and Policy* (New York, Macmillan, 1963); Townsend Hoopes and Douglas Brinkley, *Driven Patriot: The Life and Times of James Forrestal* (Annapolis, Naval Institute Press, 1992).

15 *Diaries of James V. Forrestal, 1944–1949,*

Secretary of the Navy, 1944–1947, and first Secretary of Defense, 1947–1949: Complete and Unexpurgated Diaries from the Seeley G. Mudd Manuscript Library, Princeton University (microfilm), 4–19 August 1944. An expurgated version of Forrestal's diary was published soon after his death: Walter Millis (ed.), *The Forrestal Diaries: The Inner History of the Cold War* (London, Cassell, 1952). All references are to the manuscript diary.

16 Forrestal, *Diary*, 2 February 1945; Briefing Books for Yalta Conference in *Foreign Relations of the United States: The Conferences at Malta and Yalta* (Washington, GPO, 1955), 41–428.

17 Dimitrov, *Diary*, 8 April 1945.

18 J. R. Whittam, 'Drawing the Line: Britain and the Emergence of the Trieste Question, January 1941–May 1945', *The English Historical Review*, 106 (1991), 346–70; Roberto Rabel, 'Prologue to Containment: The Truman Administration's Response to the Trieste Crisis of May 1945', *Diplomatic History*, 10 (1986), 141–60; Richard Dinardo, 'Glimpse of an Old World Order? Reconsidering the Trieste Crisis of 1945', *Diplomatic History*, 21 (1997), 365–81; Glenda Sluga, 'Trieste: Ethnicity and the Cold War, 1945–54', *Journal of Contemporary History*, 29 (1994), 285–303; Pons, 'Stalin, Togliatti, and the Origins of the Cold War in Europe', 3–27.

19 Forrestal, *Diary*, 17 July 1945; Bilqin and Morewood, 'Turkey's Reliance on Britain: British Political and Diplomatic Support for Turkey against Soviet Demands, 1943–1947', 24–58.

20 695 Rome to Washington, 1729, 14 June 1945, WO204/10300; Norman Kogan, 'The Italian Action Party and the Institutional Question', *Western Political Quarterly*, 6 (1953), 275–95.

21 Forrestal, *Diary*, 23 July 1945.

22 Jonathan Knight, 'American Statecraft and the 1946 Black Sea Straits Controversy', *Political Science Quarterly*, 90 (1975), 451–75; Melvyn Leffler, 'Strategy, Diplomacy, and the Cold War: The United States, Turkey, and NATO, 1945–1952', *Journal of American History*, 71 (1985).

23 David Dunthorn, 'The Paris Conference on Tangier, August 1945: The British Response to Soviet Interest in the Tangier Question', *Diplomacy & Statecraft*, 16 (2005), 117–37.

24 Dimitrov, *Diary*, 6 August 1945.

25 Arieh Kochavi, 'Indirect Pressure: Moscow and the End of the British Mandate in Palestine', *Israel Affairs*, 10 (2004), 60–76; Statement of Head of SIME to CIGS, 25 November 1946, KV4/234.

26 Sergei Mazov, 'The USSR and the Former Italian Colonies, 1945–1950', *Cold War History*, 3 (2003), 49–78.

27 Raymond Smith and John Zametica, 'The Cold Warrior: Clement Attlee Reconsidered, 1945–47', *International Affairs*, 61 (1985), 237–52.

28 Ankara (Wilson) to Department of State, 6 October 1945 entered in Forrestal, *Diary*.

29 H. W. Brands, *Inside the Cold War: Loy Henderson and the Rise of the American Empire, 1918–1961* (New York, OUP, 1991).

30 Forrestal, *Diary*, 2 December 1945.

31 Forrestal, *Diary*, 20 March 1946.

32 Rami Ginat, 'Syria's and Lebanon's Meandering Road to Independence: The Soviet Involvement and the Anglo-French Rivalry', *Diplomacy & Statecraft*, 13 (2002), 96–122; Zohar Segev, 'Struggle for Co-operation and Integration: American Zionists and Arab Oil in the 1940s', *Middle Eastern Studies*, 42 (2006), 819–30.

33 Michael Cohen, 'The Genesis of the Anglo-American Committee on Palestine, November 1945: A Case Study in the Assertion of American Hegemony', *Historical Journal*, 22 (1979), 185–207.

34 Stephen Xydis, 'The Genesis of the Sixth Fleet', *US Naval Institute Proceedings*, 84 (1958), 41–50; D. M. Pricolo, *Naval Presence and Cold War Foreign Policy: A Study of the Decision to Station the 6th Fleet in the Mediterranean* (Annapolis, US Naval Academy, 1978); Edward Sheehy, *The US Navy, the Mediterranean and the Cold War, 1945–1947* (Westport, Greenwood, 1992).

35 Forrestal, *Diary*, 28 February 1946.

36 Winston Churchill, 'The Sinews of Peace' (Halcyon Booklet, V), 16.

37 Forrestal, *Diary*, 10 March 1946.

38 Thanasis Sfikas, 'War and Peace in the Strategy of the Communist Party of Greece, 1945–1949', *Journal of Cold War Studies*, 3 (2001), 5–30; John Iatrides, 'Revolution or Self-Defence? Communist Goals, Strategy, and Tactics in the Greek Civil War', *Journal of Cold War Studies*, 7 (2005), 3–33.

39 Leonid Glibianskii, 'The Soviet Bloc and Initial Stage of the Cold War: Archival Documents on Stalin's Meetings with Communist Leaders of Yugoslavia and Bulgaria, 1946–1948', *Cold War International History Project Bulletin*, 10 (1998), 112–48.

40 Vladimir Pechatnov, '"The Allies are Pressing On You to Break Your Will": Foreign Policy Correspondence between Stalin and Molotov and Other Politburo Members, September 1945 to December 1946', *CWIHP Working Paper*, 26.

41 I. I. Yermashev, 'The Mediterranean Problem', minutes of a public lecture, 16 August 1946 quoted in Artiom A. Ulunian, 'Soviet Cold War Perceptions of Turkey and Greece, 1945–58', *Cold War History*, 3 (2003), 47.

42 Forrestal, *Diary*, 6 June 1946.

43 CIG Weekly Intelligence Summary, 16 August 1946 in Woodrow Kuhns (ed.), *Assessing the Soviet Threat: The Early Cold War Years* (CIA Center for the Study of Intelligence, 1997).

44 Robert Beisner, 'Patterns of Peril: Dean Acheson Joins the Cold Warriors, 1945–1946', *Diplomatic History*, 20 (1996), 321–55.

45 Forrestal, *Diary*, 14 August 1946.

46 Melvyn Leffler, *A Preponderance of Power: National Security, the Truman Administration and the Cold War* (Stanford, Stanford University Press, 1992), 121–5.

47 George Baer, *One Hundred Years of Seapower: The US Navy, 1890–1990* (Stanford, Stanford University Press, 1993), 283.

48 Stephen Xydis, 'America, Britain and the USSR in the Greek Arena, 1944–1947', *Political Science Quarterly*, 78 (1963), 581–96.

49 Forrestal, *Diary*, 30 September 1946.

50 Stalin to Molotov, 21 October 1946 in 'Break Your Will'.

51 Forrestal, *Diary*, 22 August 1946; Michael Hogan, *A Cross of Iron: Harry S. Truman and the Origins of the National Security State* (Cambridge, CUP, 1998), 81–2.

52 CIG Weekly Summary, 3 January 1947, *Assessing the Soviet Threat*.

53 Alexandra Nocke, 'Israel and the Emergence of Mediterranean Identity: Expressions of Locality, Music and Literature', *Israel Studies*, 11 (2006), 143–73.

54 Dixon, *Diary*, 7 and 18 December 1946; Dalia Ofer, 'Holocaust Survivors as Immigrants: The Case of Israel and the Cyprus Detainees', *Modern Judaism*, 16 (1996), 1–23.

55 David Charters, *The British Army and Jewish Insurgency in Palestine, 1945–1947* (London, Macmillan, 1989).

56 Ritchie Ovendale, 'The Palestine Policy of the British Labour Government, 1945–1946', *International Affairs*, 55 (1979), 409–31; Alan Bullock, *Ernest Bevin: Foreign Secretary* (Oxford, OUP, 1985), 307–54.

57 Simon Ball, 'Bomber Bases and British Strategy in the Middle East, 1945–1949', *Journal of Strategic Studies*, 14 (1991), 515–33.

58 CIG, ORE 6/1, 7 February 1947, *Assessing the Soviet Threat*.

59 Forrestal, *Diary*, 24 February 1947.

60 Robert Frazier, 'Did Britain Start the Cold War? Bevin and the Truman Doctrine', *Historical Journal*, 27 (1984), 715–27.

61 Keith Legg, 'Musical Chairs in Athens: Analyzing Political Instability, 1946–52' in John Iatrides, Lars Baerentzen and Ole Smith (eds), *Studies in the History of the Greek Civil War* (Copenhagen, Museum Tusculanum Press, 1987), 9–24.

62 MacVeagh, Porter and Ethridge to State Department, 20 February 1947, *Ambassador MacVeagh Reports*.

63 Forrestal, *Diary*, 7 March 1947.

64 Iatrides, 'Revolution or Self-Defence?', 3–33.

65 Forrestal, *Diary*, 7 March 1947.

66 *New York Times*, 5 March 1947, quoted in William Reitzel, *The Mediterranean: Its Role in American Foreign Policy* (New York, Harcourt Brace, 1948), 90; Daniel

Chomsky, 'Advance Agent of the Truman Doctrine: The United States, the *New York Times*, and the Greek Civil War', *Political Communication*, 17 (2000), 415–32.

67 Forrestal, *Diary*, 9 October 1947; Andrew Rathmell, *The Secret War in the Middle East: The Covert Struggle for Syria, 1949–1961* (London, 1995); Douglas Little, 'Pipeline Politics: America, TAPLINE and the Arabs', *Business History Review*, 64 (1990), 255–85.

68 Forrestal to Marshall, 6 November 1947, DDRS.

69 Elsey to Clifford, 8 March 1947 and Memorandum for the File: The Drafting of the President's Message to Congress, 12 March 1947, Harry S. Truman Library and Museum Online Archive.

70 Robert Ivie, 'Fire, Flood, and Red Fever: Motivating Metaphors of Global Emergency in the Truman Doctrine Speech', *Presidential Studies Quarterly*, 29 (1999), 570–91; Dennis Merrill, 'The Truman Doctrine: Containing Communism and Modernity', *Presidential Studies Quarterly*, 36 (2006), 27–37; Robert Frazier, 'Acheson and the Formulation of the Truman Doctrine', *Journal of Modern Greek Studies*, 17 (1999), 229–51.

71 Marx Leva (Special Assistant to the Secretary of the Navy) to Clark Clifford (Special Assistant to the President), 6 March 1947, DDRS.

72 Hogan, *Cross of Iron*, 23–68.

73 'Man in Motion', *Time*, 29 September 1947.

74 George McGhee, *The US-Turkish-NATO Connection: How the Truman Doctrine and Turkey's NATO Entry Contained the Soviets* (Basingstoke, Macmillan, 1990), 35–50.

75 Reitzel, *Mediterranean*, 169.

76 Forrestal, *Diary*, 26 September 1947.

77 CIA Weekly Summary, 12 September 1947, *Assessing the Threat*. As it turned out, the Italians had been summoned to western Poland so that Stalin's representative, Andrei Zhdanov, could pillory them for their failure, not in the Mediterranean, but in destroying the Marshall Plan in Europe. Stalin was already measuring the comrades for their coffins. Eugenio Reale,

'The Founding of the Cominform', in M. Drachkovitch (ed.), *The Comintern: Historical Highlights* (New York, Praeger, 1966), 253–68 and Giuliano Procacci (ed.), *The Cominform: Minutes of the Three Conferences, 1947/1948/1949* (Milan, Fondazione Giangiacomo Feltrinelli, 1994).

78 Forrestal, *Diary*, 26 September 1947.

79 James Miller, 'Taking Off the Gloves: The United States and the Italian Elections of 1948', *Diplomatic History*, 7 (1983), 35–55; Mario Del Pero, 'The United States and "Psychological Warfare" in Italy, 1948–1955', *The Journal of American History*, 87 (2001), 1304–34; Kaeten Mistry, 'The Case for Political Warfare: Strategy, Organization and US Involvement in the 1948 Italian Election', *Cold War History*, 6 (2006), 301–29.

80 Bruce Kuniholm, 'US Policy in the Near East: The Triumphs and Tribulations of the Truman Administration' in Michael Lacey (ed.), *The Truman Presidency* (New York, 1991).

81 Forrestal, *Diary*, 4 September 1947.

82 Forrestal, *Diary*, 24 January 1948.

83 Forrestal, *Diary*, 8 August 1947.

84 Reitzel, *Mediterranean*, 161.

85 Memorandum for the Secretary of Defense by Admiral William Leahy, 'Conversations with the British in regard to the Eastern Mediterranean and the Middle East', 19 November 1947 and Memorandum for the Secretary of Defense by Sidney Souers, Executive Secretary, NSC, 'Conversations with the British in regard to the Eastern Mediterranean and the Middle East', 25 November 1947, *Records of the Joint Chiefs of Staff, 1946–1953* (microfilm, Washington, University Publications of America, 1979–1981).

86 Forrestal, *Diary*, 7 January 1948.

87 Ball, 'Bomber Bases', 522–7.

88 Forrestal, *Diary*, 7 November 1947.

89 RAFDEL to VCAS, 11 September 1947, AIR20/2461.

90 Brands, *Inside the Cold War*, 182–3.

91 Forrestal, *Diary*, 26 November 1947.

92 Forrestal, *Diary*, 1 December 1947.

93 CIA, Office of Reports and Estimates, ORE 69, 9 February 1948, DDRS.

94 Howard Jones, 'Mistaken Prelude to Vietnam: The Truman Doctrine and a "New Kind of War" in Greece', *Journal of Modern Greek Studies*, 10 (1992), 121–43.

95 There are various versions of Stalin's statement: all agree on the sentiment behind the words. Jeronim Perović, 'The Tito–Stalin Split: A Reassessment in Light of New Evidence', *Journal of Cold War Studies*, 9 (2007), 32–63; Glibianskii, 'The Soviet Bloc and Initial Stage of the Cold War', 112–48.

96 Bruce Kuniholm, 'US Policy in the Near East'.

97 David Tal, 'The Forgotten War: Jewish-Palestinian Strife in Mandatory Palestine, December 1947 to May 1948', *Israel Affairs*, 6 (2000), 3–21; *idem*, 'The Historiography of the 1948 War in Palestine: The Missing Dimension', *Journal of Israeli History*, 24 (2005), 183–202.

98 Forrestal, *Diary*, 3 February 1948.

99 Rogow, *Forrestal*, 306–7.

100 Bruce Evensen, 'A Story of "Ineptness": The Truman Administration's Struggle to Shape Conventional Wisdom on Palestine at the Beginning of the Cold War', *Diplomatic History*, 15 (1991), 339–59; *idem*, 'Truman, Palestine and the Cold War', *Middle Eastern Studies*, 28 (1992), 120–56.

101 Forrestal, *Diary*, 26 May 1948; Mark Byrnes, '"Overruled and Worn Down": Truman Sends an Ambassador to Spain', *Presidential Studies Quarterly*, 29 (1999), 263–79.

102 Rosa Pardo Sanz, 'The Mediterranean Policy of Franco's Spain', *Mediterranean Historical Review*, 16 (2001), 45–68; Edward Johnson, 'Early Indications of a Freeze: Greece, Spain and the United Nations, 1946–47', *Cold War History*, 6 (2006), 43–61.

103 Troutbeck (British Middle East Office, Cairo) to Secretary of State for Foreign Affairs, 11 October 1948 with covering minute by Bernard Burrows, 20 October 1948, FO371/68435.

104 Minute by Peck, 3 May 1948, FO371/72348.

105 Minute by Geoffrey Wallinger on a Memorandum left by the Greek Ambassador with the Foreign Secretary, 8 June 1948, FO371/72349.

106 Sir Orme Sargent, Interview with the Greek Ambassador, 3 June 1948, FO371/72349.

107 Cees Wiebes and Bert Zeeman, 'The Pentagon Negotiations, March 1948: The Launching of the North Atlantic Treaty', *International Affairs*, 59 (1983), 351–63.

108 Timothy Smith, 'The Fear of Subversion: The United States and the Inclusion of Italy in the North Atlantic Treaty', *Diplomatic History*, 7 (1983), 139–55.

109 Brief on the Washington Talks for the Secretary of State, FO371/72349.

110 Forrestal, *Diary*, 30 July 1948.

111 Smith, 'Fear of Subversion', 151.

112 Forrestal, *Diary*, 13 November 1948.

113 Forrestal, *Diary*, 21 October 1948.

114 Forrestal, *Diary*, Notes taken at Budget Meeting in Secretary Forrestal's Office, 15 October 1948.

115 Merriam to Kennan, 18 March 1949, quoted in Michael Cohen, 'William A. Eddy, the Oil Lobby and the Palestine Problem', *Middle Eastern Studies*, 30 (1994), 166–80, 178–9.

116 George McGhee, *Envoy to the Middle World: Adventures in Diplomacy* (New York, Harper & Row, 1983).

117 Moscow to Foreign Office, 4 April 1950, FO371/87465.

118 NCT (NSC) 1092, Statement of Policy by the Psychological Strategy Board (Robert Cutler) on the Position of the US with Respect to the General Area of the Eastern Mediterranean, Red Sea and Persian Gulf, 23 October 1951, DDRS.

119 M. Hill Goodspeed, *US Navy: A Complete History* (Washington, Naval Historical Foundation, 2003), 12 February 1950.

120 James Keeley (US Minister in Damascus) to Berry, 16 December 1949, discussed in Rathmell, *The Secret War in the Middle East*, 43–4.

121 Behcet Yesilbursa, 'Turkey's Participation in the Middle East Command and its Admission to NATO, 1950–52', *Middle Eastern Studies*, 35 (1999), 70–102, 73.

122 JCS 1887/7, 7 November 1950, *Records of JCS*.

123 Minutes of a meeting between SACEUR

(Eisenhower), CNO (Forrest Sherman) and CINCNELM (Carney) held at SHAPE, Paris, 3 March 1951, and Carney to Eisenhower, 8 March 1951, *Records of JCS*.

124 McGhee, *Middle World*, 381.

125 NSC 114/3, 5 June 1952, *FRUS 1952*, II, 20–47.

126 Michael Cohen, 'From "Cold" to "Hot" War: Allied Strategic and Military Interests in the Middle East after the Second World War', *Middle Eastern Studies*, 43 (2007), 725–48; Toru Onozawa, 'Formation of American Regional Policy for the Middle East, 1950–1953: The Middle East Command Concept and its Legacy', *Diplomatic History*, 29 (2005), 117–48; Elie Podeh, 'The Desire to Belong Syndrome: Israel and Middle Eastern Defense, 1948–1954', *Israel Studies*, 4 (1999), 121–48.

127 Leffler, 'Strategy, Diplomacy, and the Cold War', 807–25.

128 JCS 1887/12, 20 March 1951, *Records of the JCS*.

129 Eisenhower to JCS, 23 April 1951, DDRS.

130 Eisenhower to Carney, 19 June 1951, DDRS.

131 'Ike Reviews the Fleet', *Time*, 29 October 1951.

132 Joel Gordon, 'The False Hopes of 1950: The Wafd's Last Hurrah and the Demise of Egypt's Old Order', *International Journal of Middle East Studies*, 21 (1989), 193–214; Michael Mason, '"The Decisive Volley": the Battle of Ismailia and the Decline of British Influence in Egypt, January to July 1952', *Journal of Imperial and Commonwealth History*, 19 (1991), 45–64; Michael Thornhill, 'Britain and the Collapse of Egypt's Constitutional Order, 1950–52', *Diplomacy & Statecraft*, 13 (2002), 121–52; Laila Amin Morsy, 'American Support for the 1952 Egyptian Coup: Why?', *Middle Eastern Studies*, 31 (1995), 307–16.

133 Jerauld Wright to Bradley, 30 October 1951; Bradley to Eisenhower, 3 January 1952, *Records of the JCS*.

134 CINCNELM became a desk job in London. JCS 1868/316, 11 November 1951, 'Advice for Bradley'; Eisenhower to Bradley, 5 January 1952; JSPC 684/97, 15 January 1952; JCS 1259/233, CNO, 'Relief of Commander-in-Chief, US Naval Forces,

Eastern Atlantic and the Mediterranean', 22 April 1952, *Records of the JCS*; Alessandro Brogi, '"Competing Missions": France, Italy, and the Rise of American Hegemony in the Mediterranean', *Diplomatic History*, 30 (2006), 741–70.

CONCLUSION

1 Lisa Chaney, *Elizabeth David* (London, Pan, 1999) and Artemis Cooper, *Writing at the Kitchen Table: Elizabeth David* (London, Penguin, 2000).

2 George Sarton, 'The Unity and Diversity of the Mediterranean World', *Osiris*, 2 (1936), 406–63, 409.

3 Edward Hungerford, 'Durrell's Mediterranean Paradise', *Studies in the Literary Imagination*, 24 (1991), 57–69, 57.

4 Gordon East, 'The Mediterranean Problem', *Geographical Review*, 28 (January 1938), 83–101, 85.

5 Gordon East, 'The Mediterranean: Pivot of Peace and War', *Foreign Affairs*, 31 (1952/1953), 619–33, 621.

6 W. B. Fisher, 'The Problems of Modern Libya', *The Geographical Journal*, 119 (1953), 183–95, 183. Fisher was the leader of the Aberdeen University Expedition to Cyrenaica in 1951. Commercial oil reserves were finally located in 1959.

7 'The Fleet's In', *Time*, 21 January 1952.

8 East, 'The Mediterranean: Pivot of Peace and War' (1952), 632.

9 Gershoni, *Beyond Anti-Semitism*.

10 Michael Thornhill, 'Britain, the United States and the Rise of an Egyptian Leader: The Politics and Diplomacy of Nasser's Consolidation of Power, 1952–1954', *The English Historical Review*, CXIX (2004), 892–921.

11 Percy Loraine, 'Perspectives of the Near East', *The Geographical Journal*, 102 (July 1943), 6–13.

12 Robert Montagne, 'Modern Nations and Islam', *Foreign Affairs*, 30 (1951/52), 580–92, 586.

13 Albert Hourani, 'How Should We Write the History of the Middle East?', *International Journal of Middle East Studies*, 23 (1991), 125–36.

14 Montagne, 'Modern Nations and Islam', 585.

15 H. A. R. Gibb, 'Toward Arab Unity', *Foreign Affairs*, 24 (1945/46), 119–29; W. B. Fisher, 'Unity and Diversity in the Middle East', *Geographical Review*, 37 (July 1947), 414–35.

16 Montagne, 'Modern Nations and Islam', 588.

17 H. A. R. Gibb, 'Middle Eastern Perplexities', *International Affairs*, 20 (October 1944 – publication of lecture given on 11 July 1944), 458–72, 462.

18 Joseph Roucek, 'The Geopolitics of the Mediterranean, I', *American Journal of Economics and Sociology*, 12 (1953), 347–54.

19 East, 'The Mediterranean: Pivot of Peace and War' (1952).

20 Joseph Roucek, 'The Geopolitics of the Mediterranean, II', *American Journal of Economics and Sociology*, 13 (1953), 71–86, 86.

21 Robert Norris, William Arkin and William Burr, 'Where They Were', *Bulletin of the Atomic Scientists*, 55 (1999), 26–35.

INDEX

p. 56 hôtel providence